SCREENSHOT HONG KONG
A PHOTOGRAPHIC EXPLORATION

SCOTT SHAW

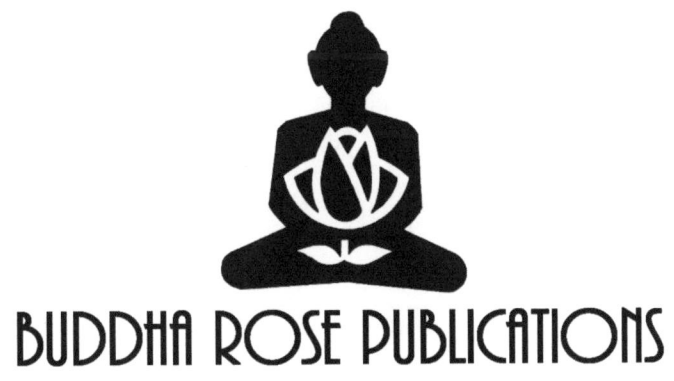

BUDDHA ROSE PUBLICATIONS

Screenshot Hong Kong
A Photographic Exploration
Copyright © 2019 By Scott Shaw
www.scottshaw.com
All Rights Reserved

No part of this book may be reproduced
in any manner without the expressed
permission of the author or the publishing company.

ISBN: 10: 1-949251-11-X
ISBN: 13: 978-1-949251-11-1

Printed in the United States of America

10 9 8 7 6 5 4 3 2 1

SCREENSHOT
HONG KONG

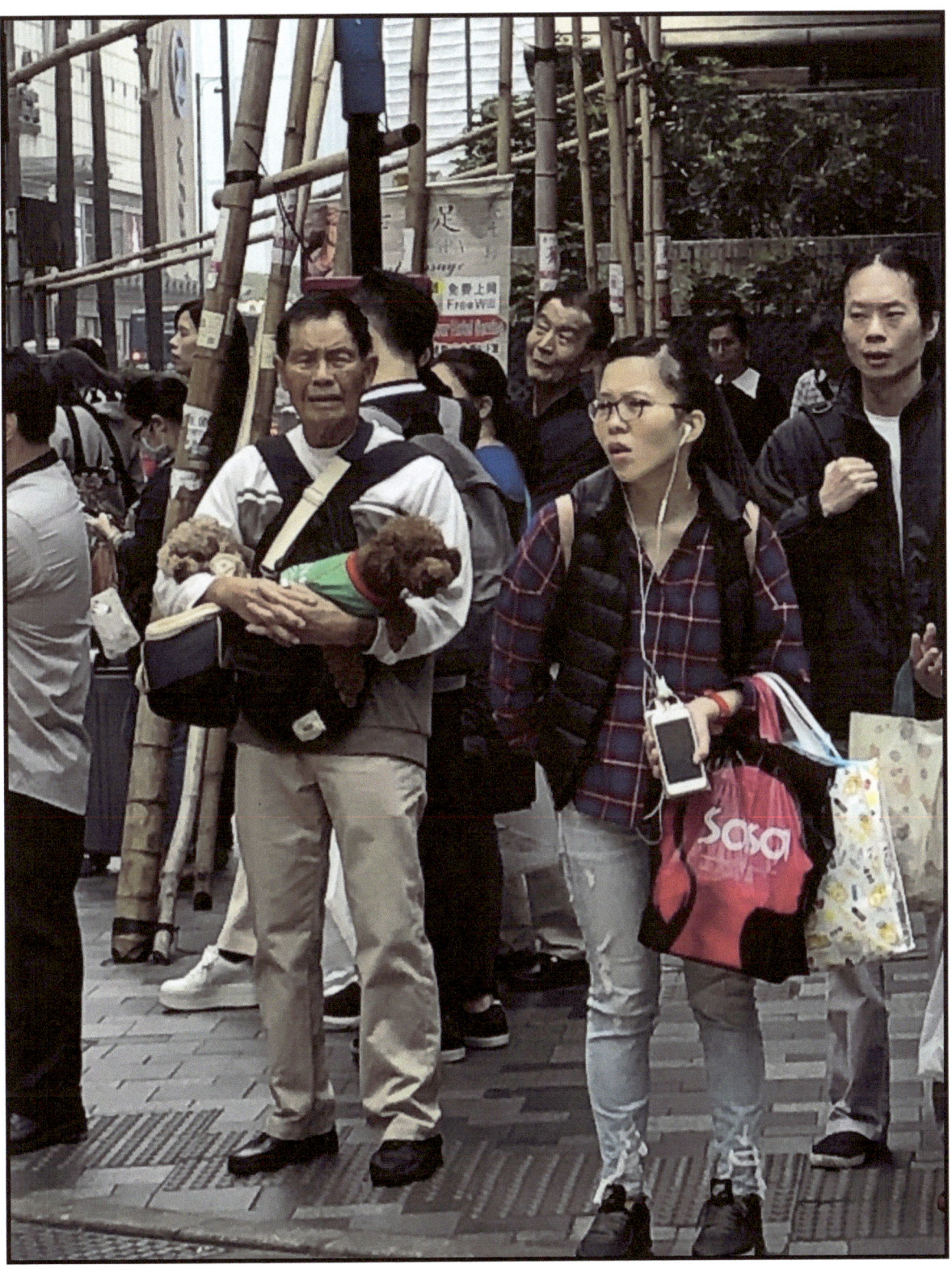

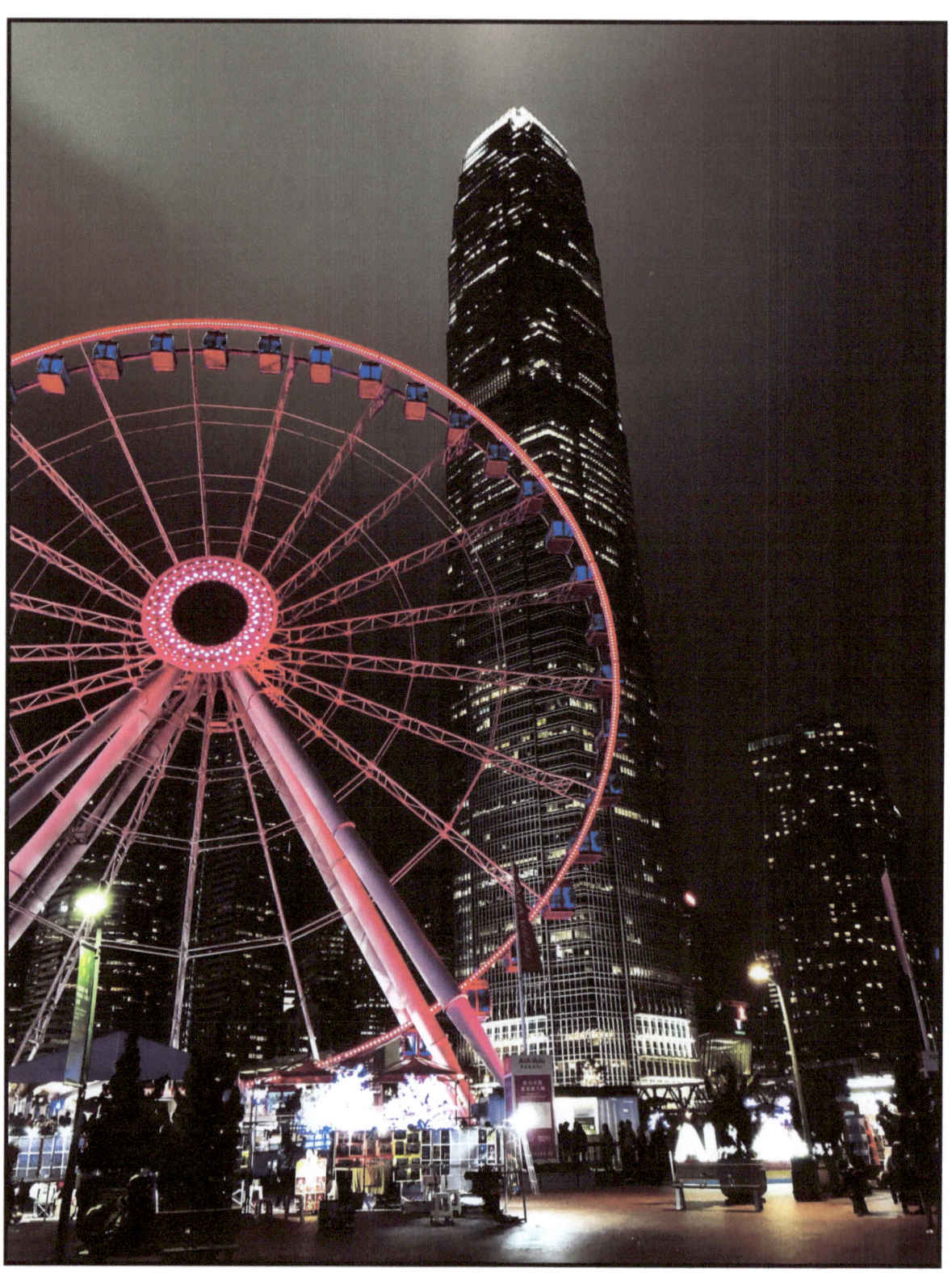

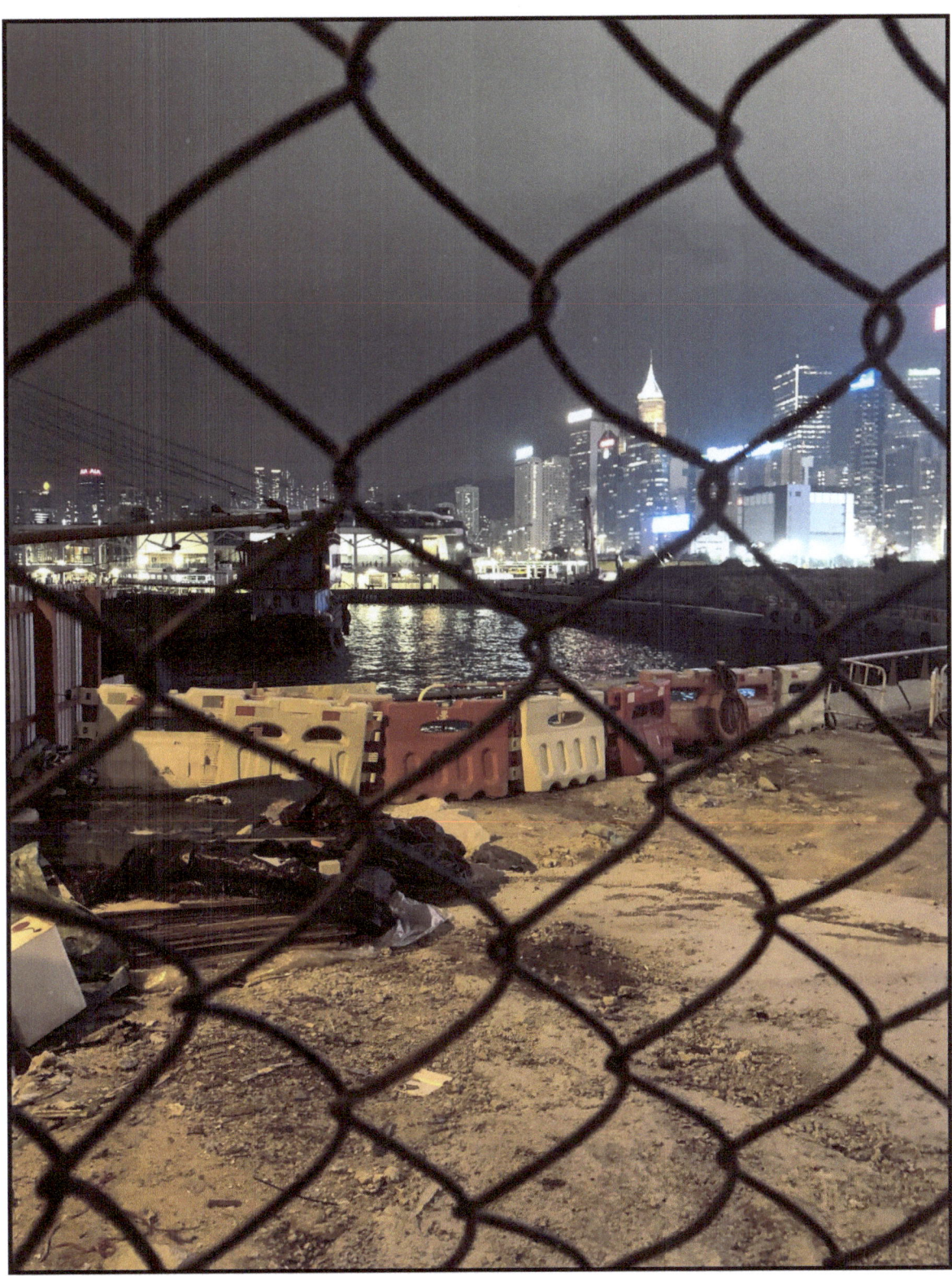

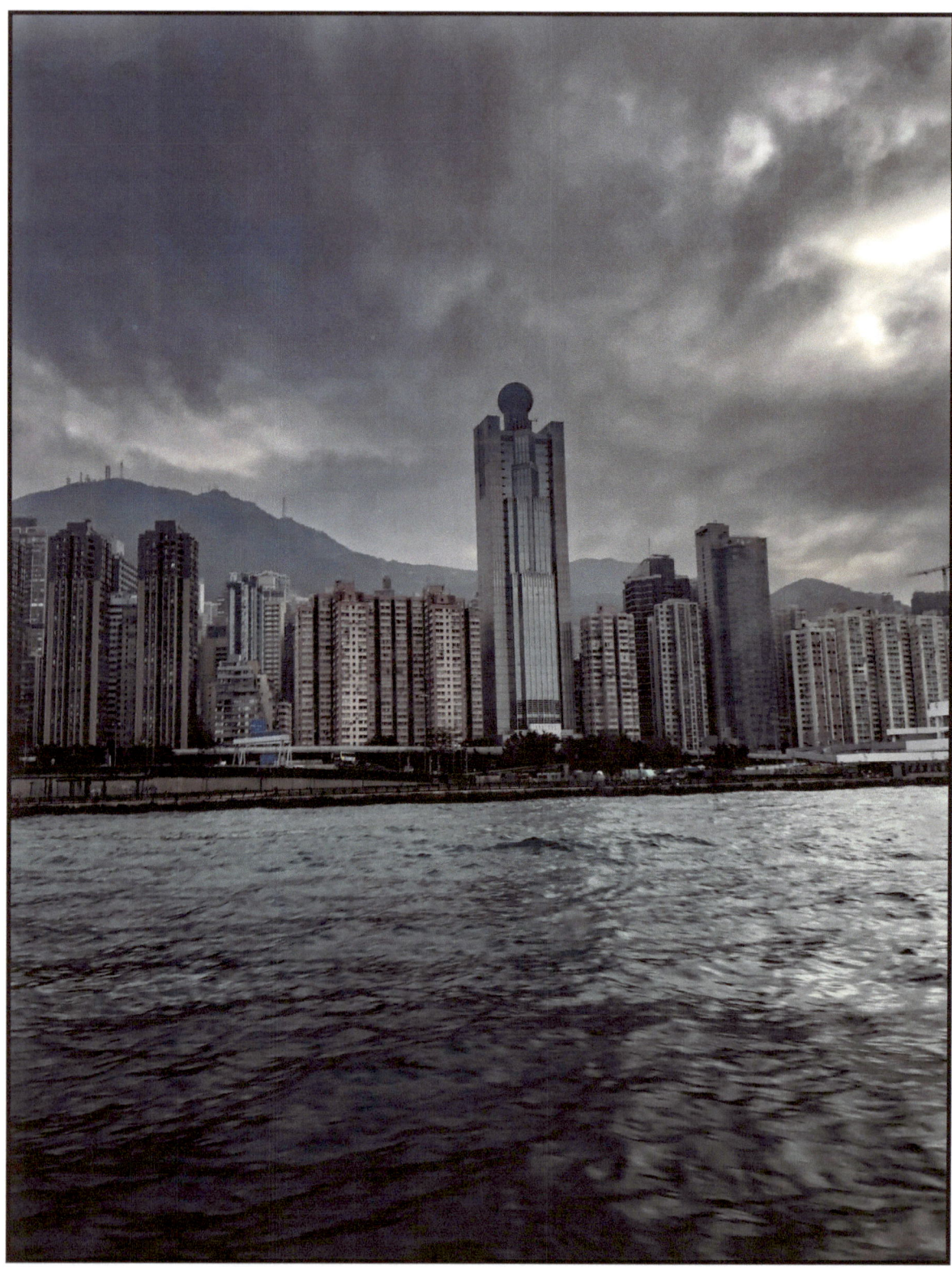

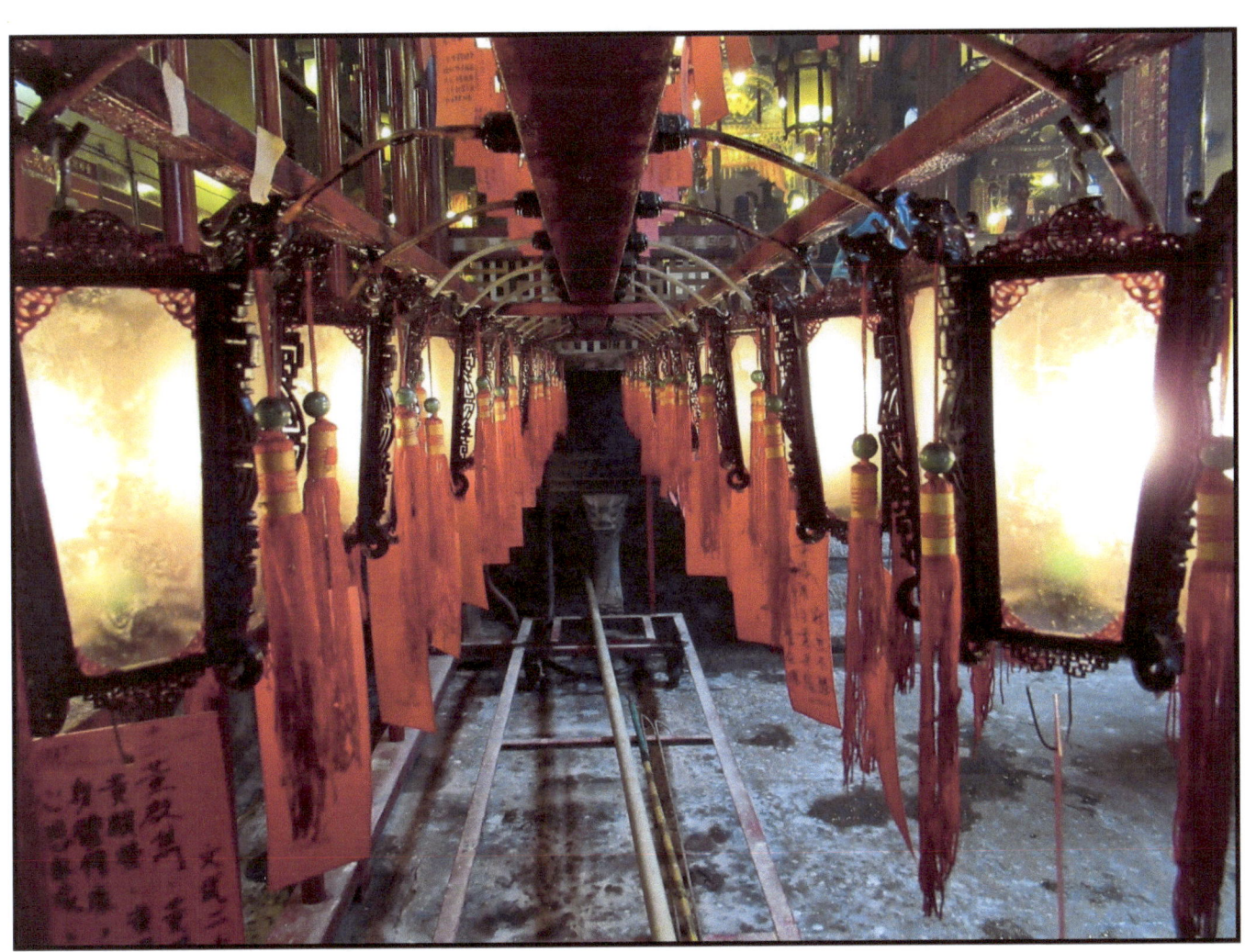

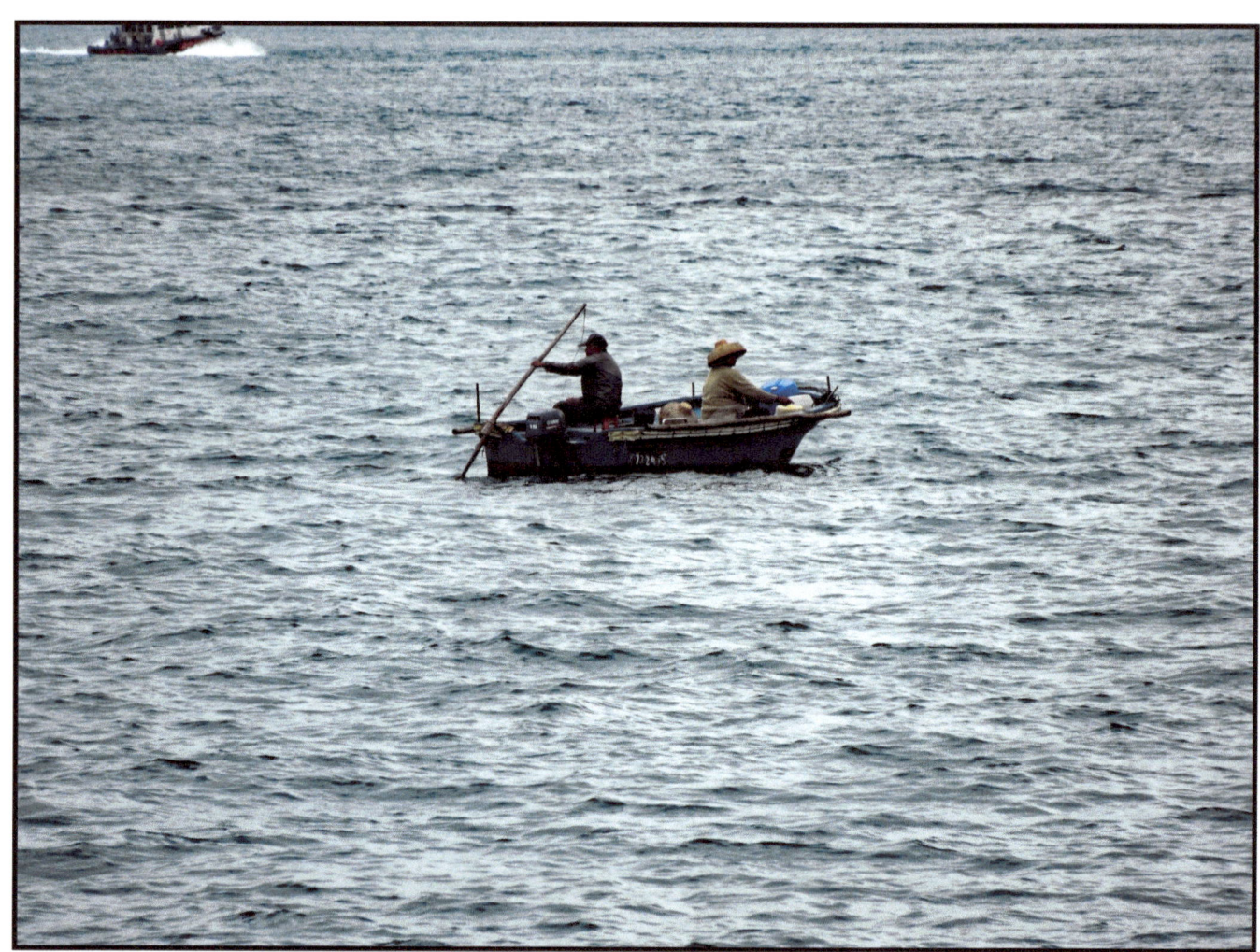

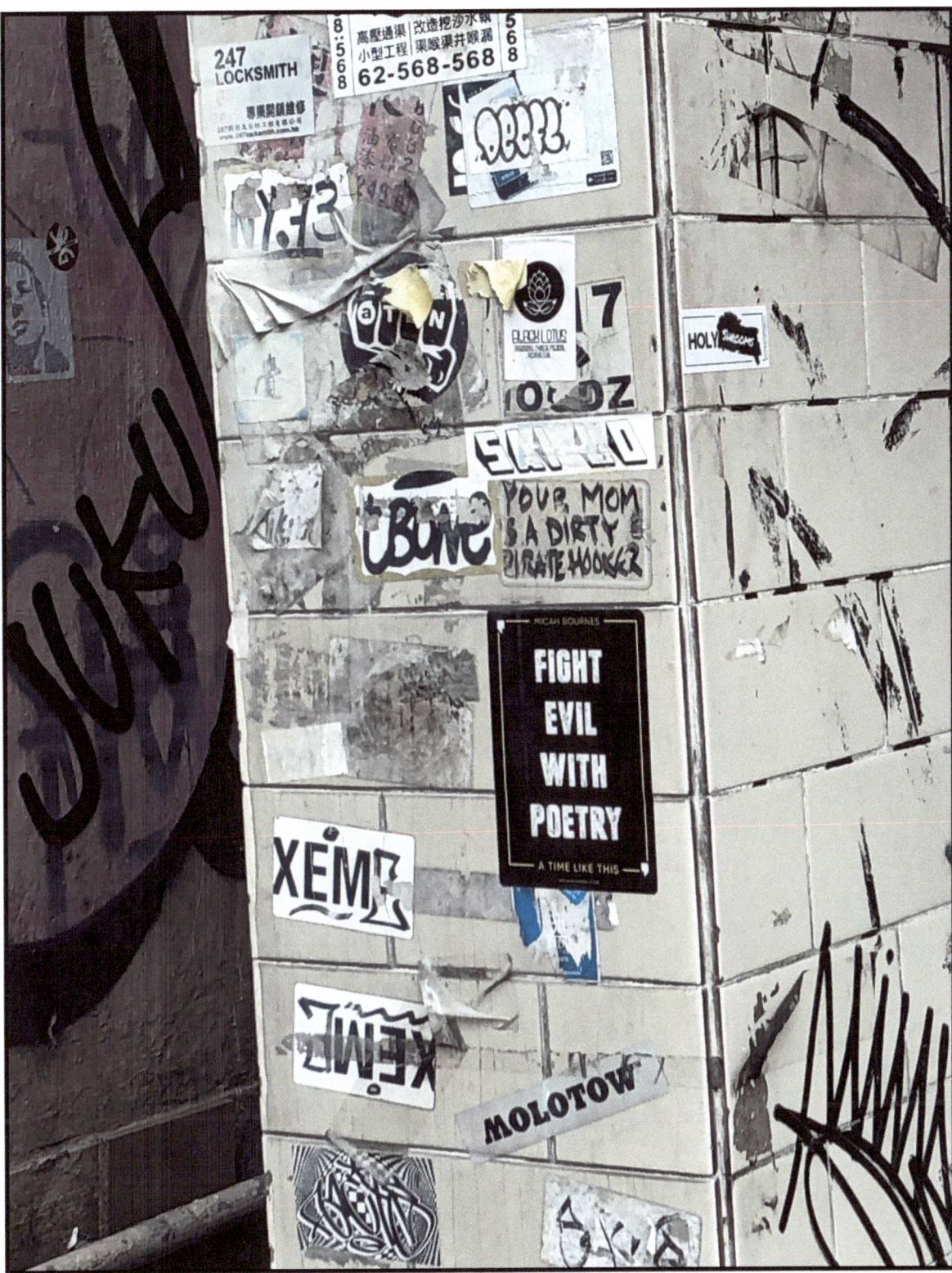

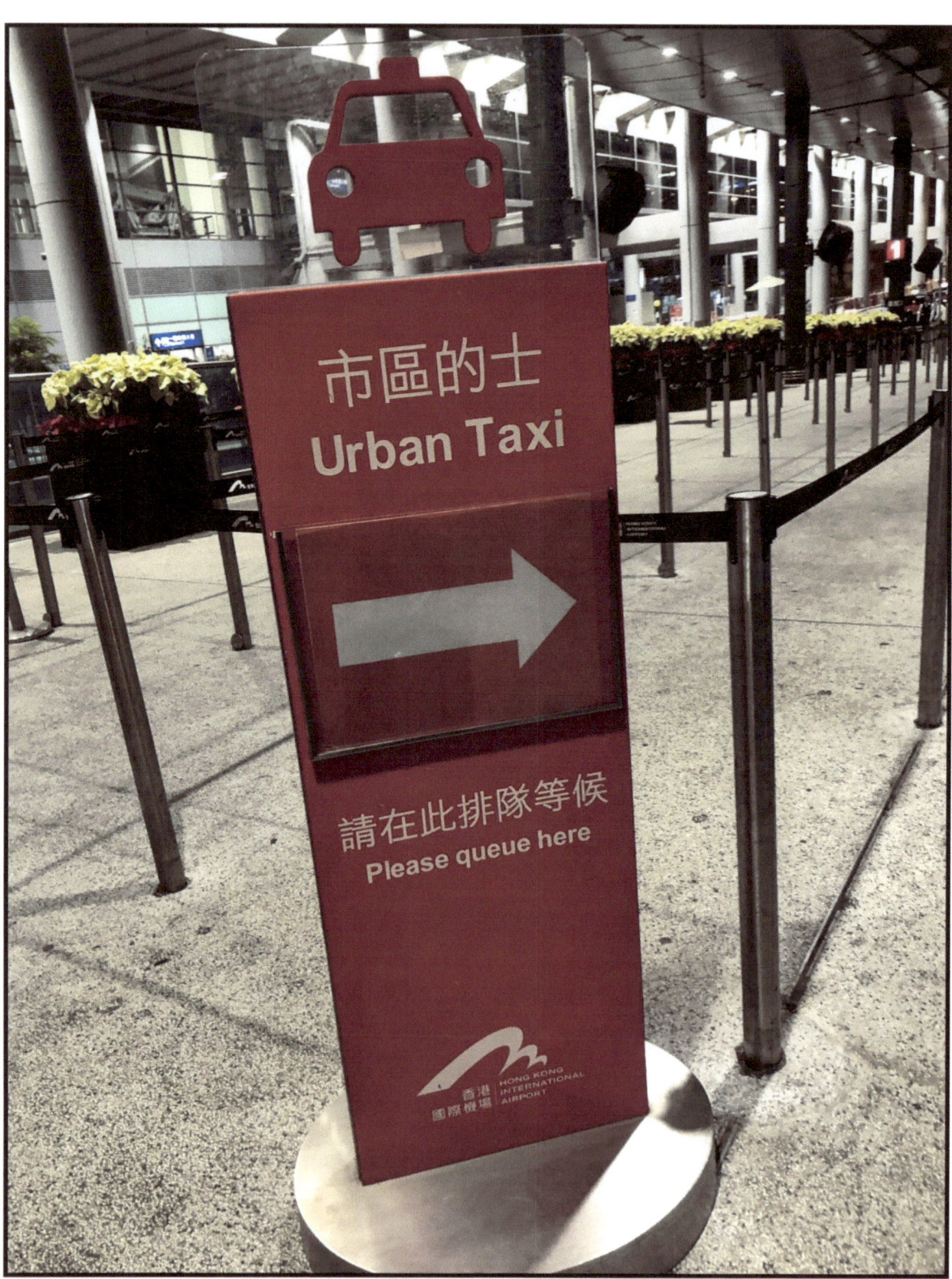

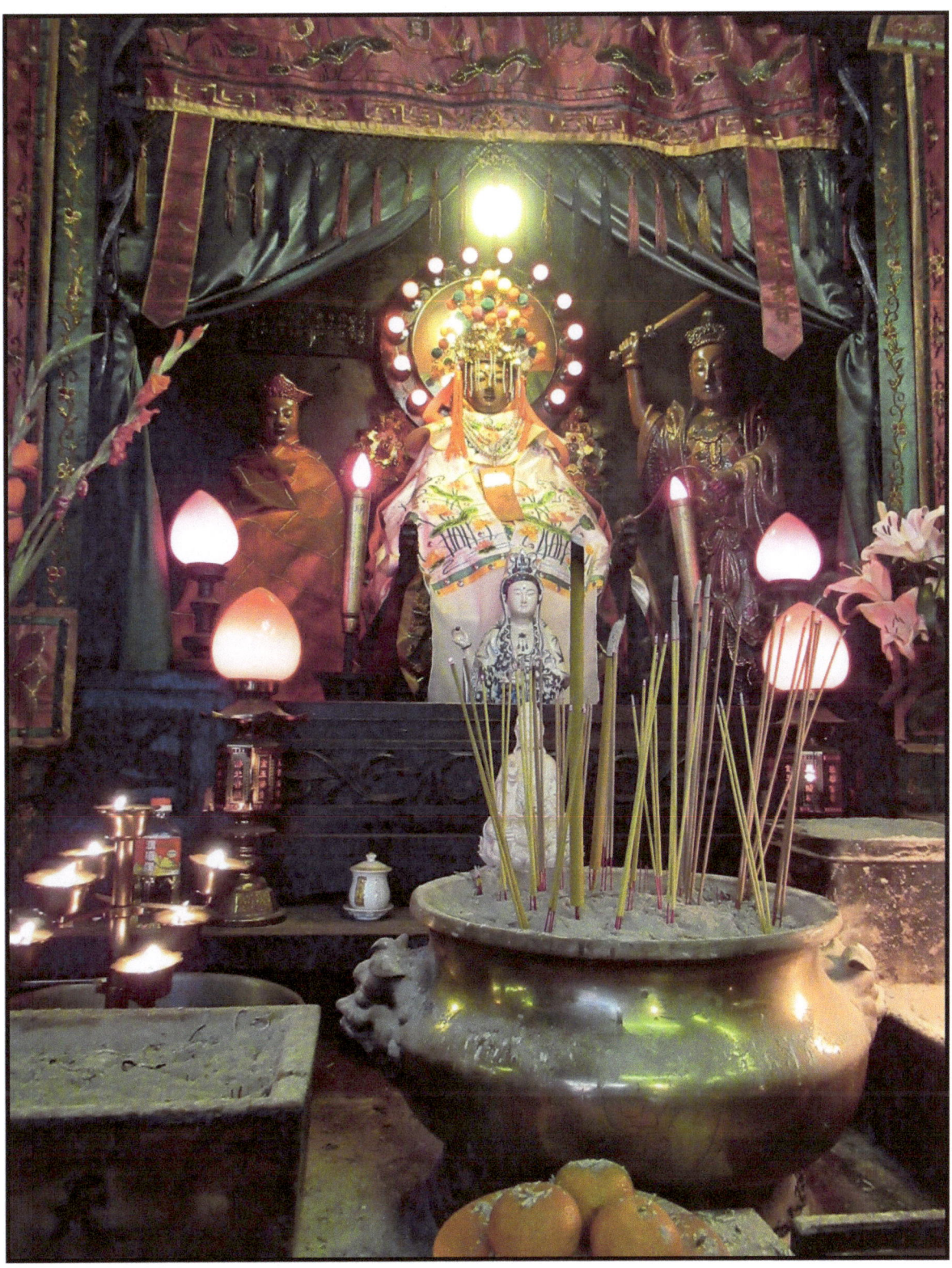

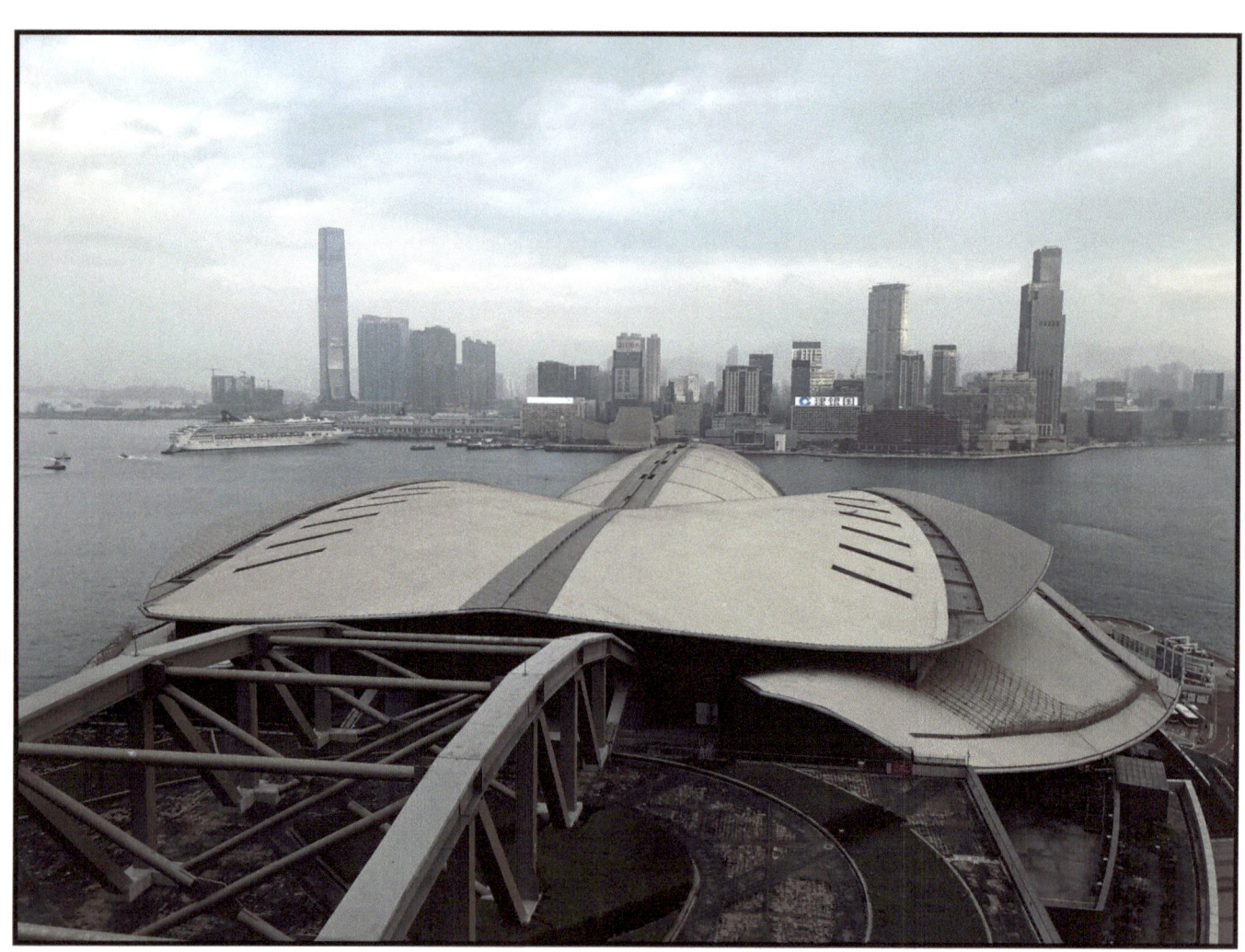

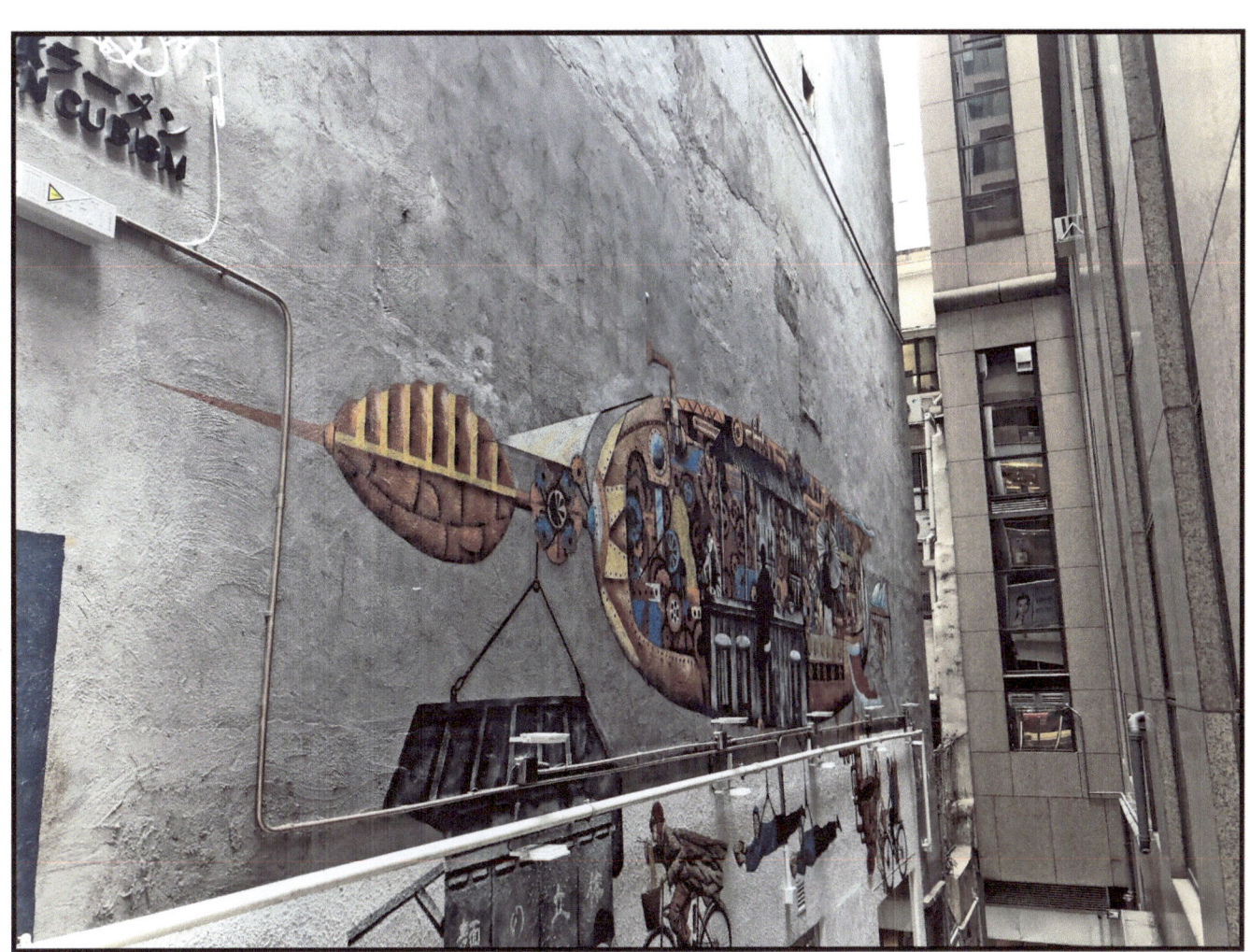

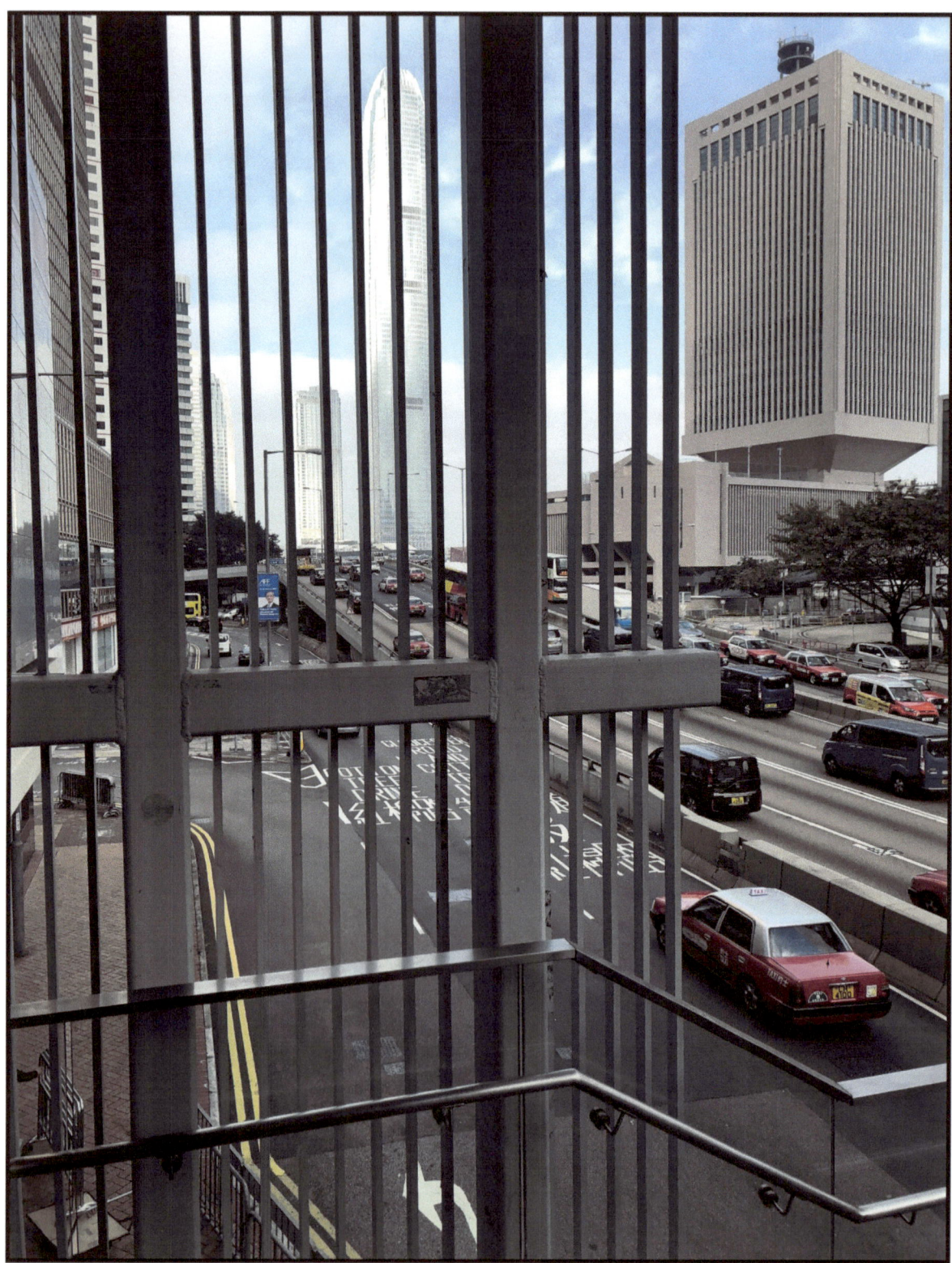

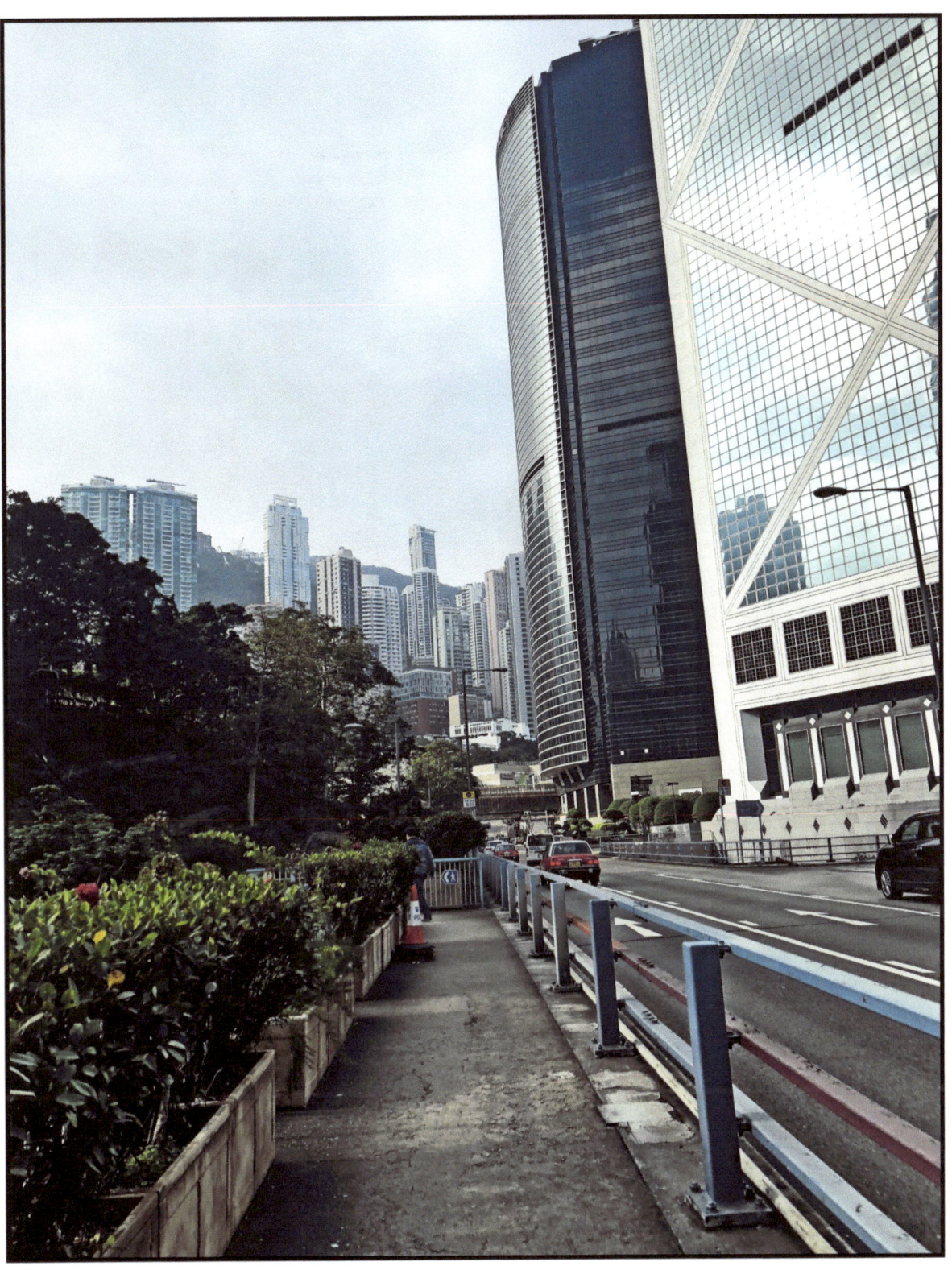

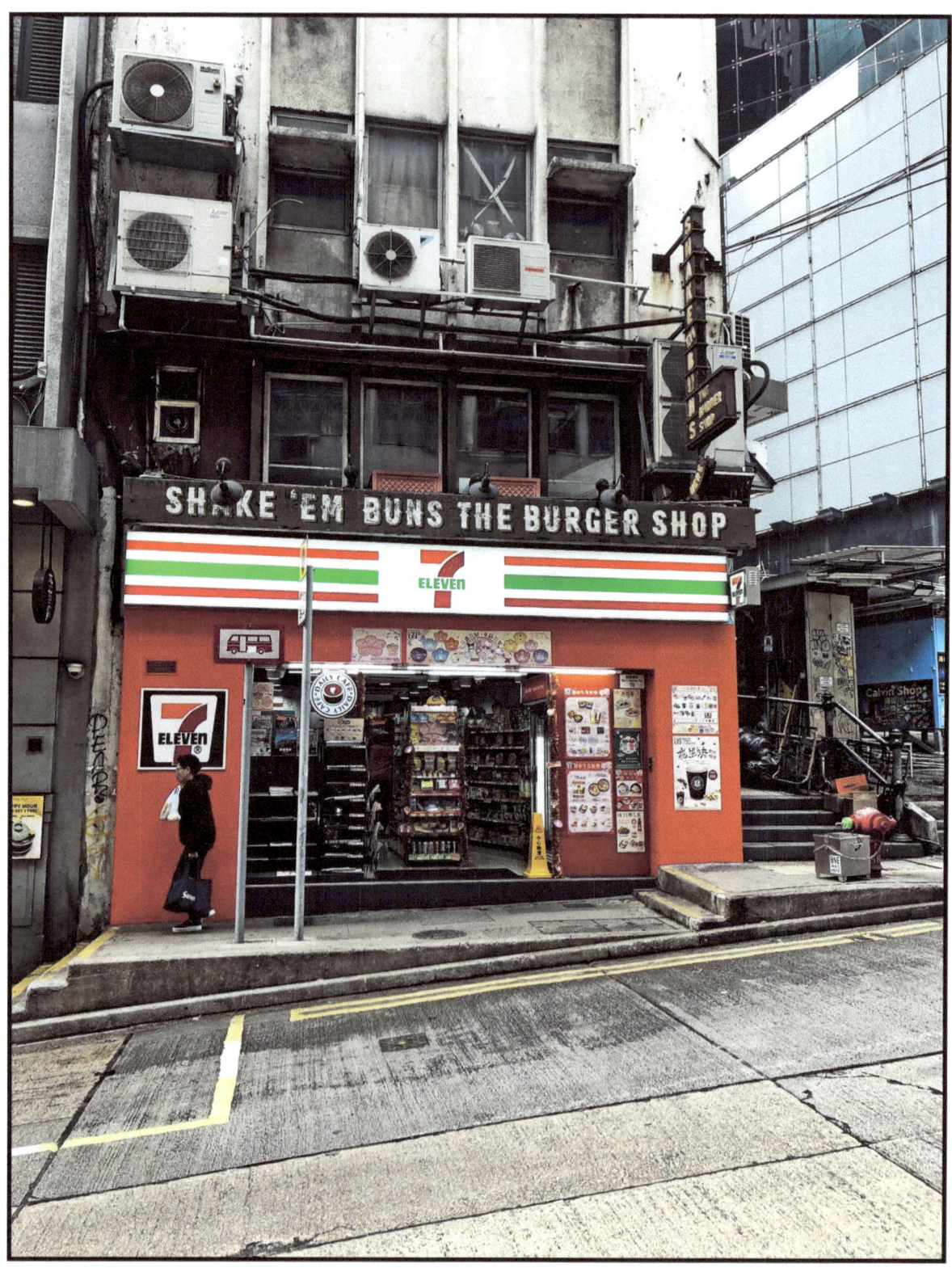

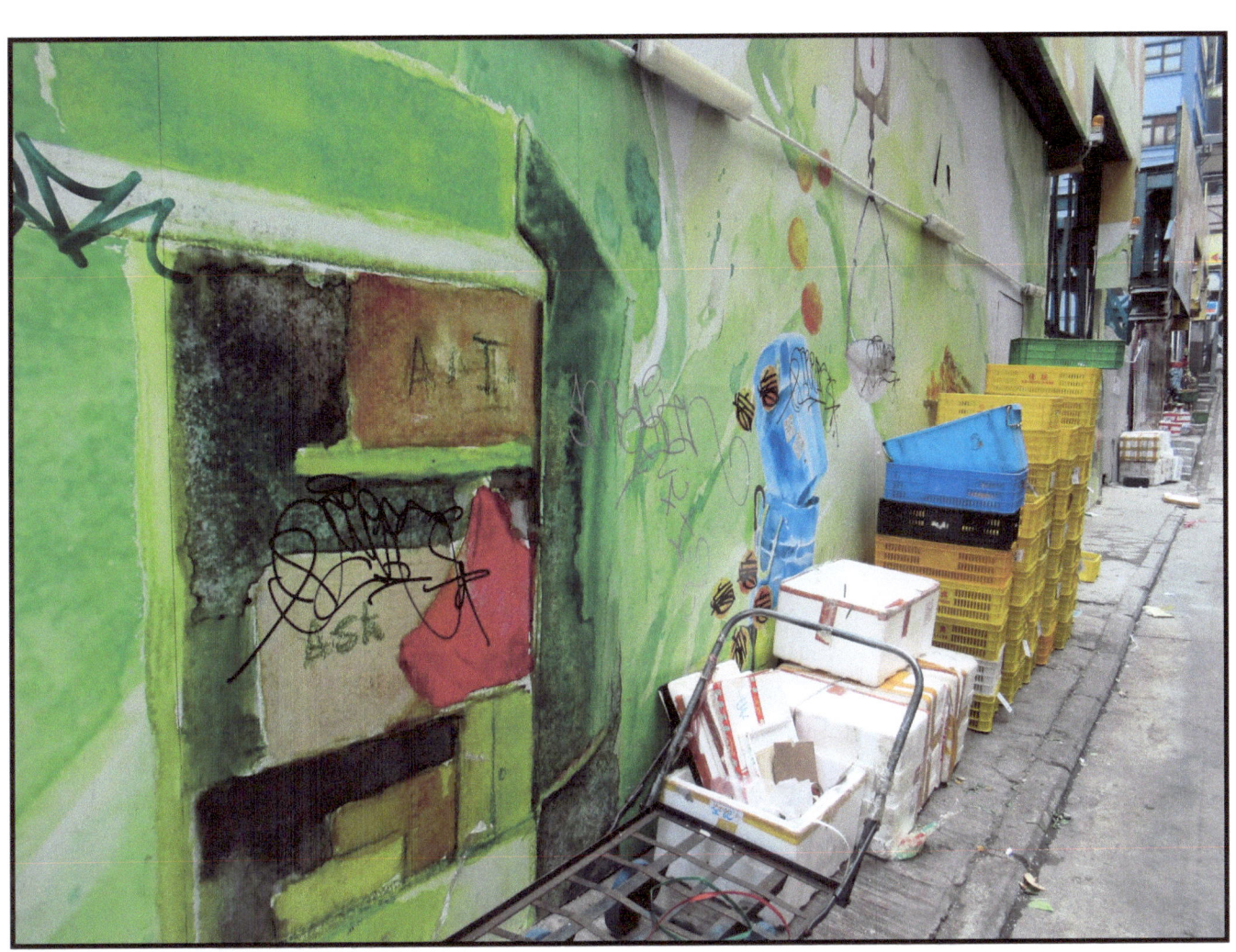

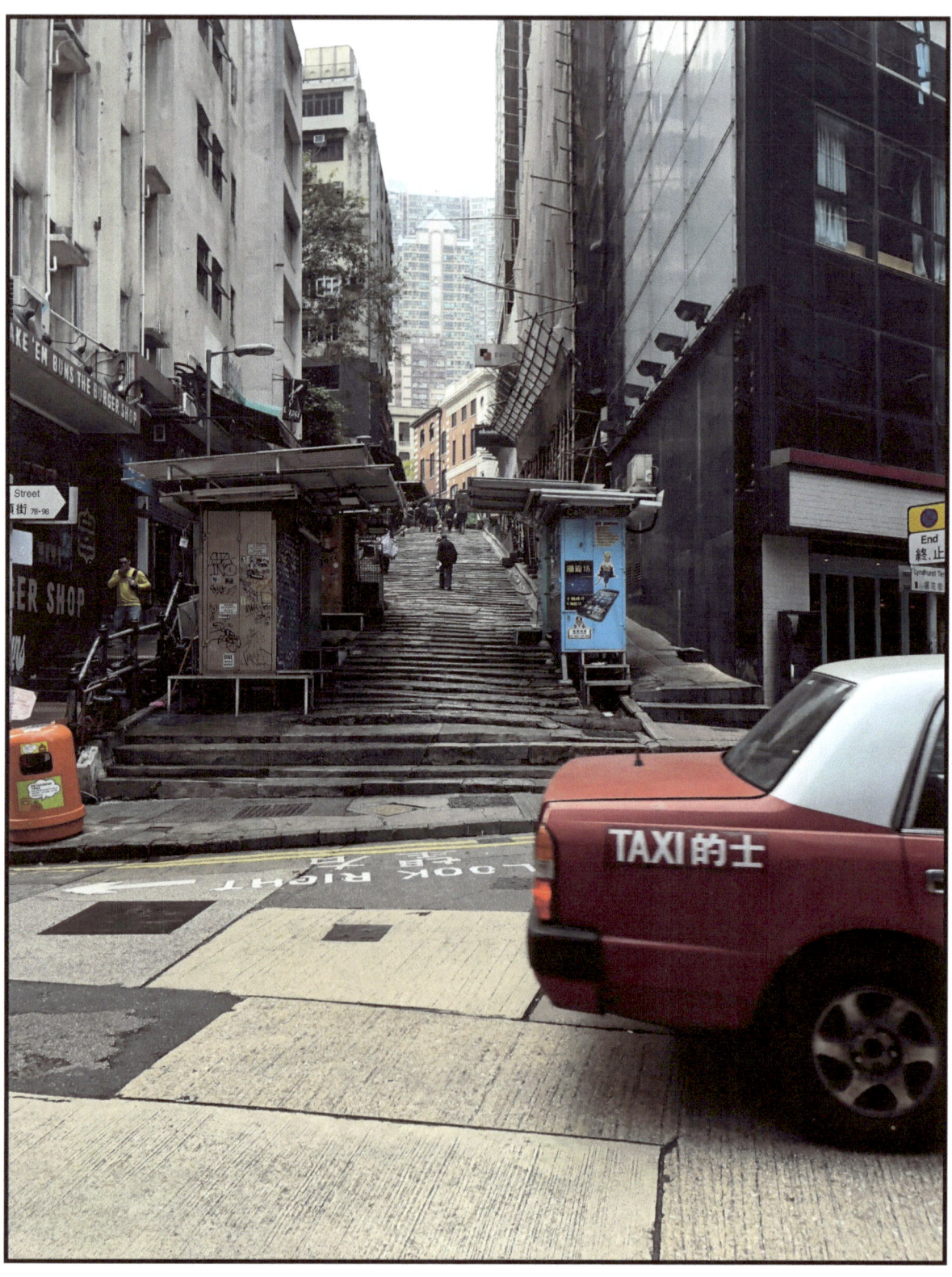

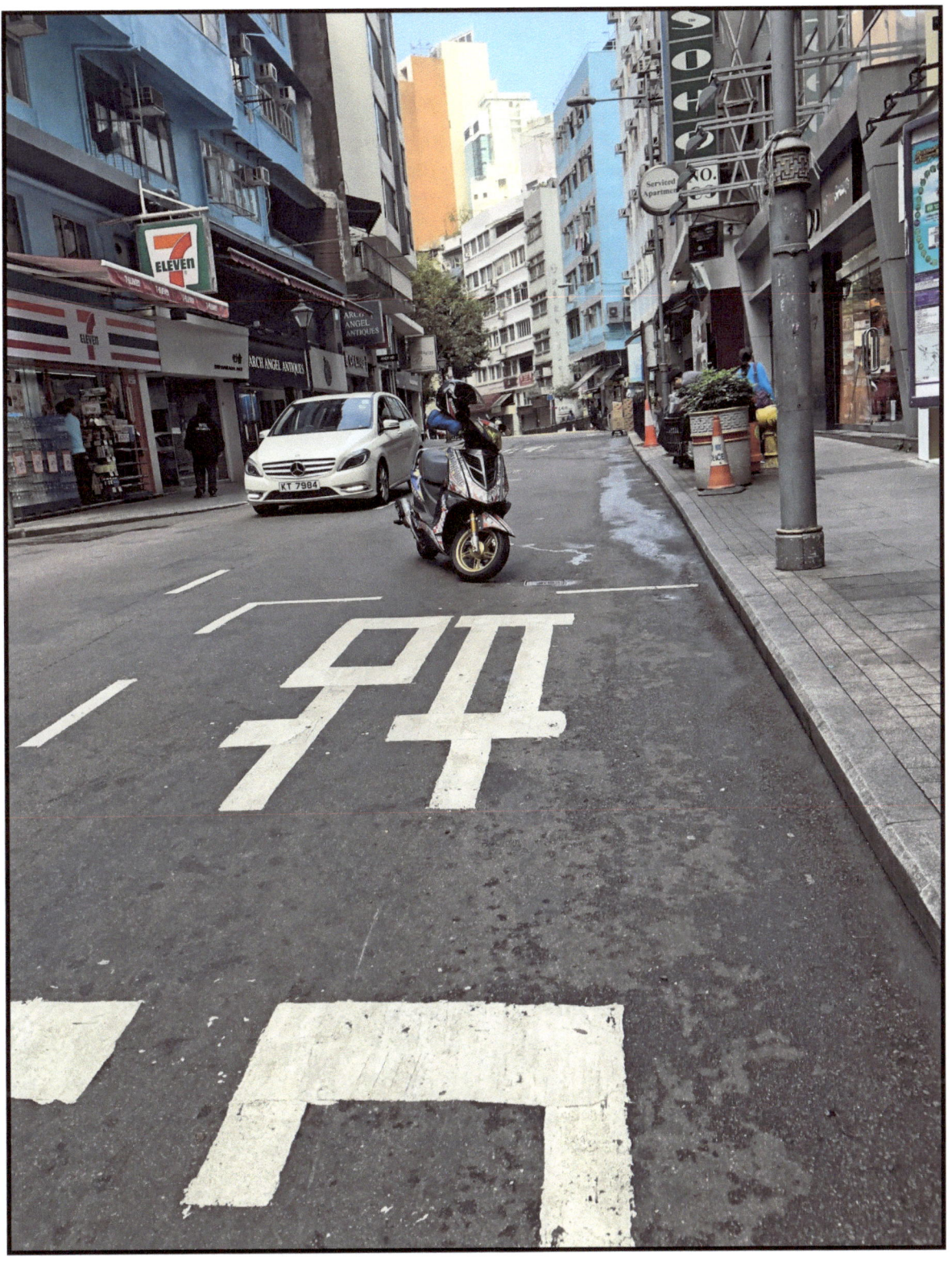

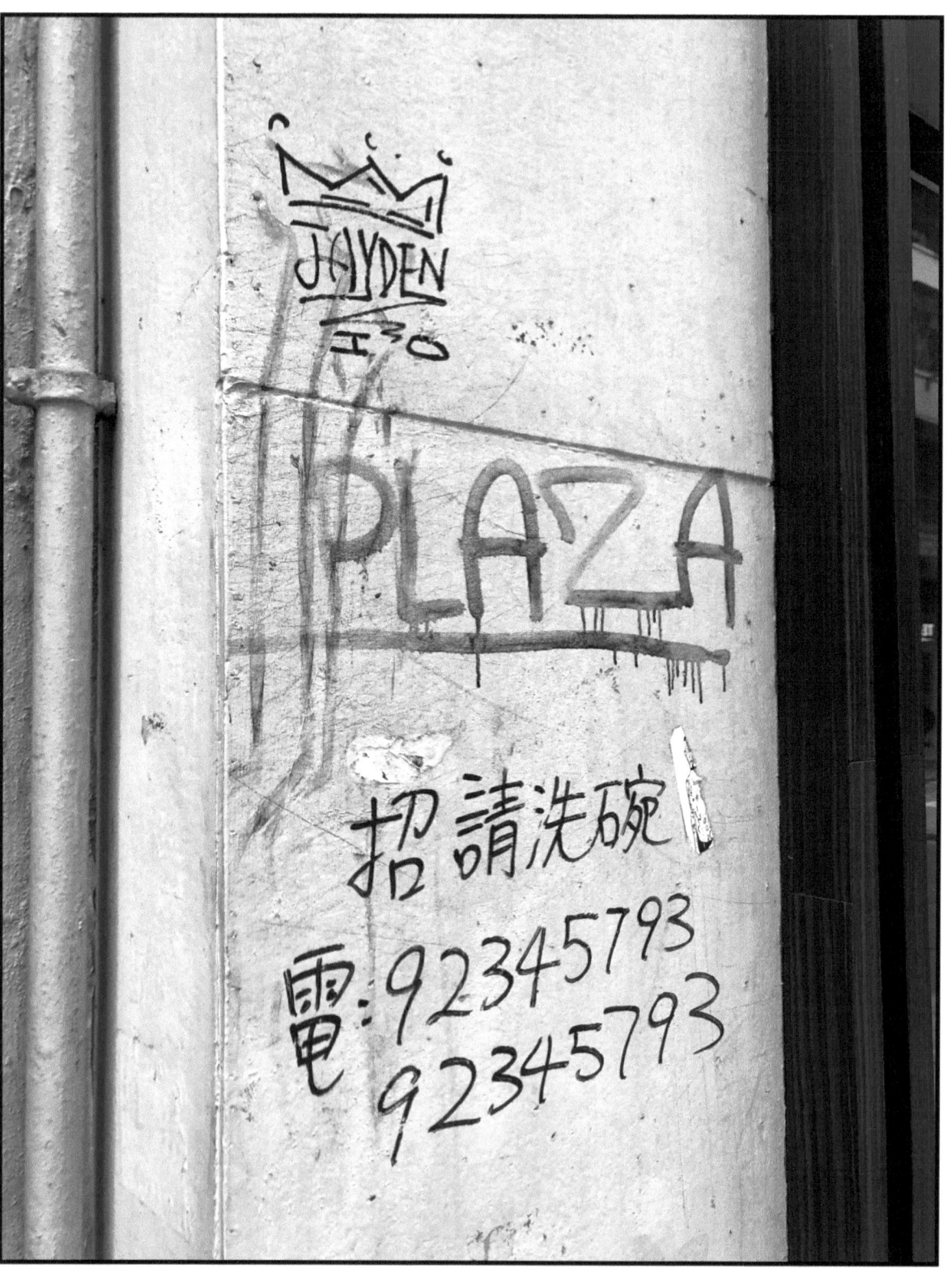

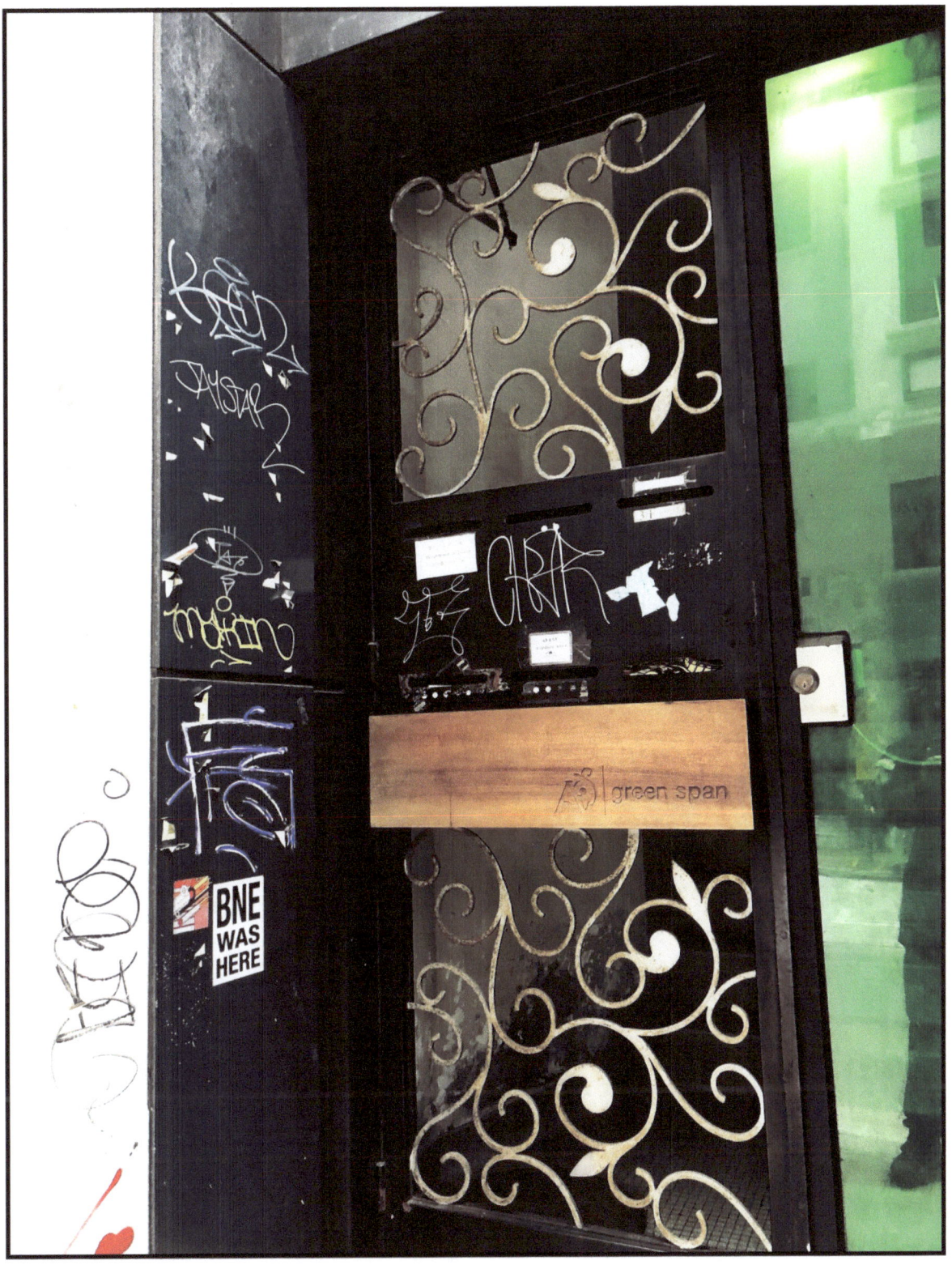

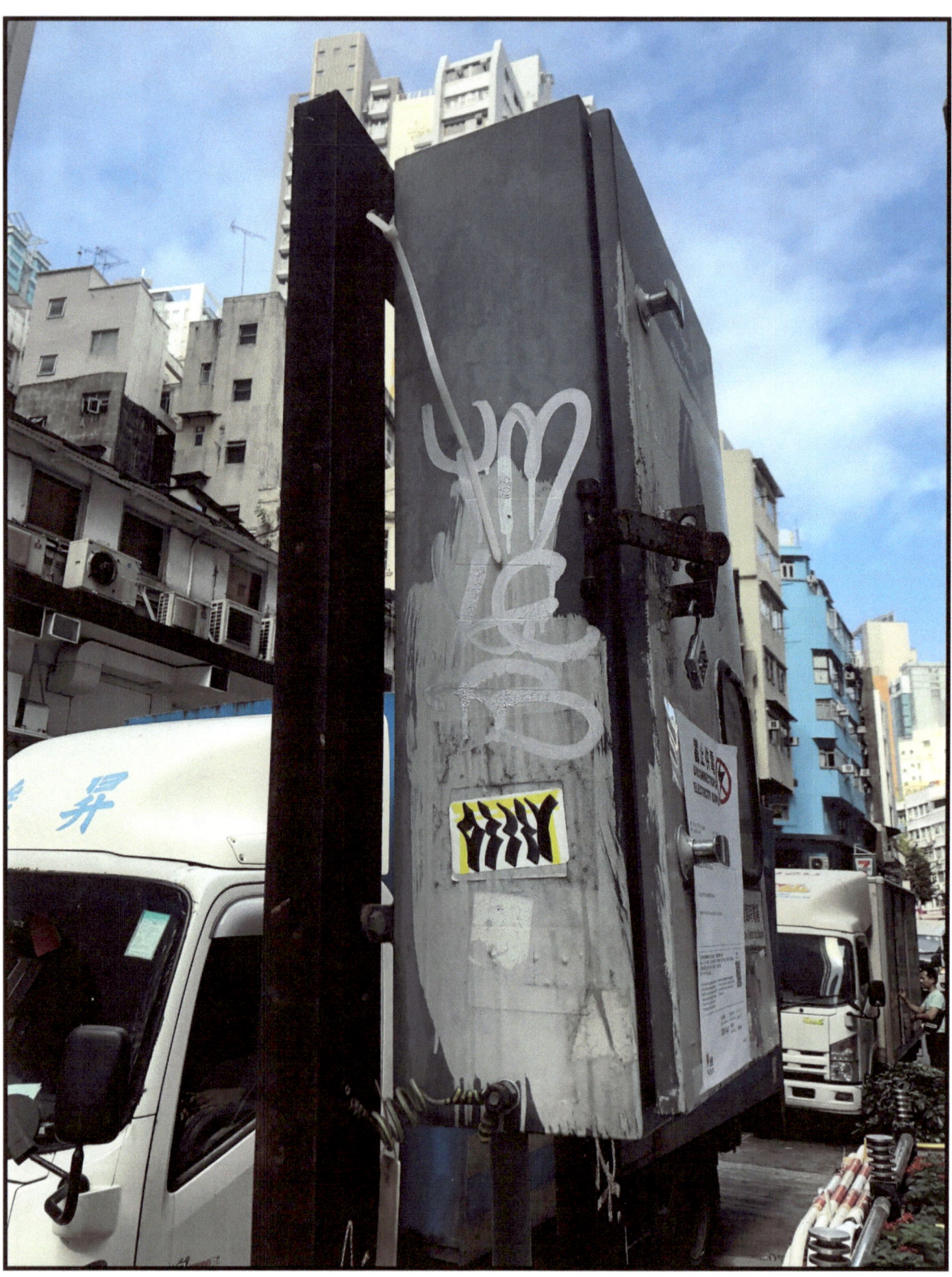

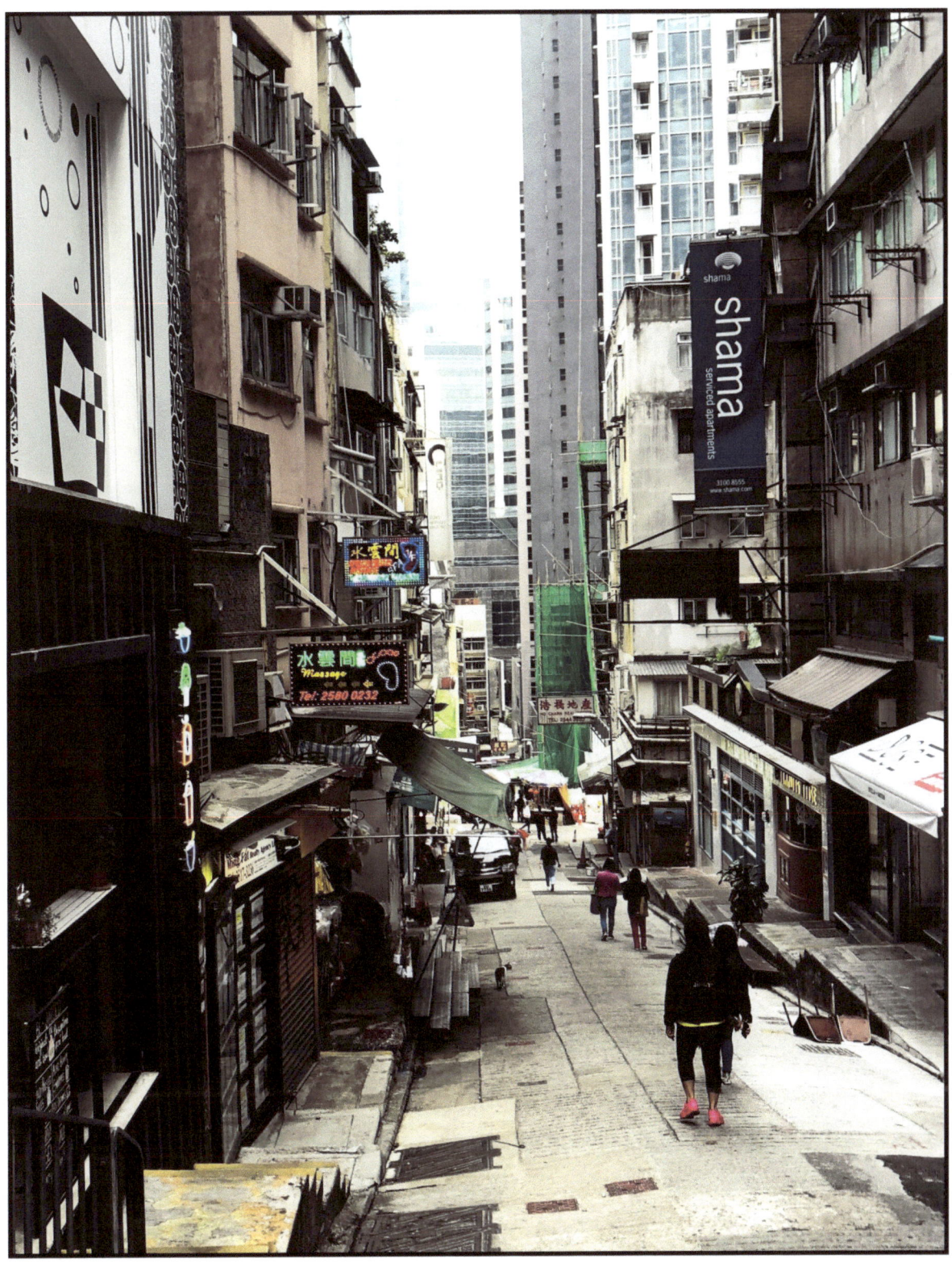

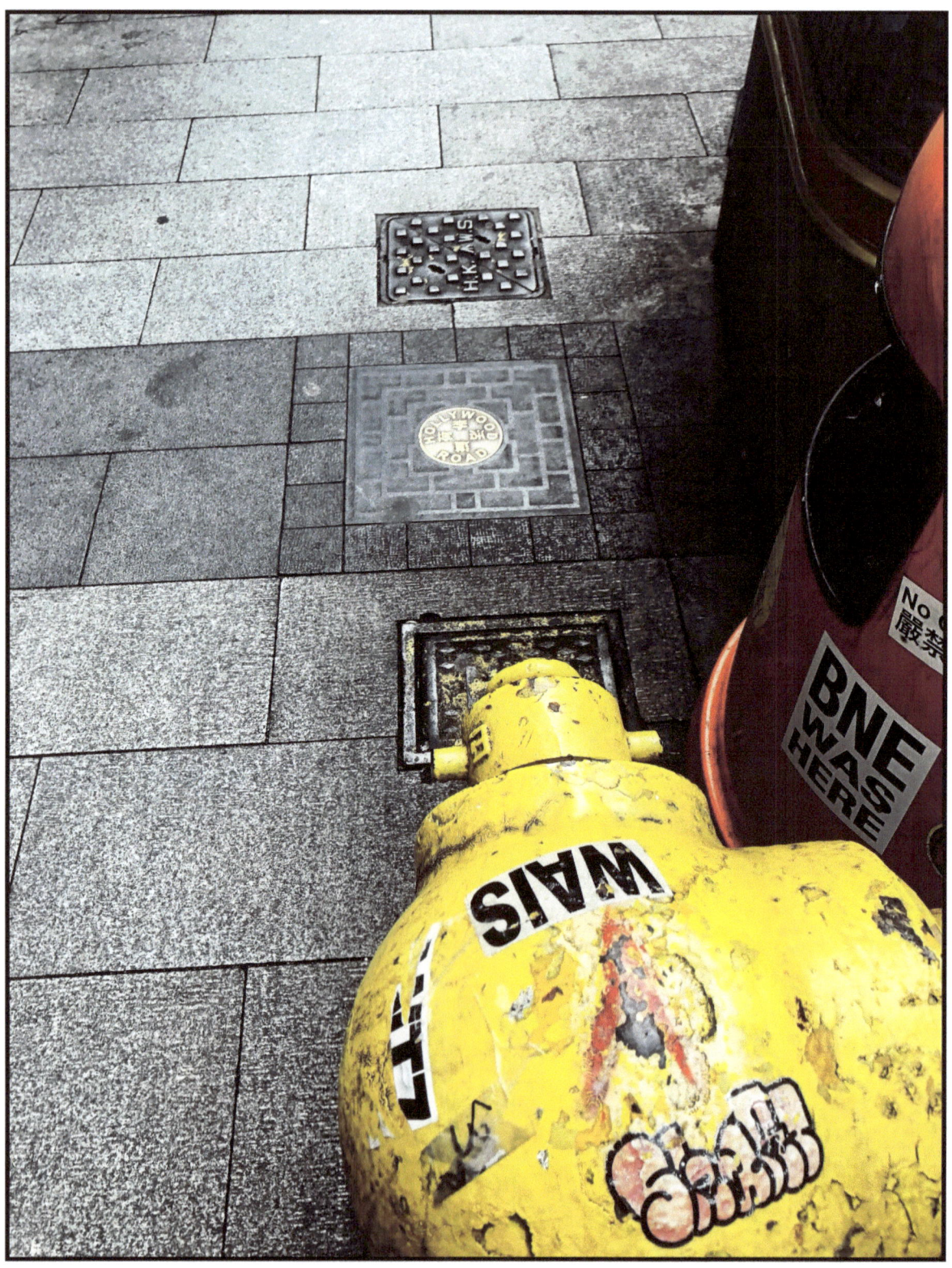

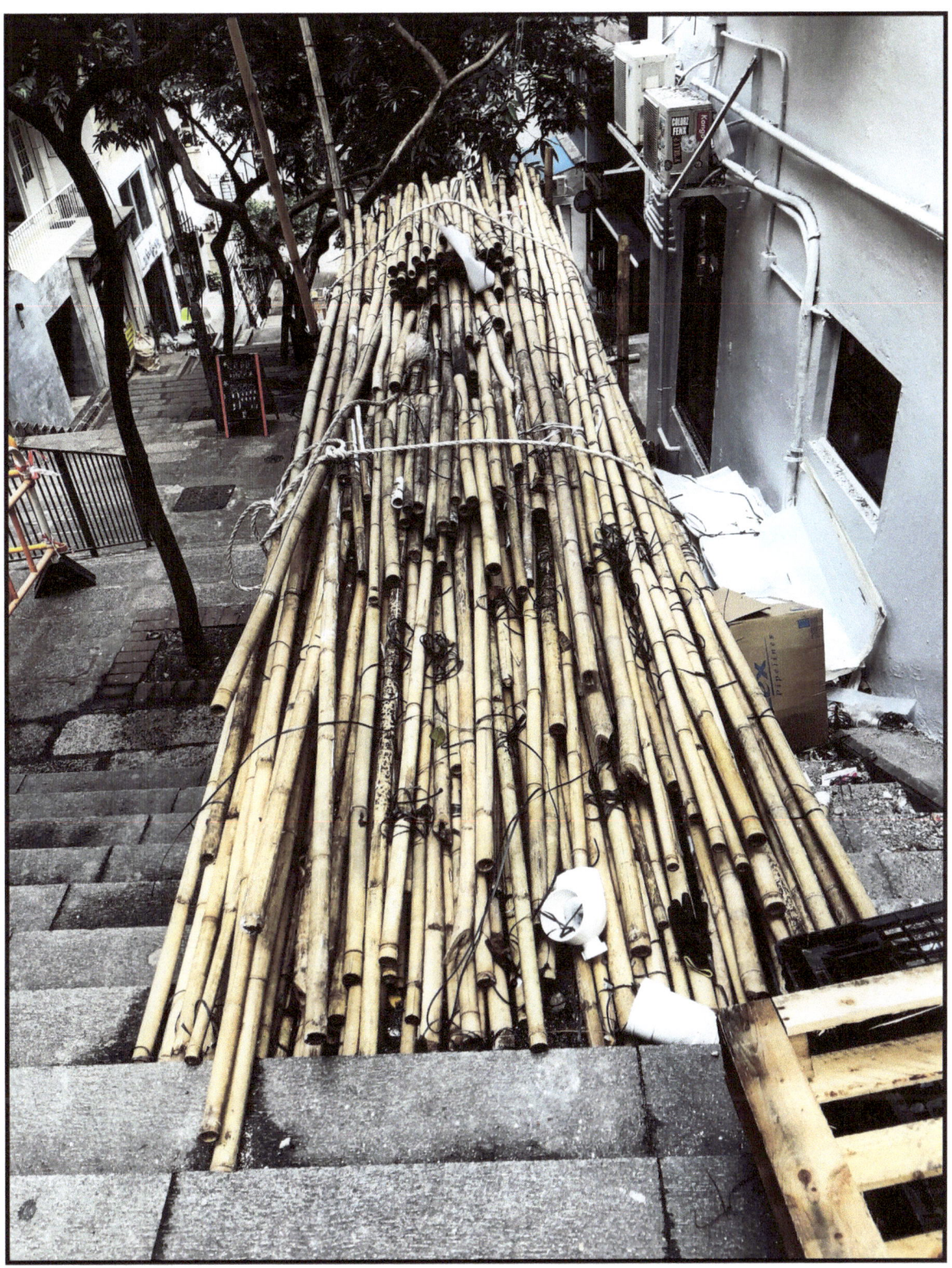

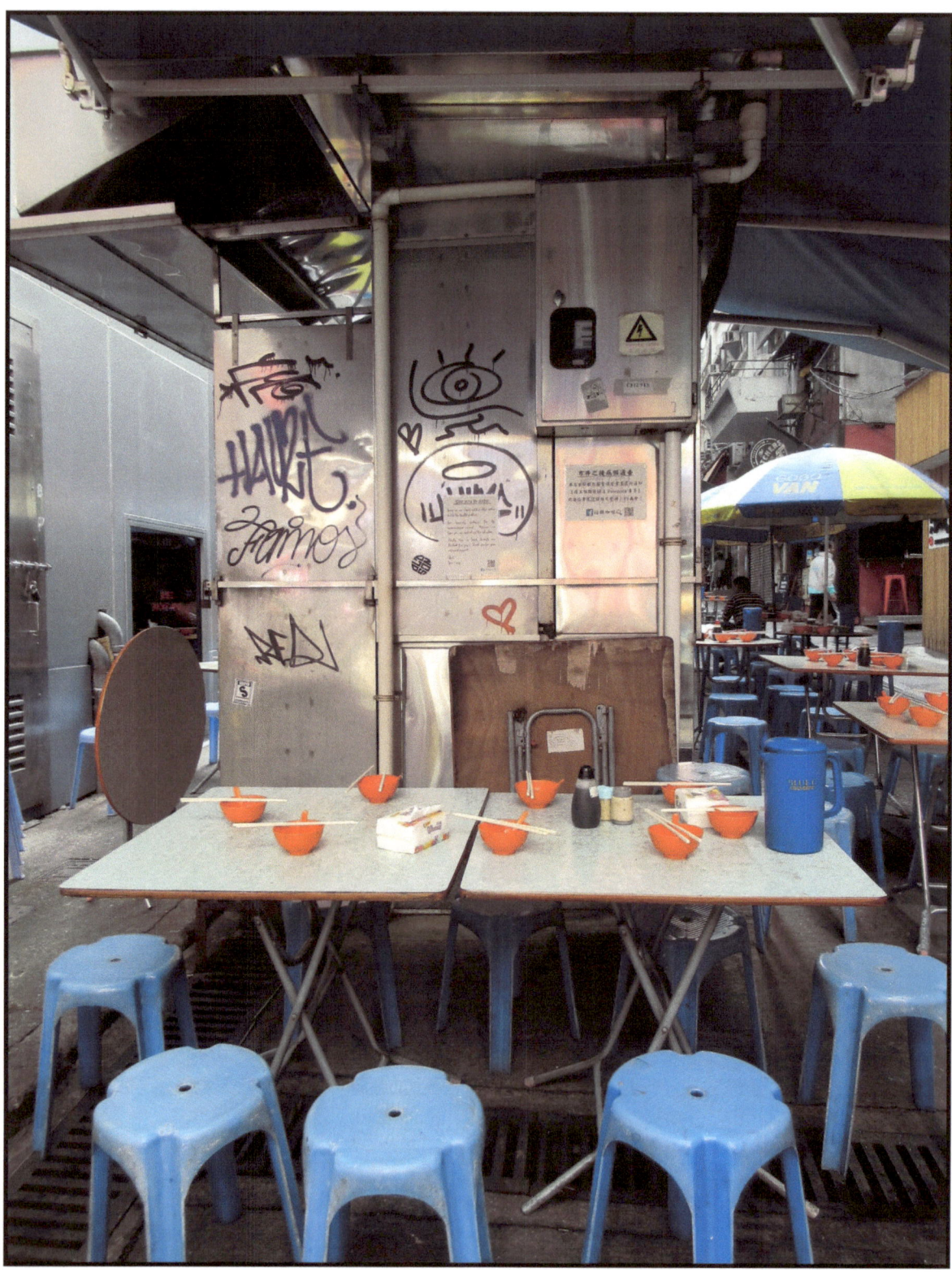

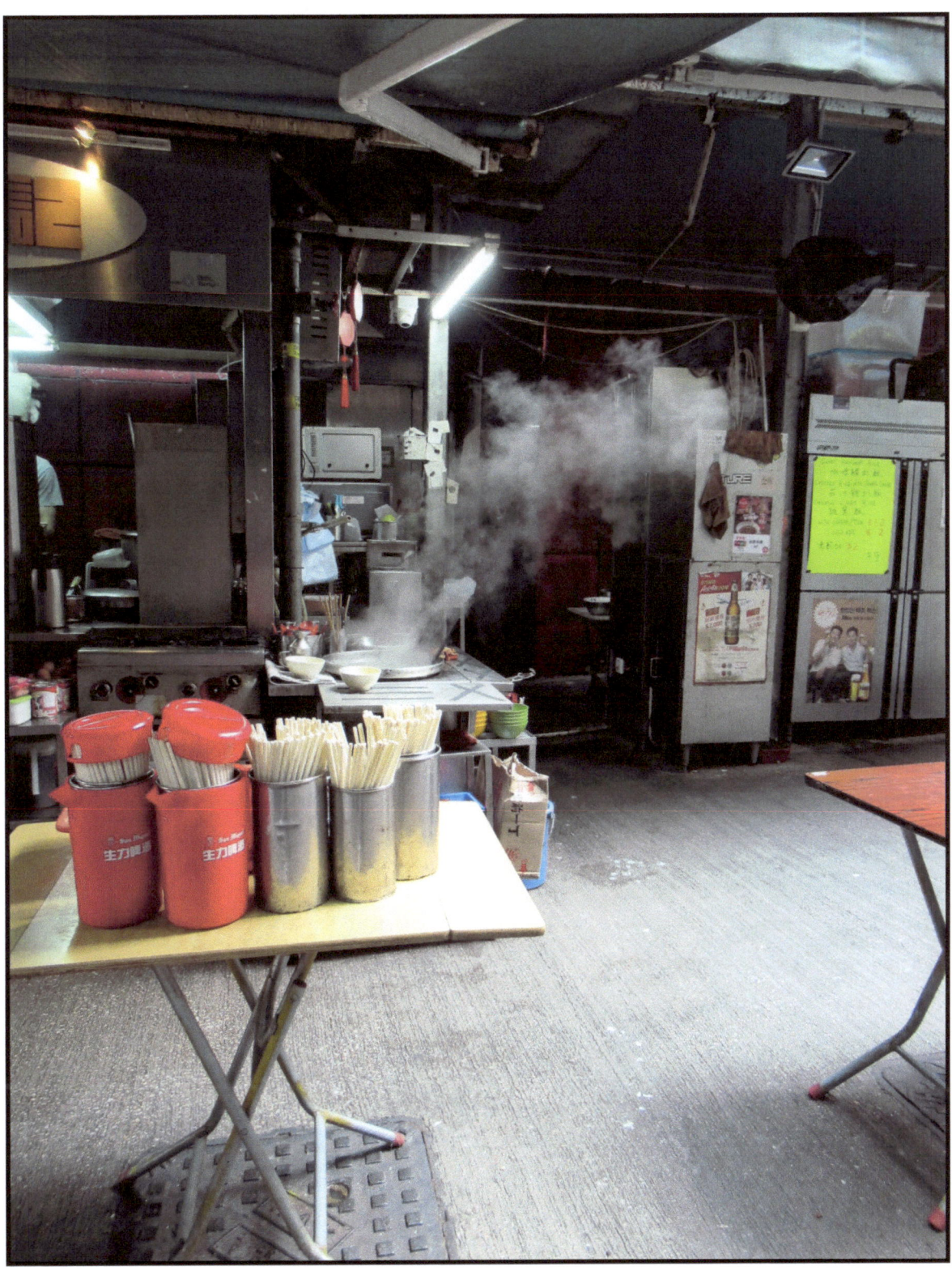

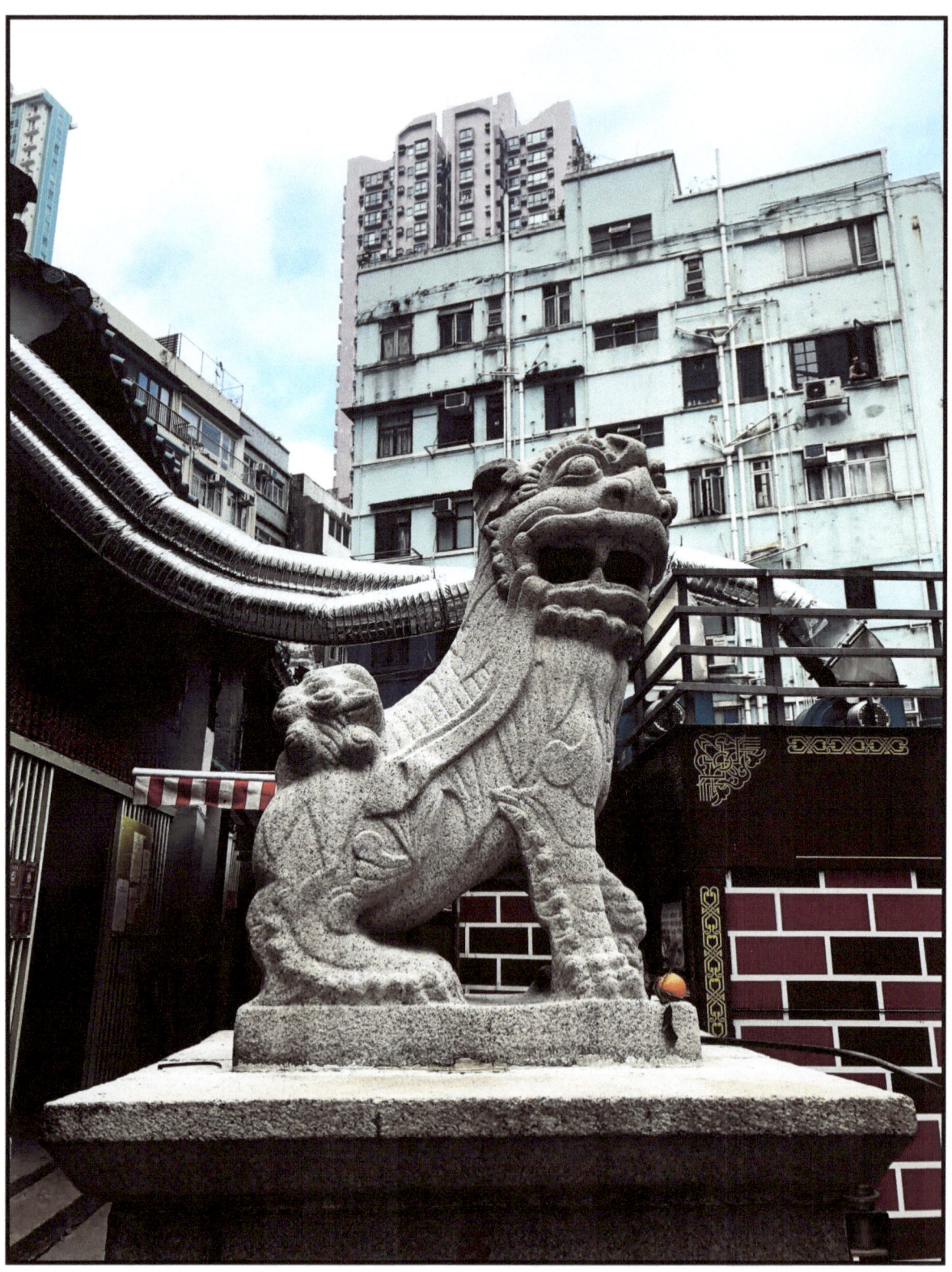

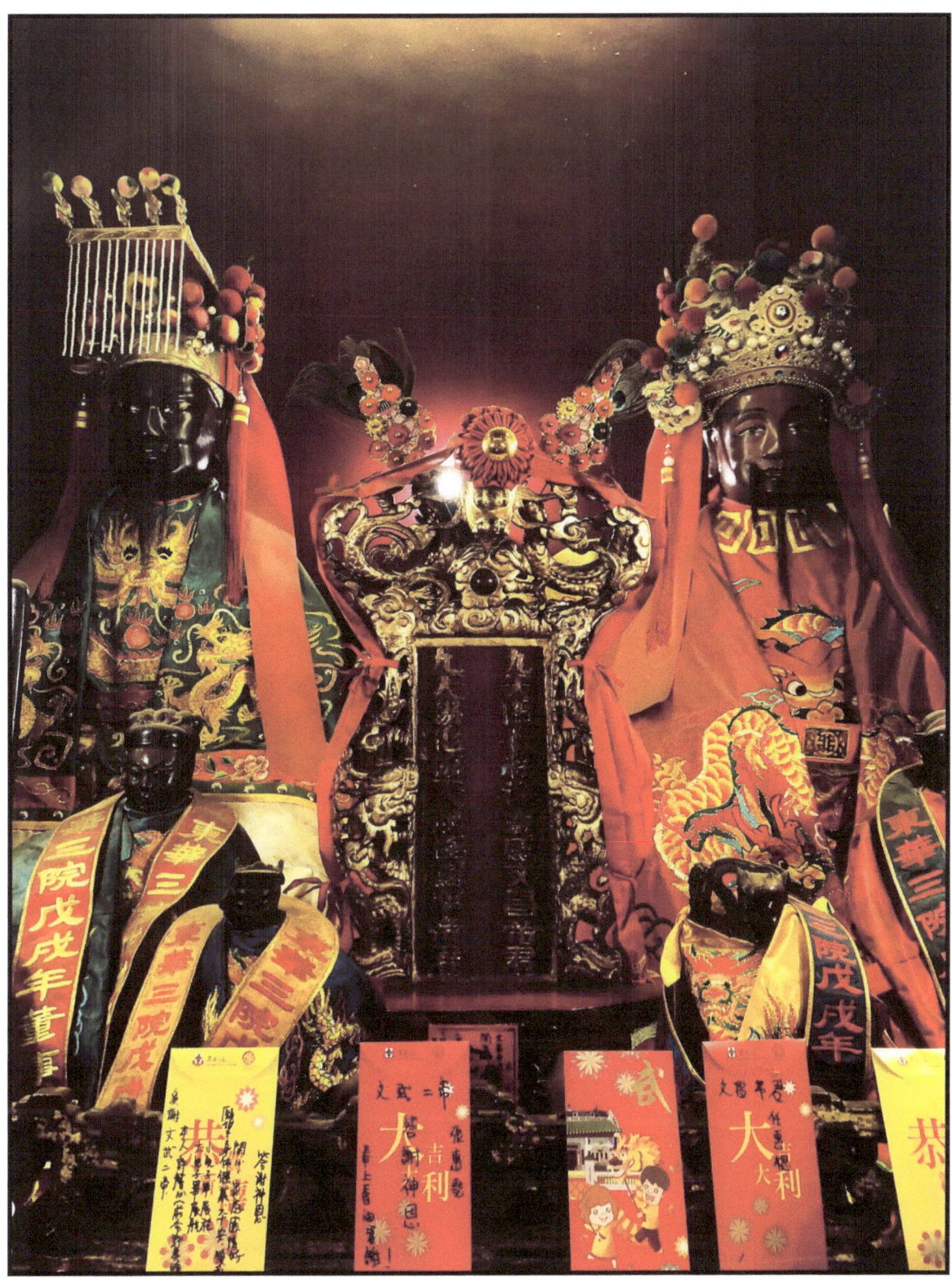

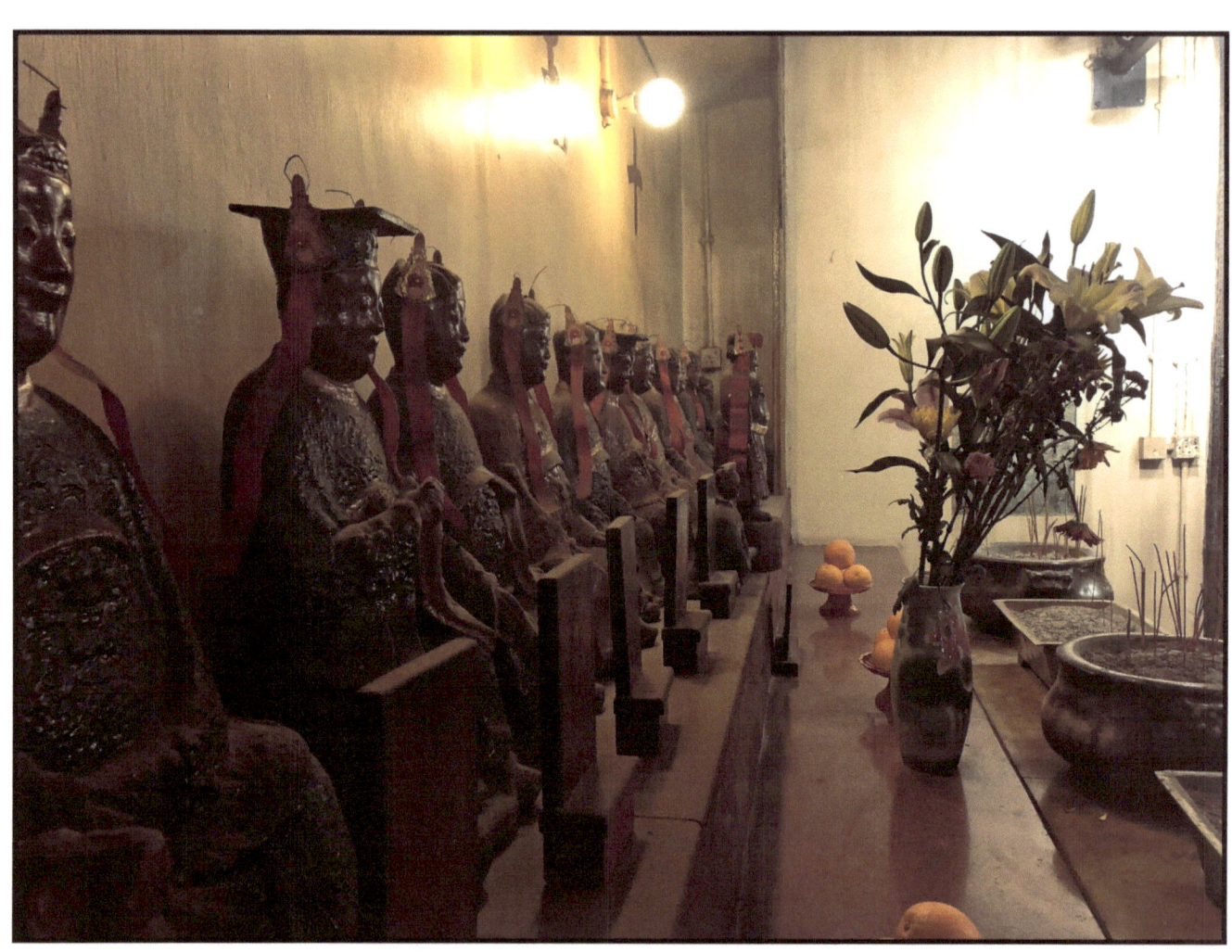

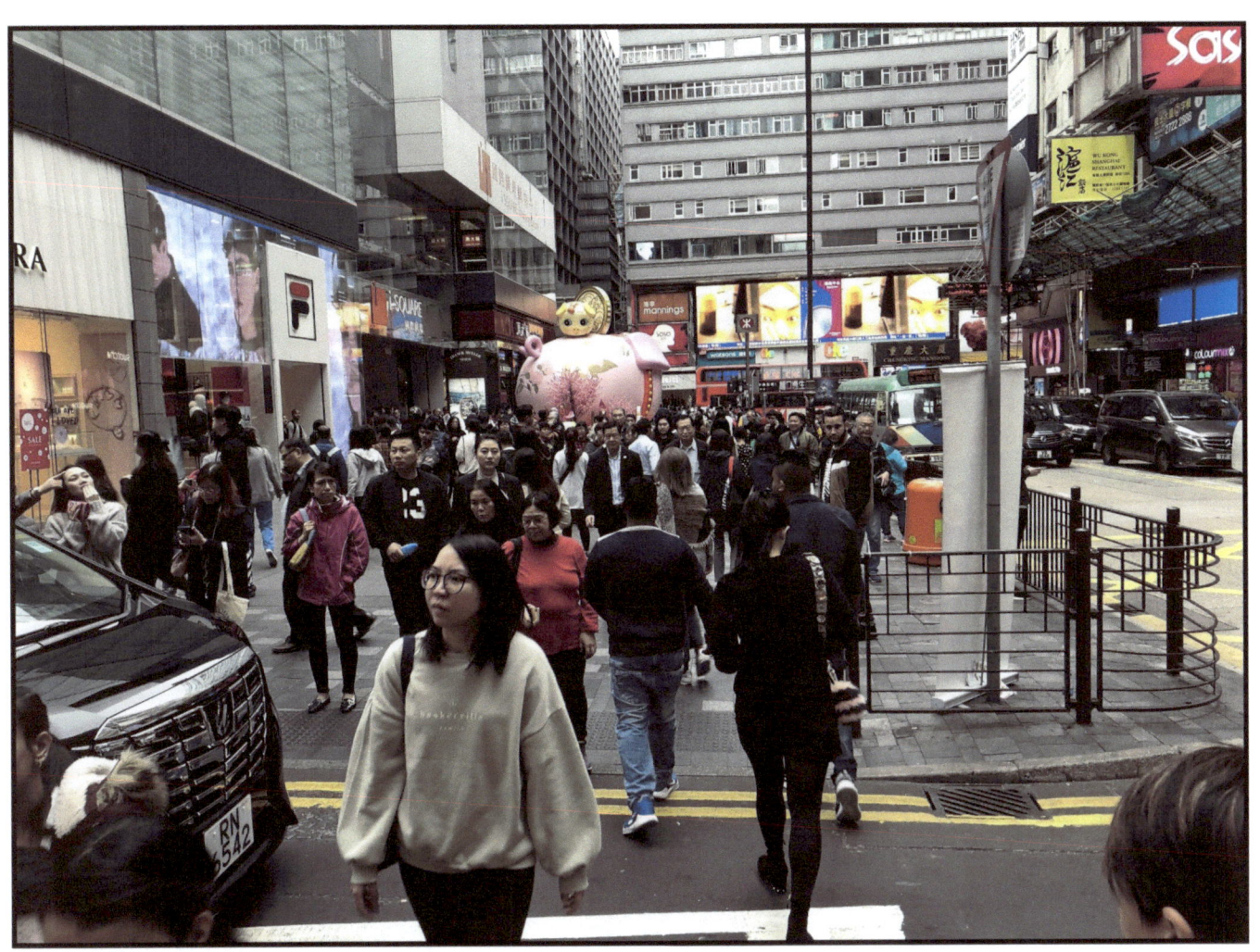

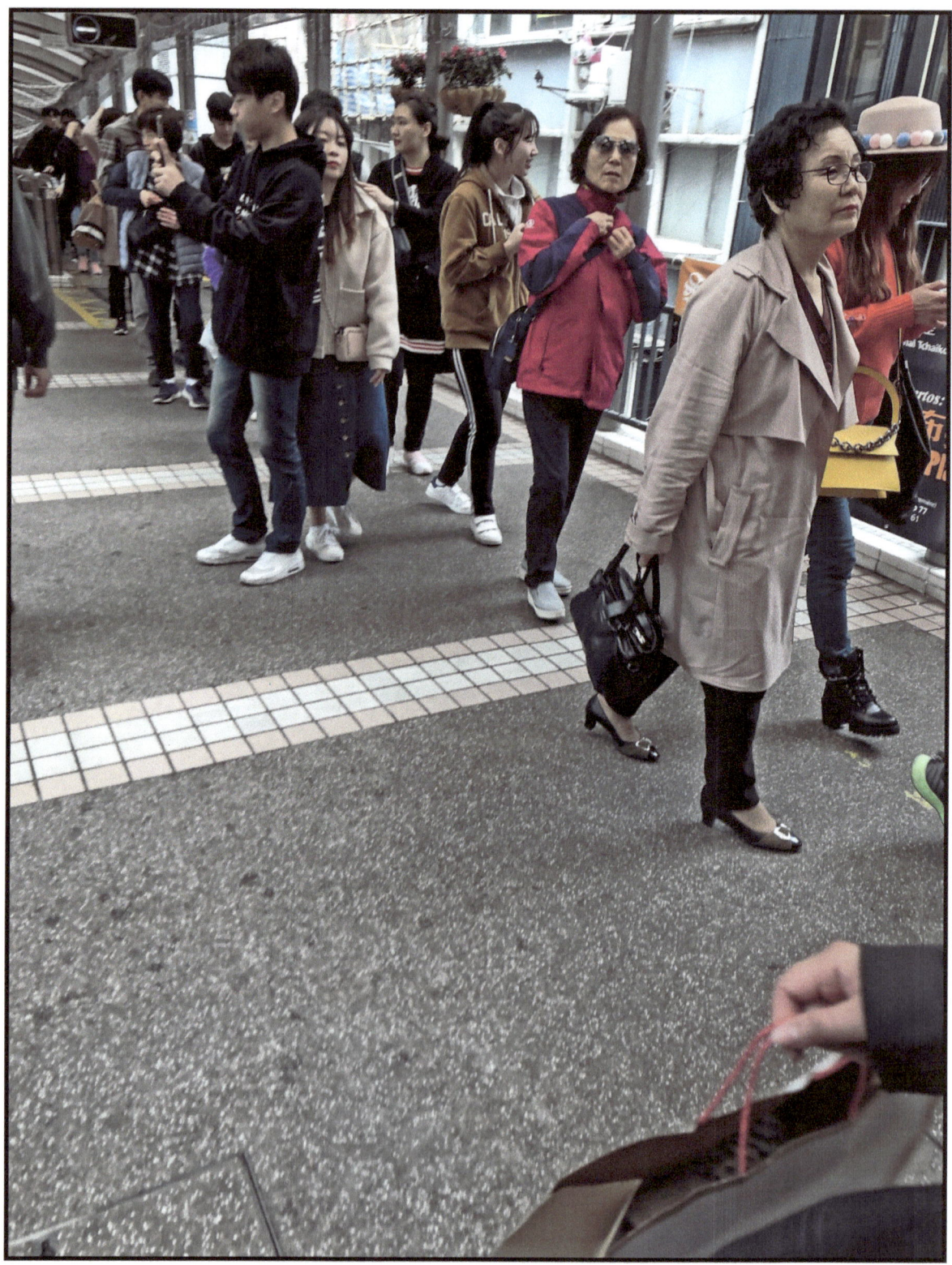

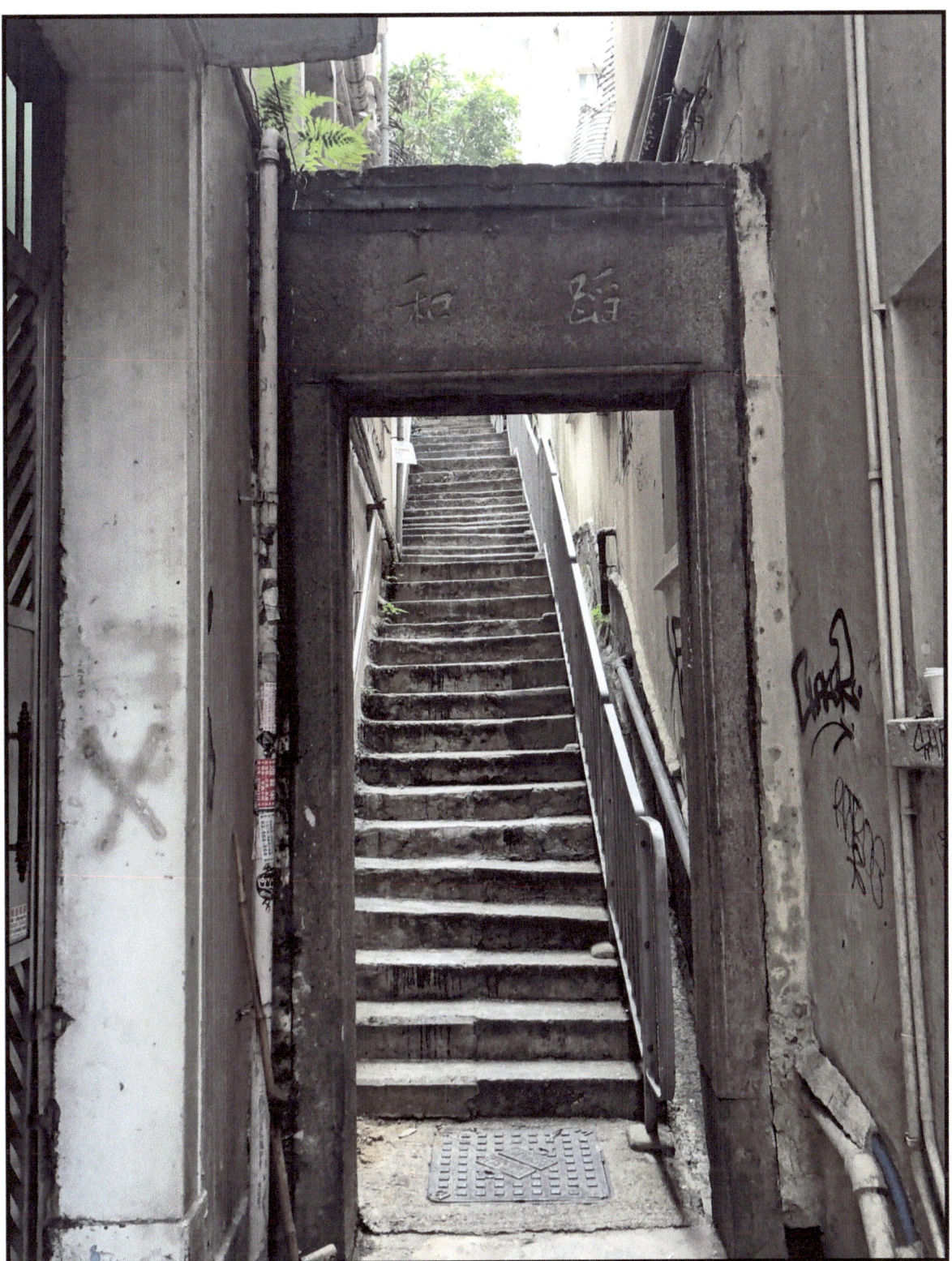

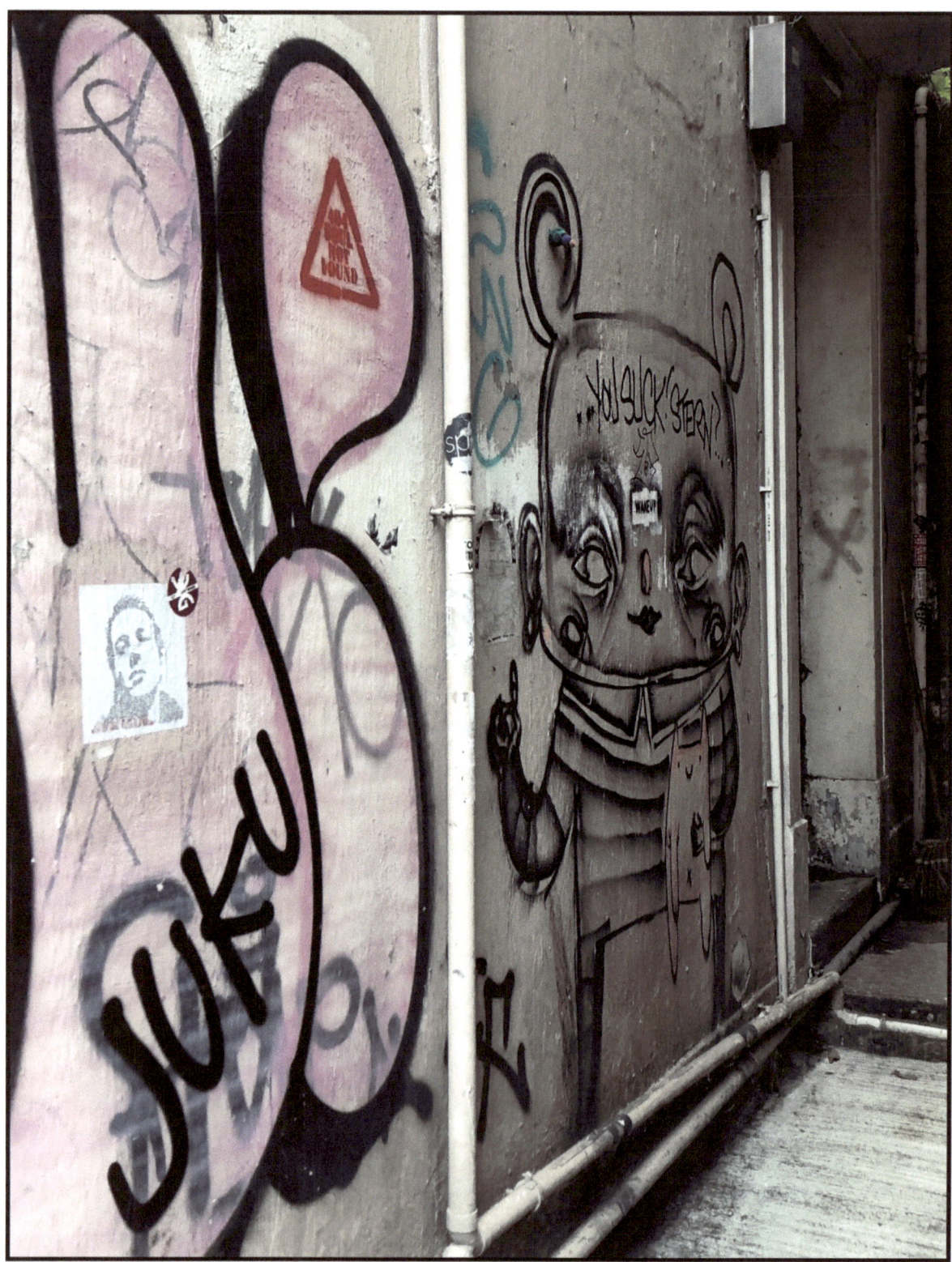

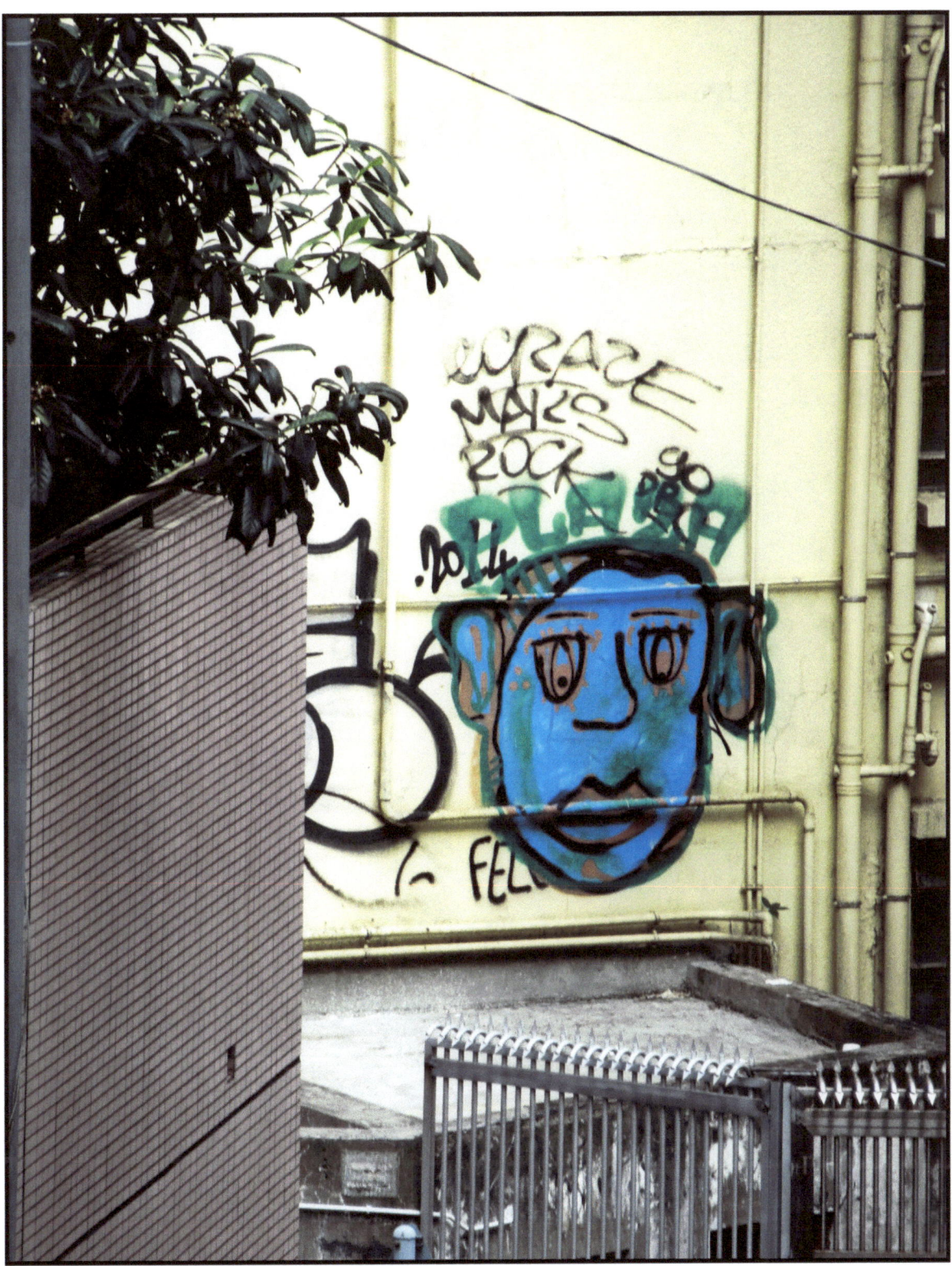

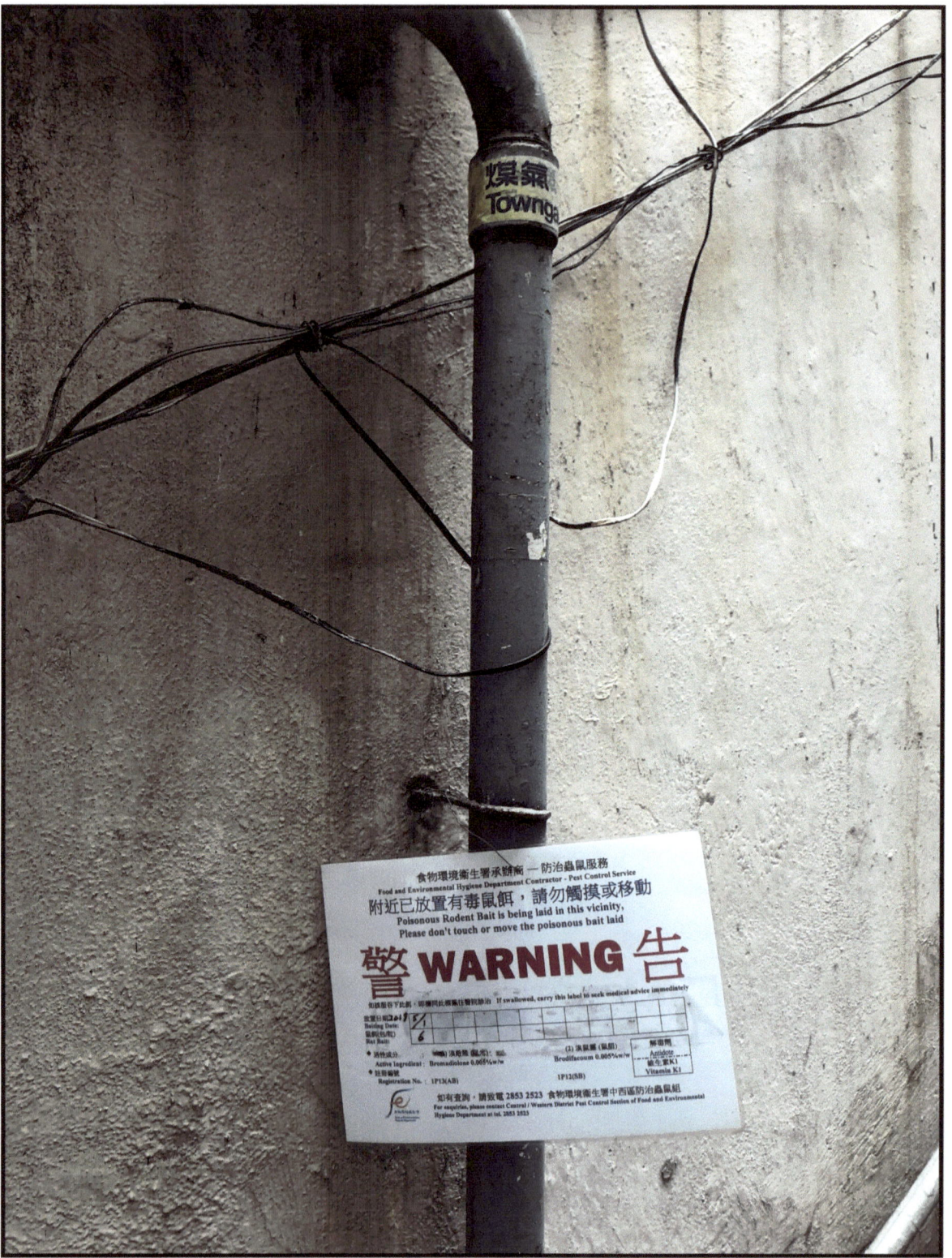

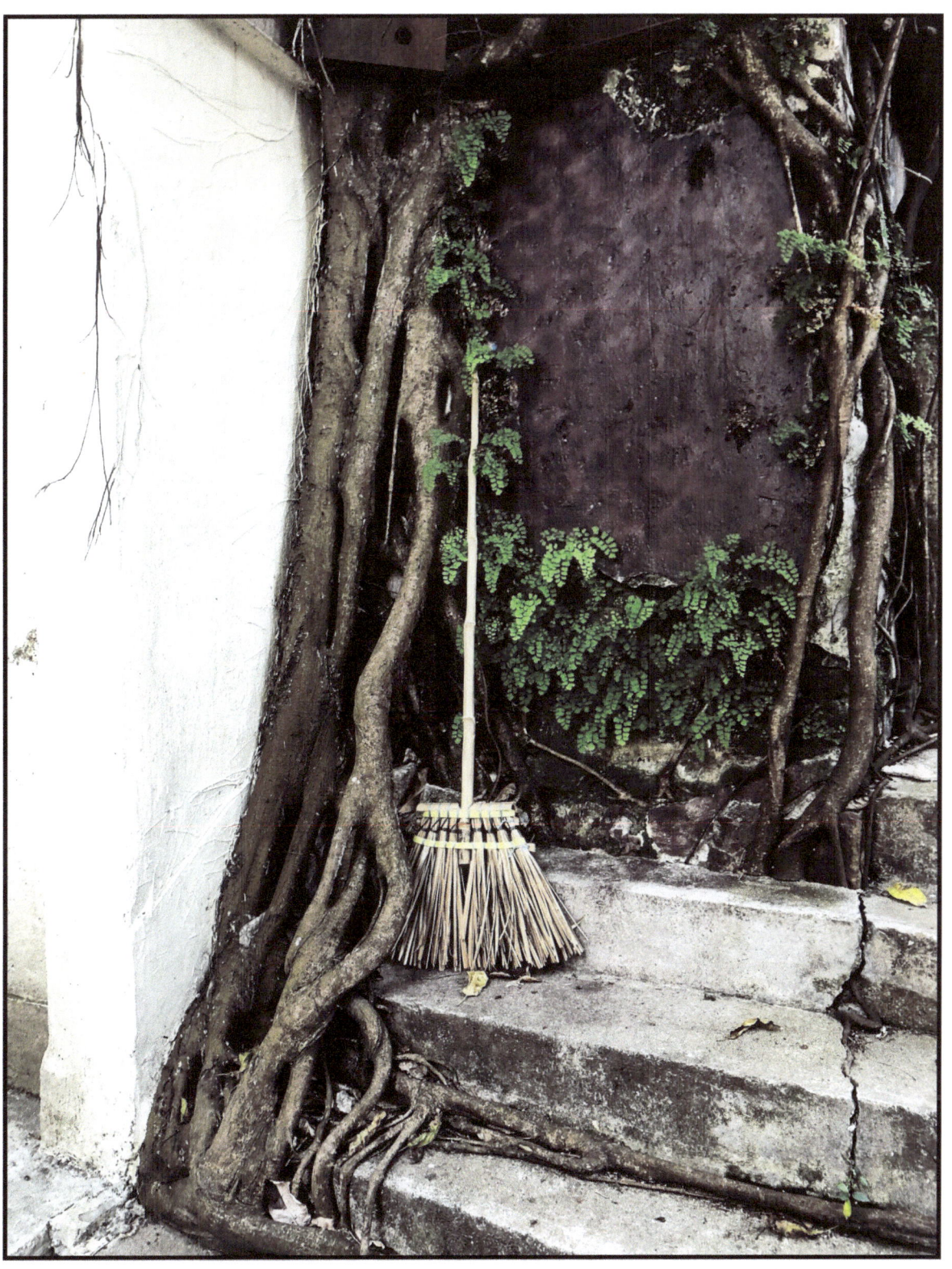

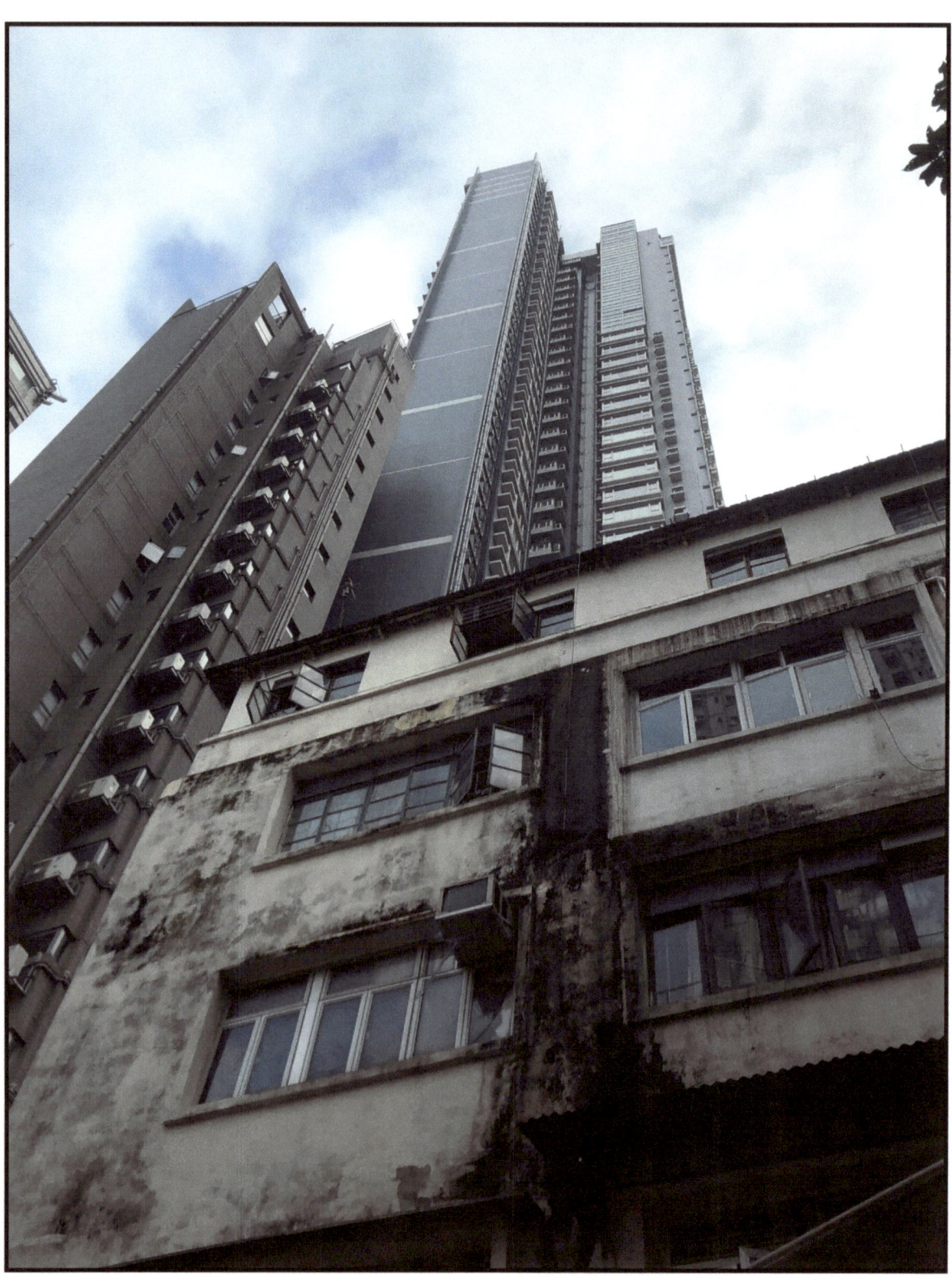

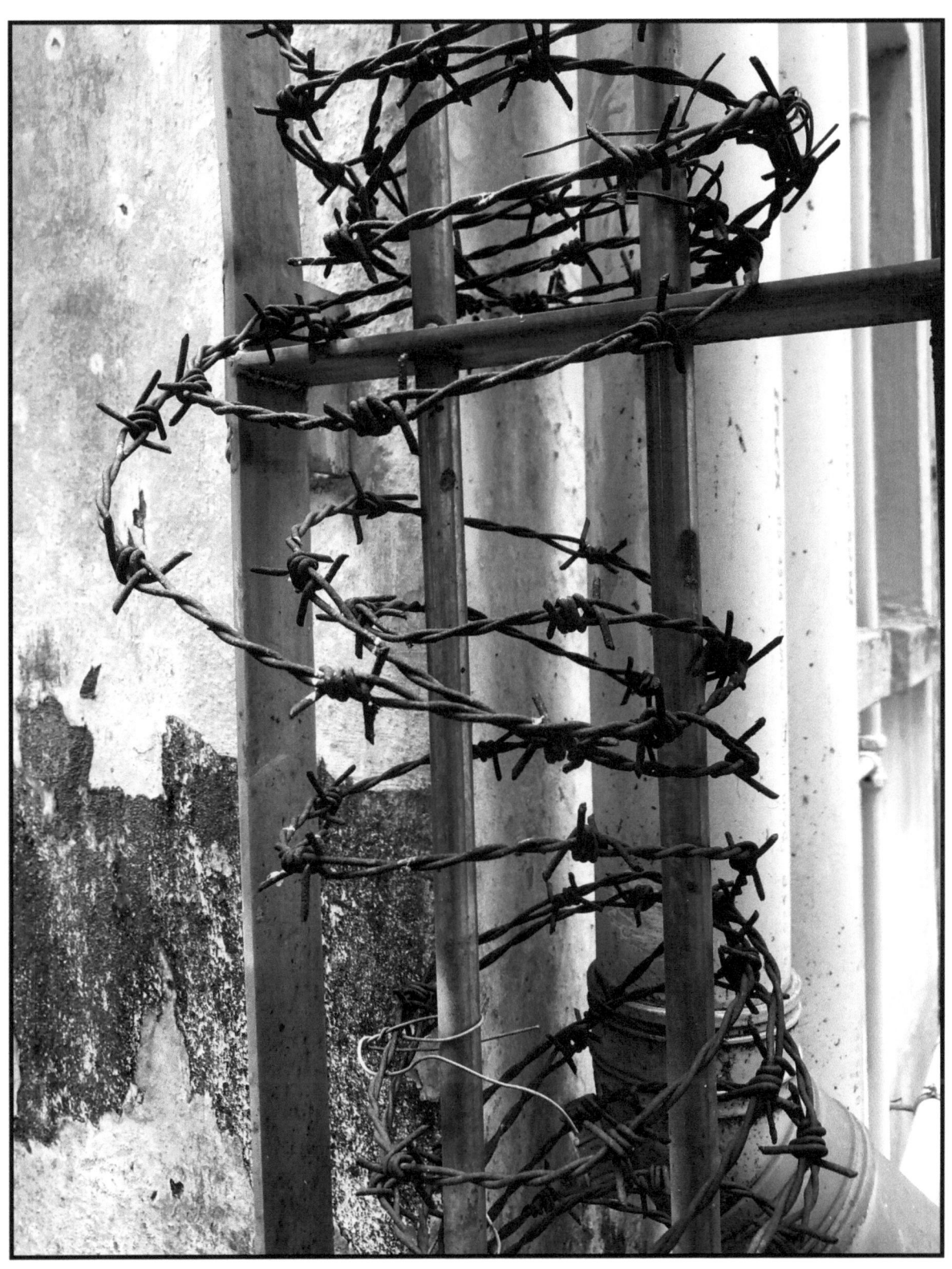

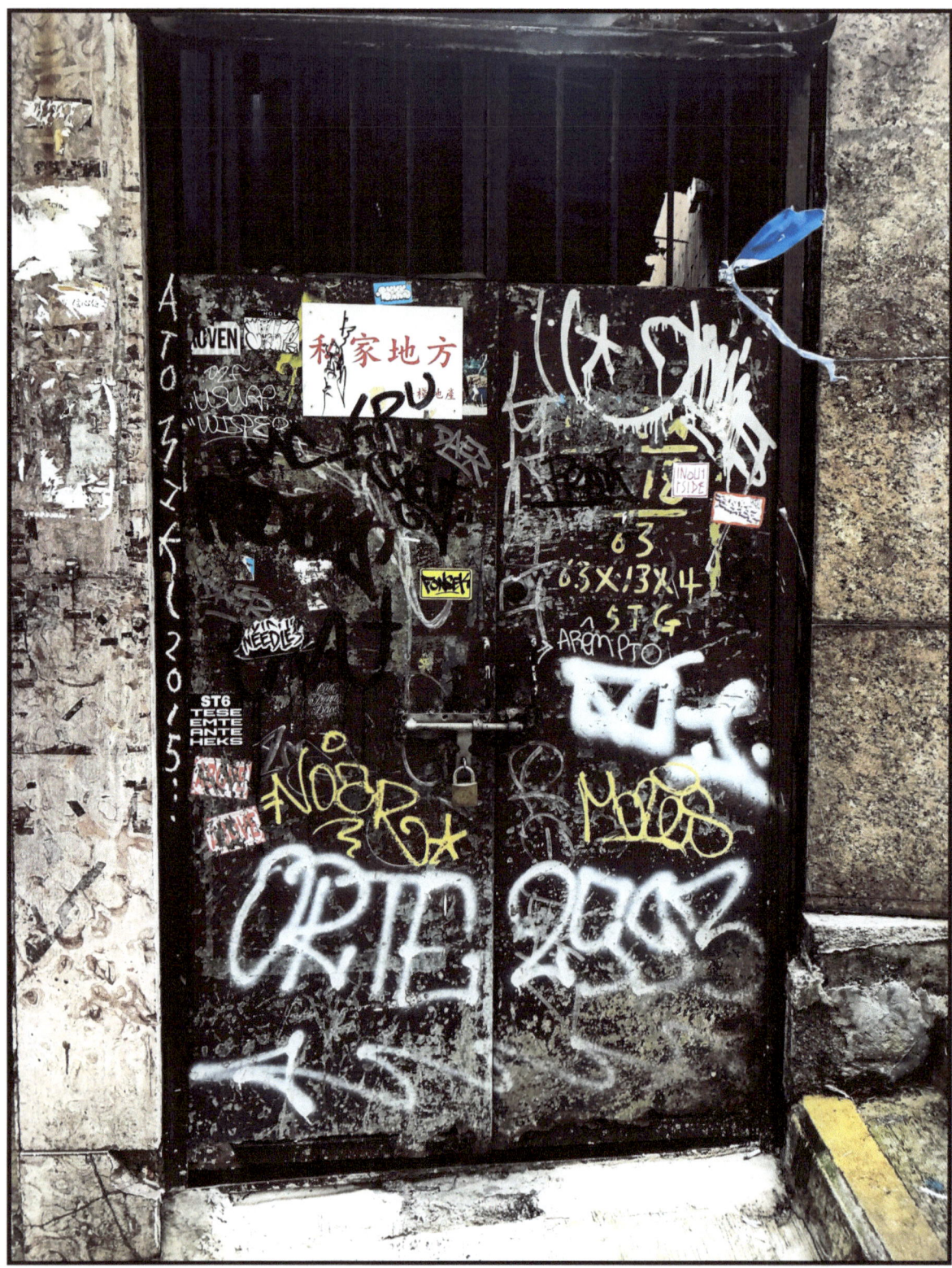

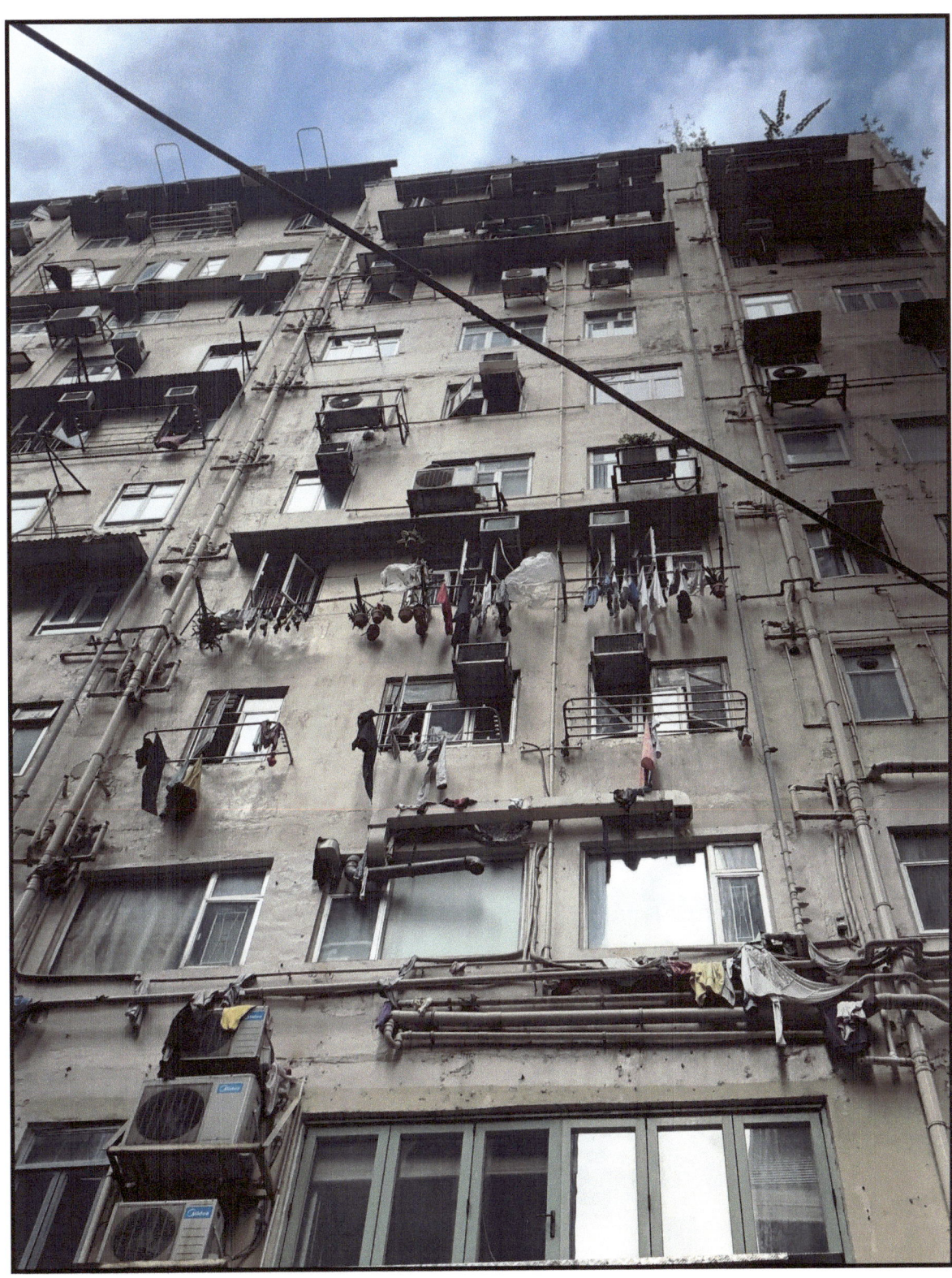

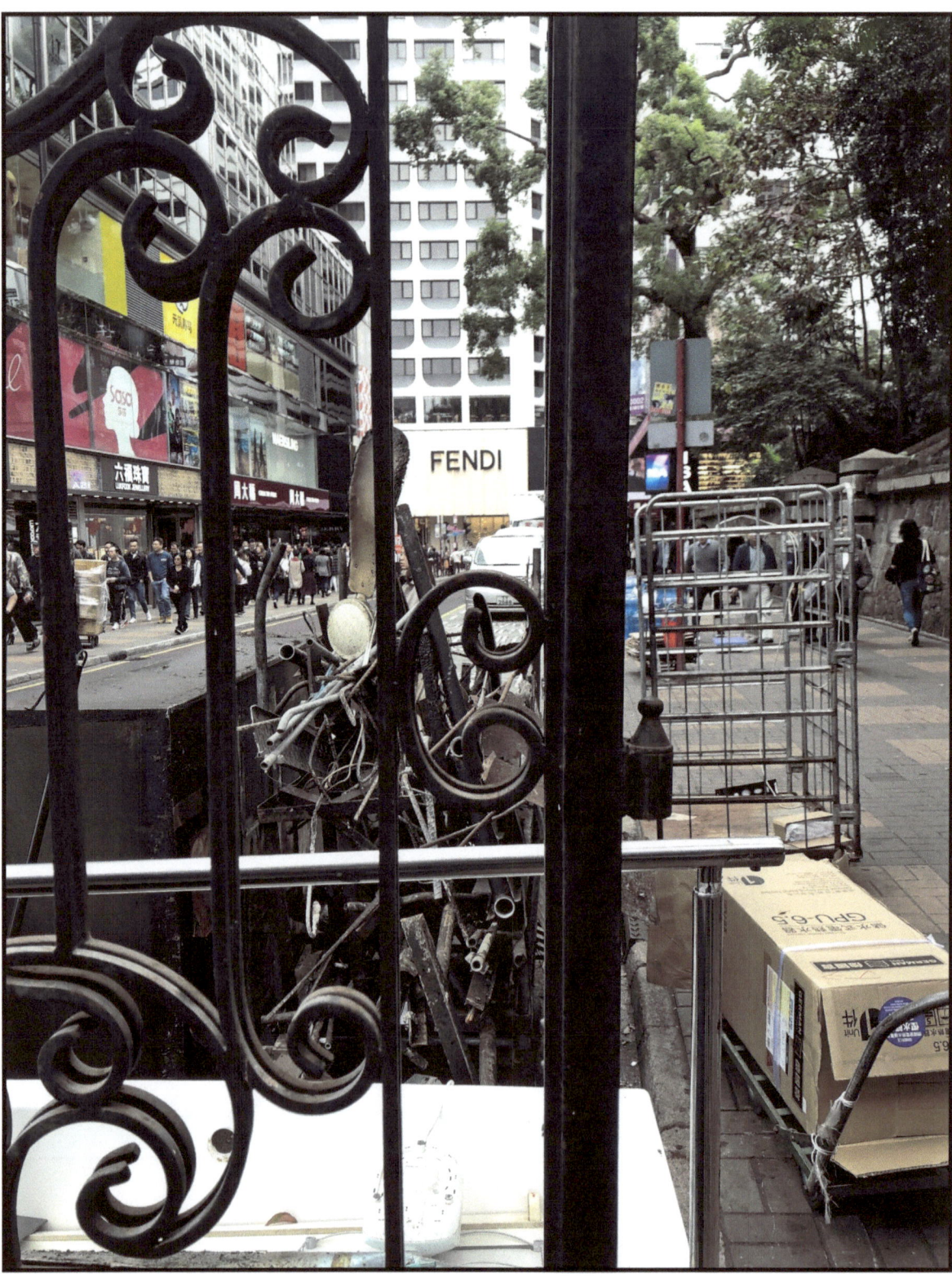

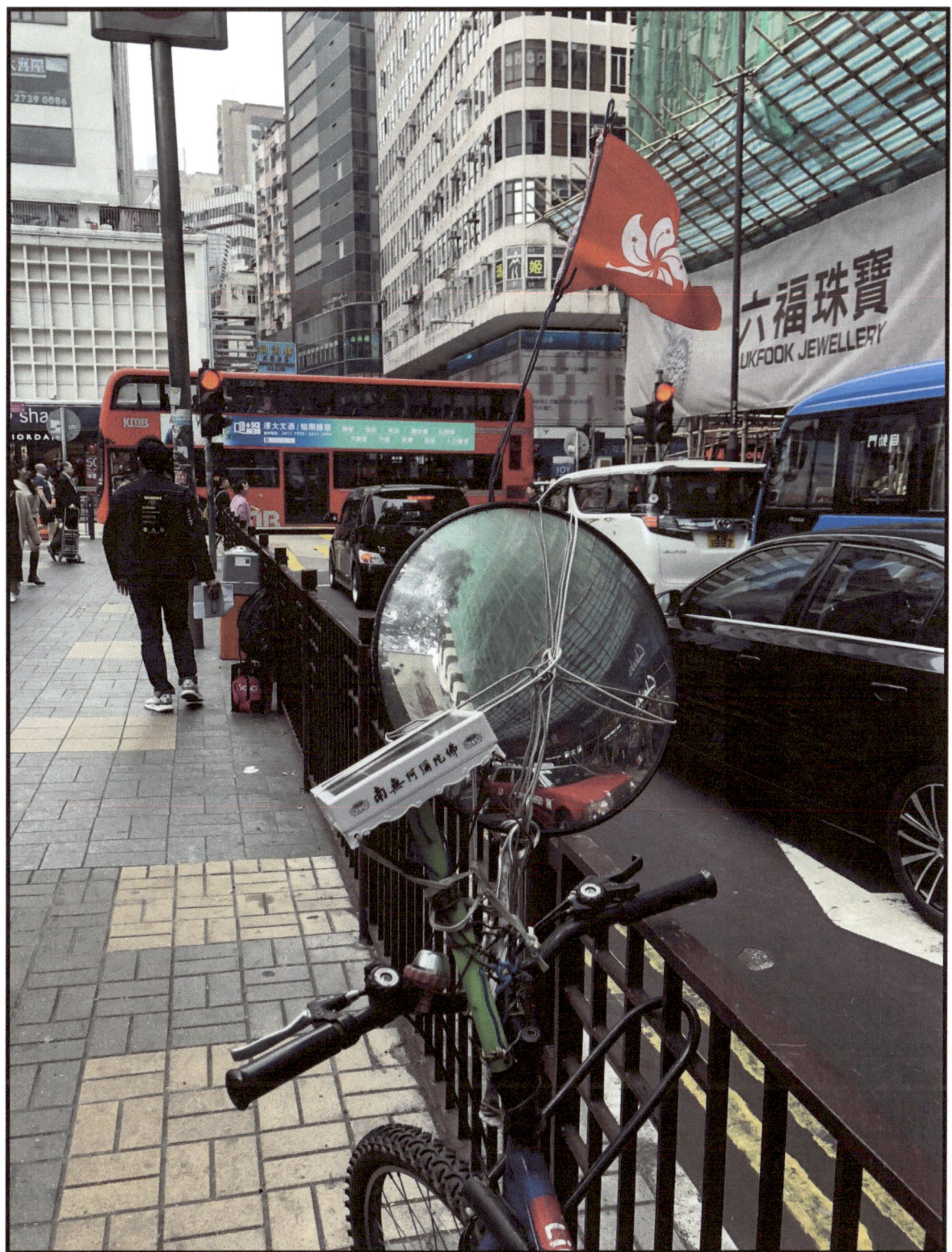

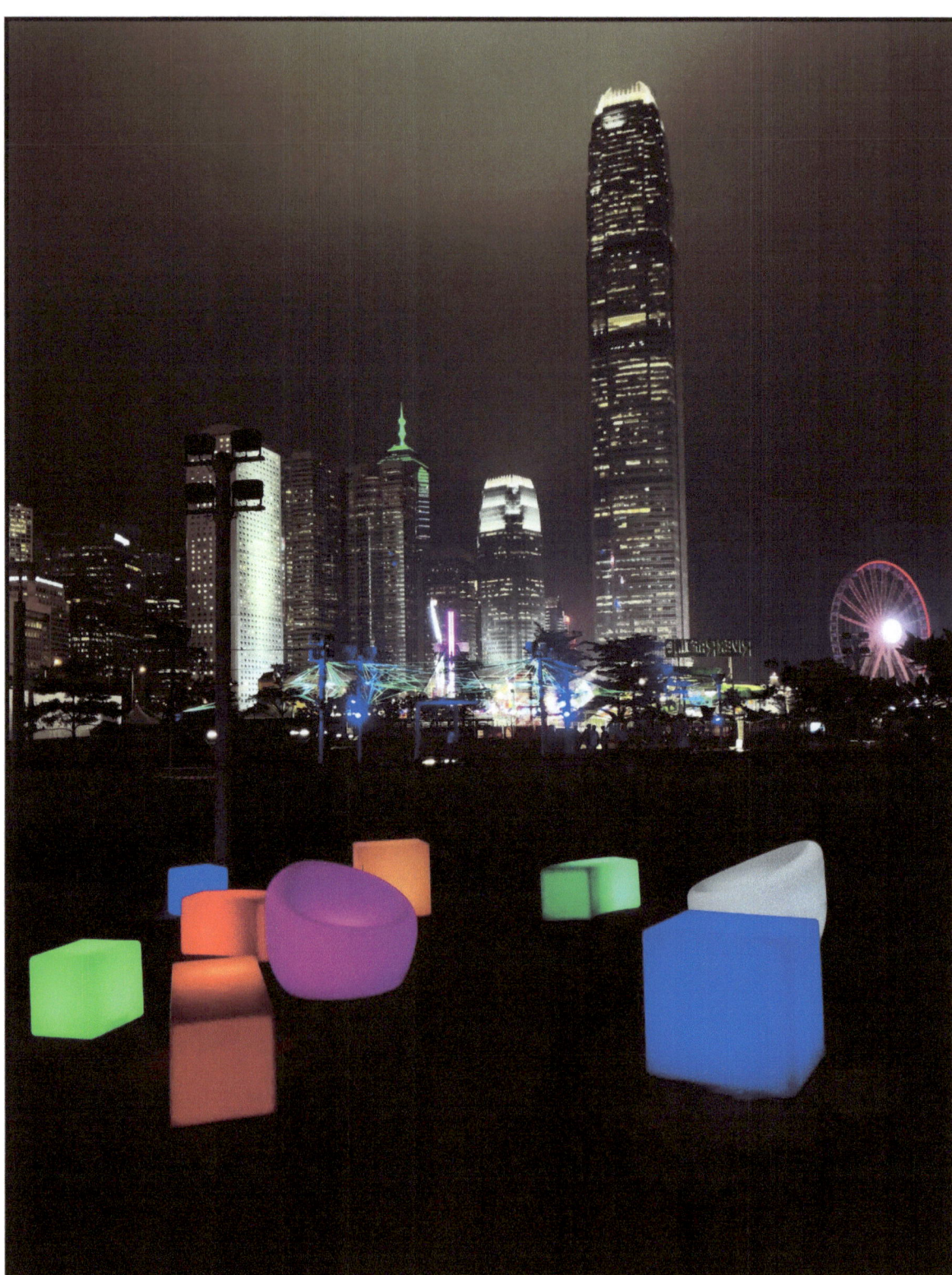

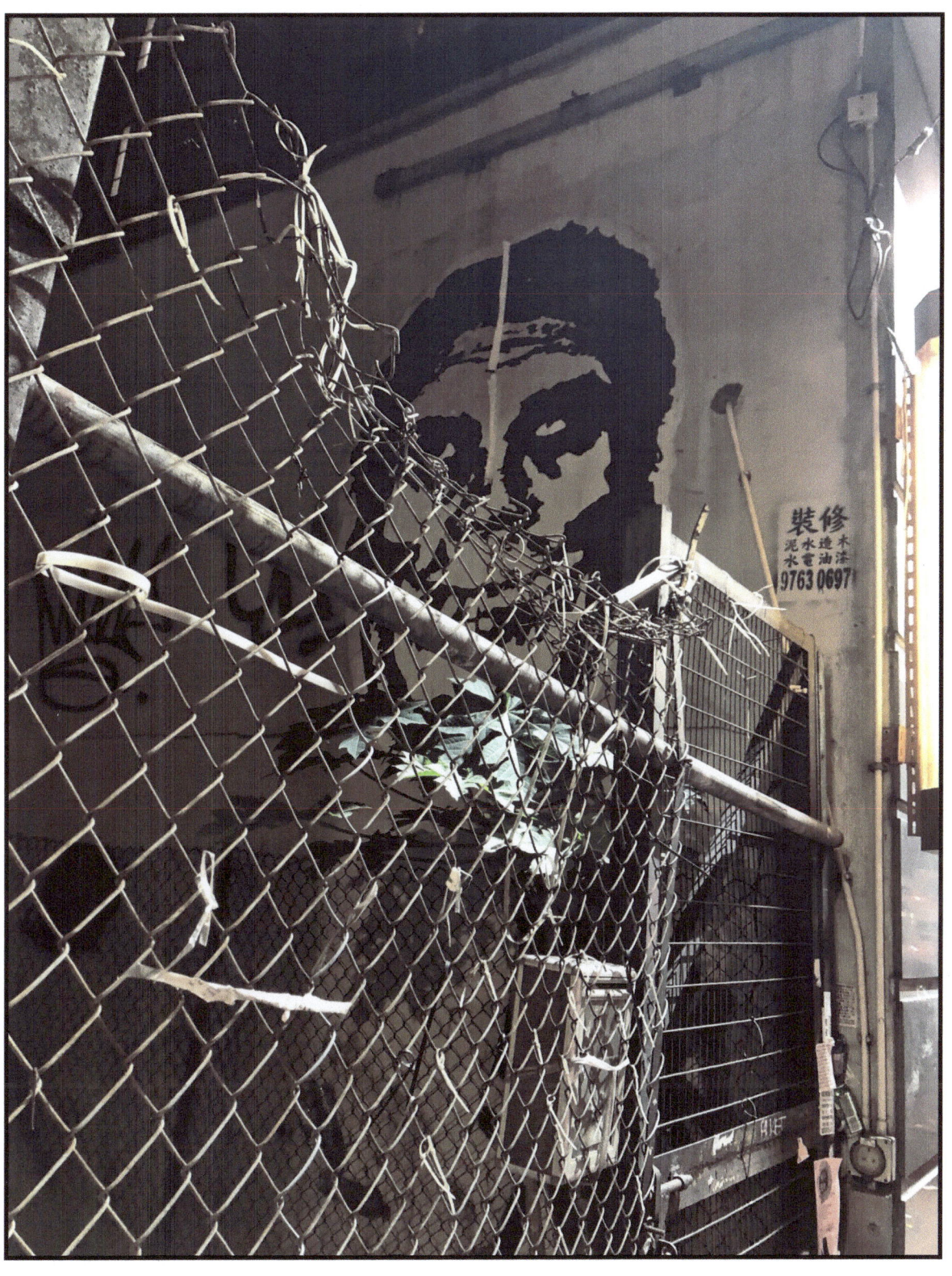

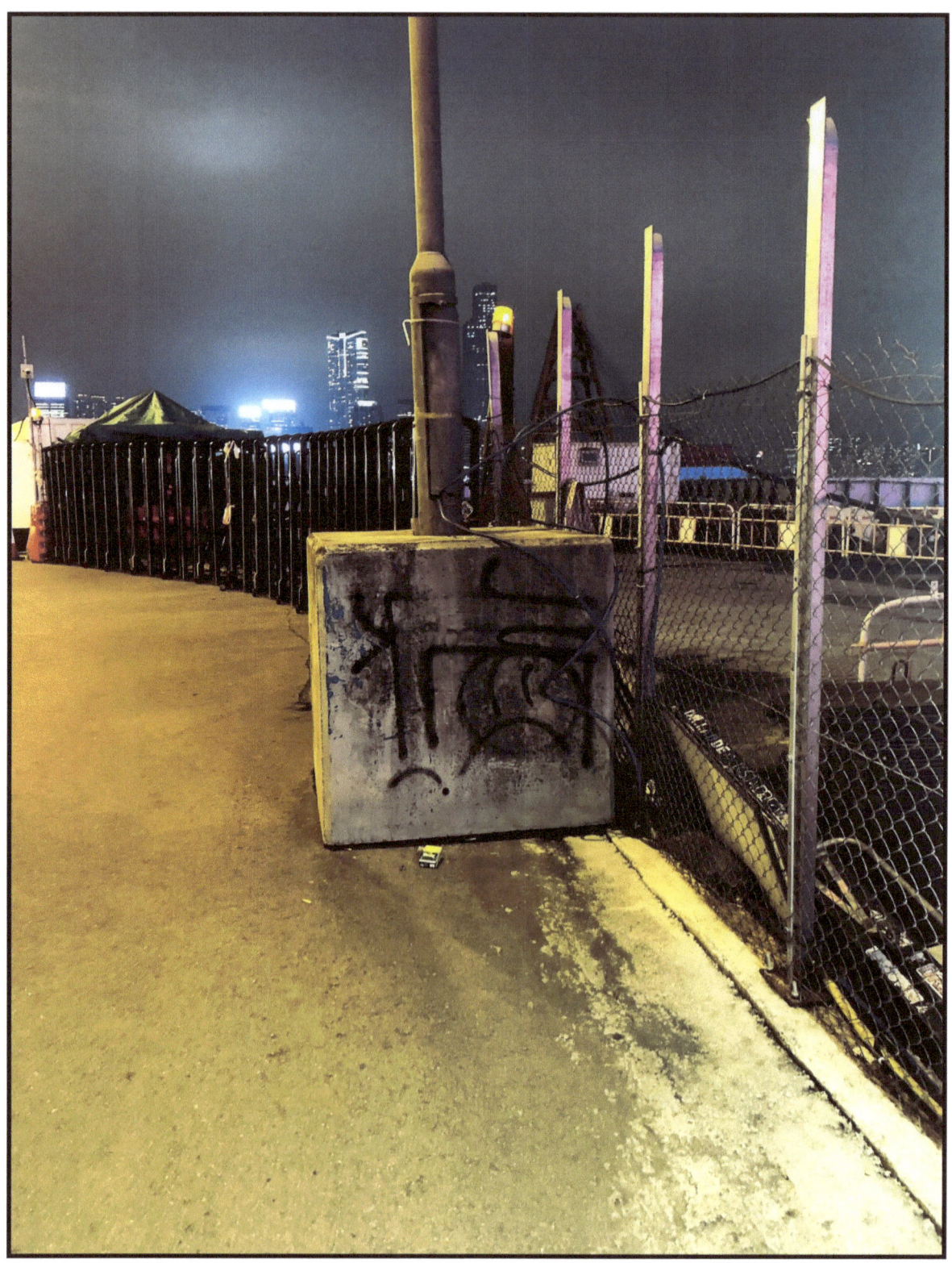

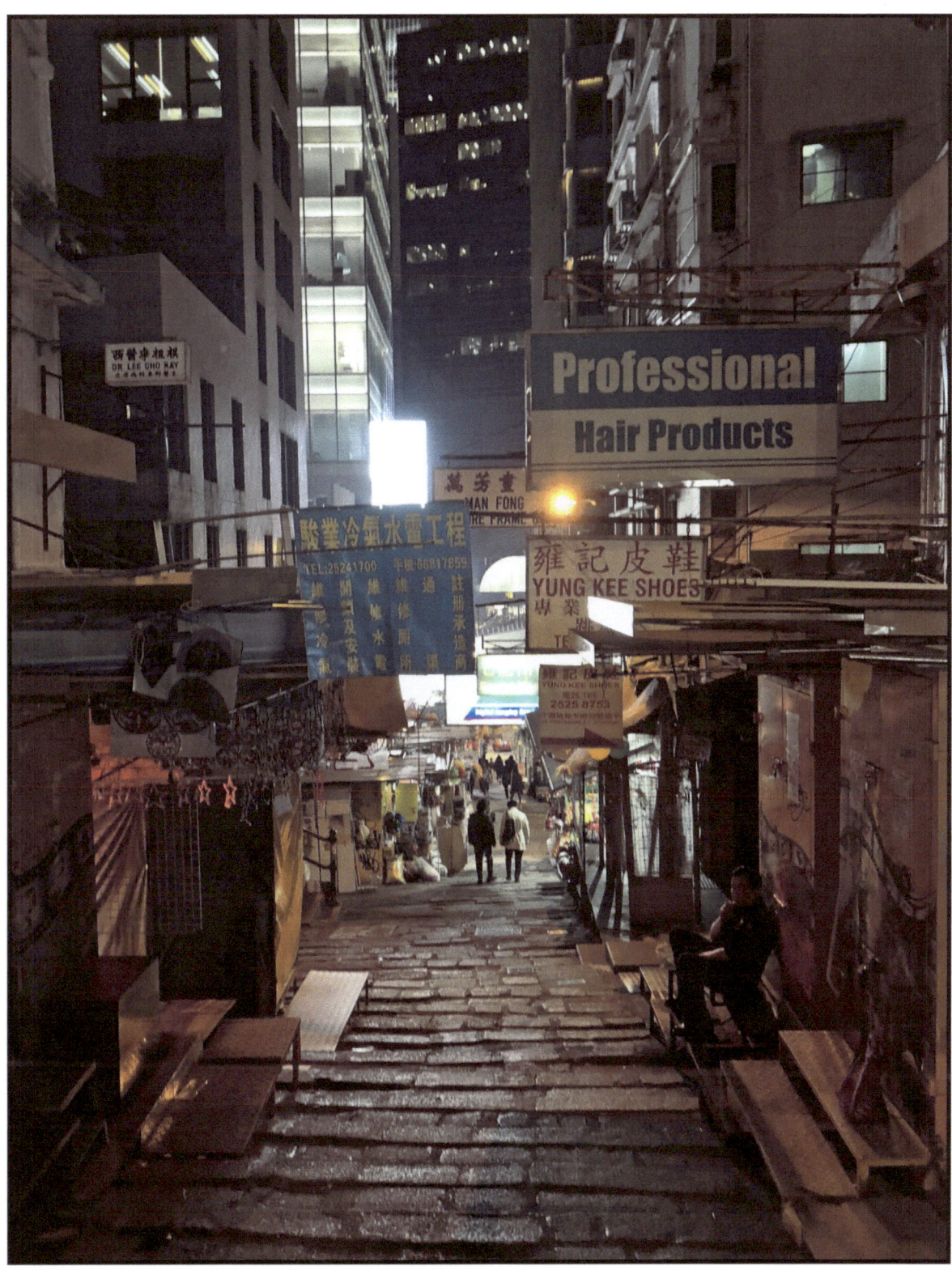

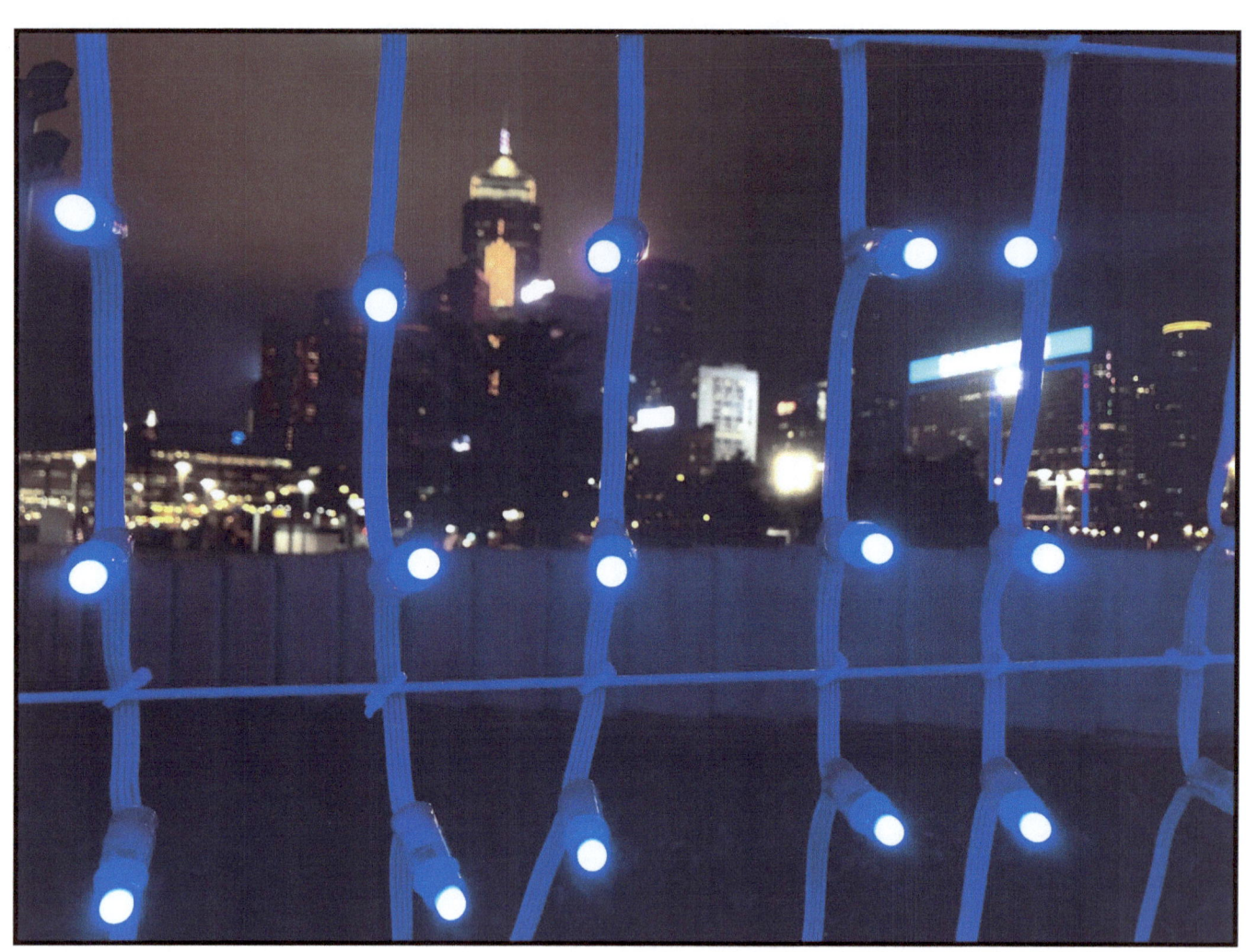

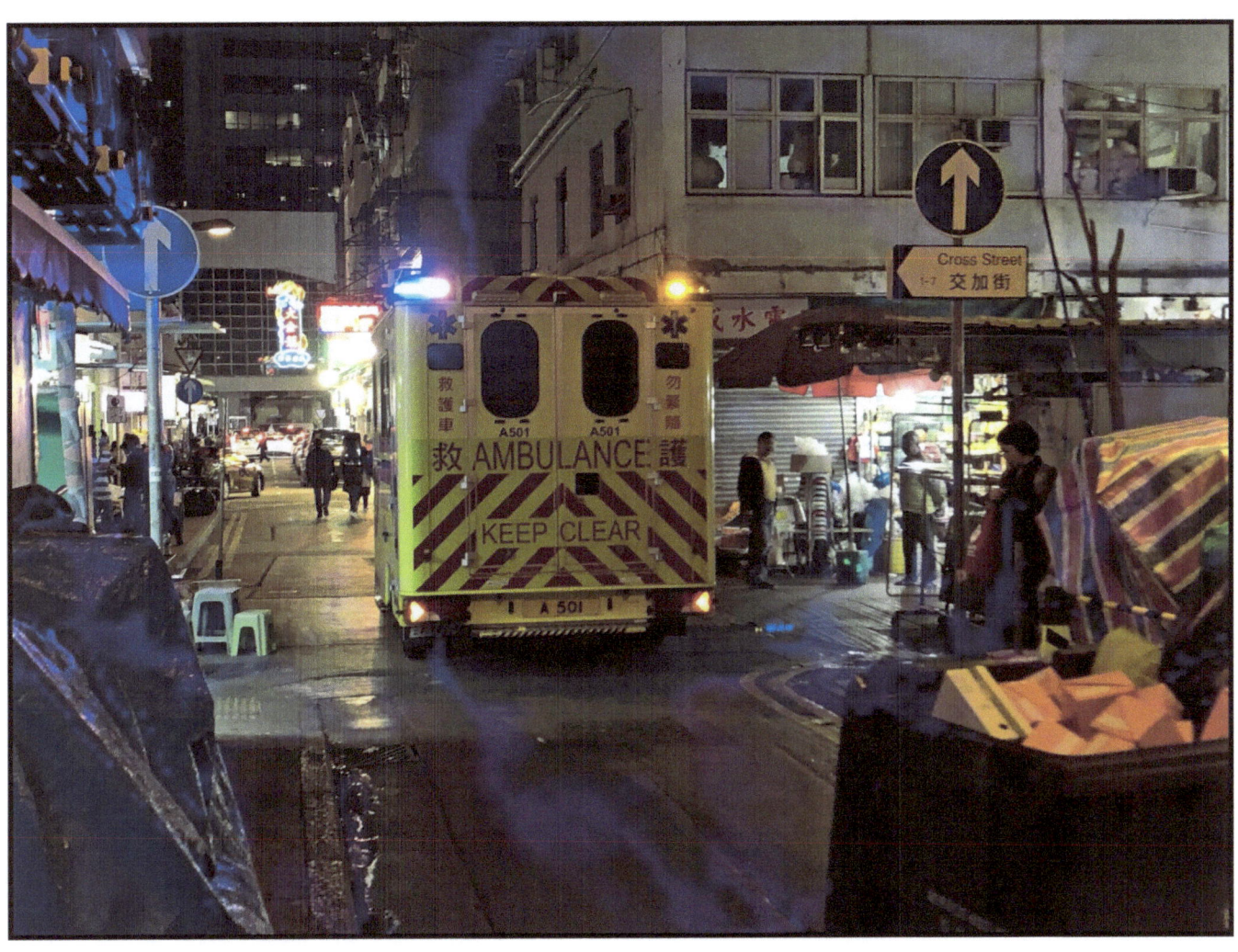

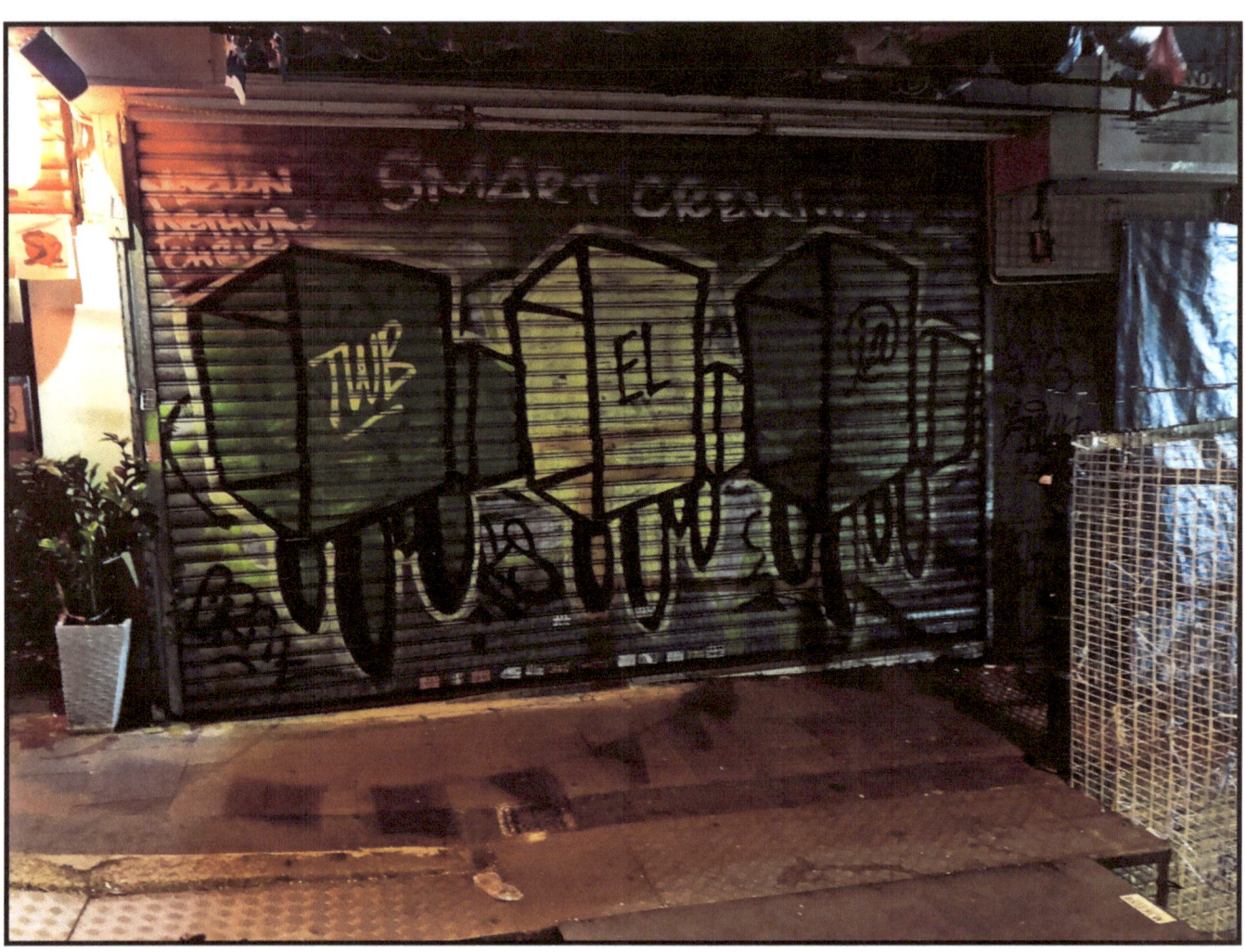

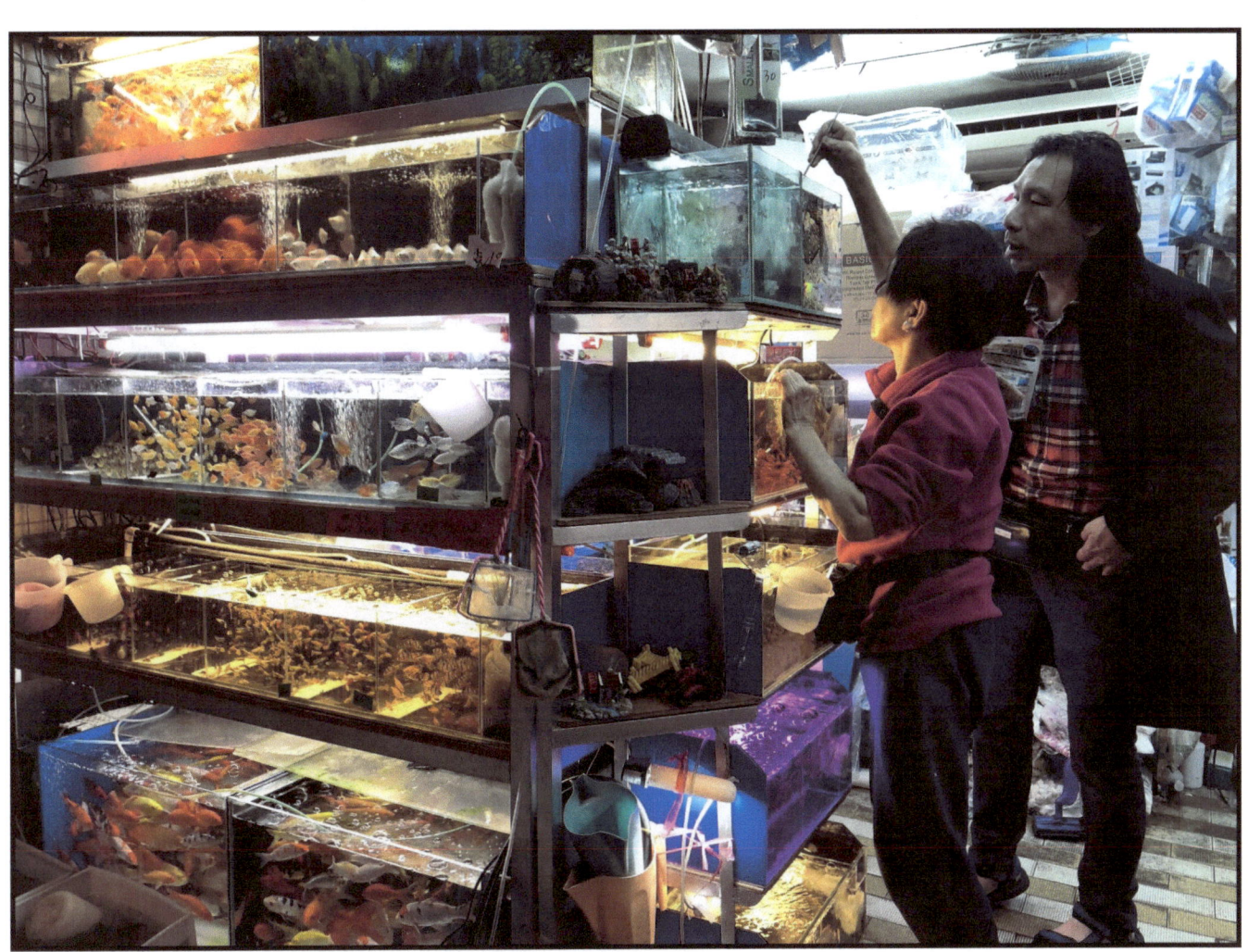

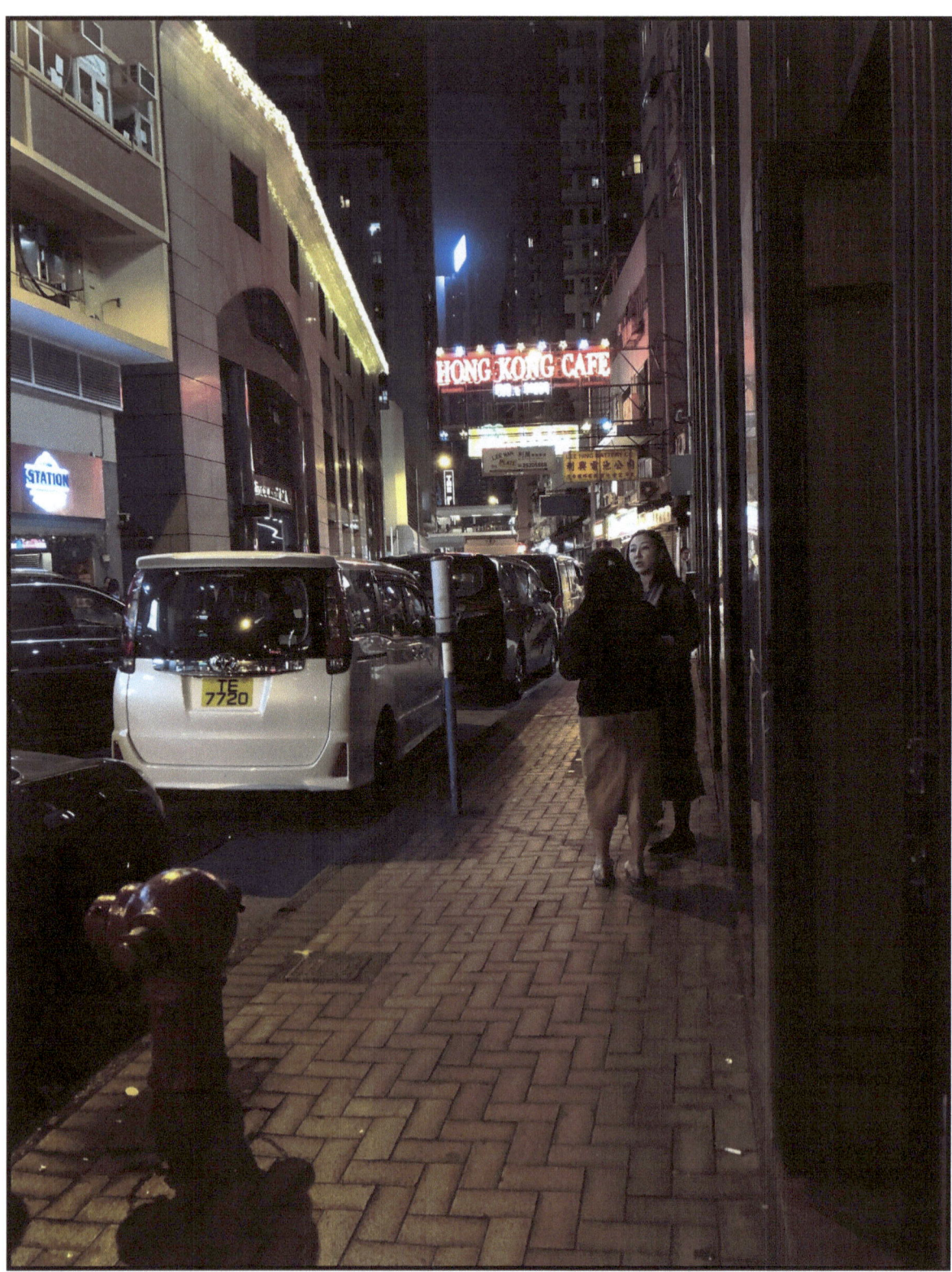

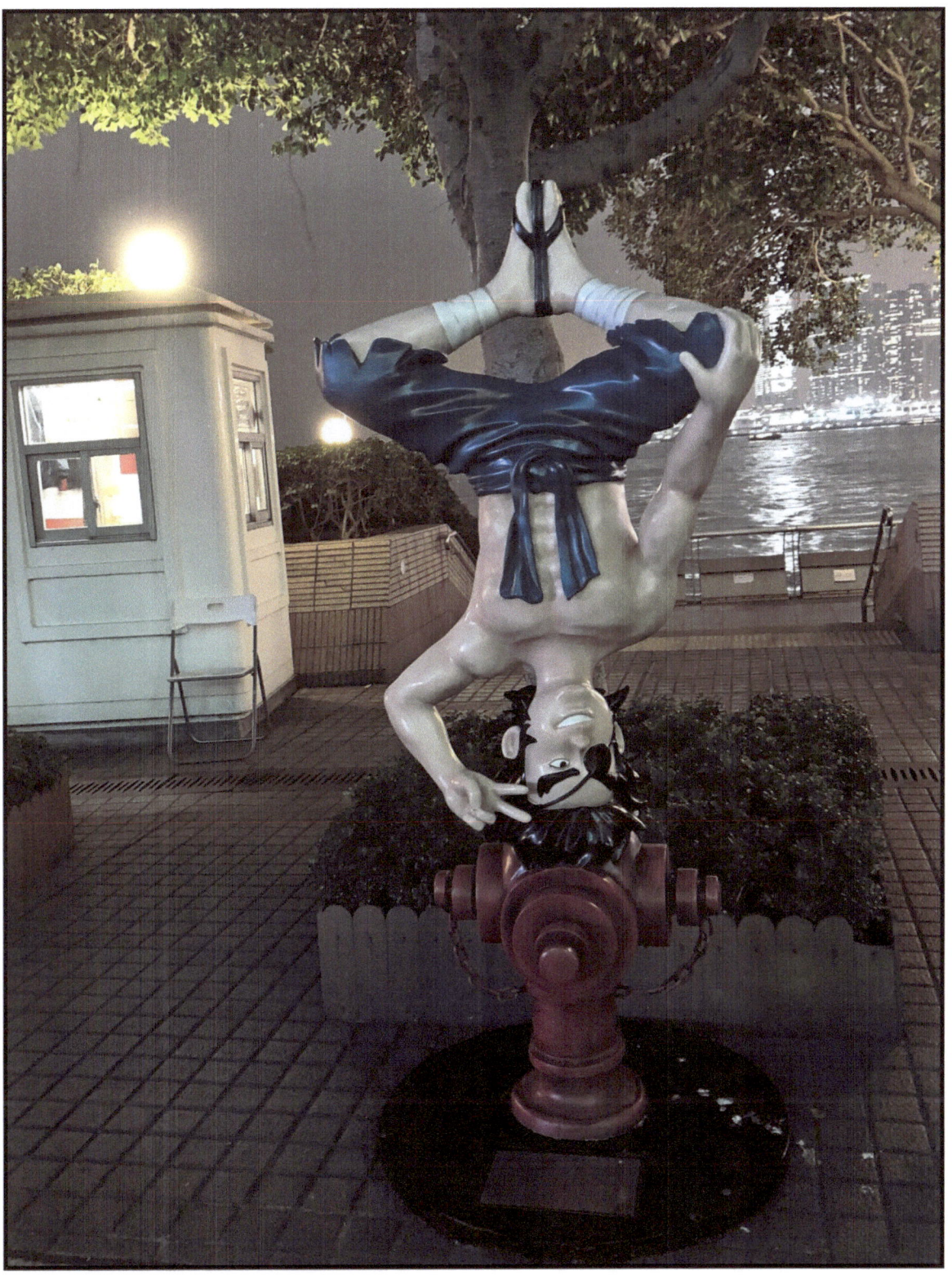

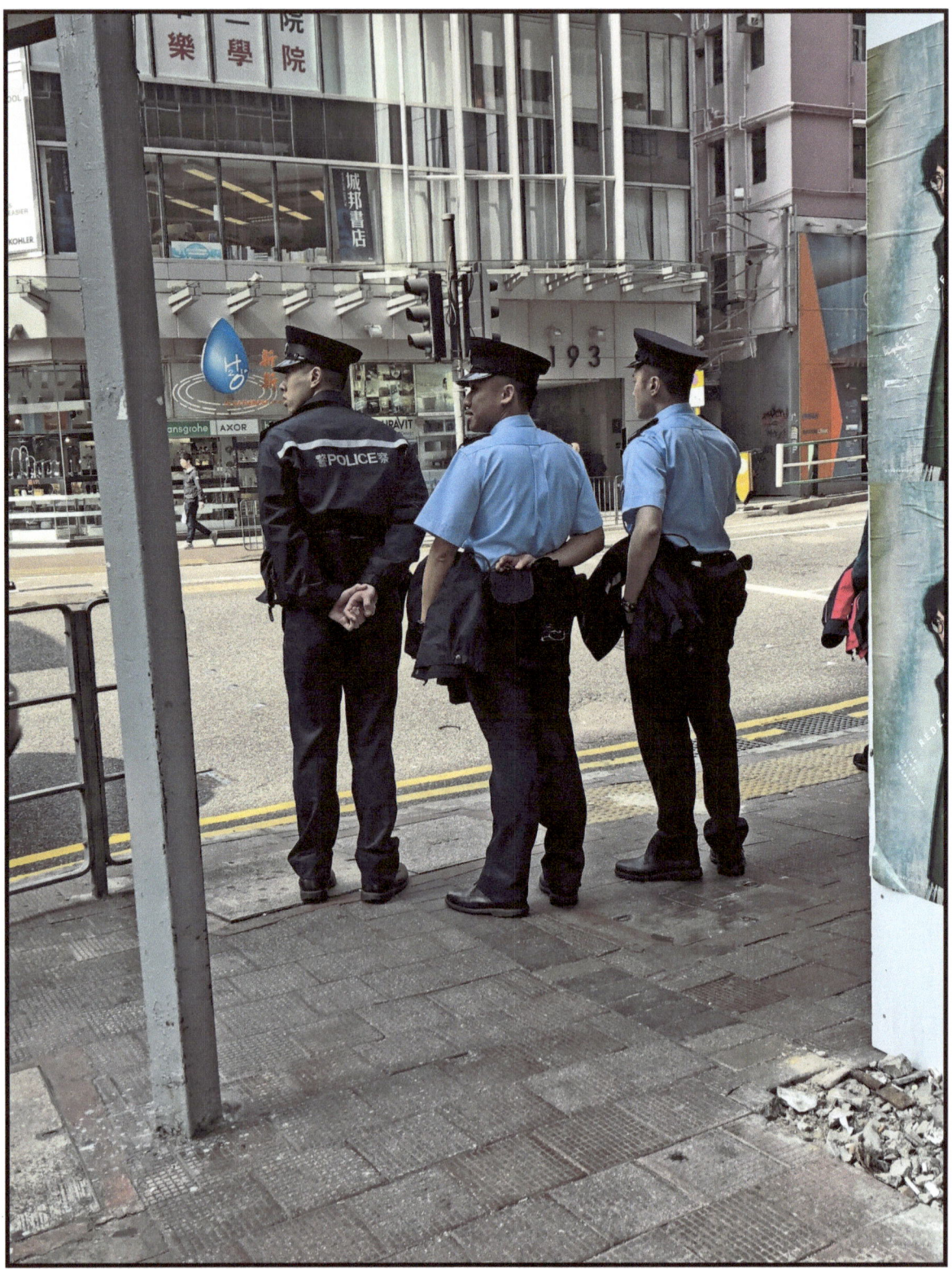

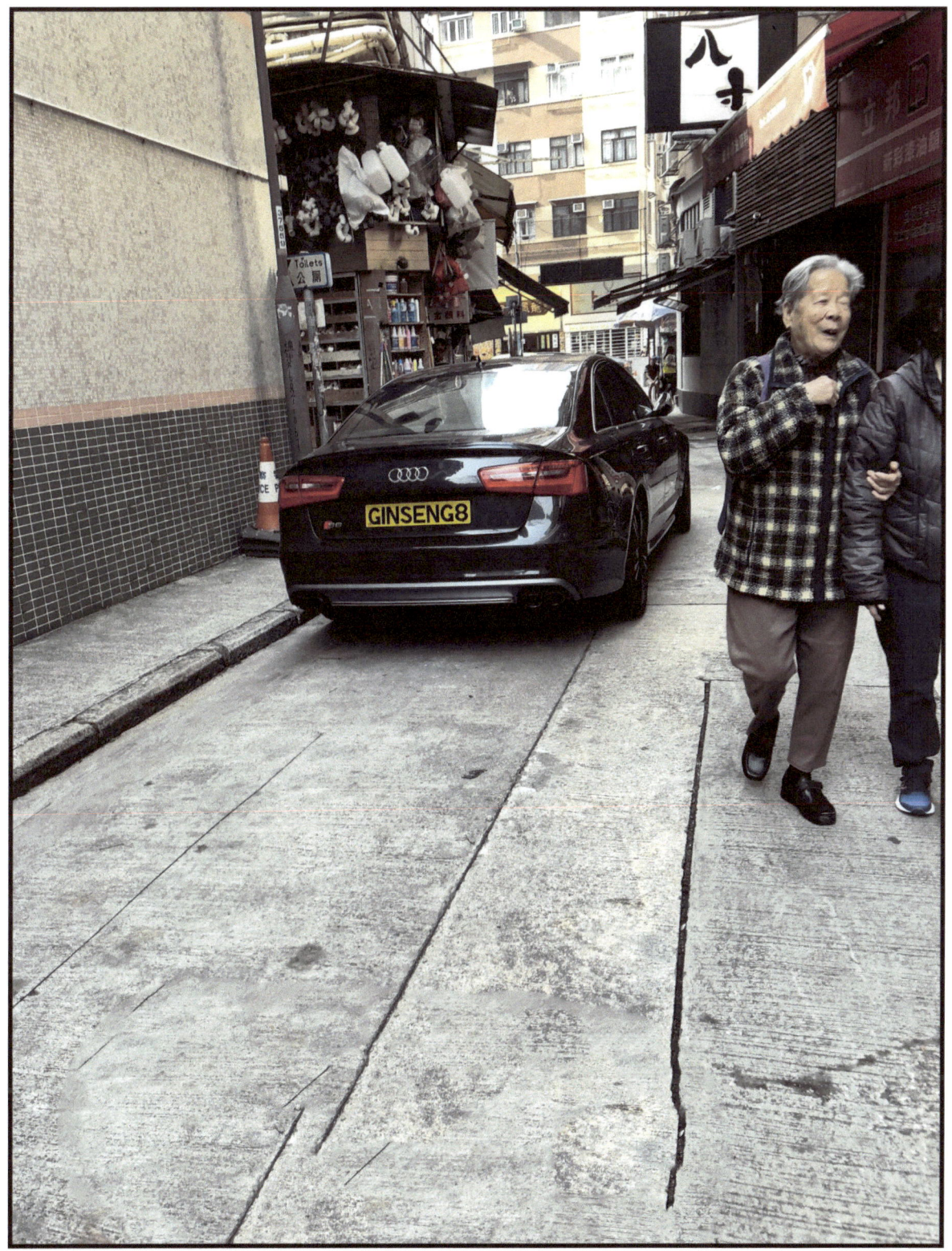

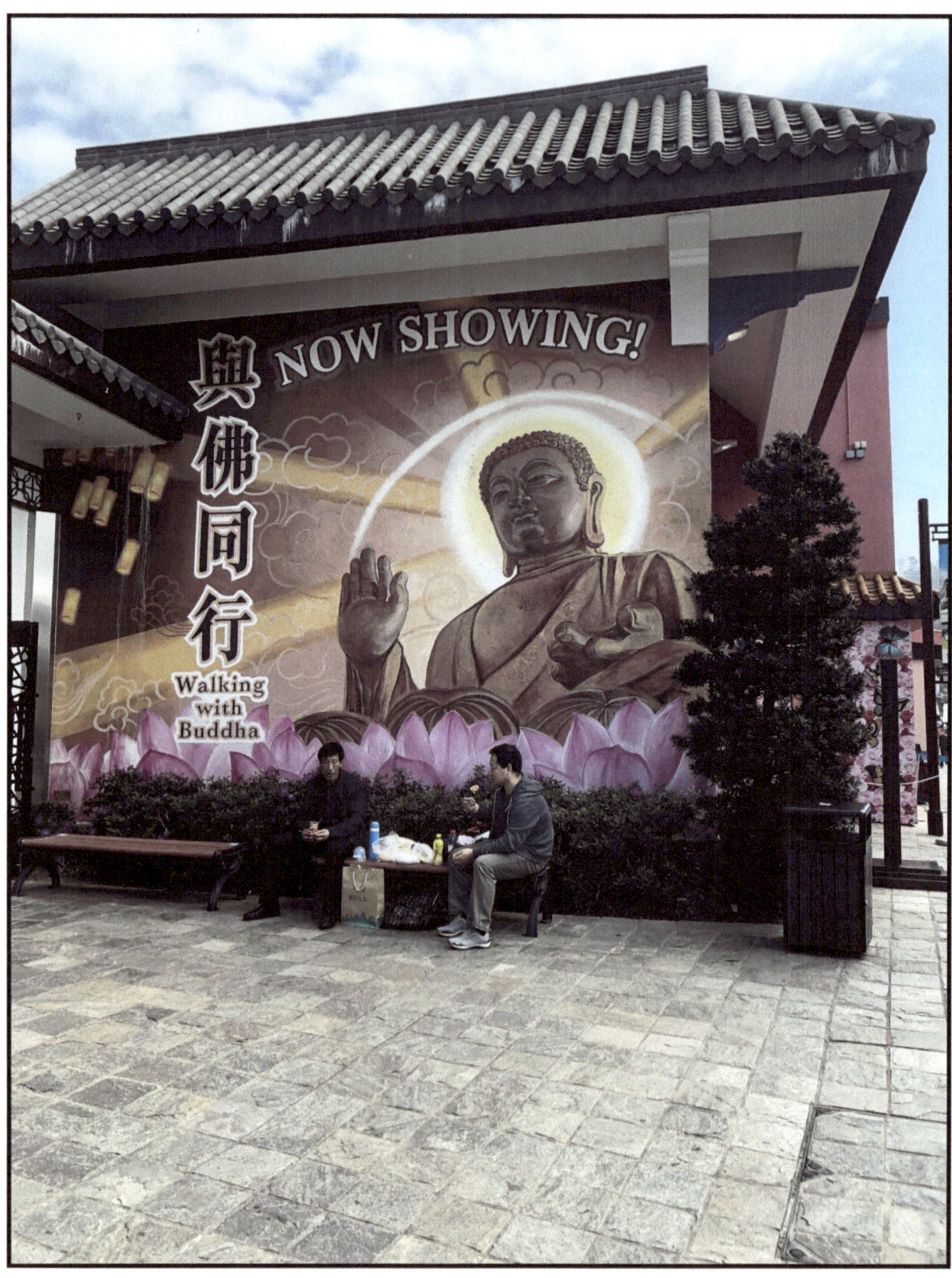

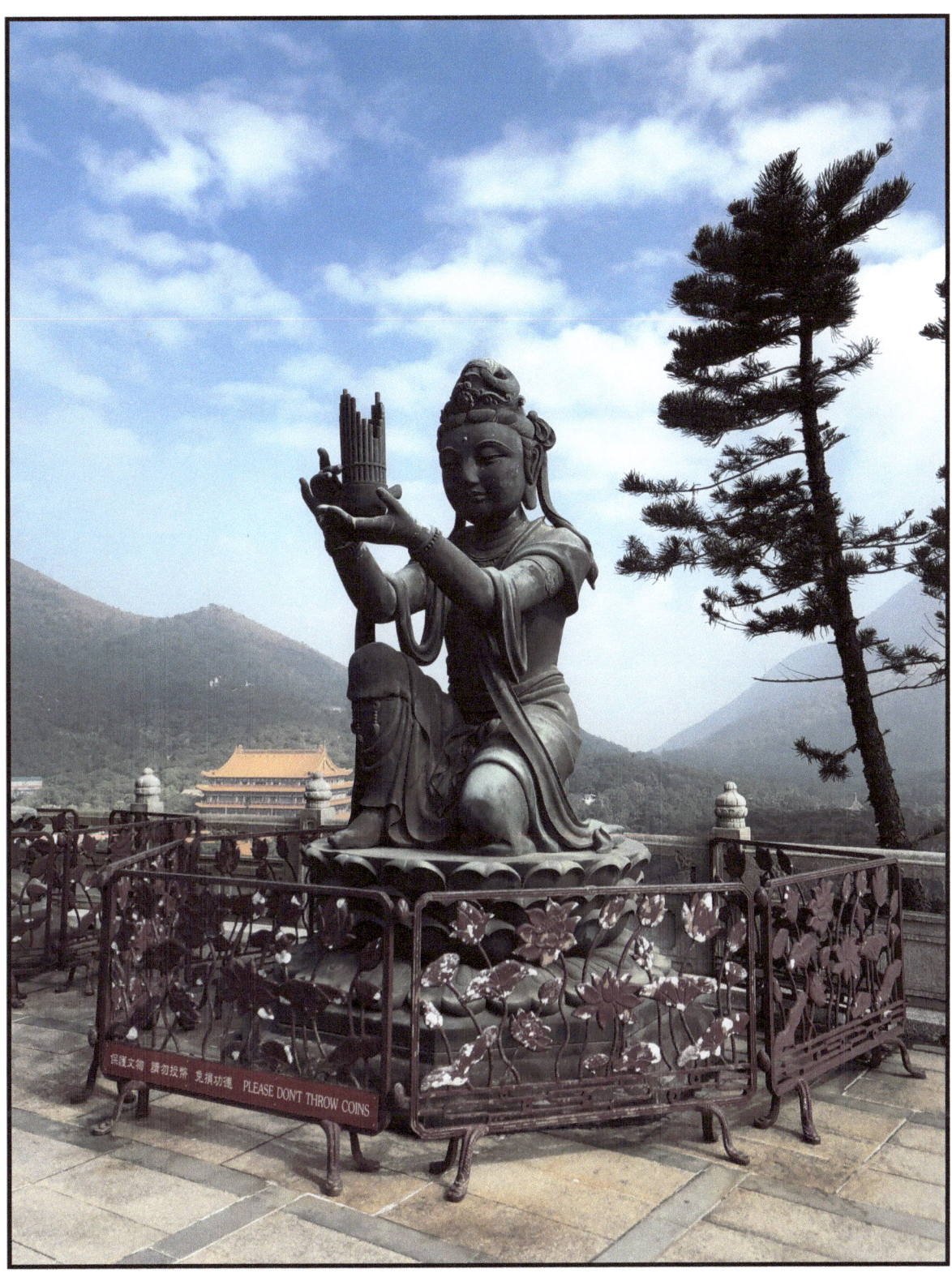

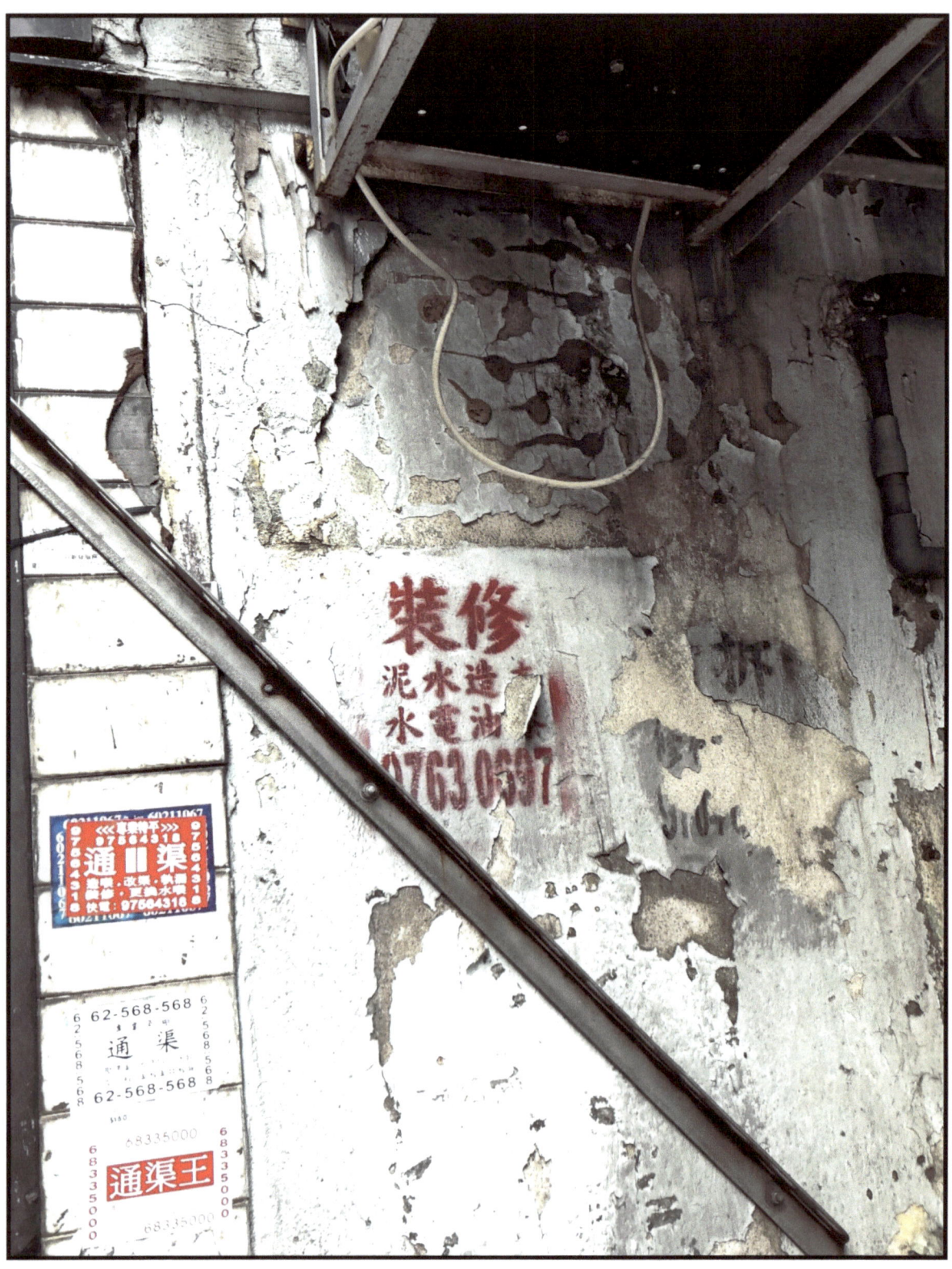

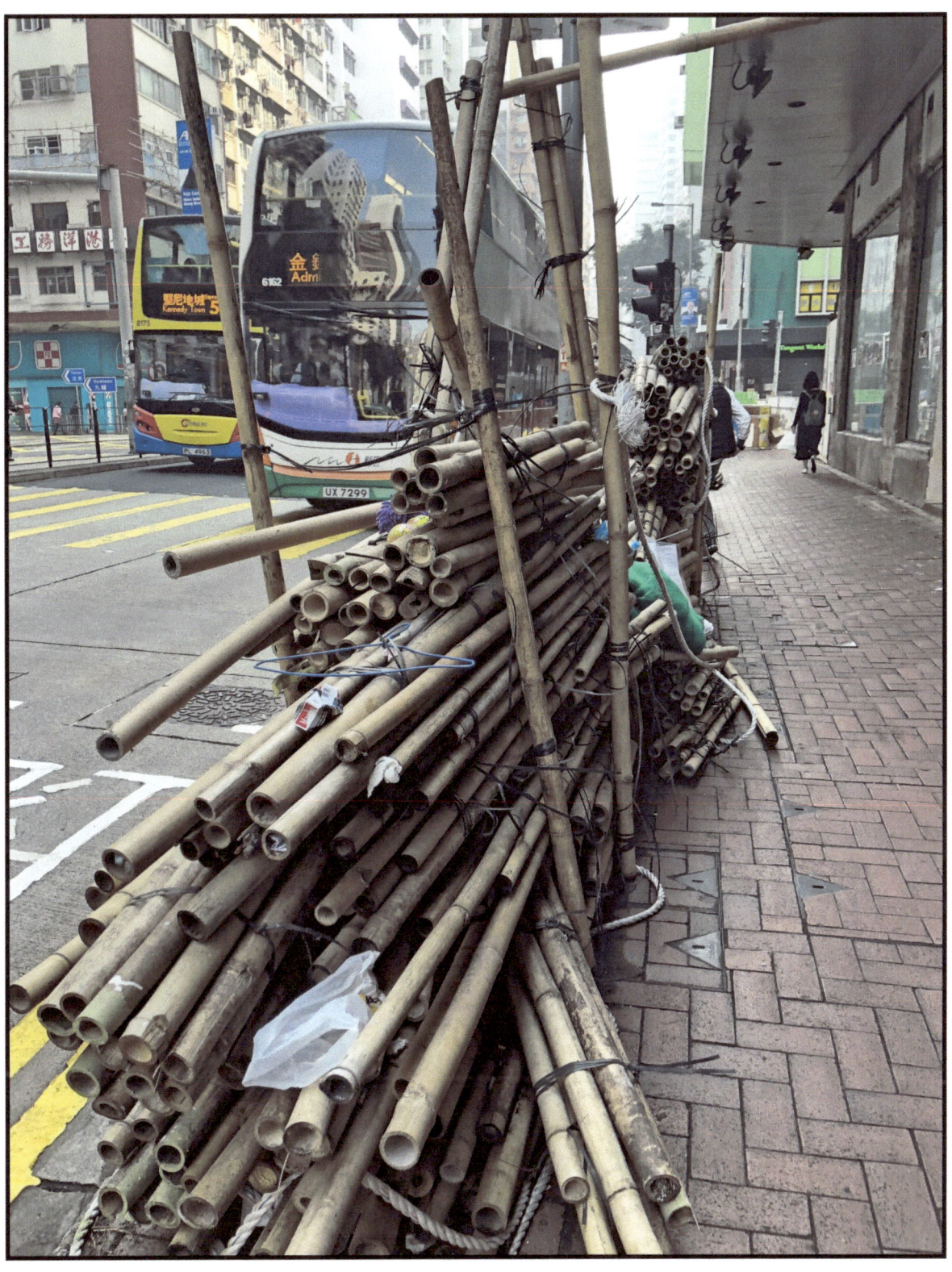

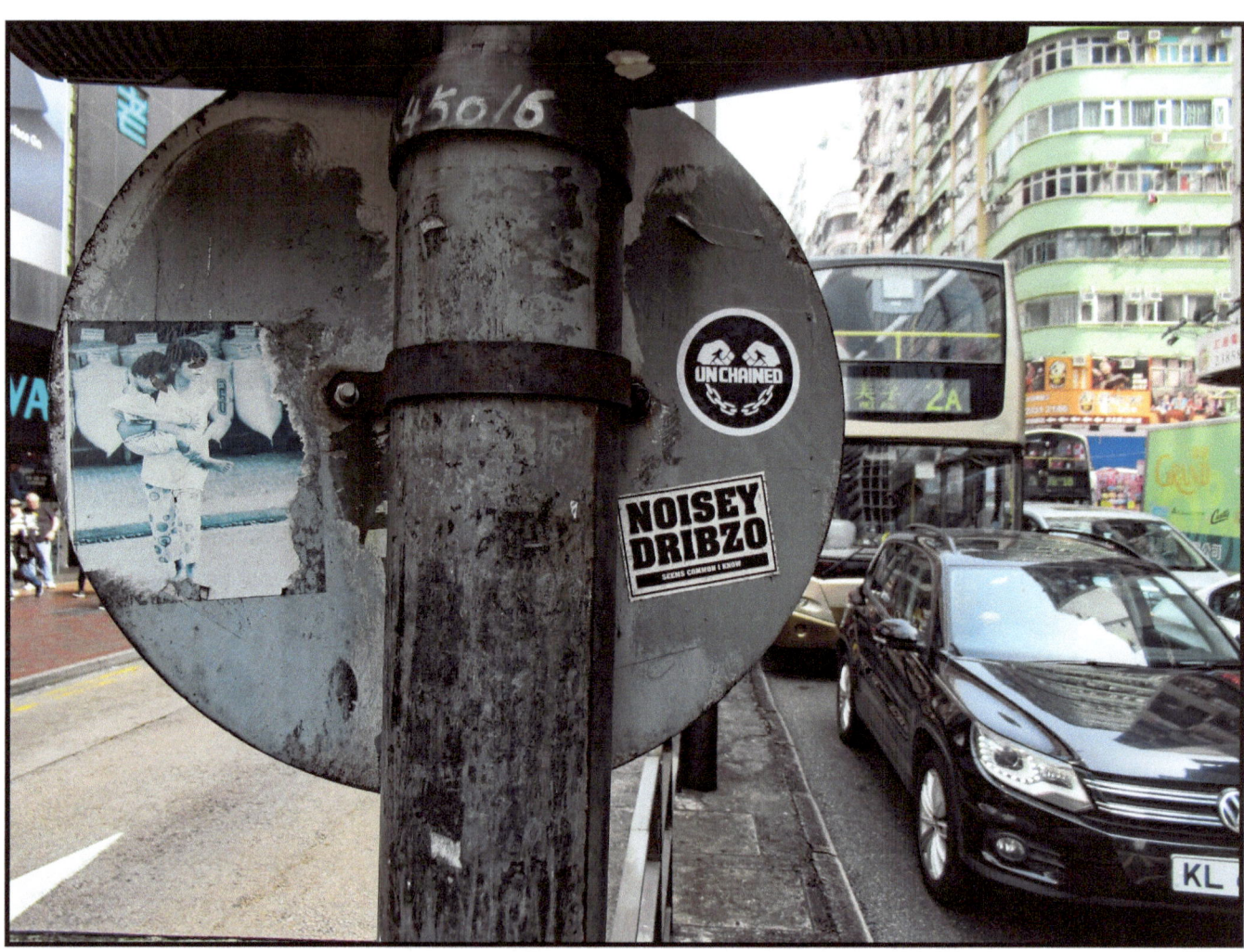

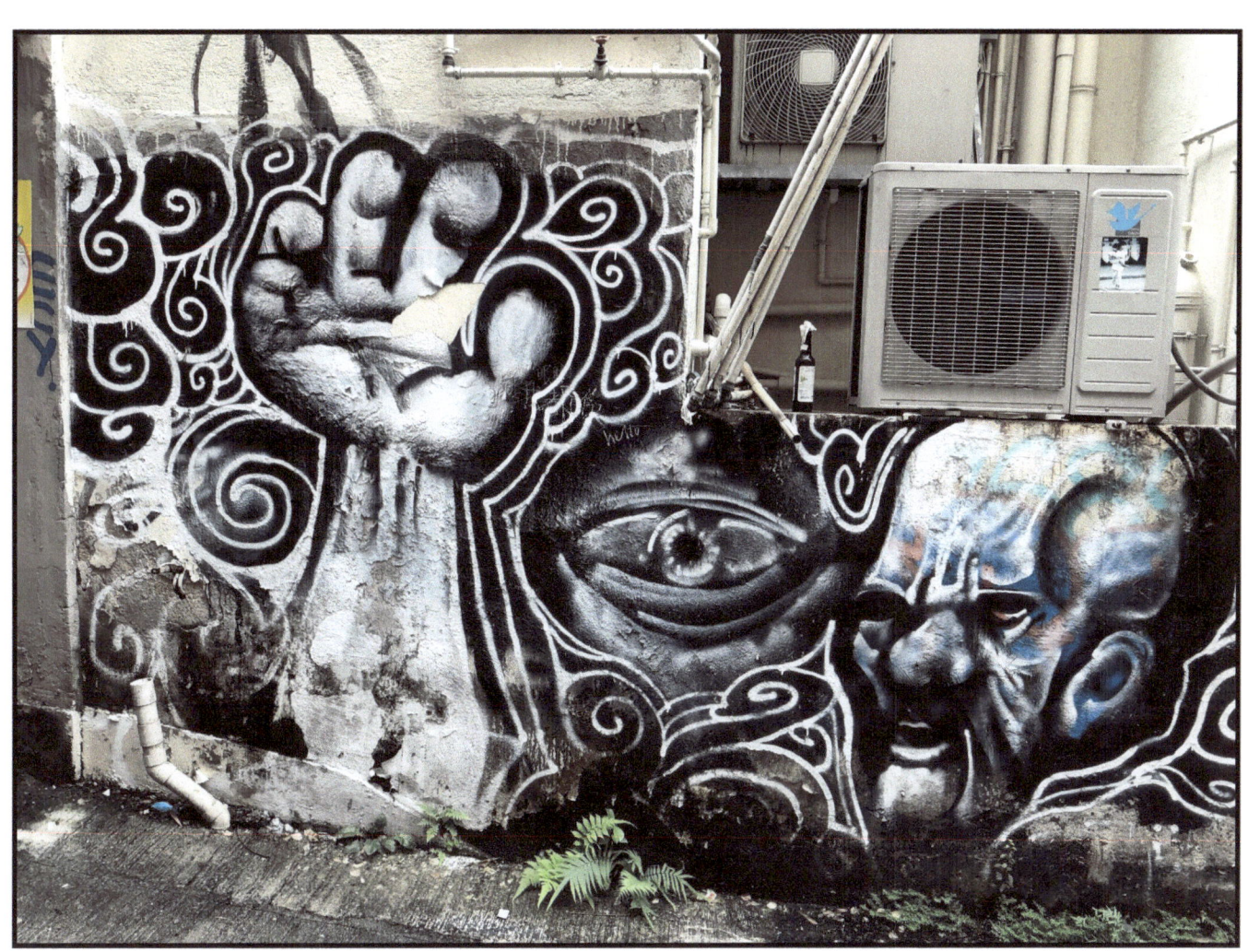

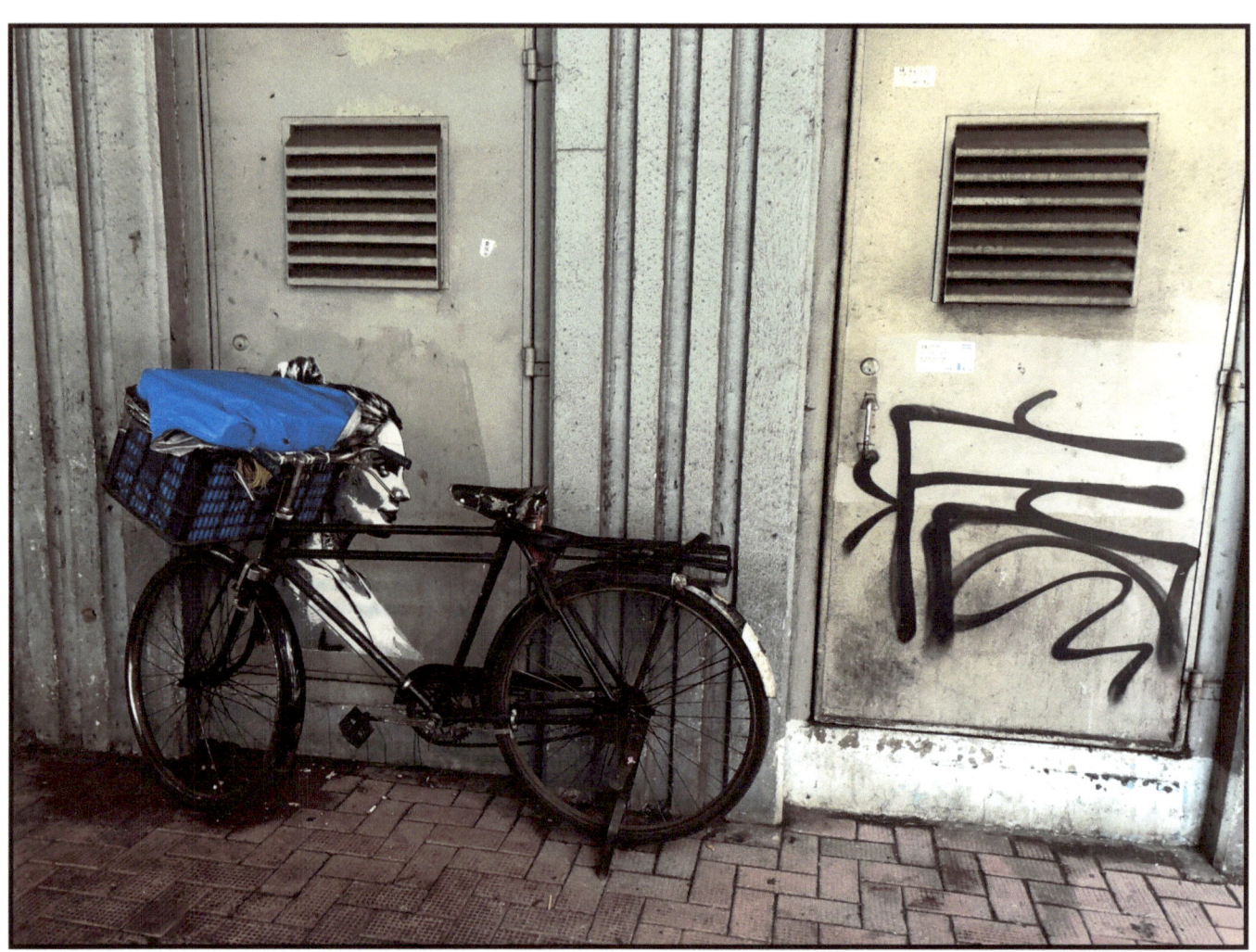

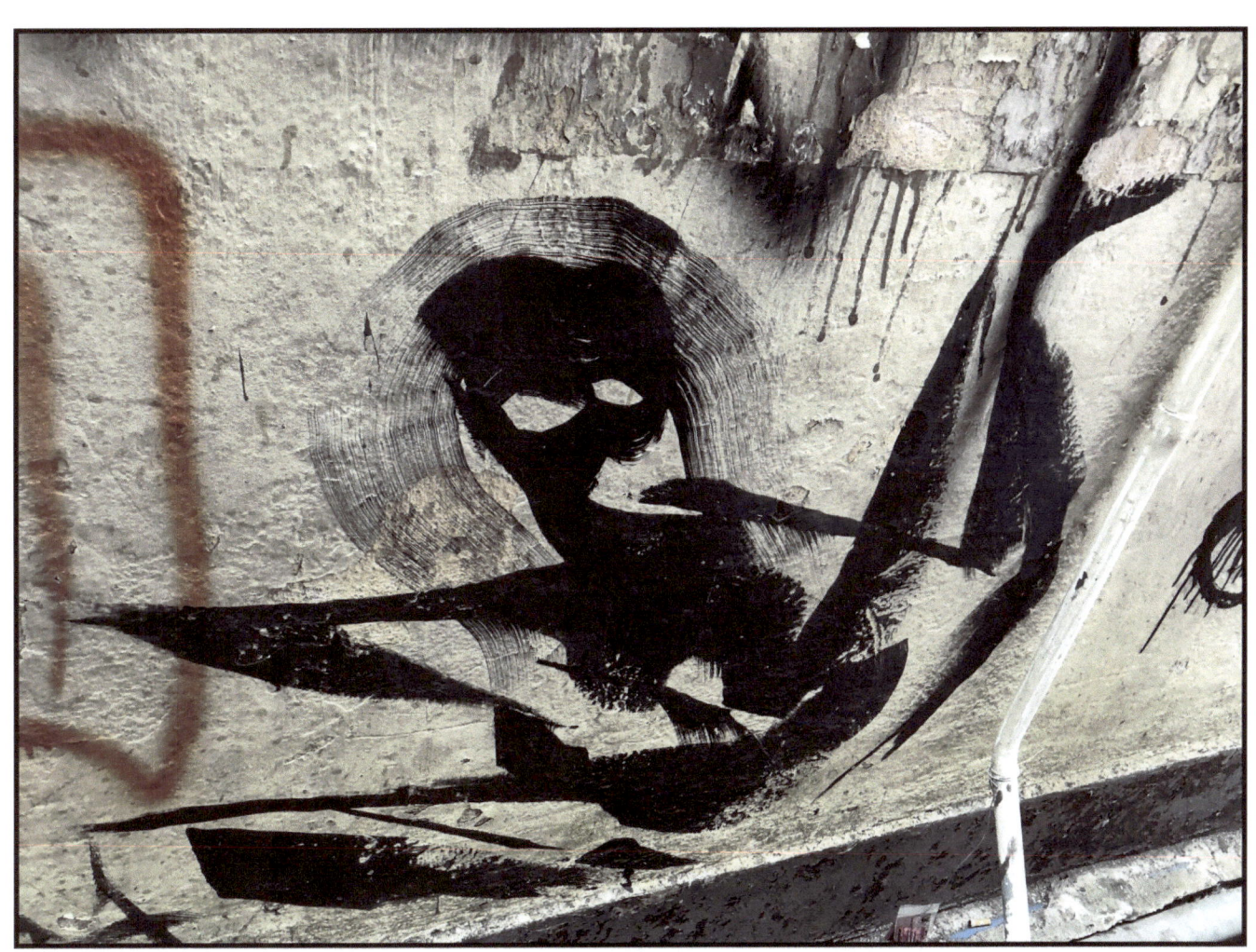

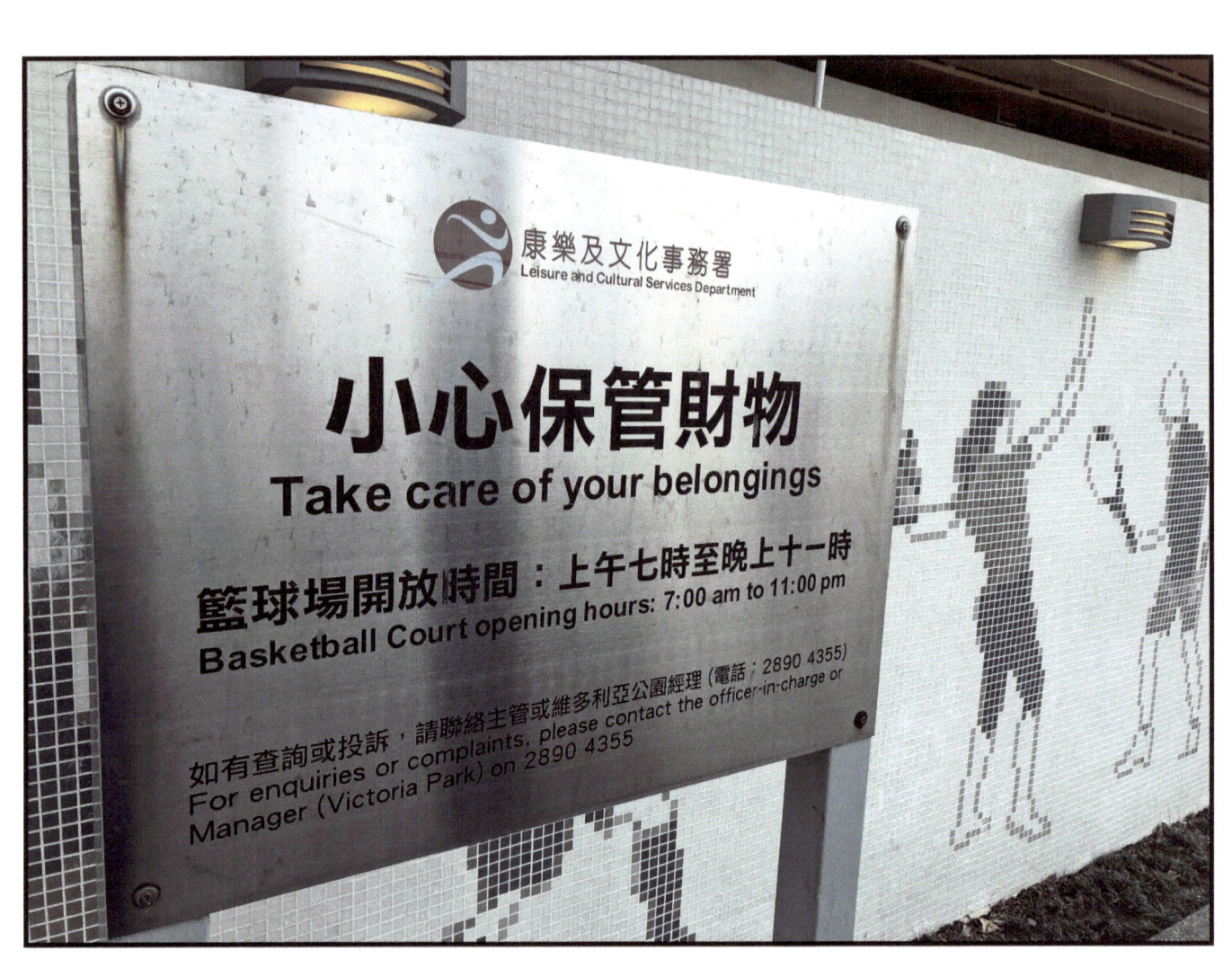

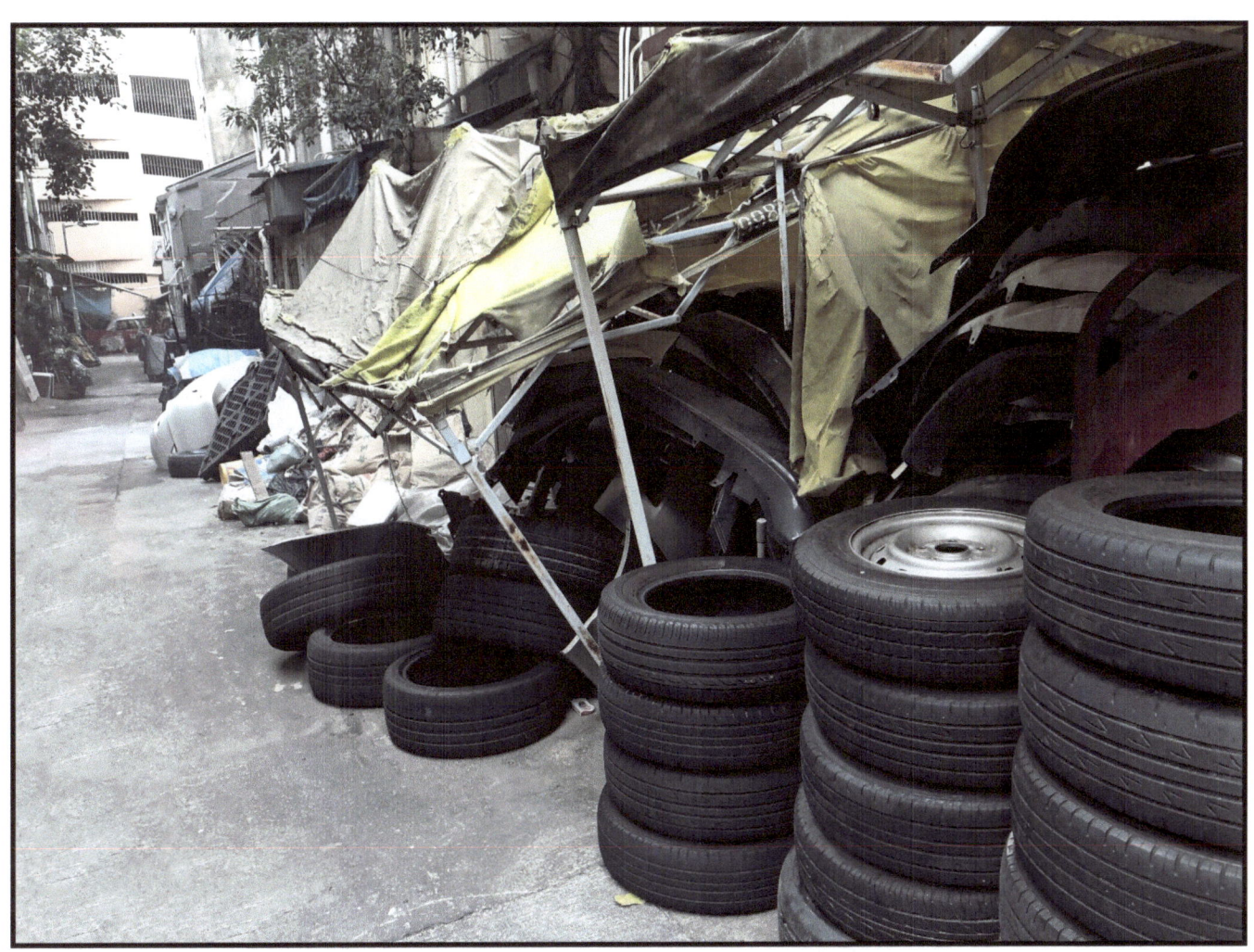

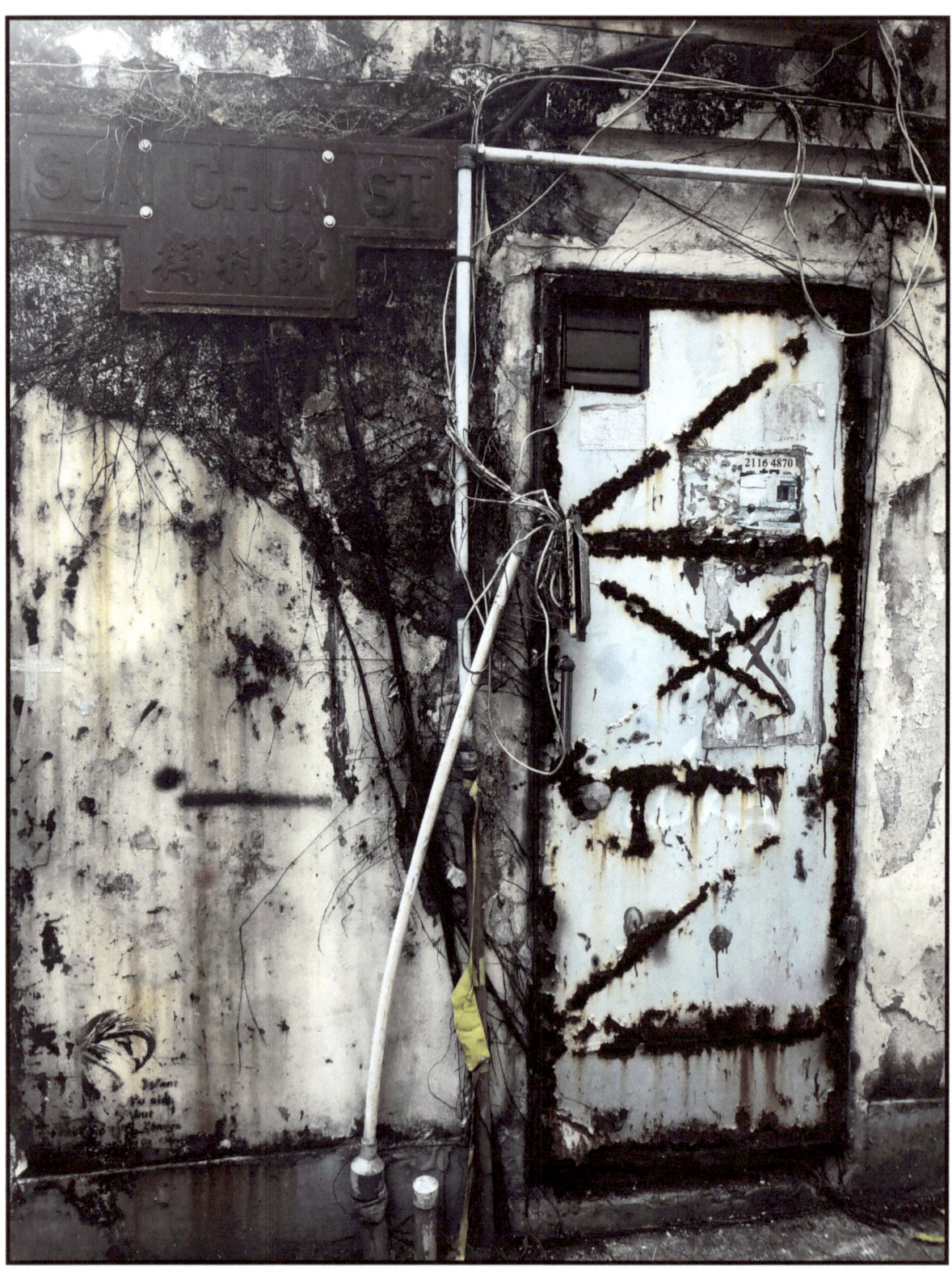

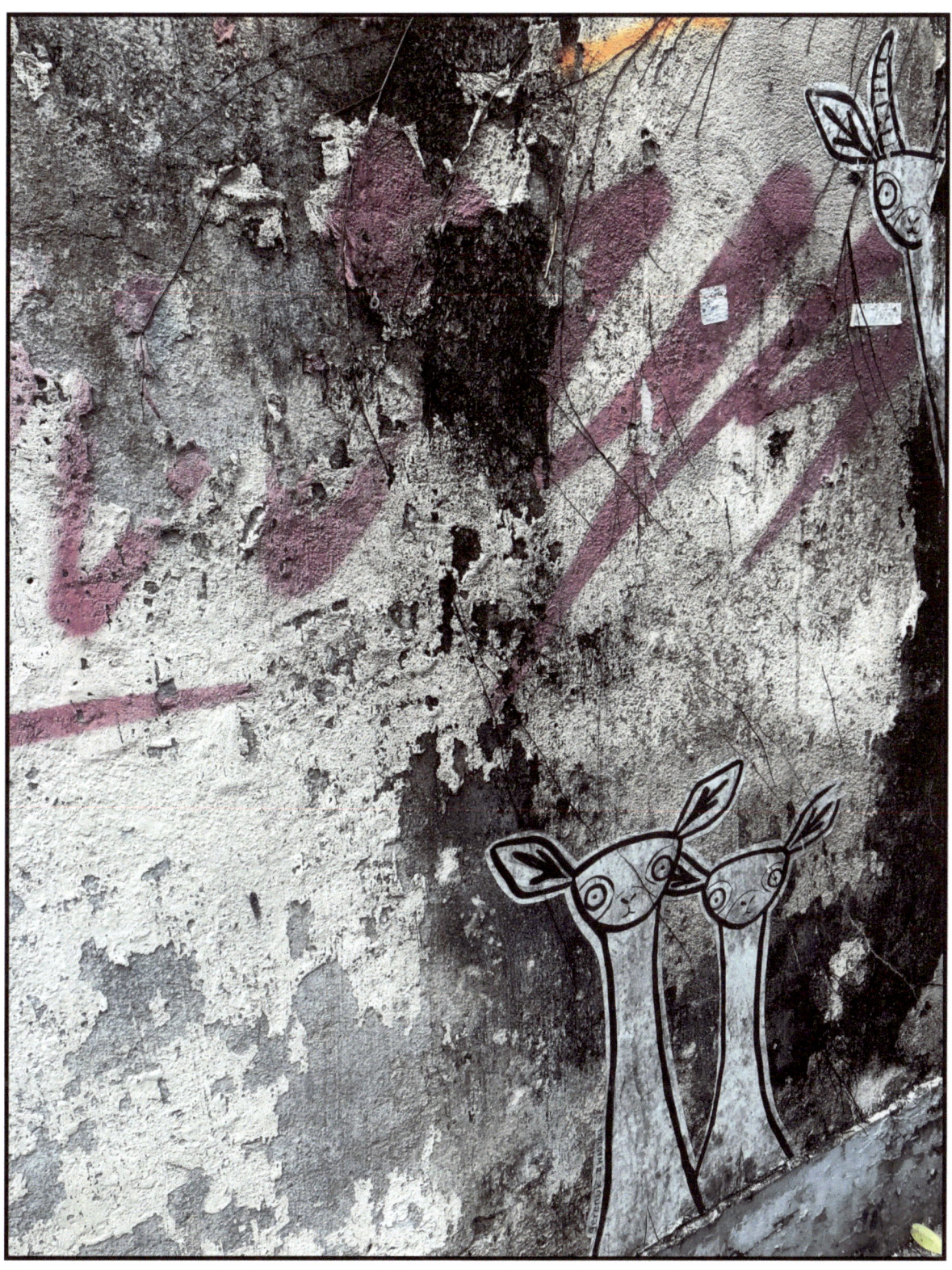

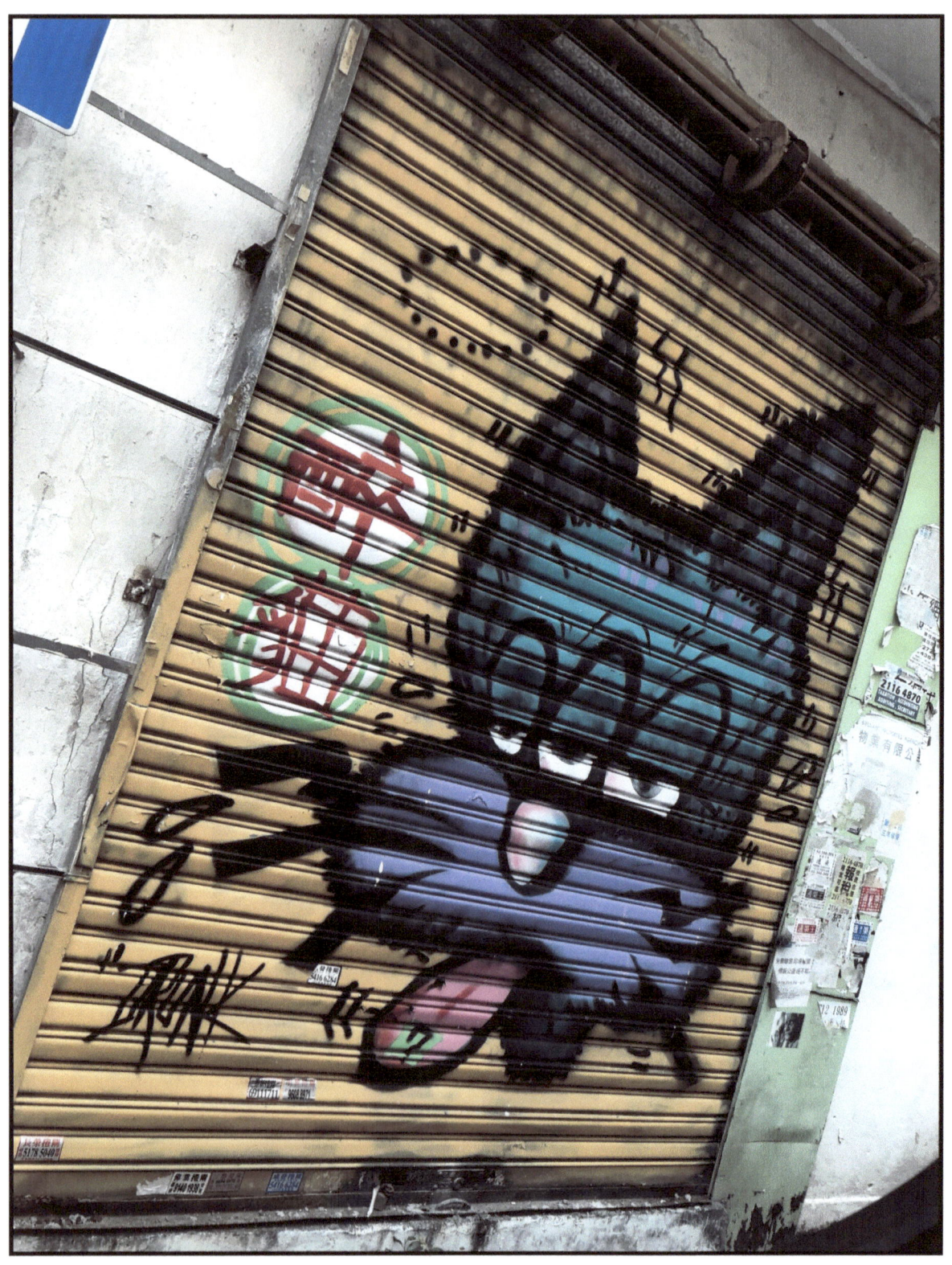

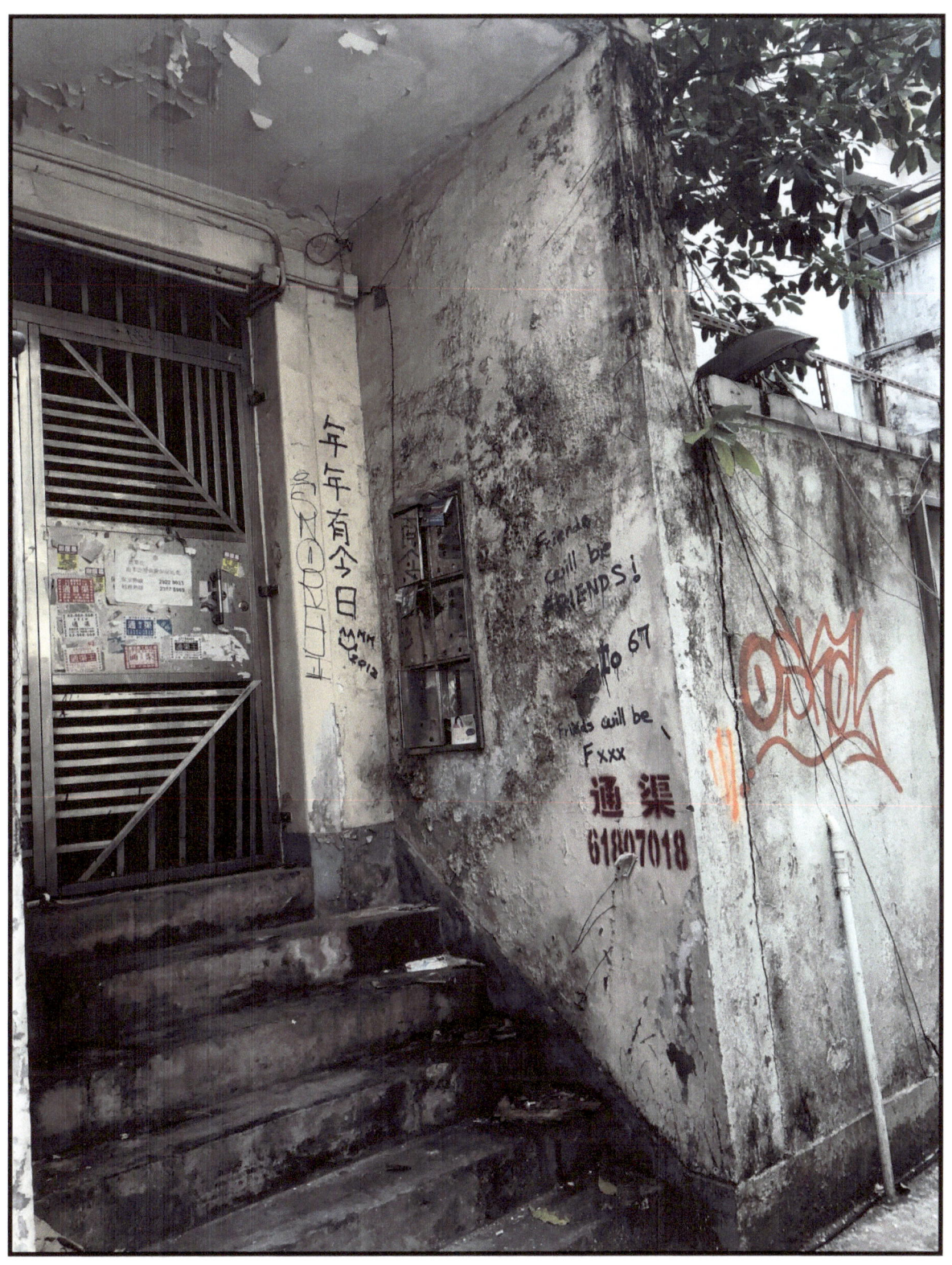

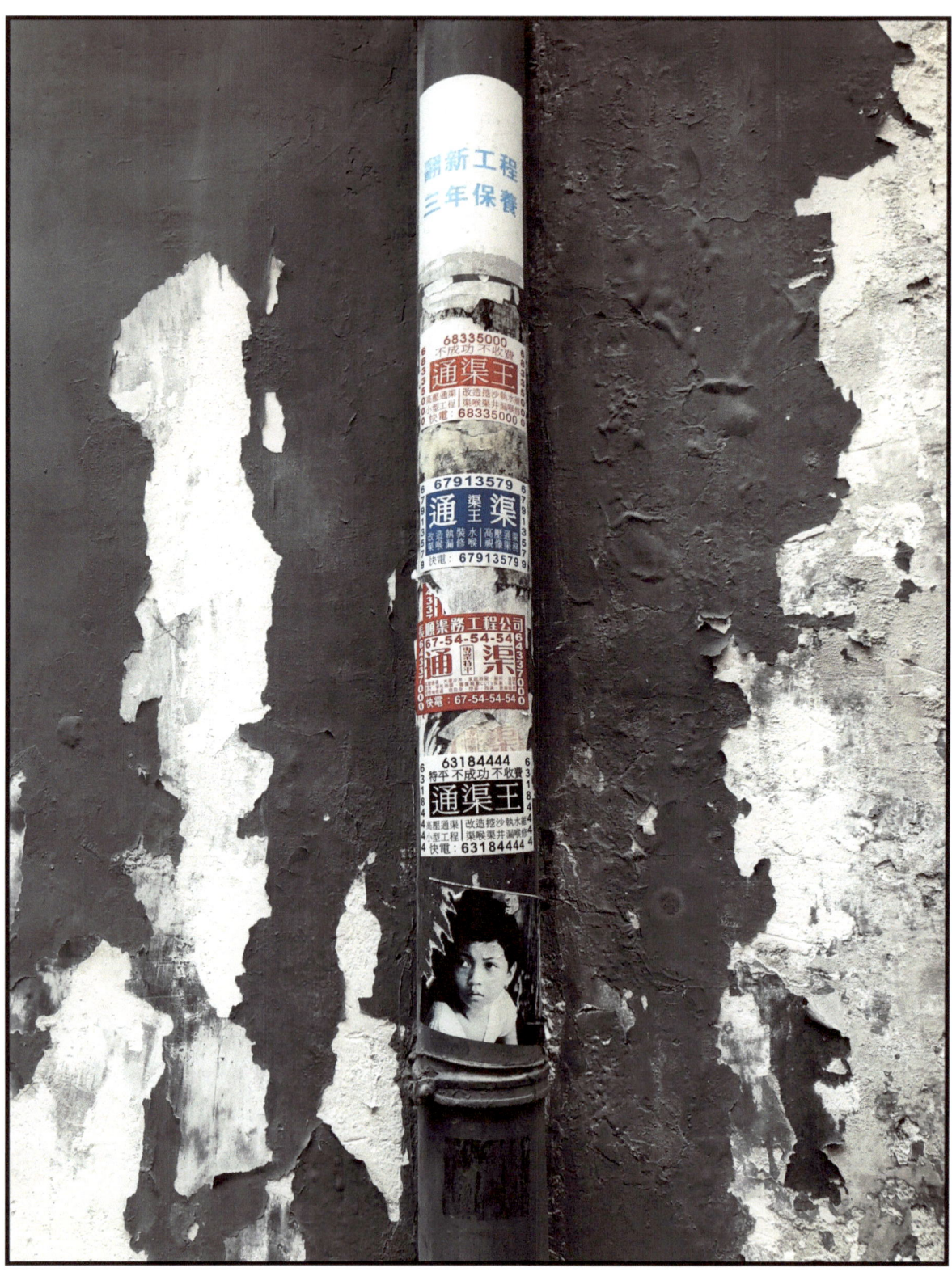

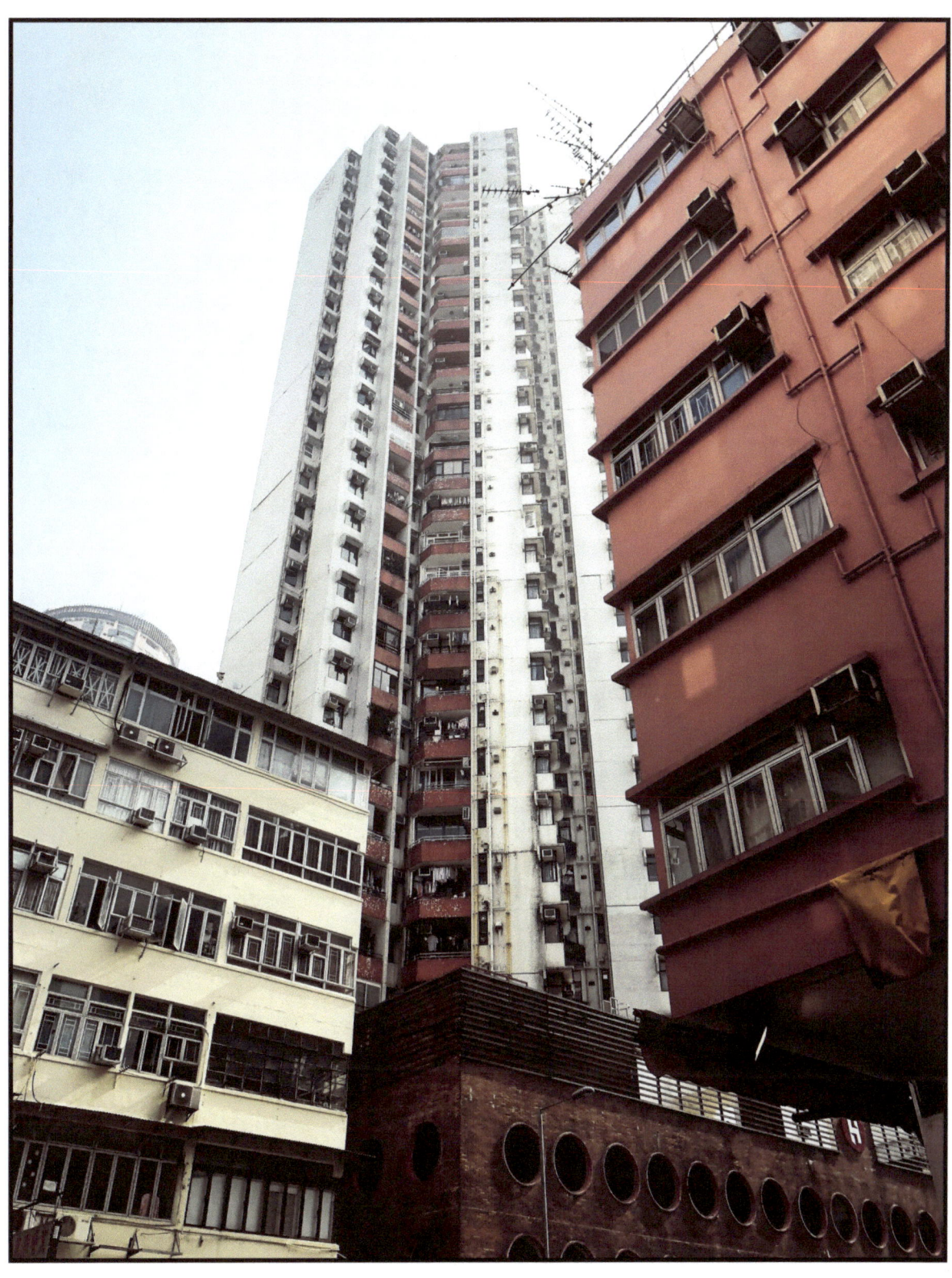

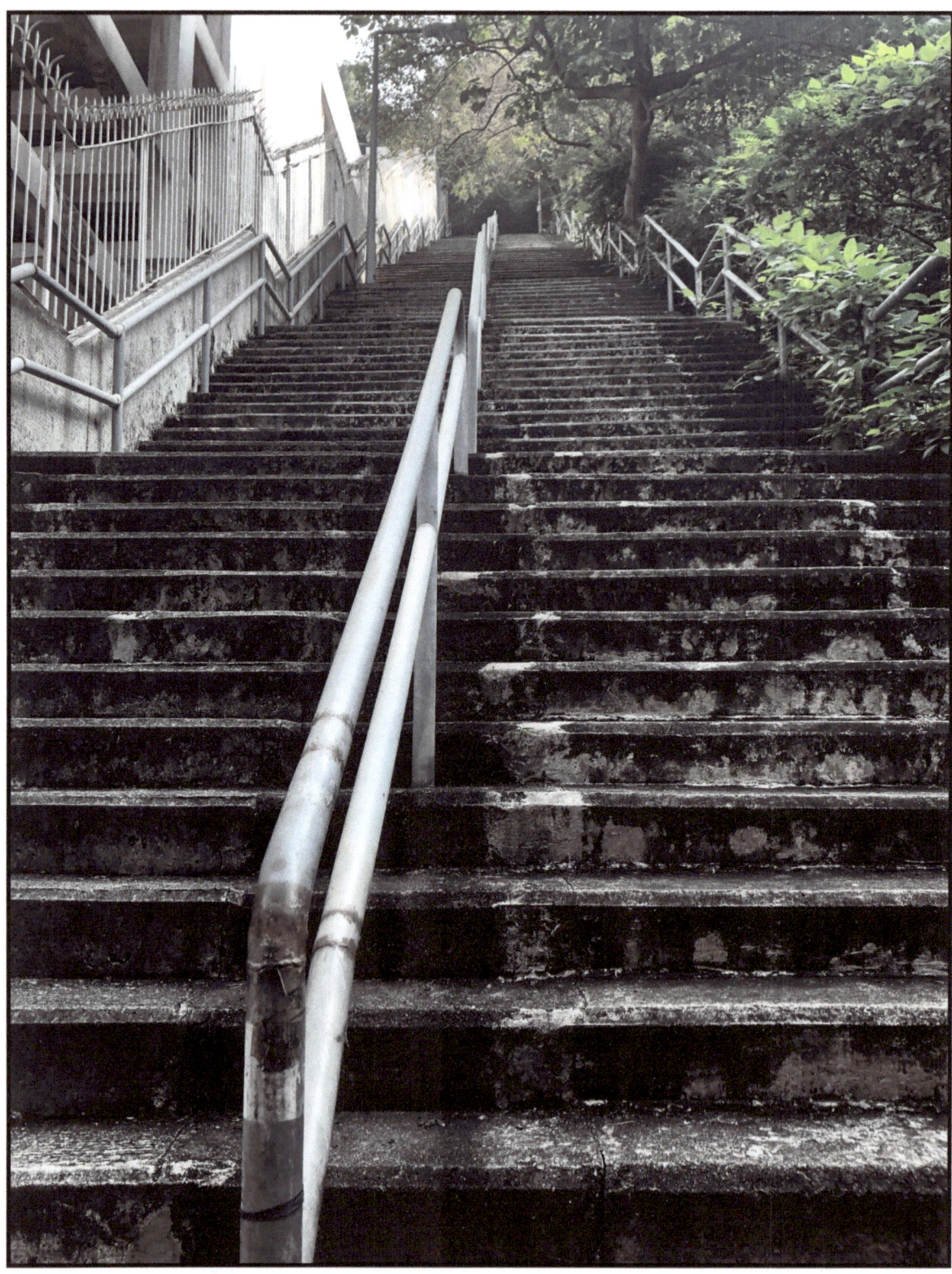

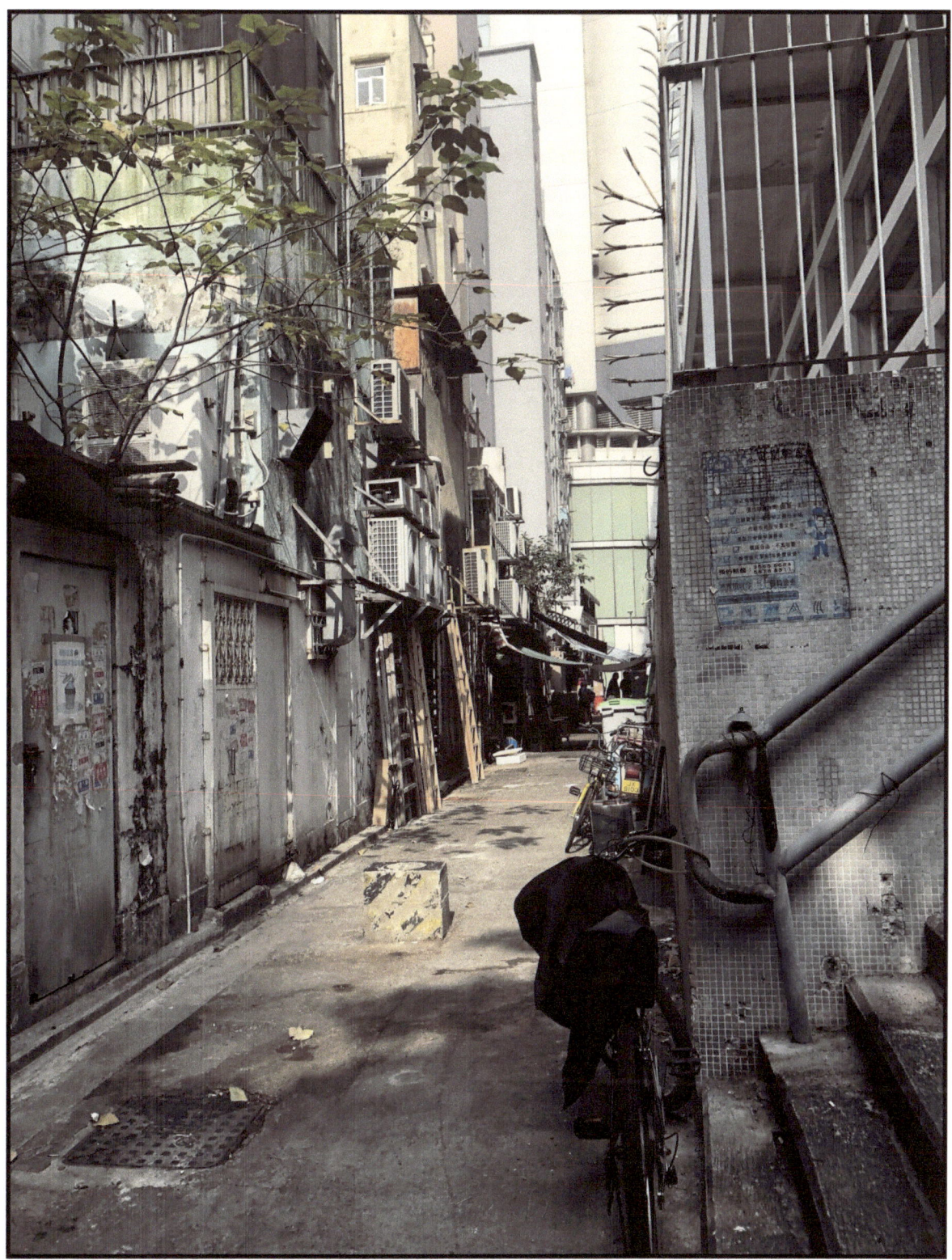

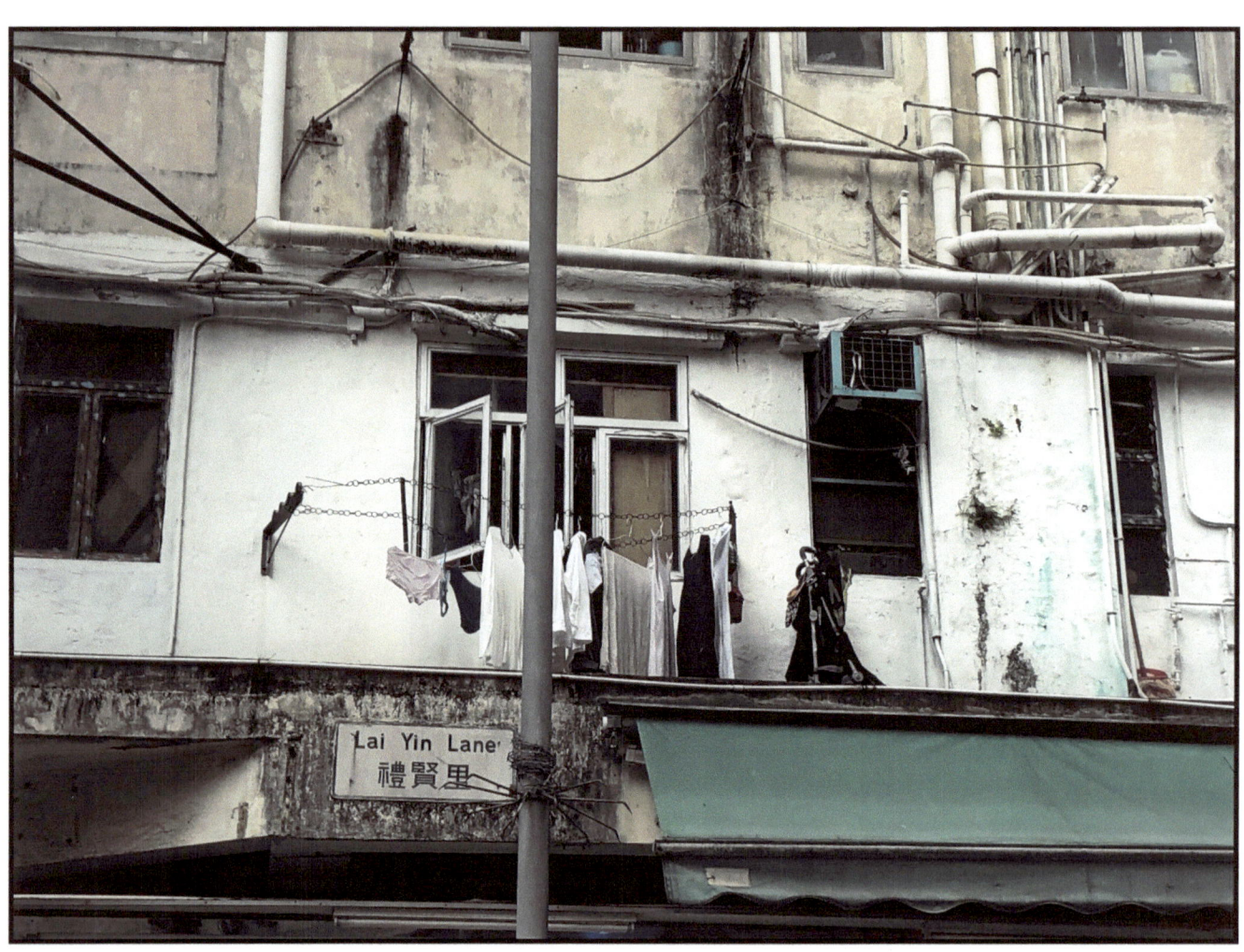

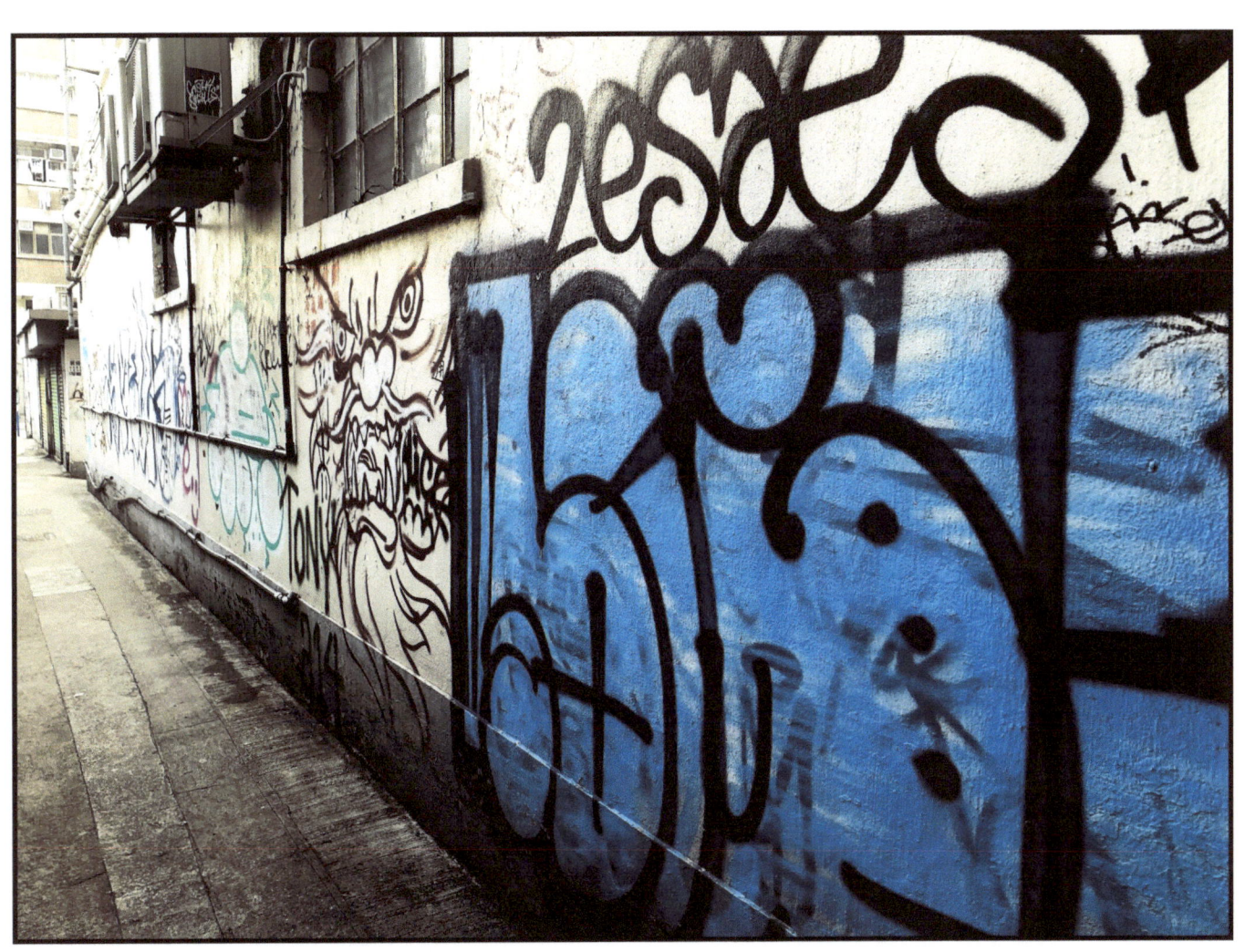

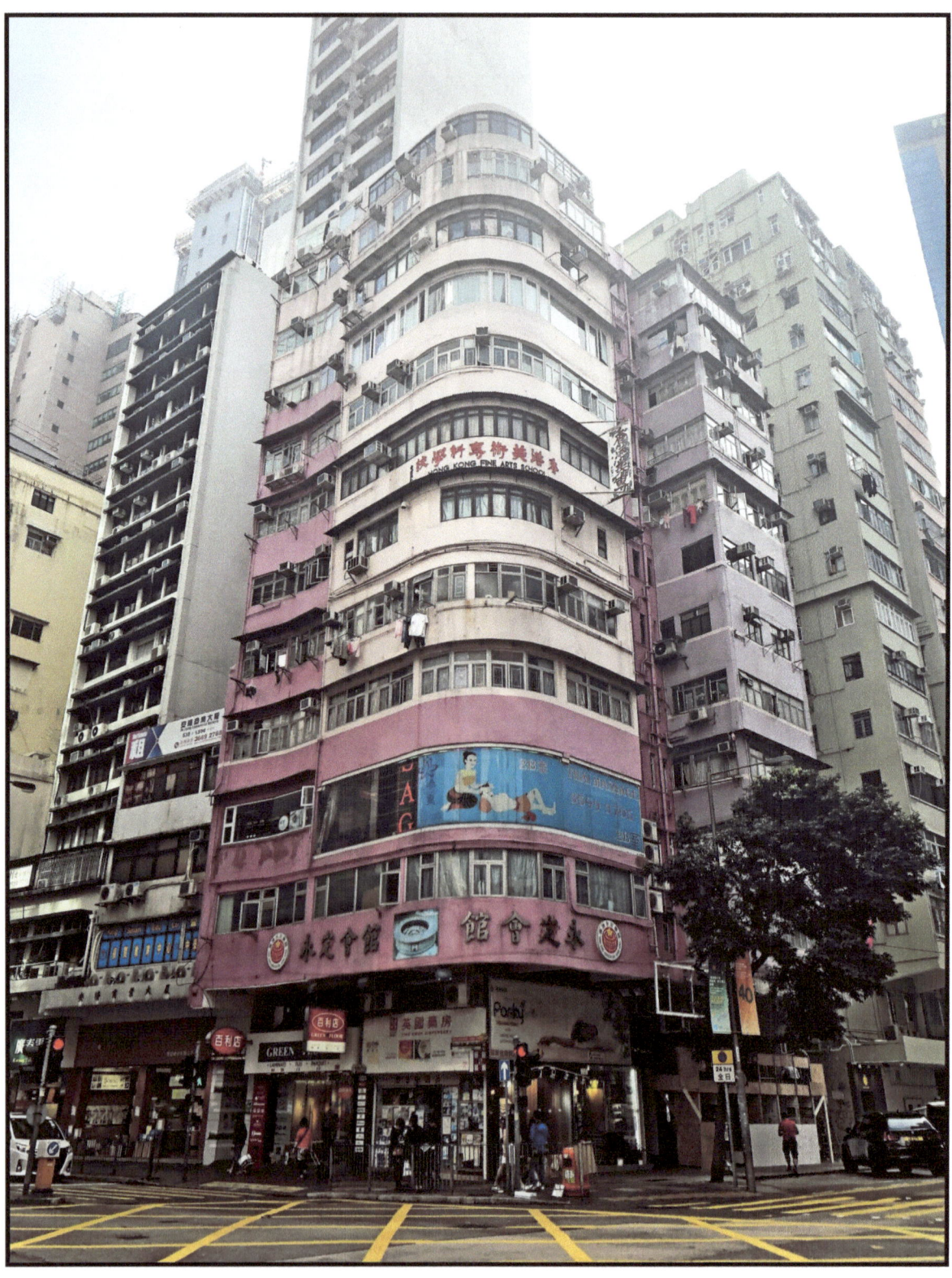

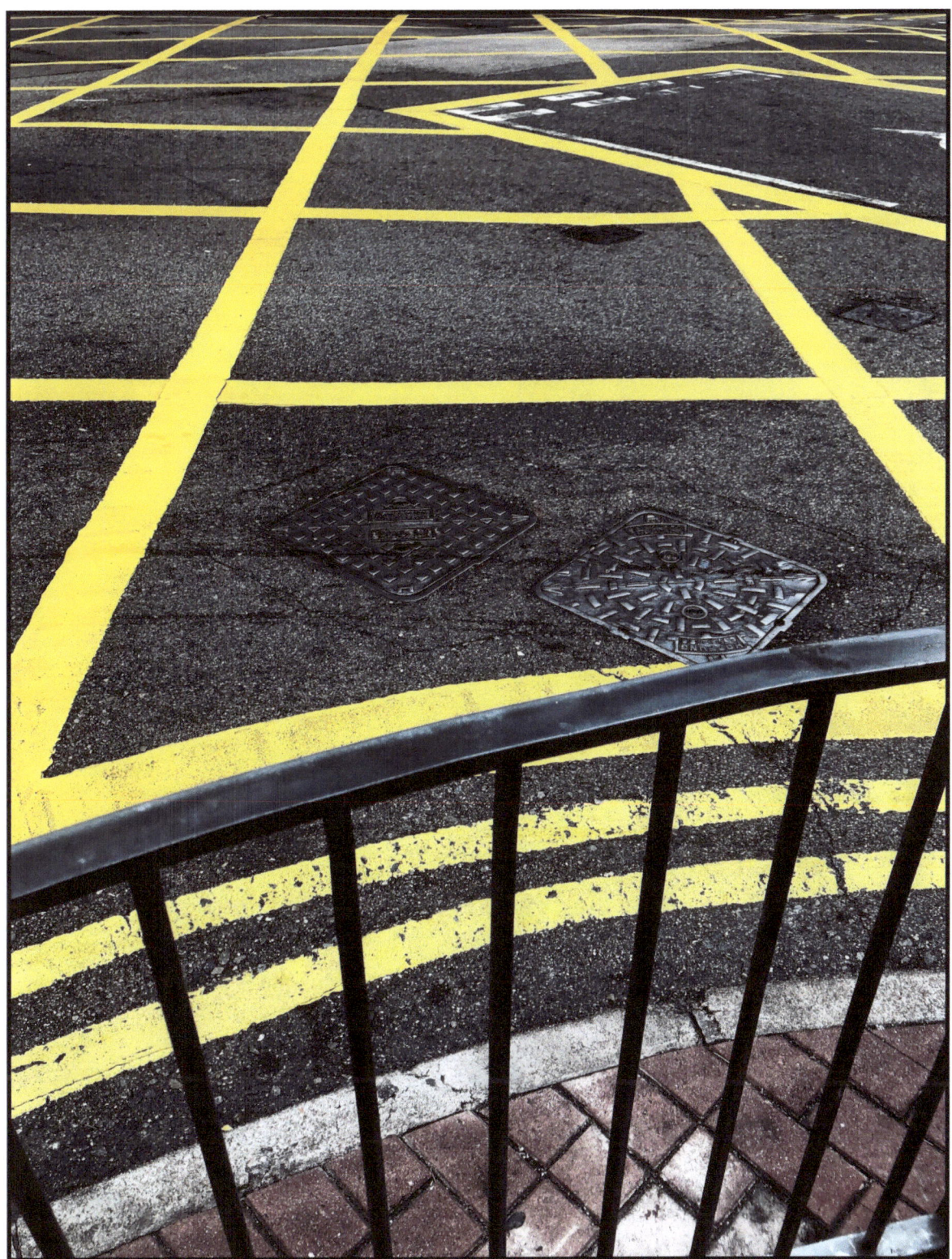

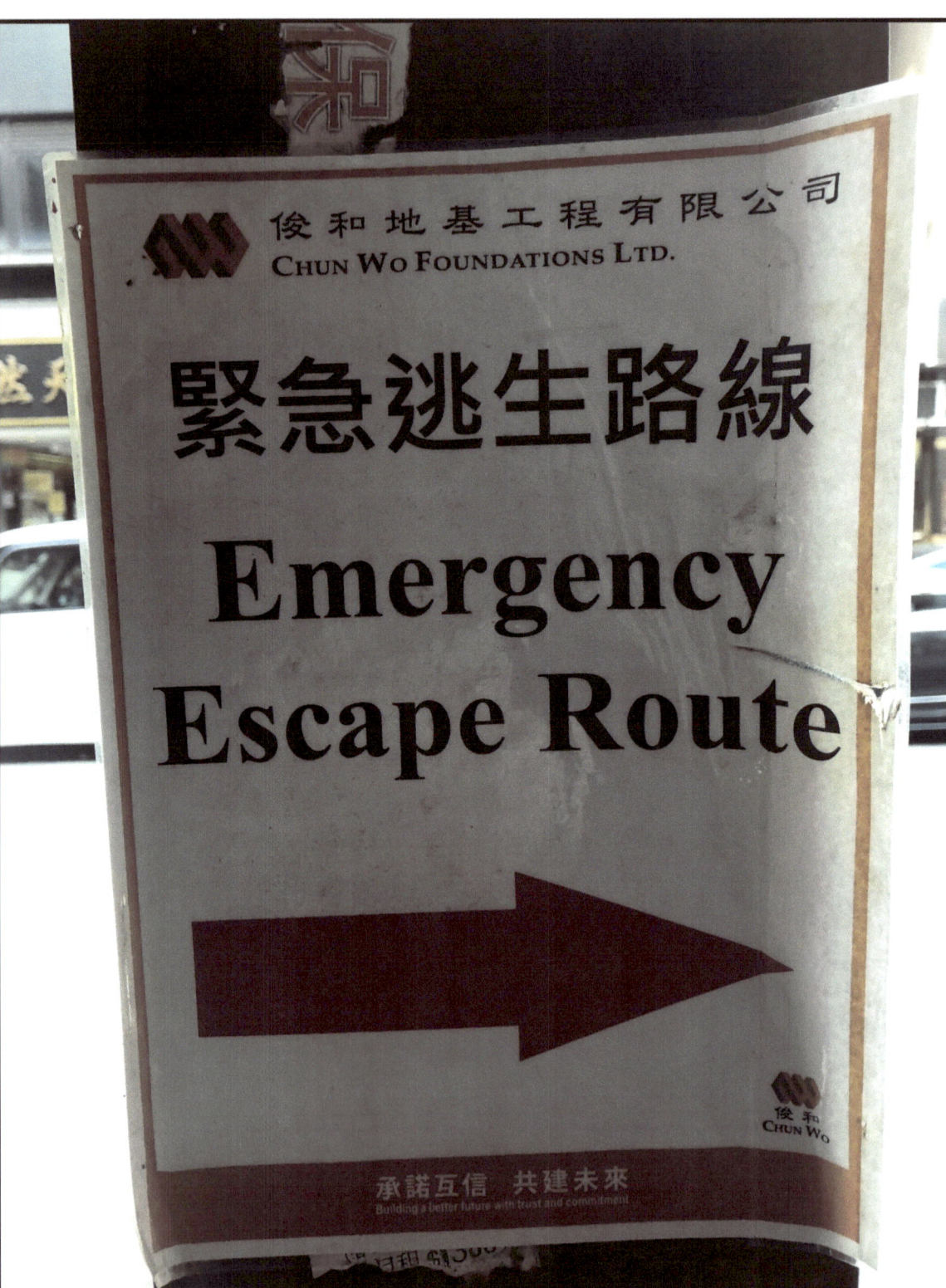

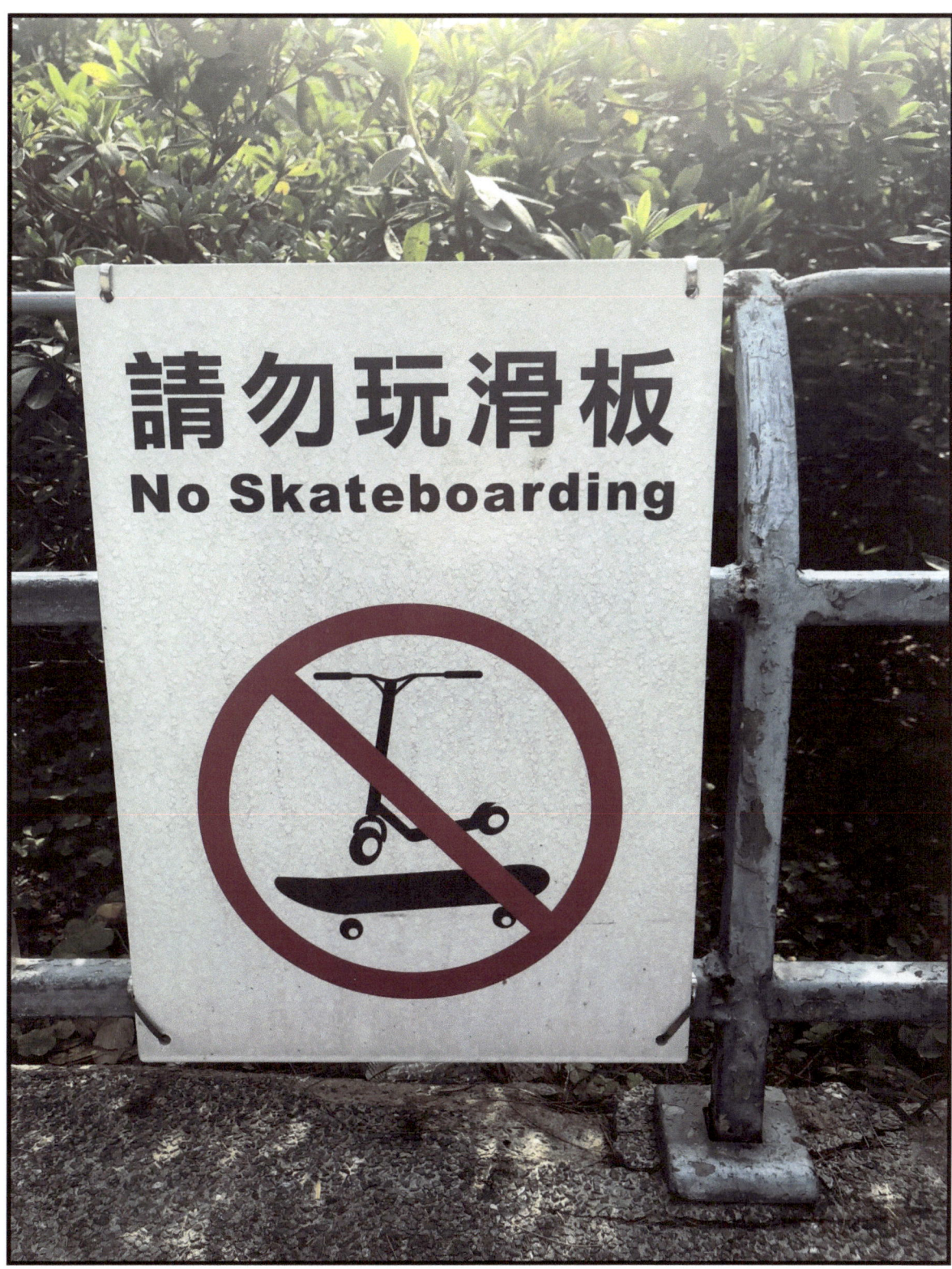

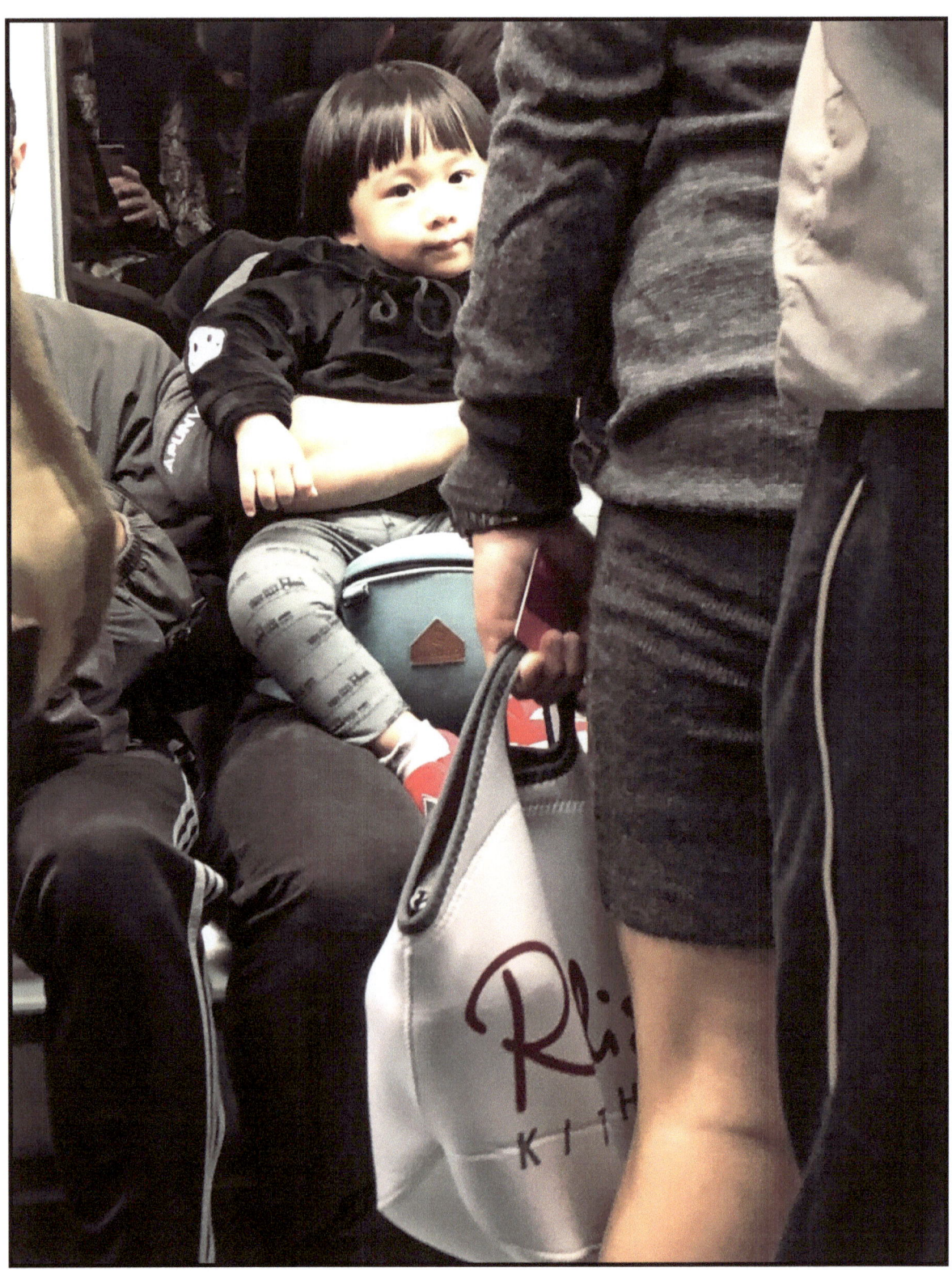

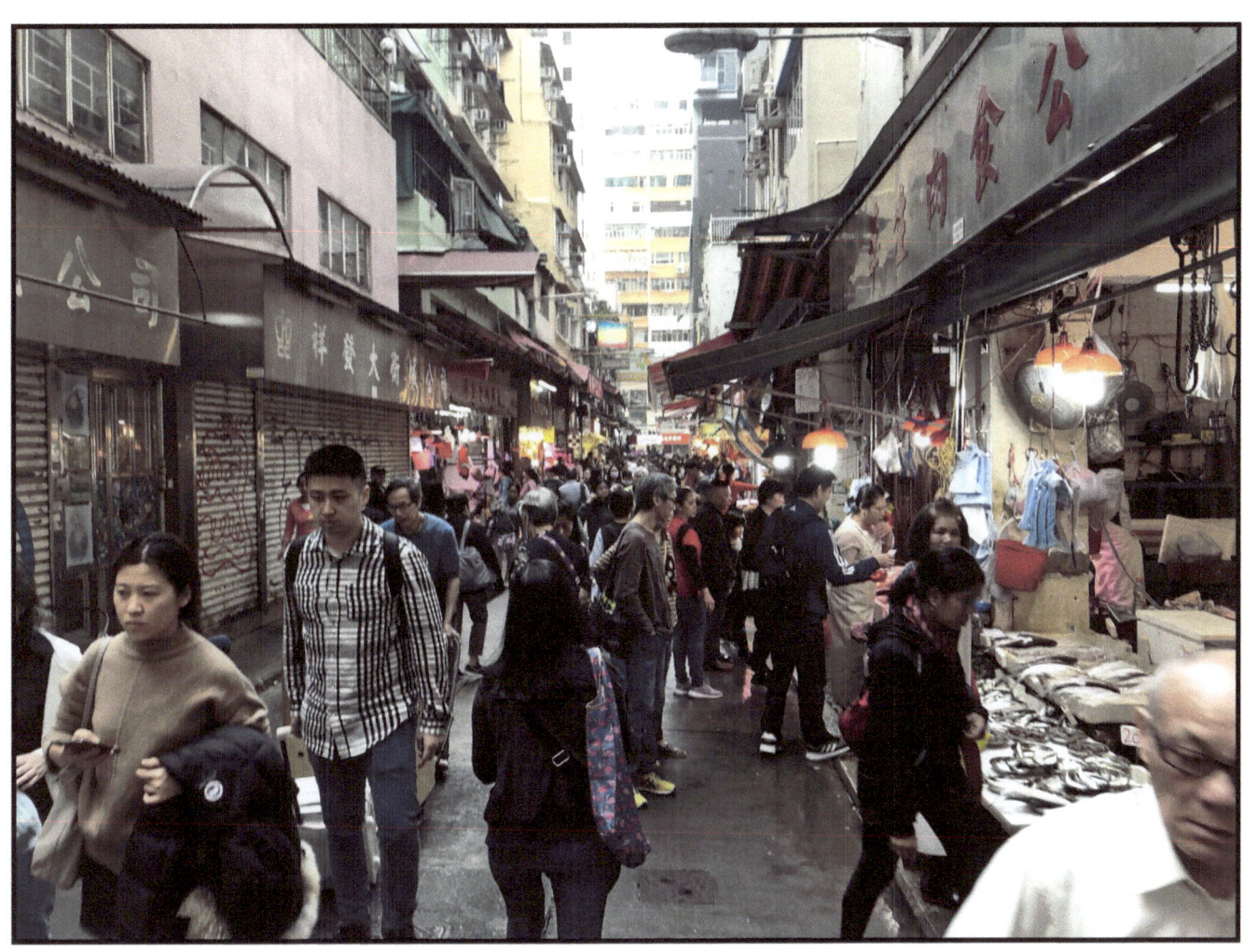

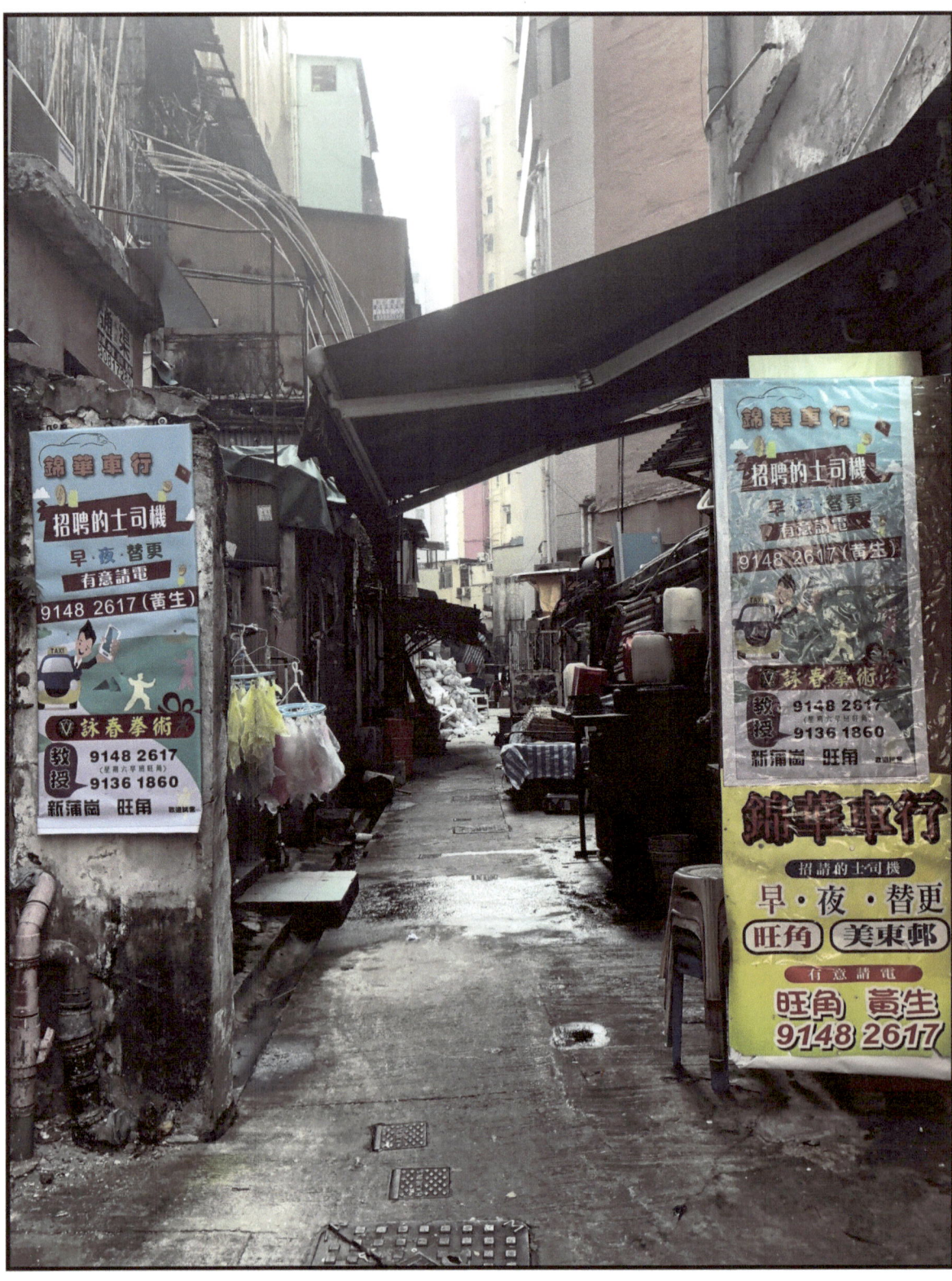

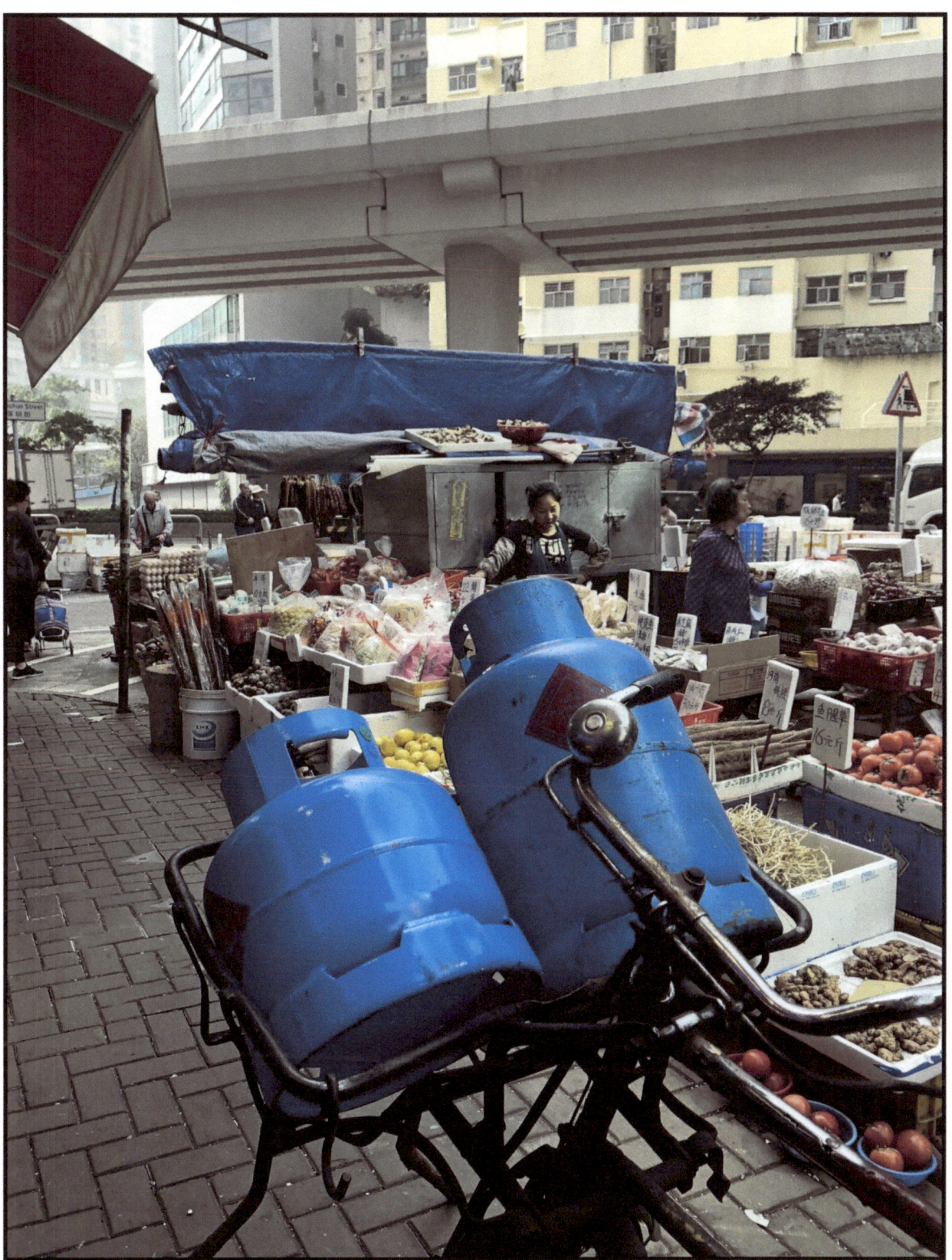

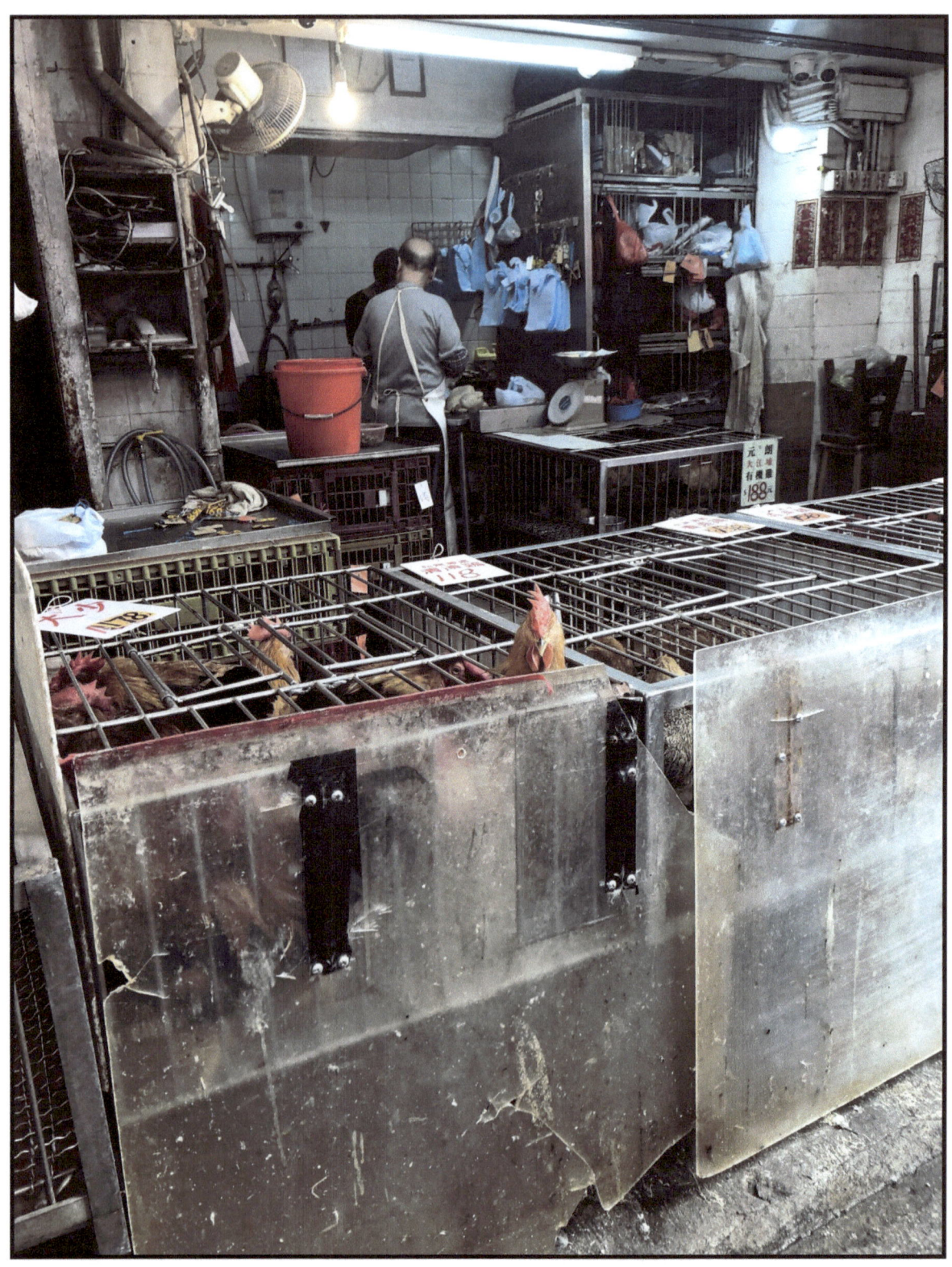

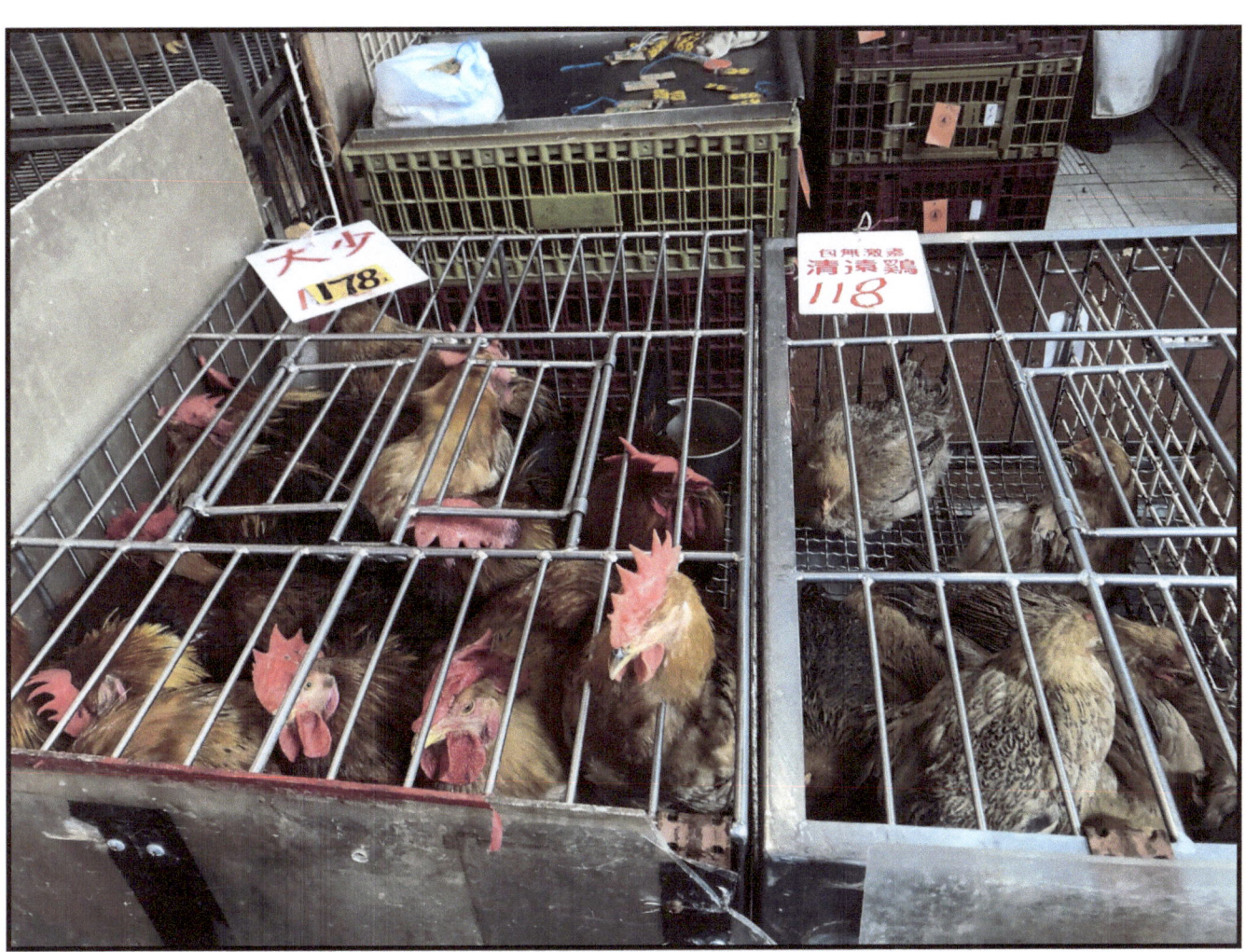

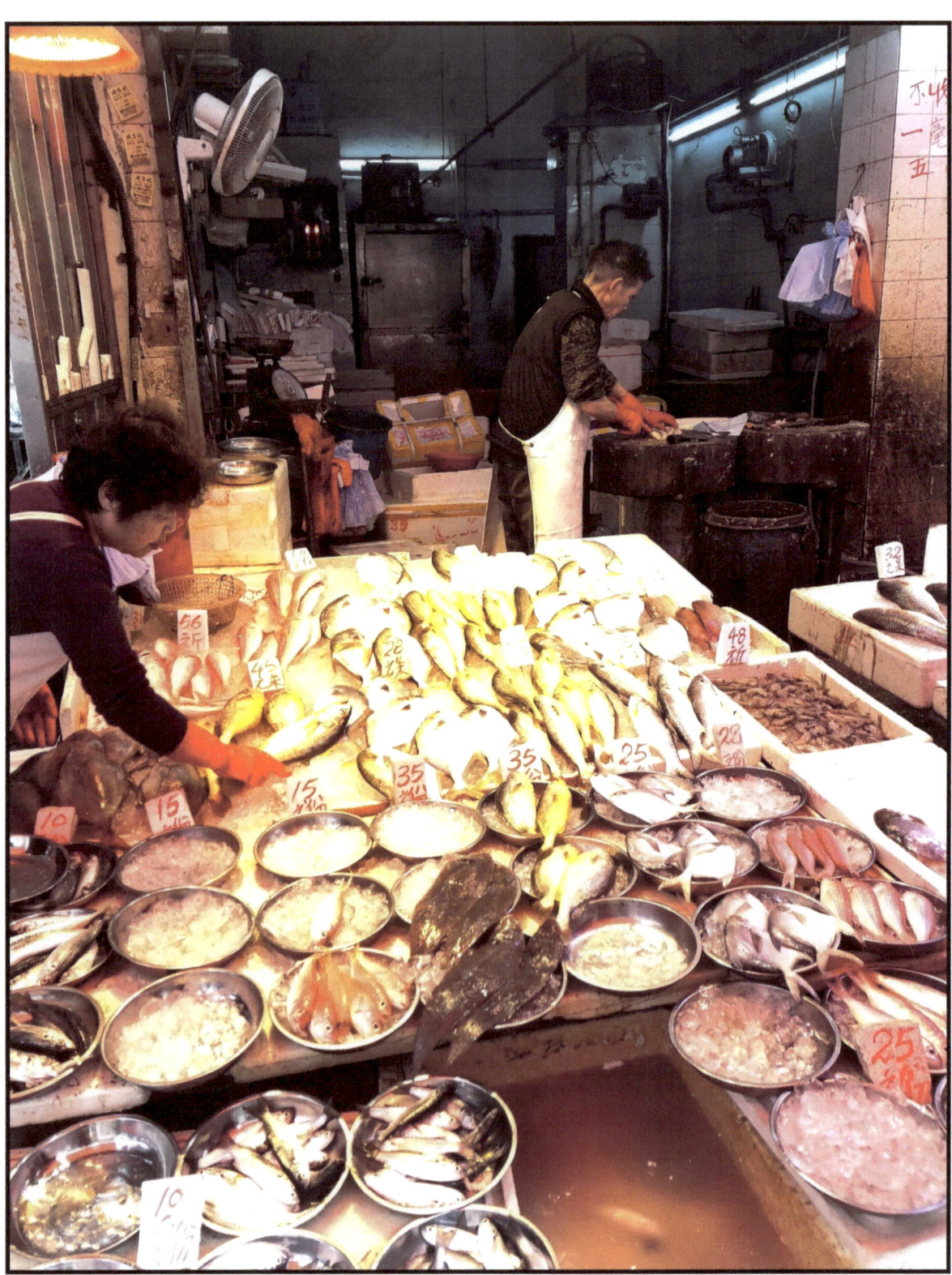

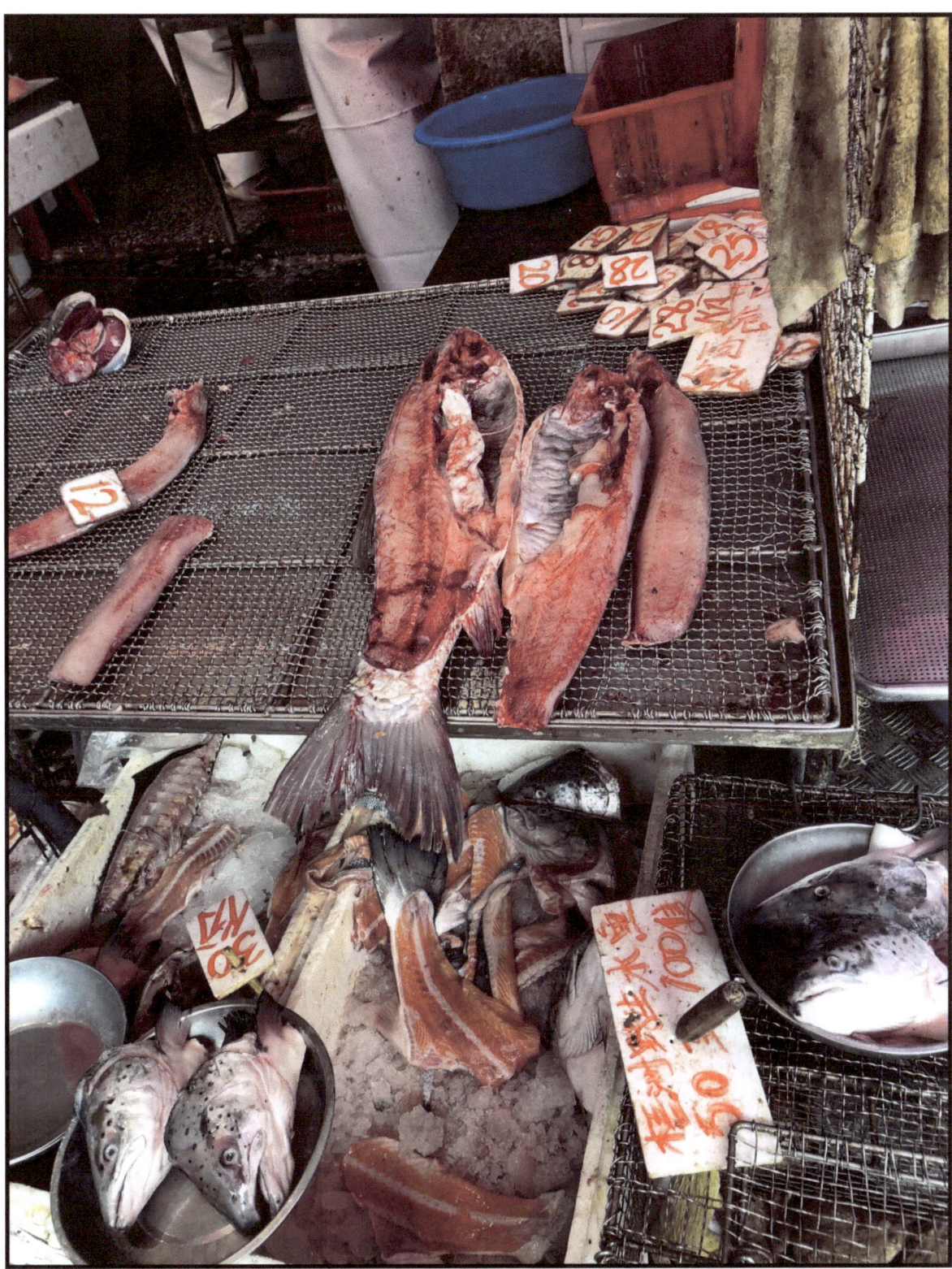

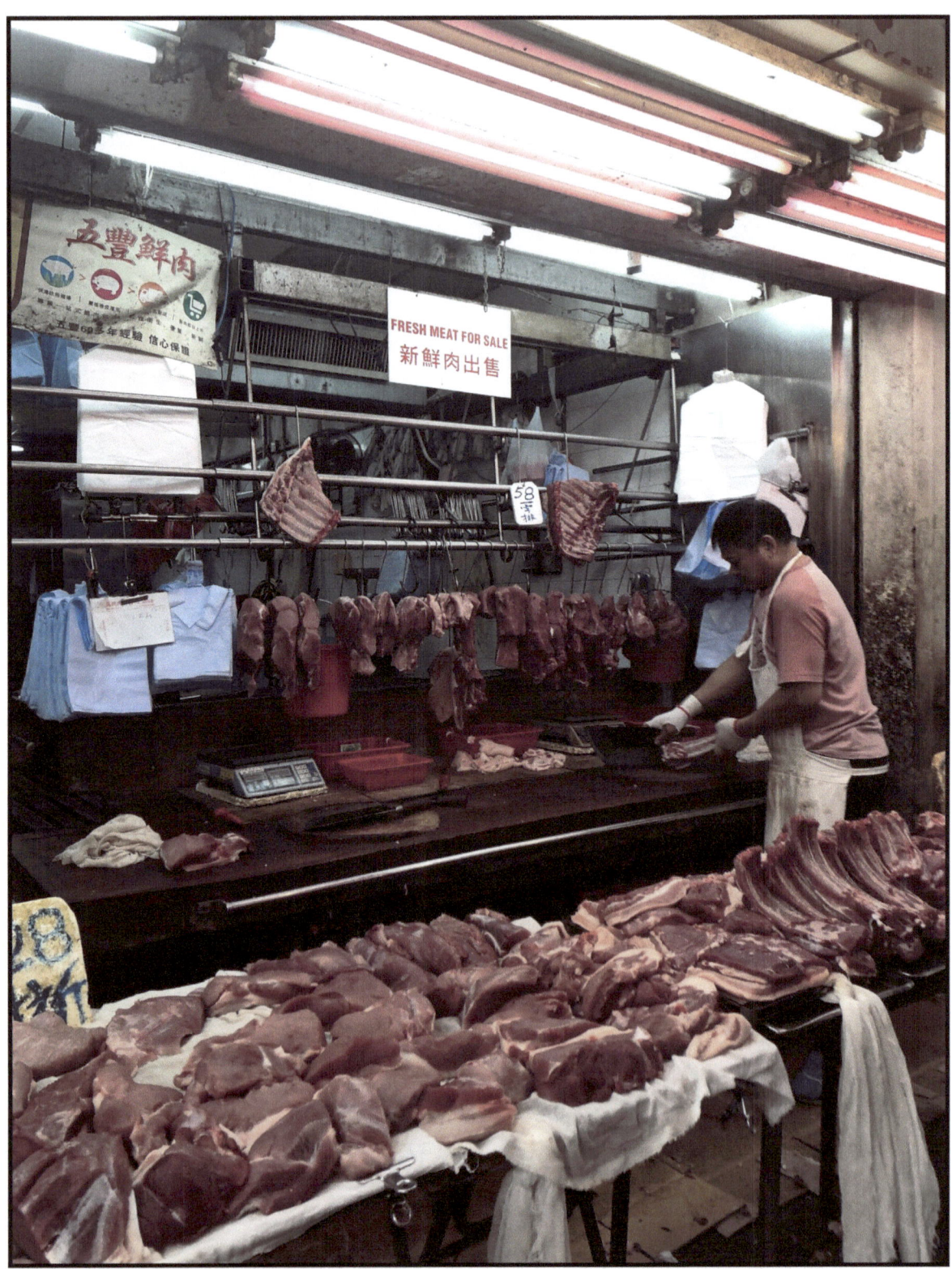

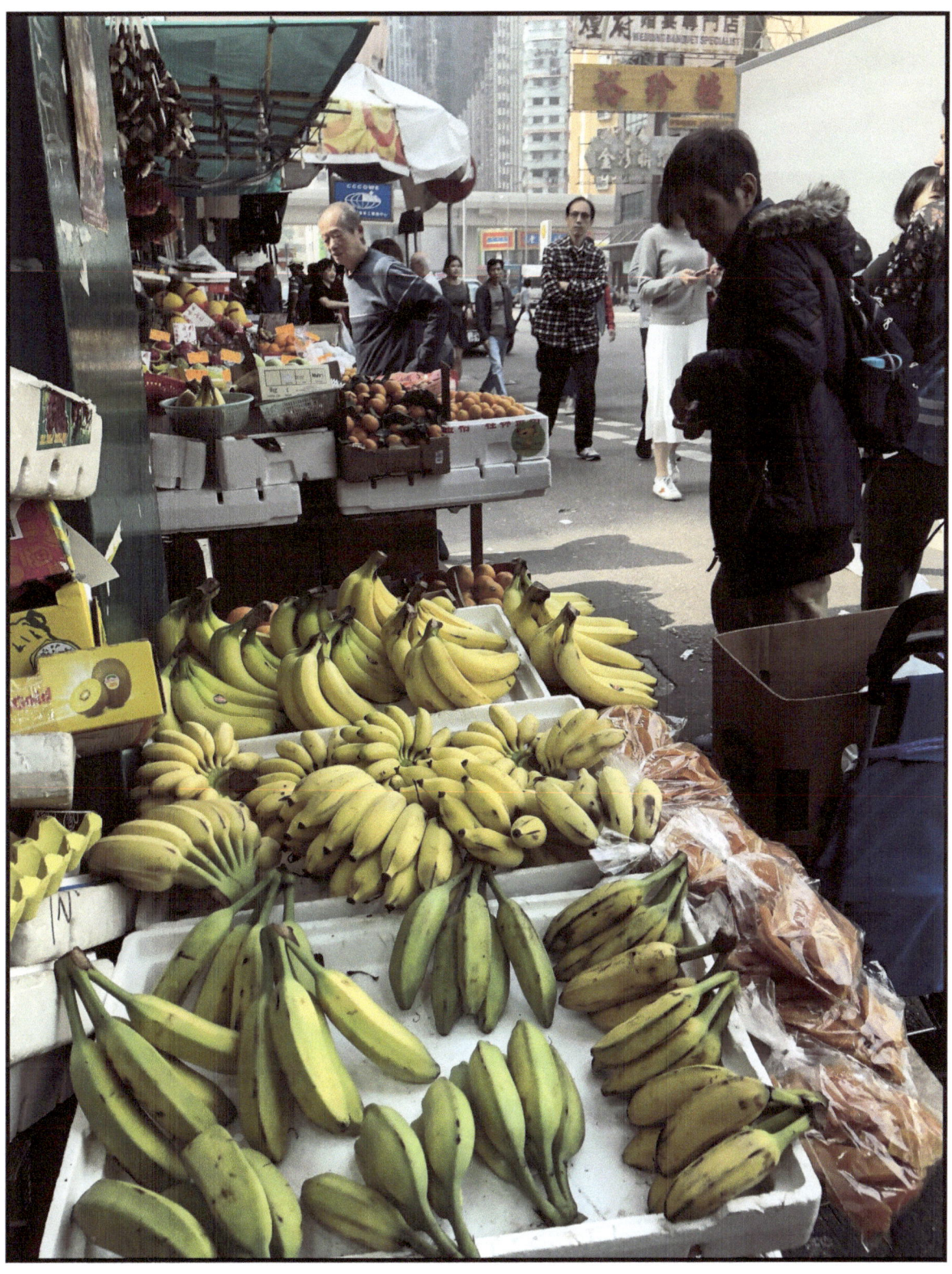

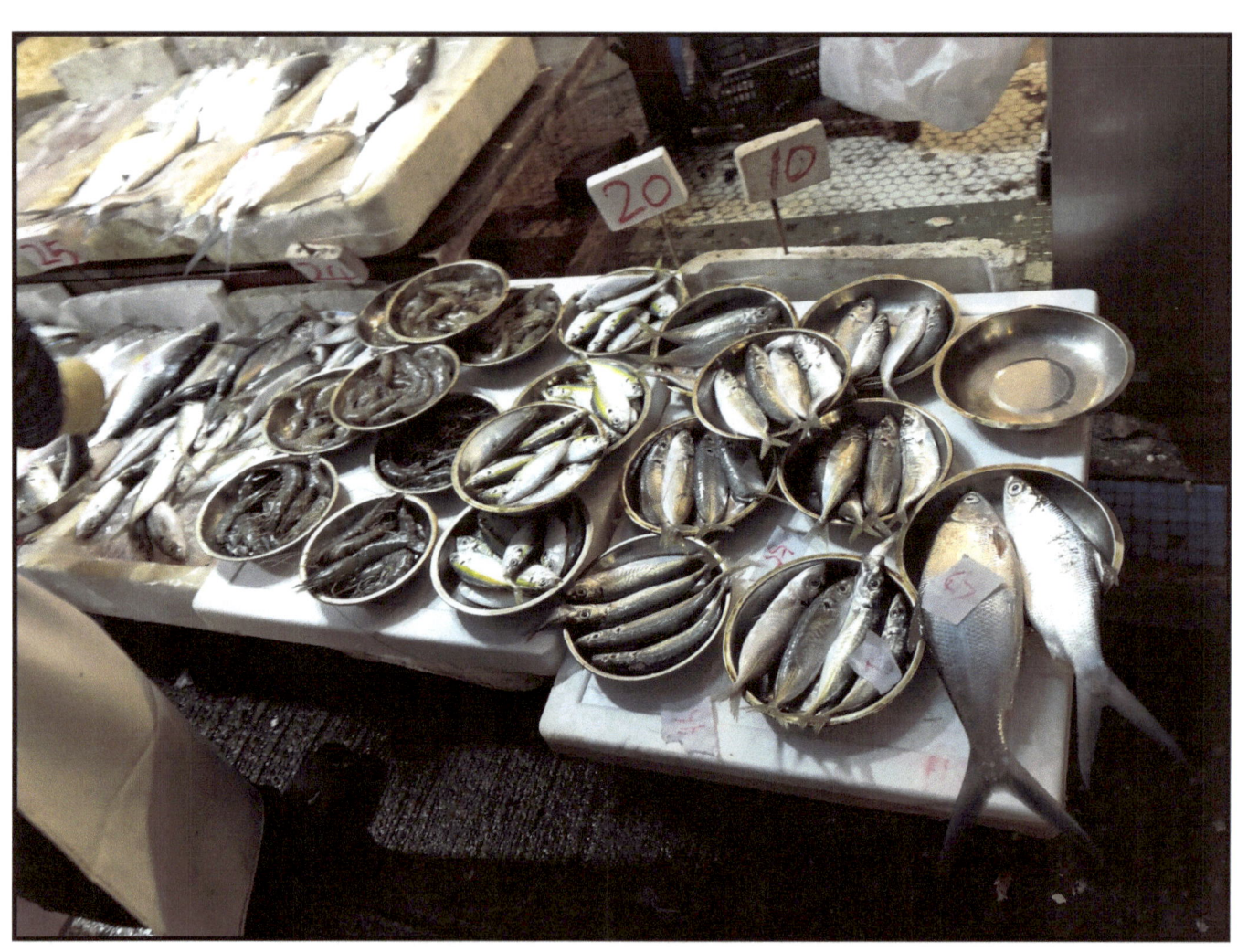

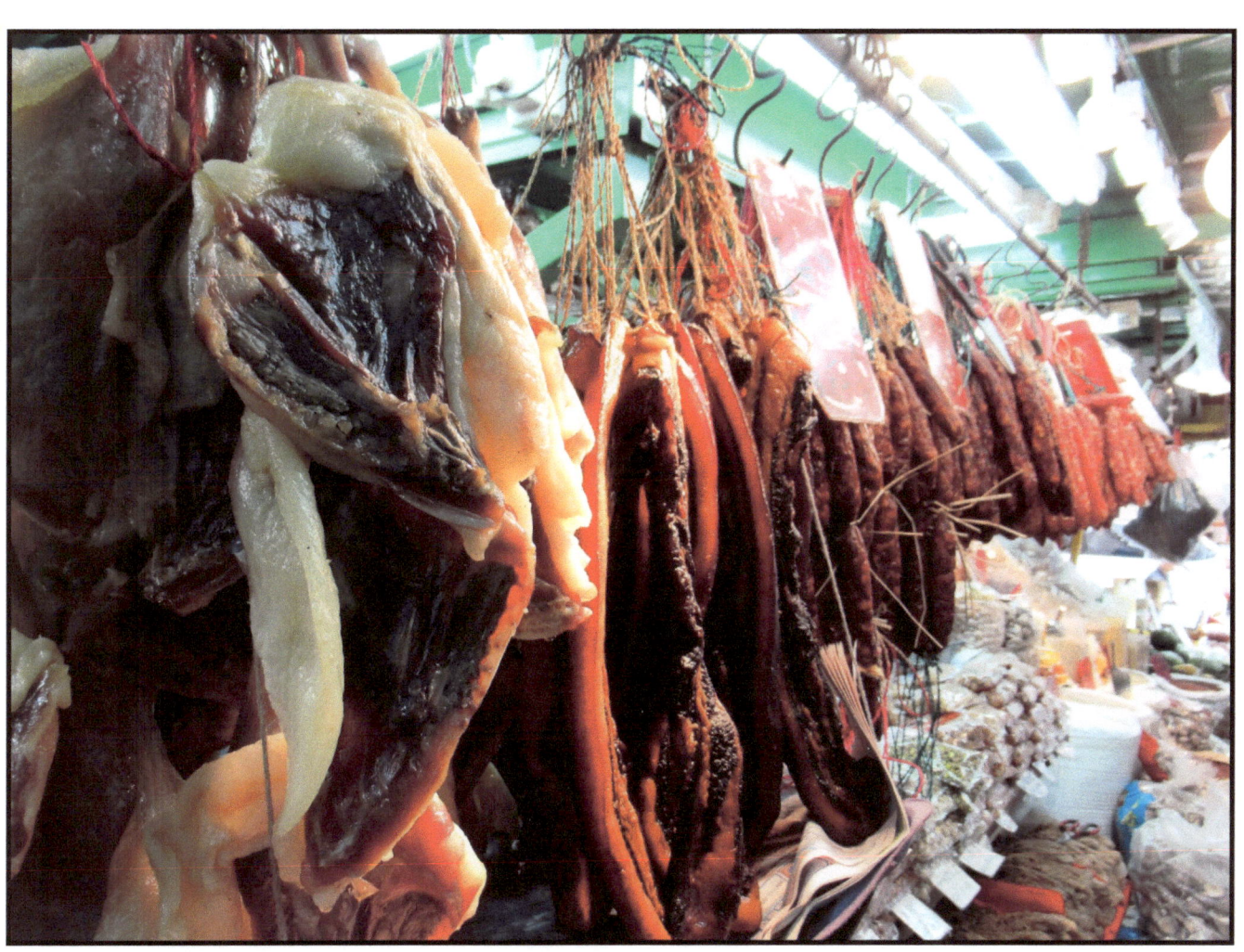

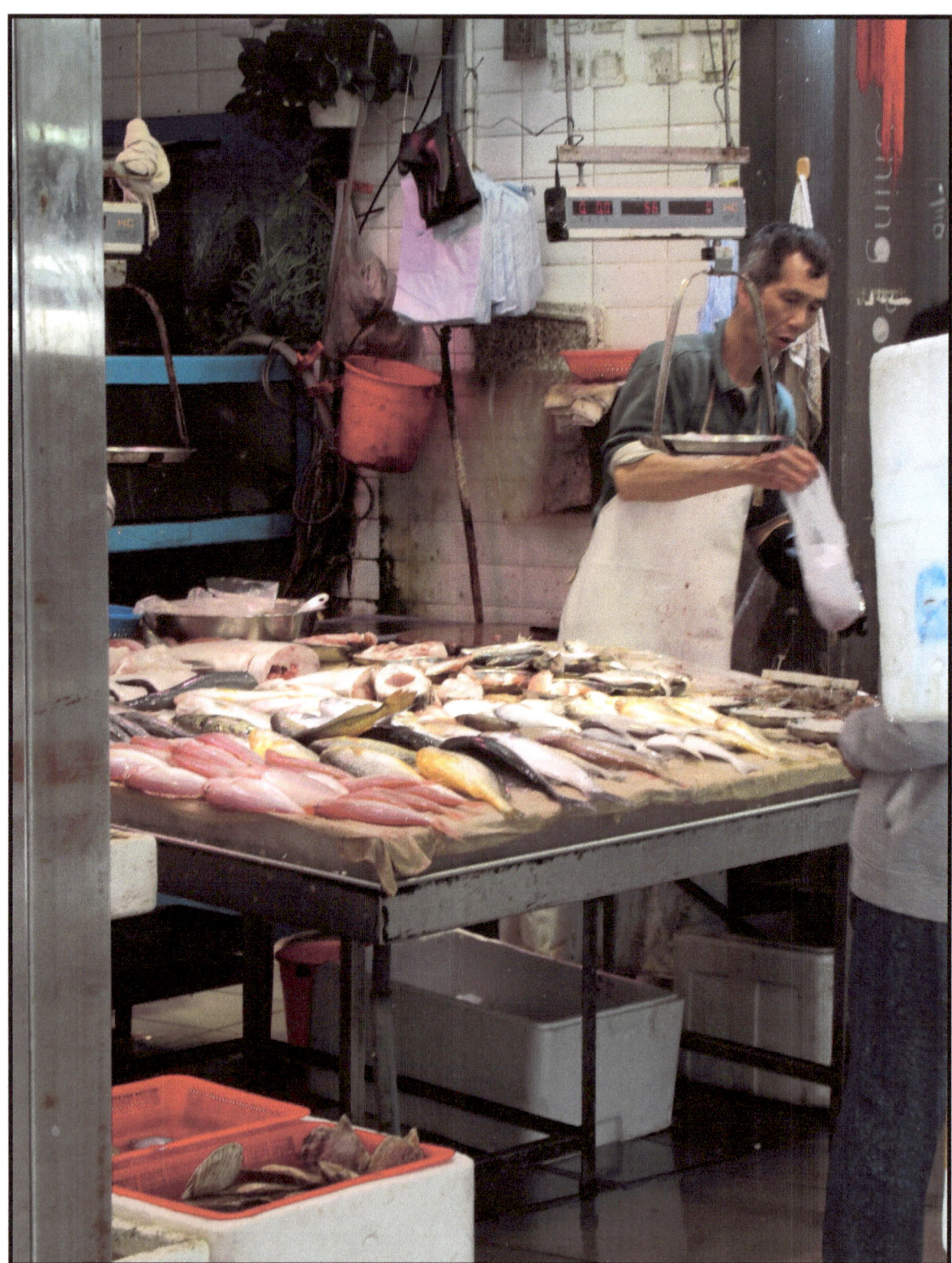

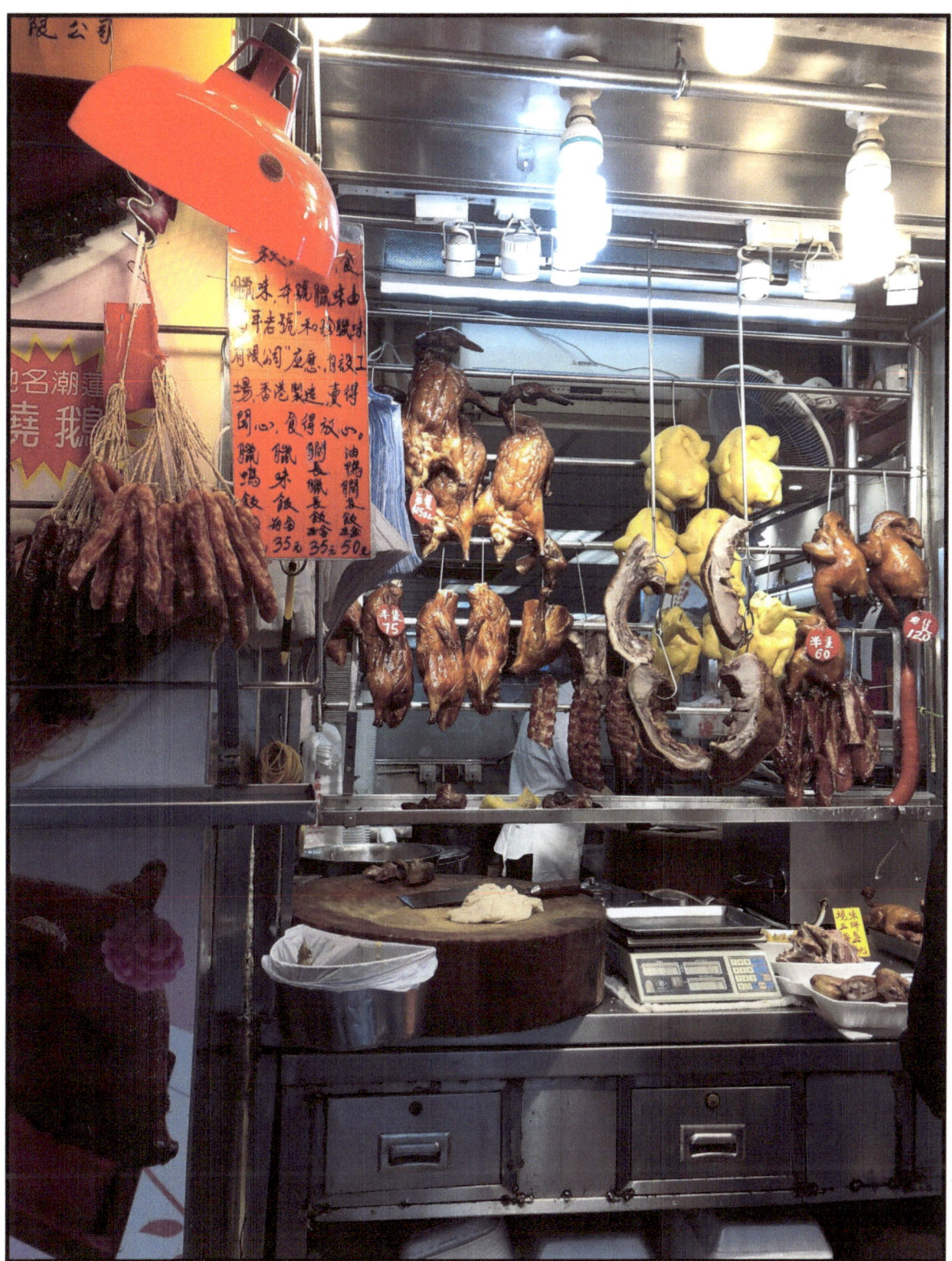

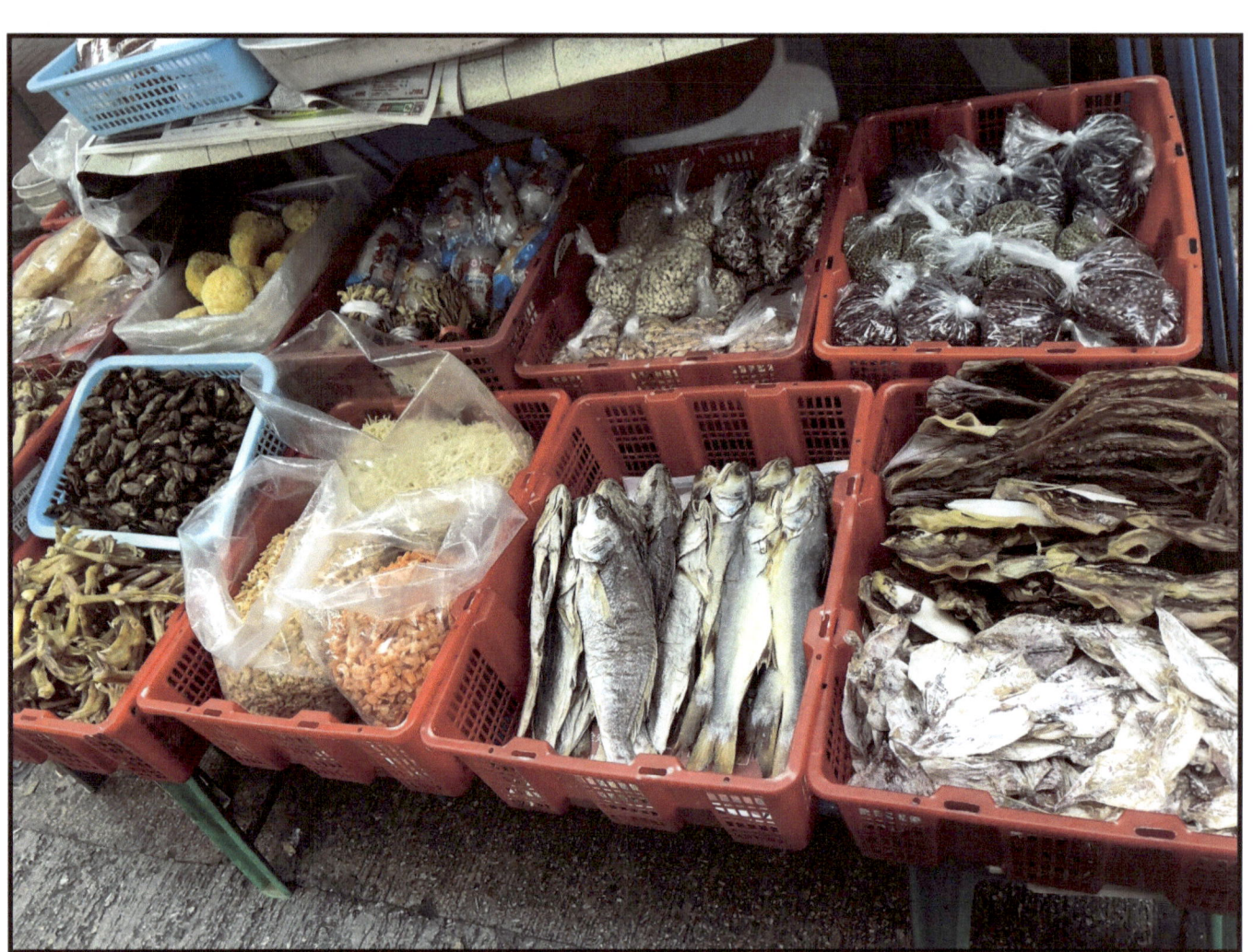

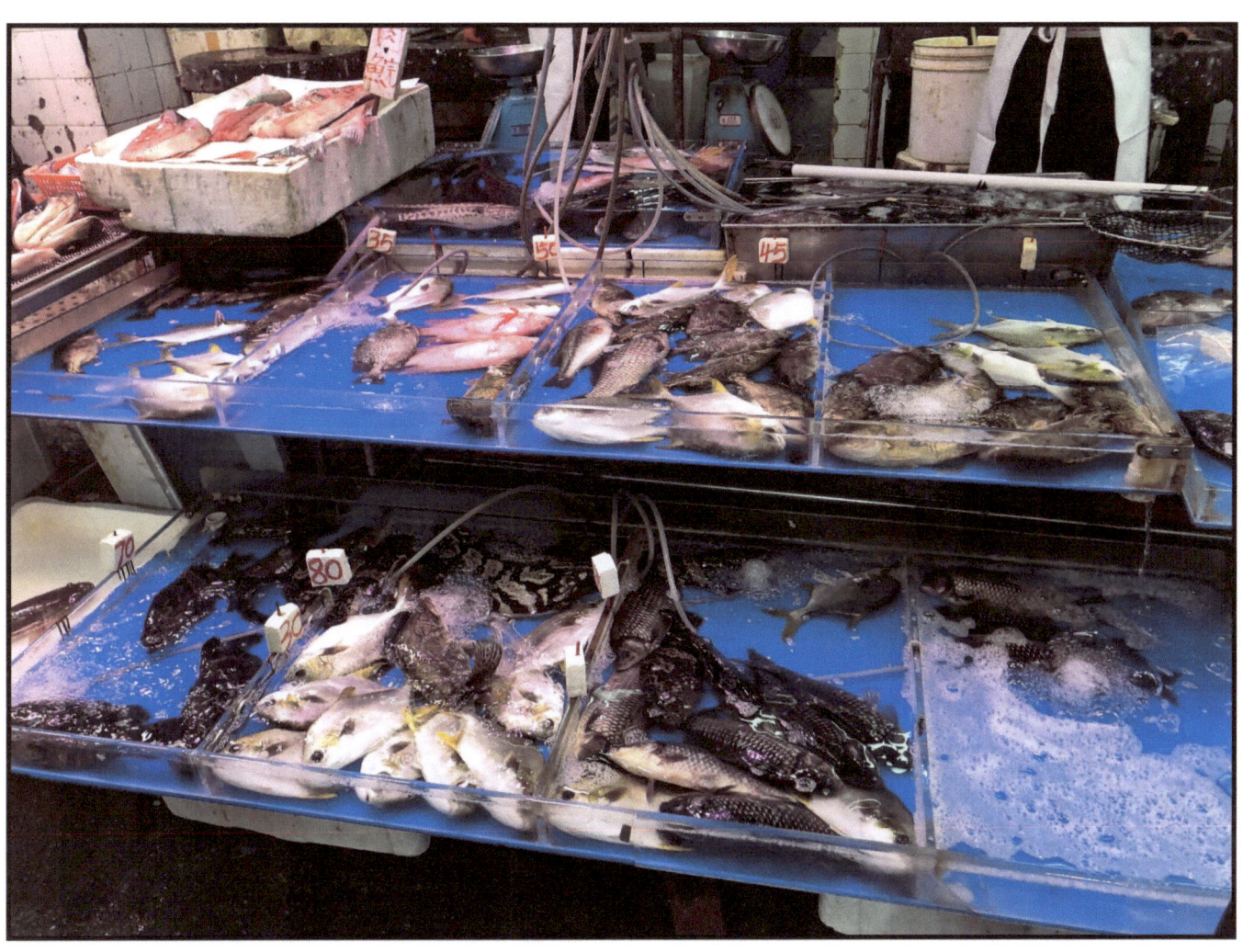

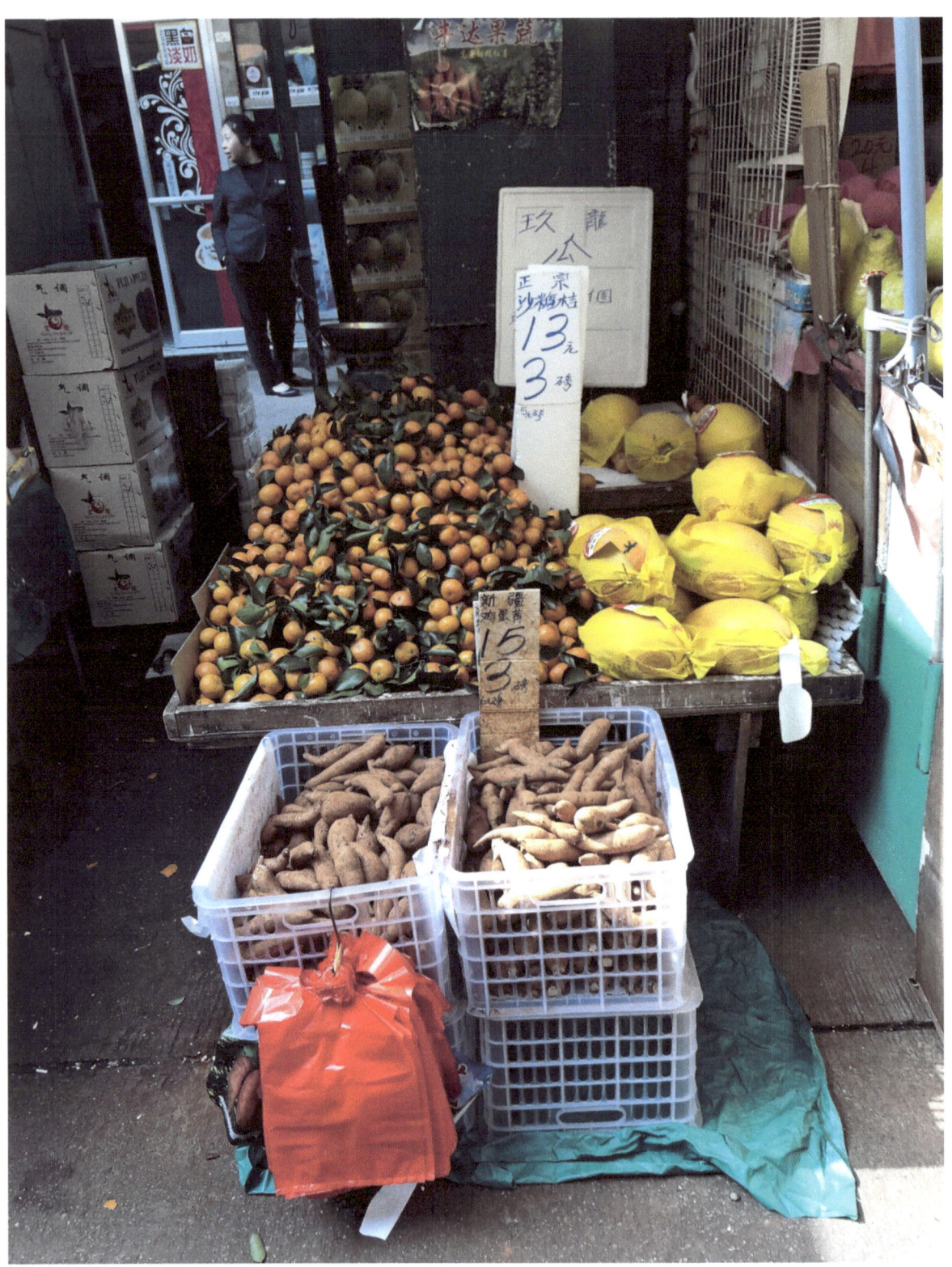

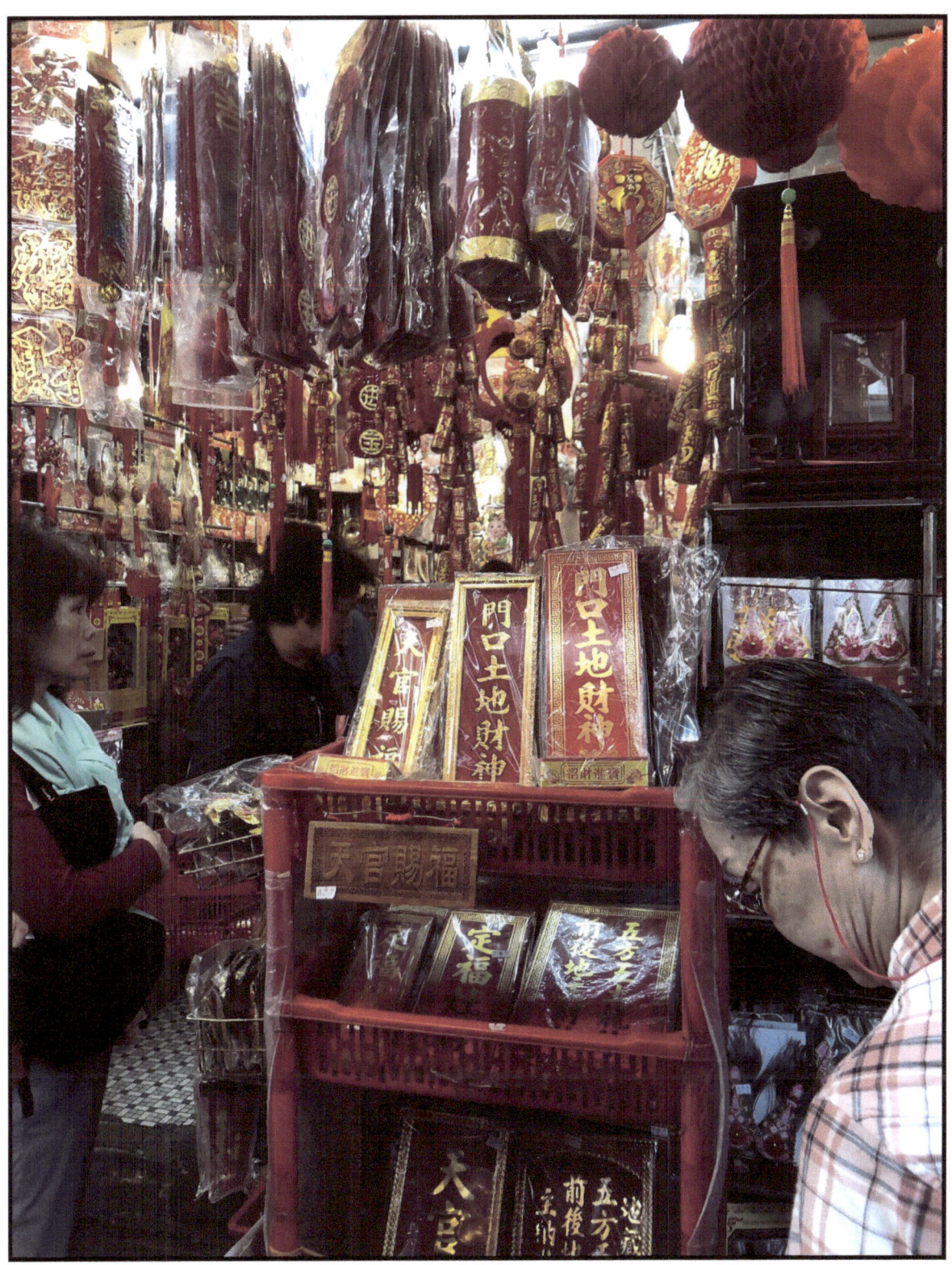

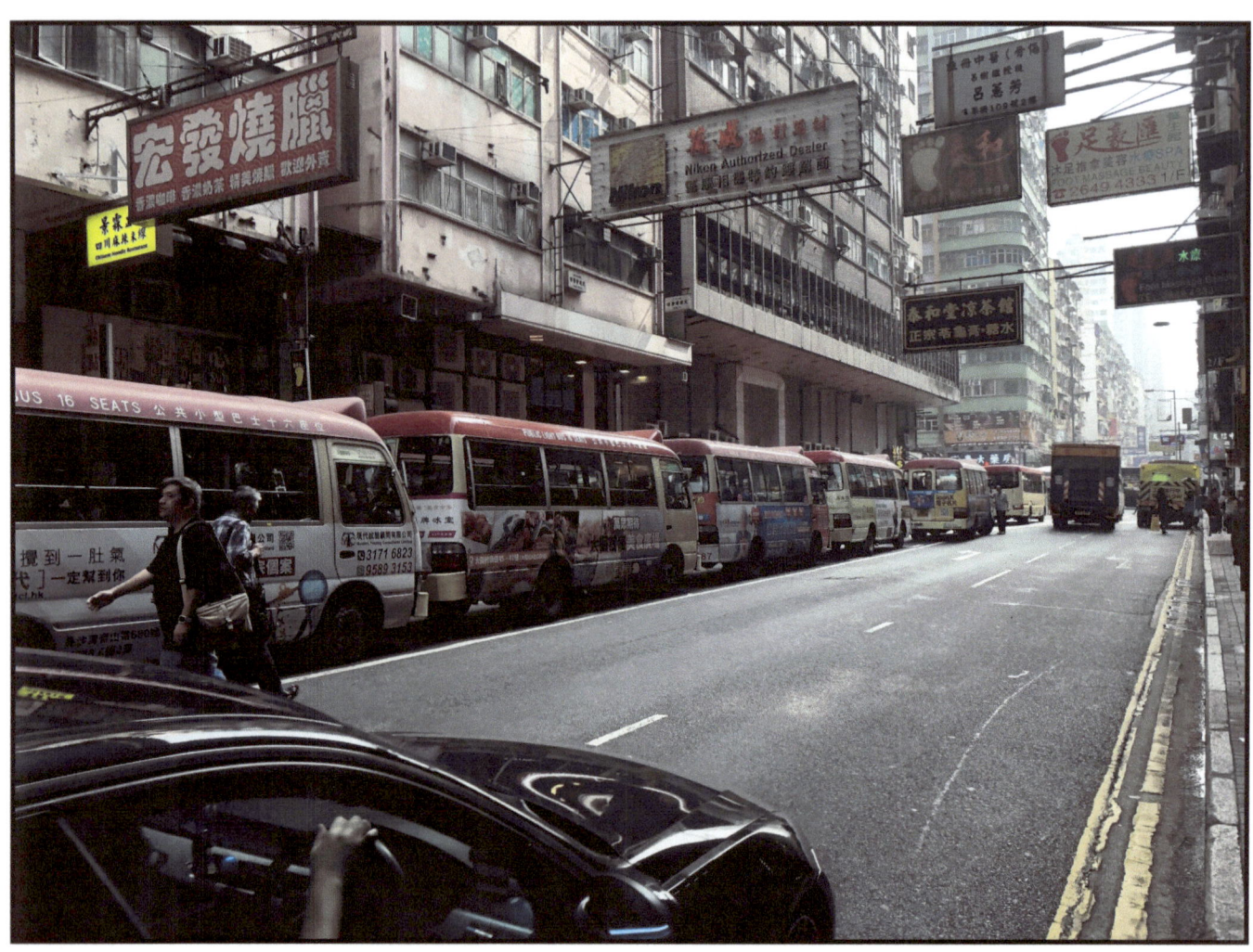

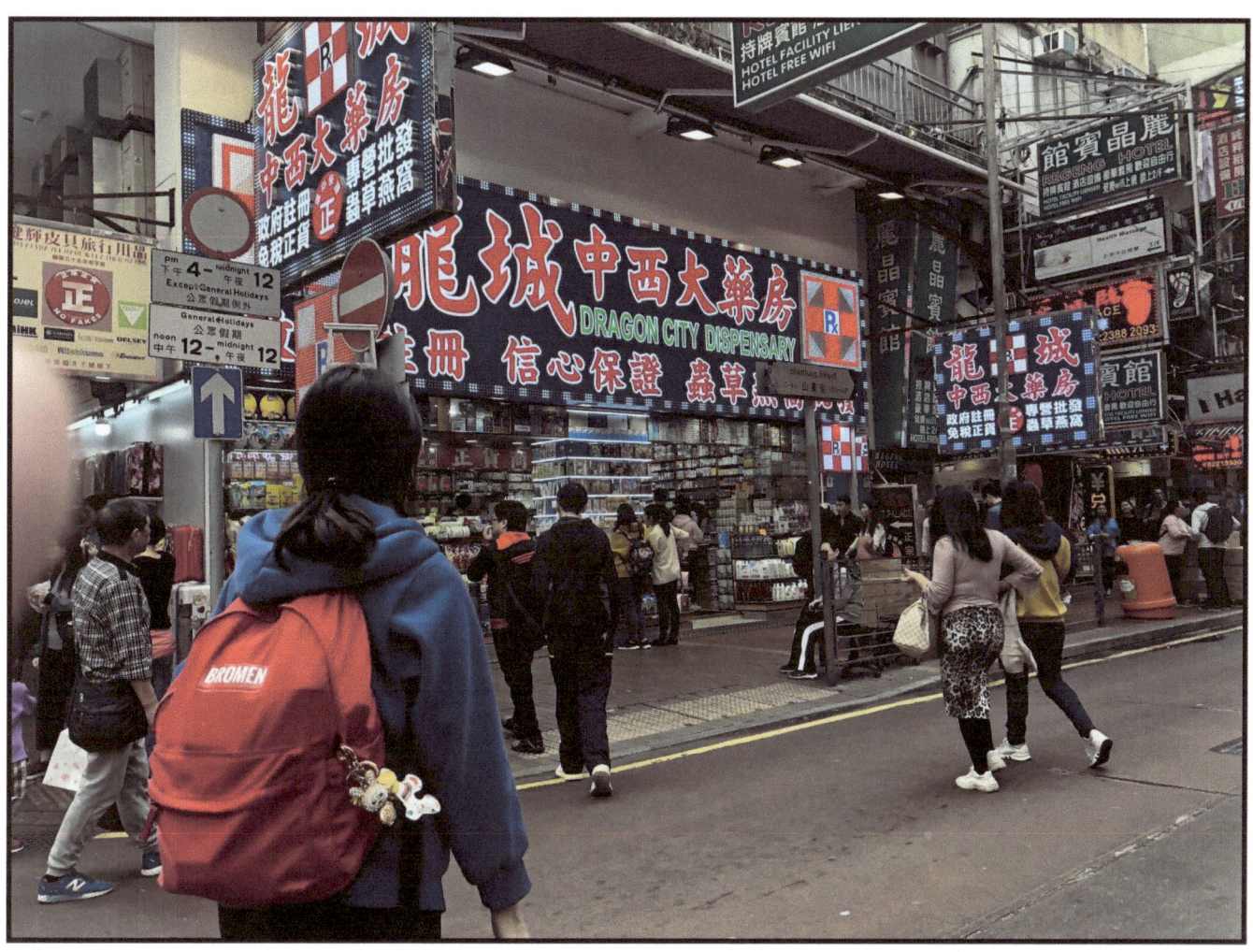

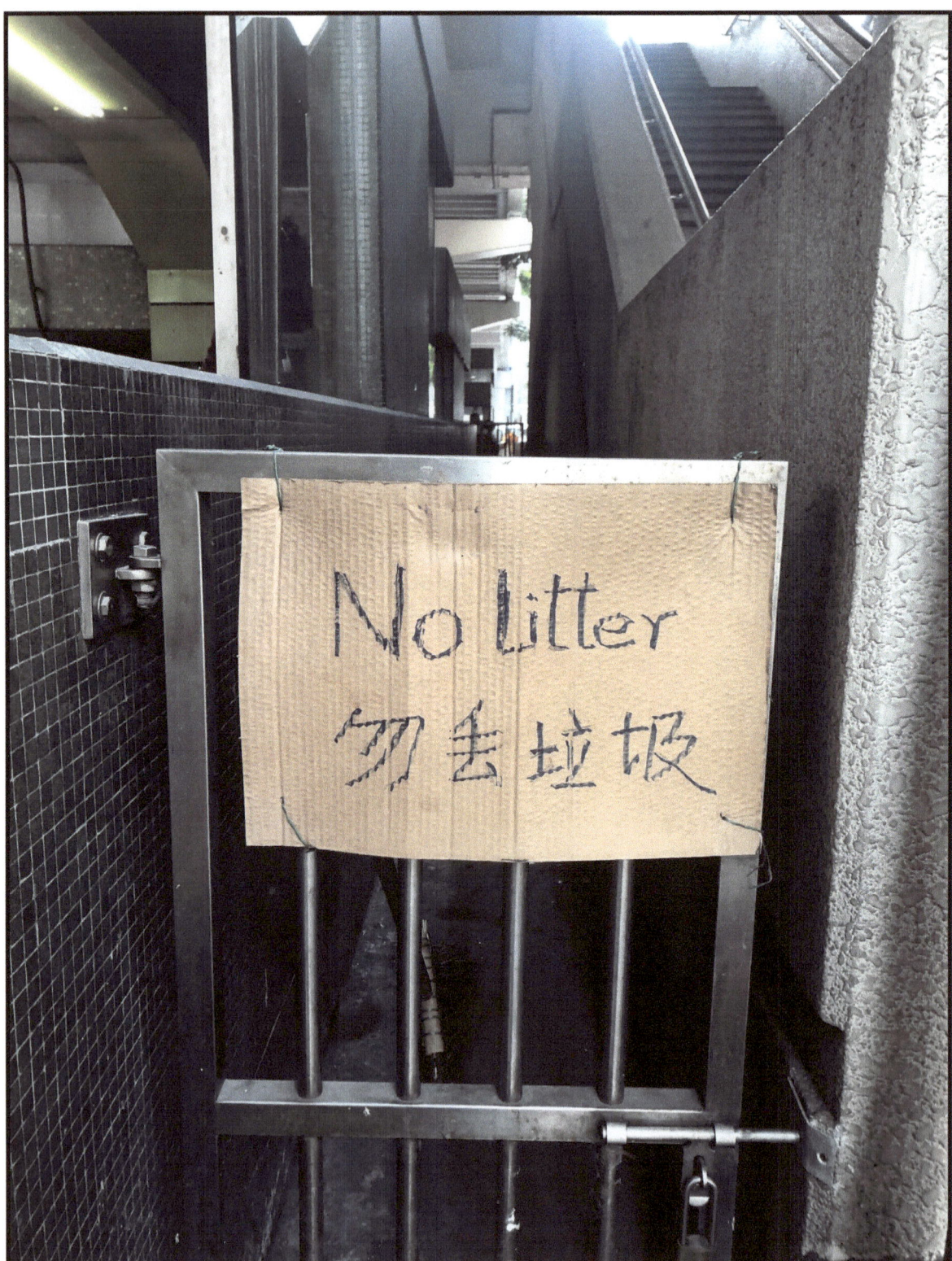

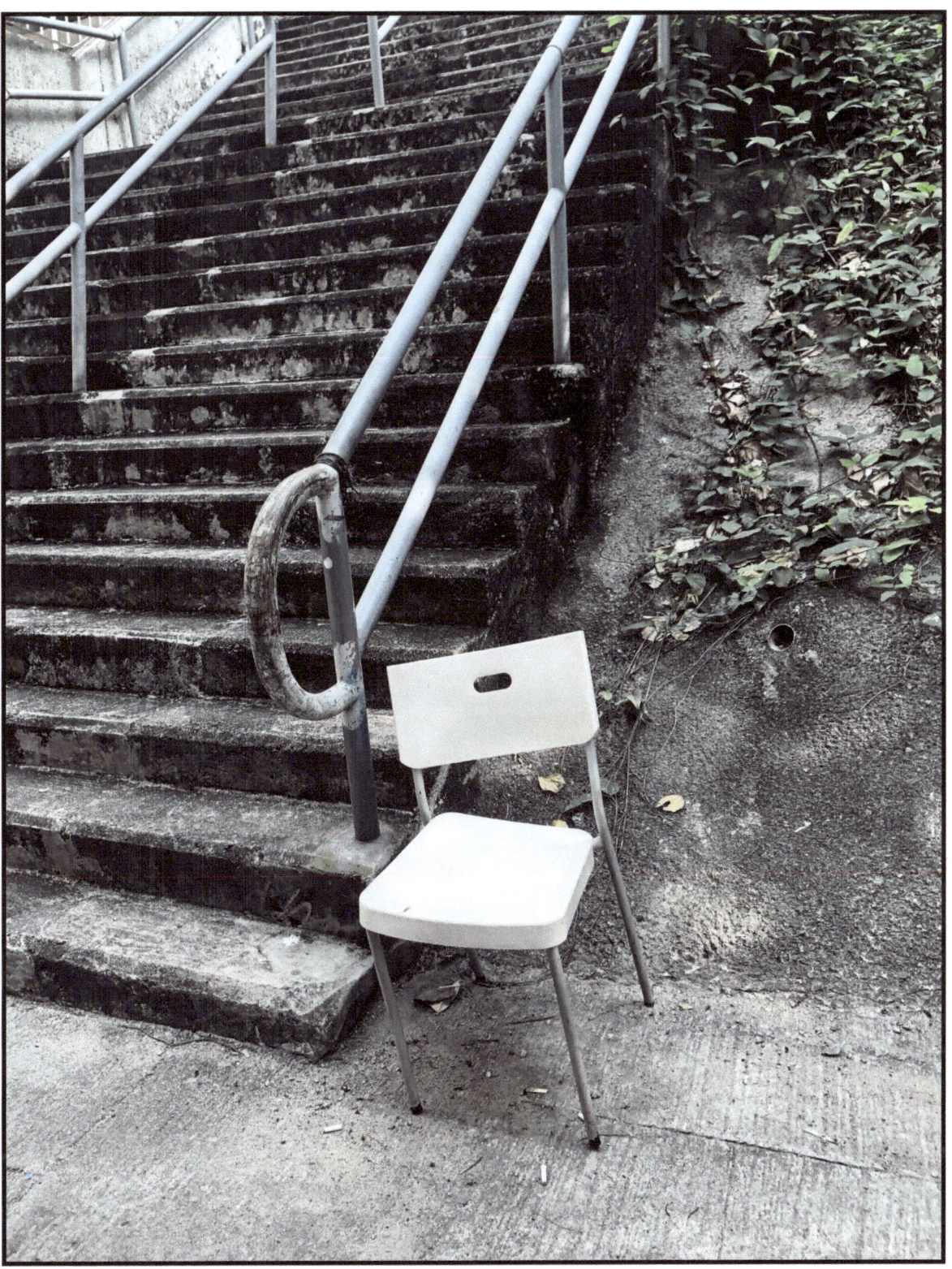

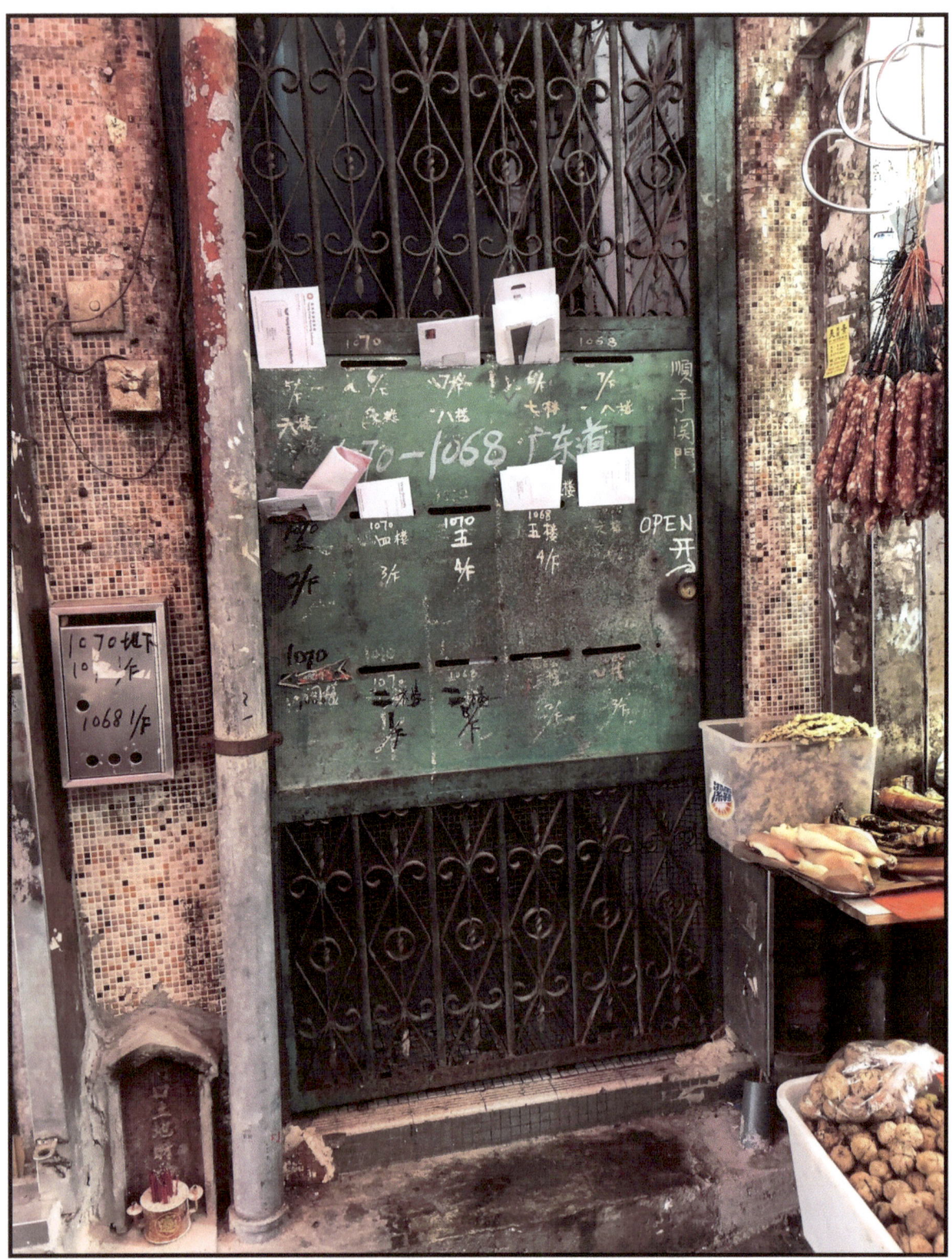

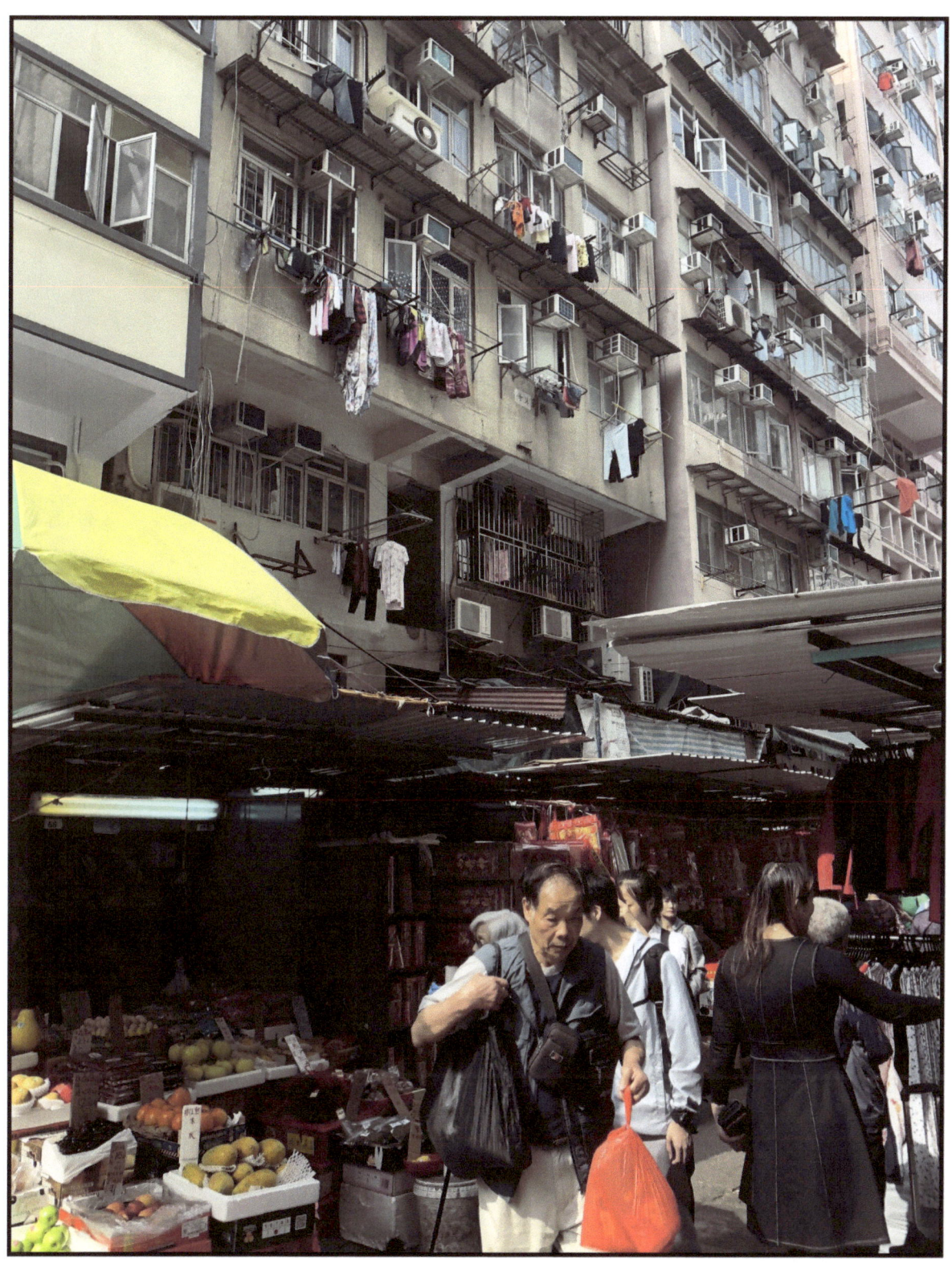

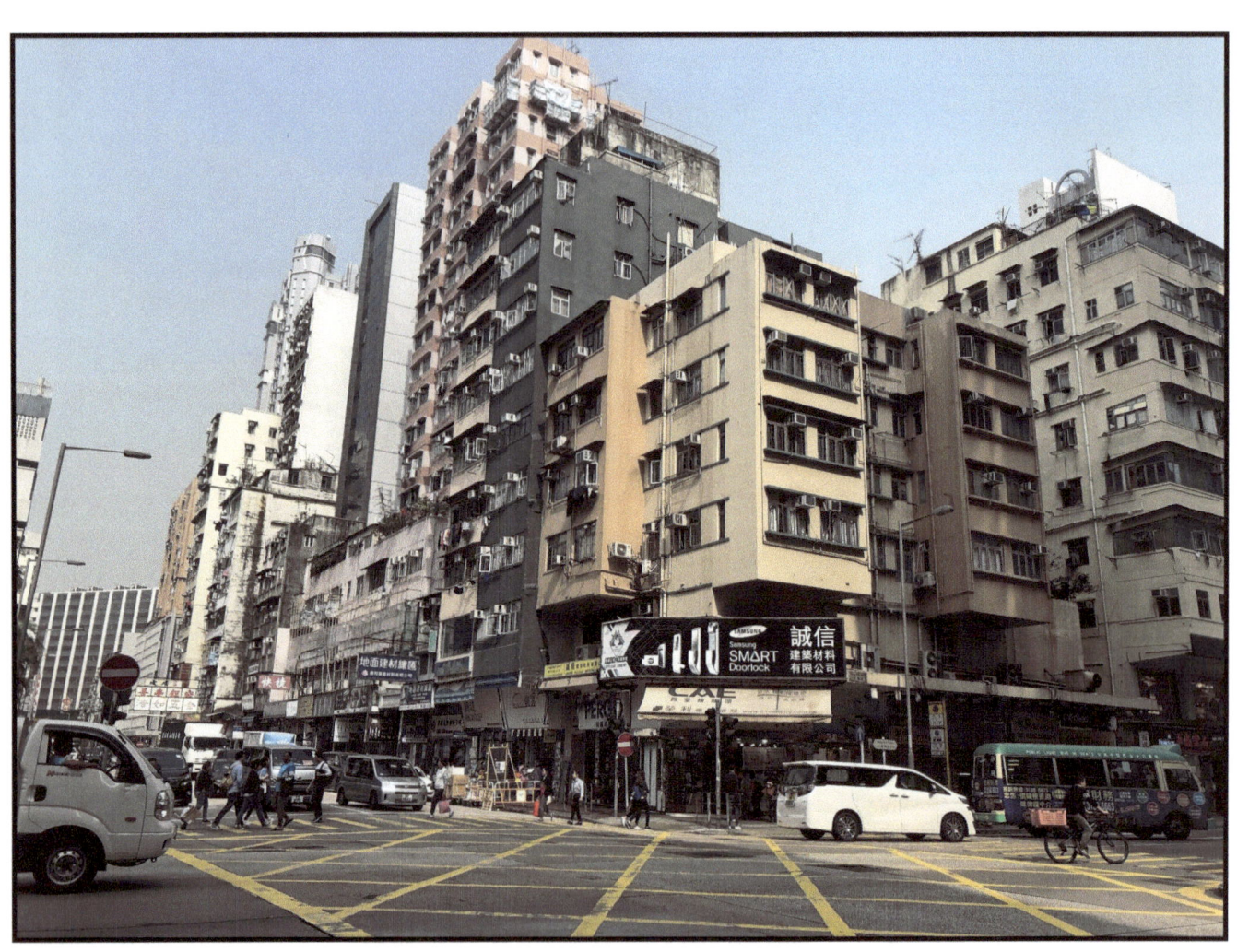

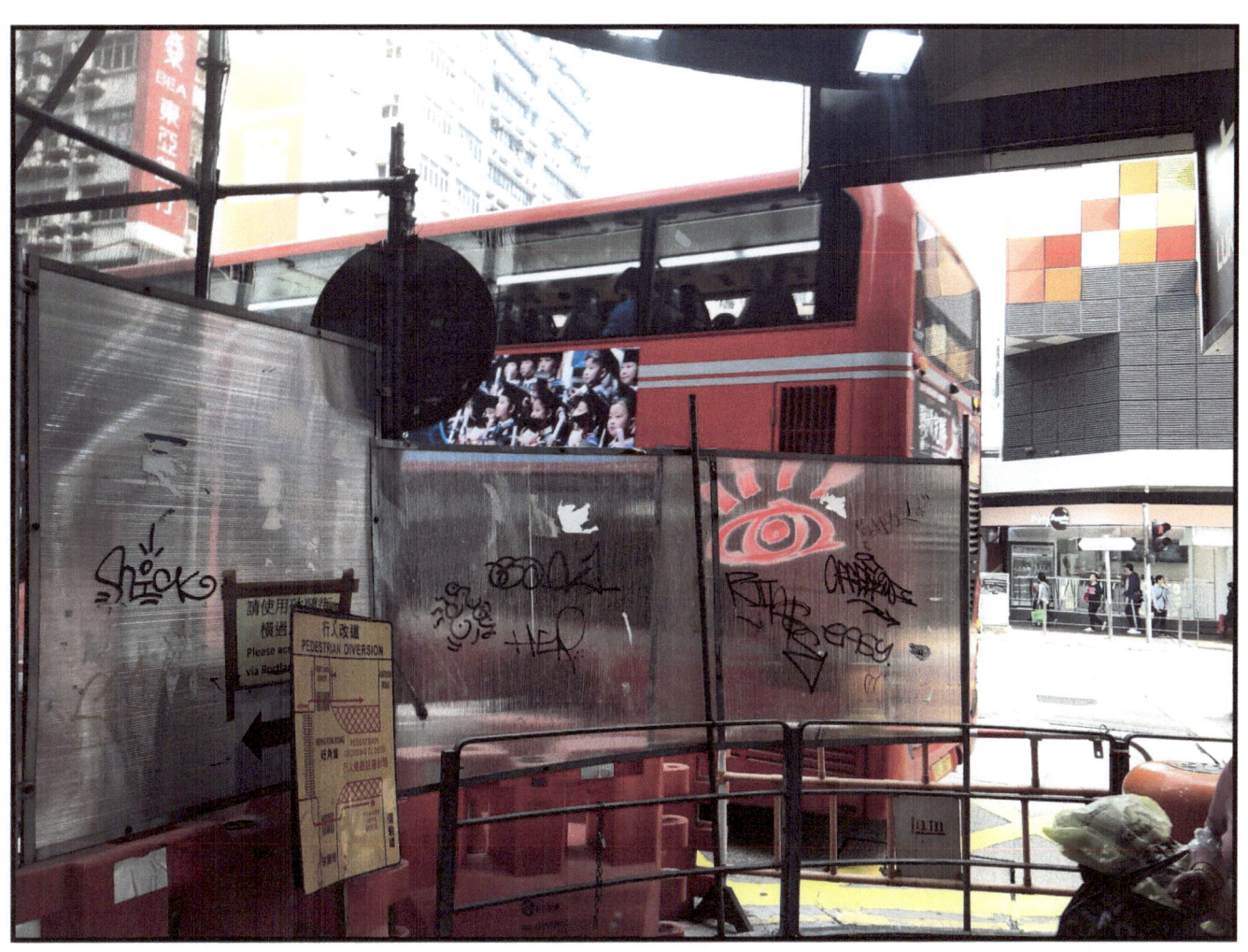

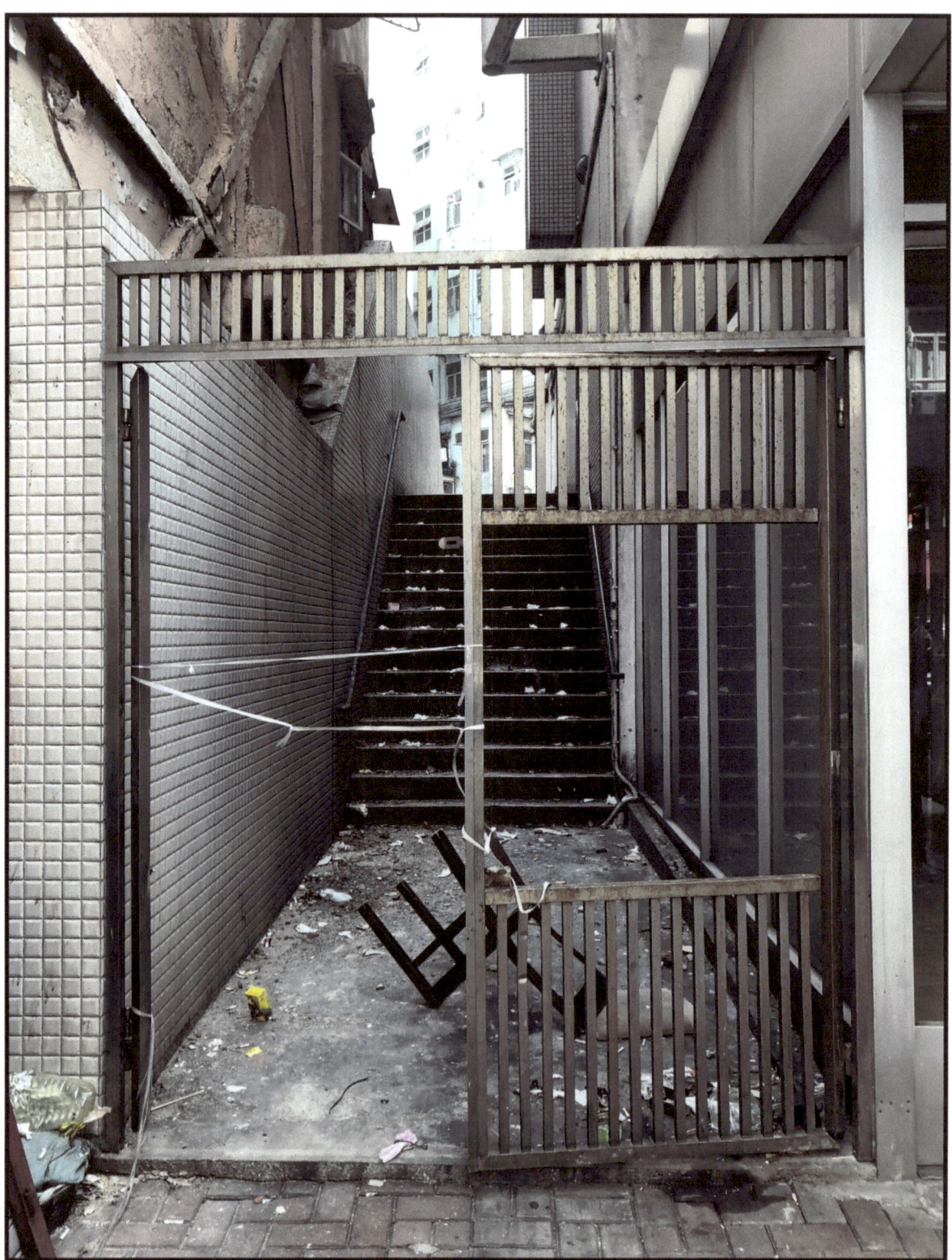

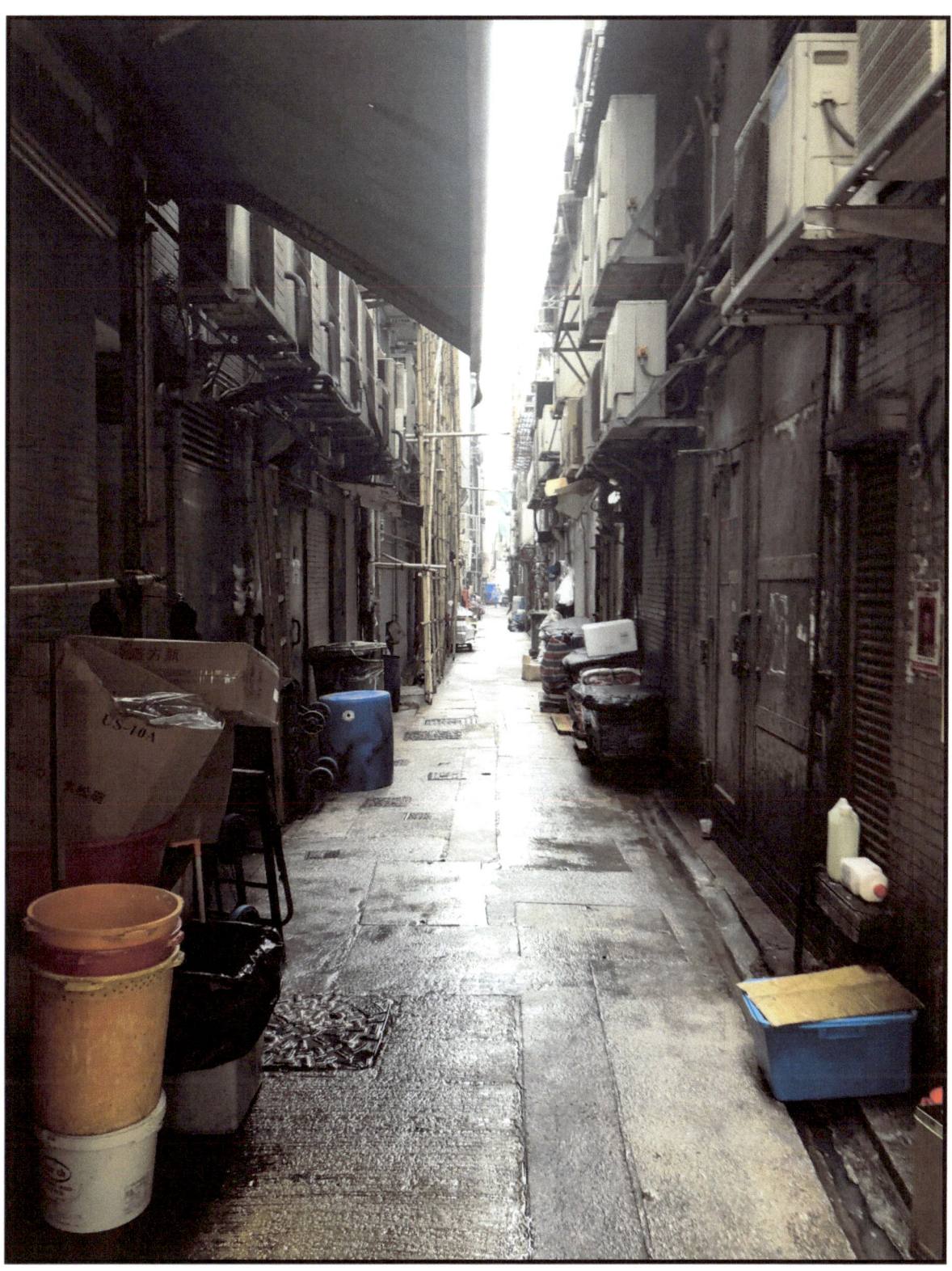

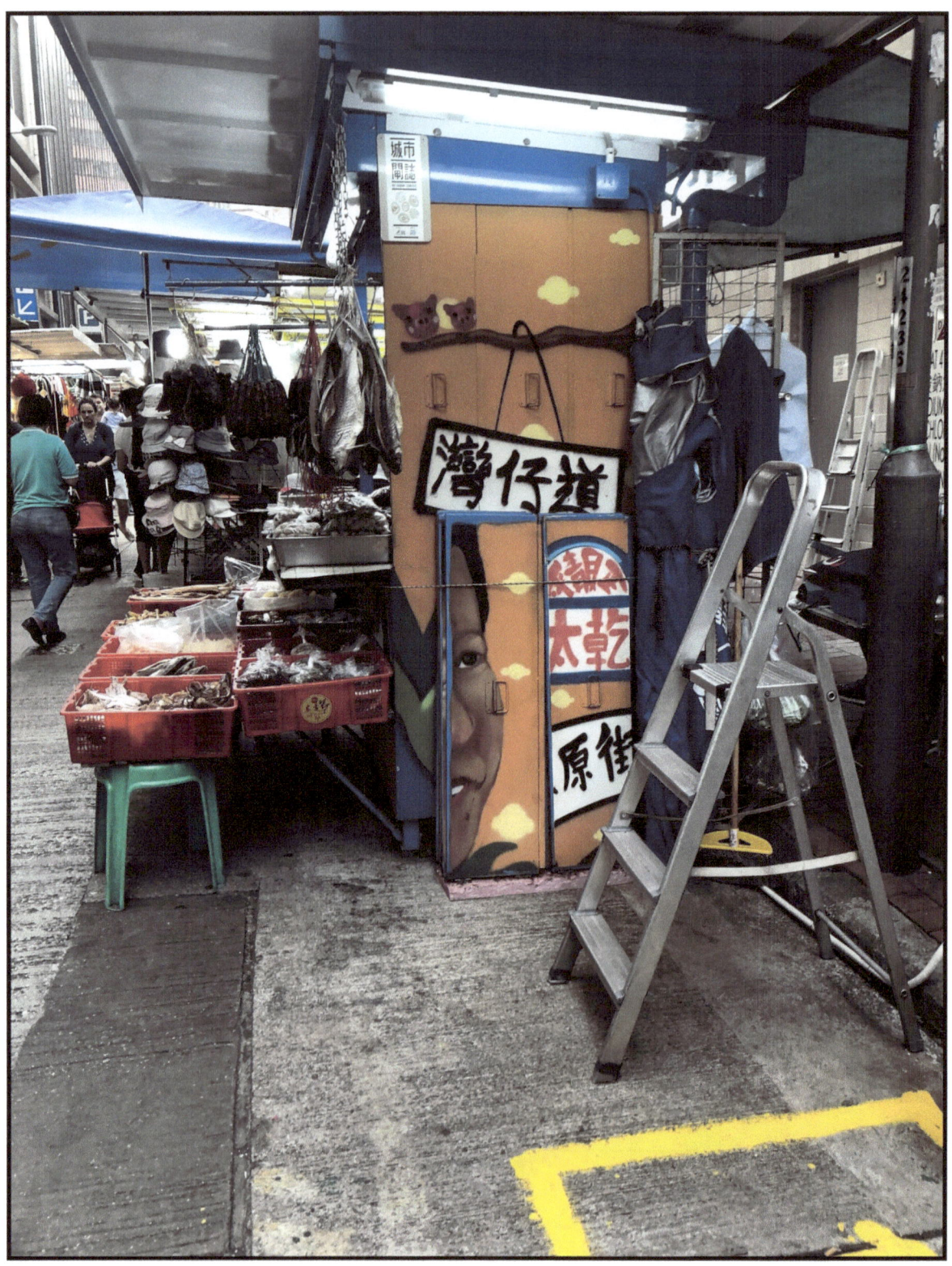

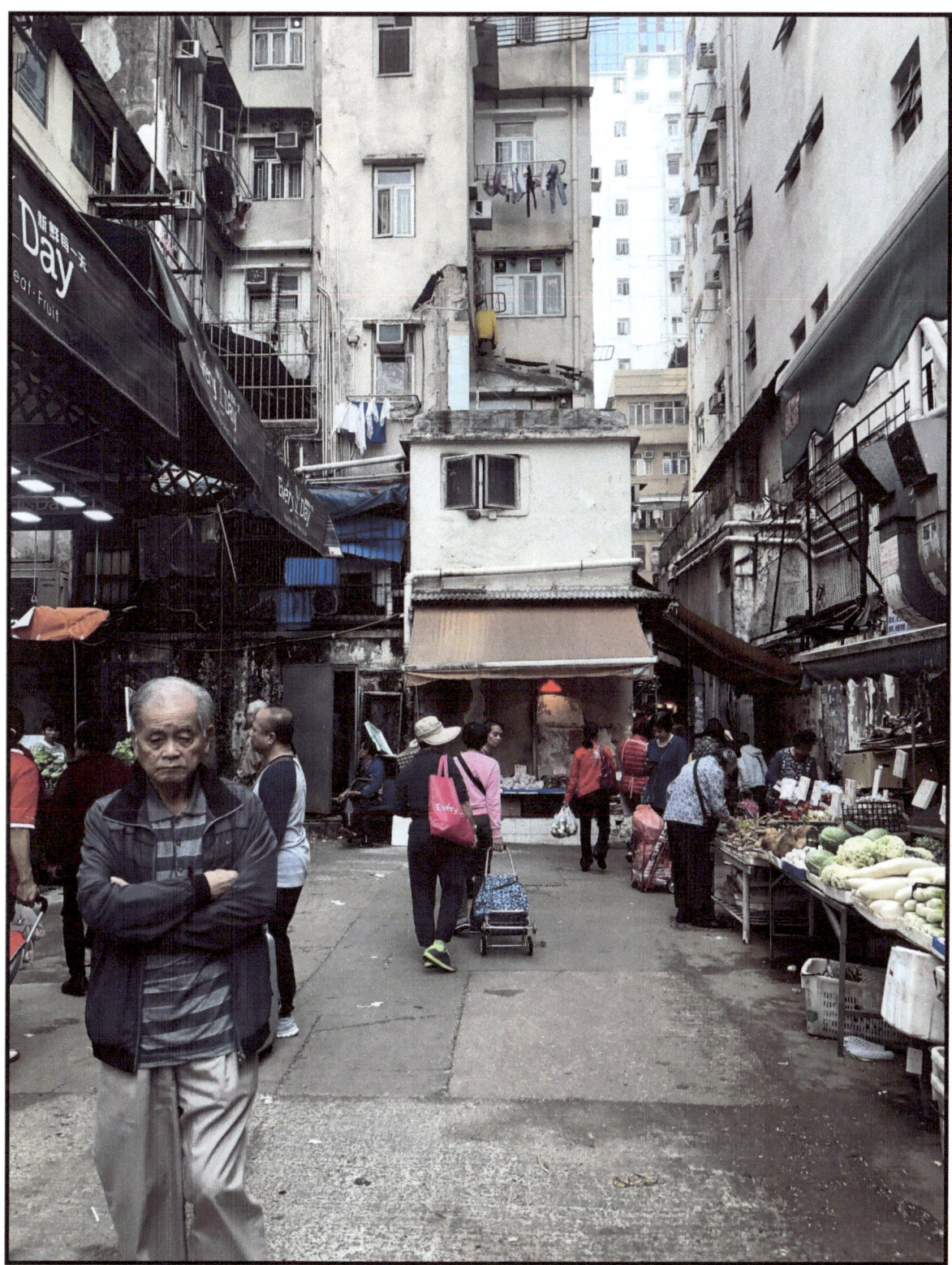

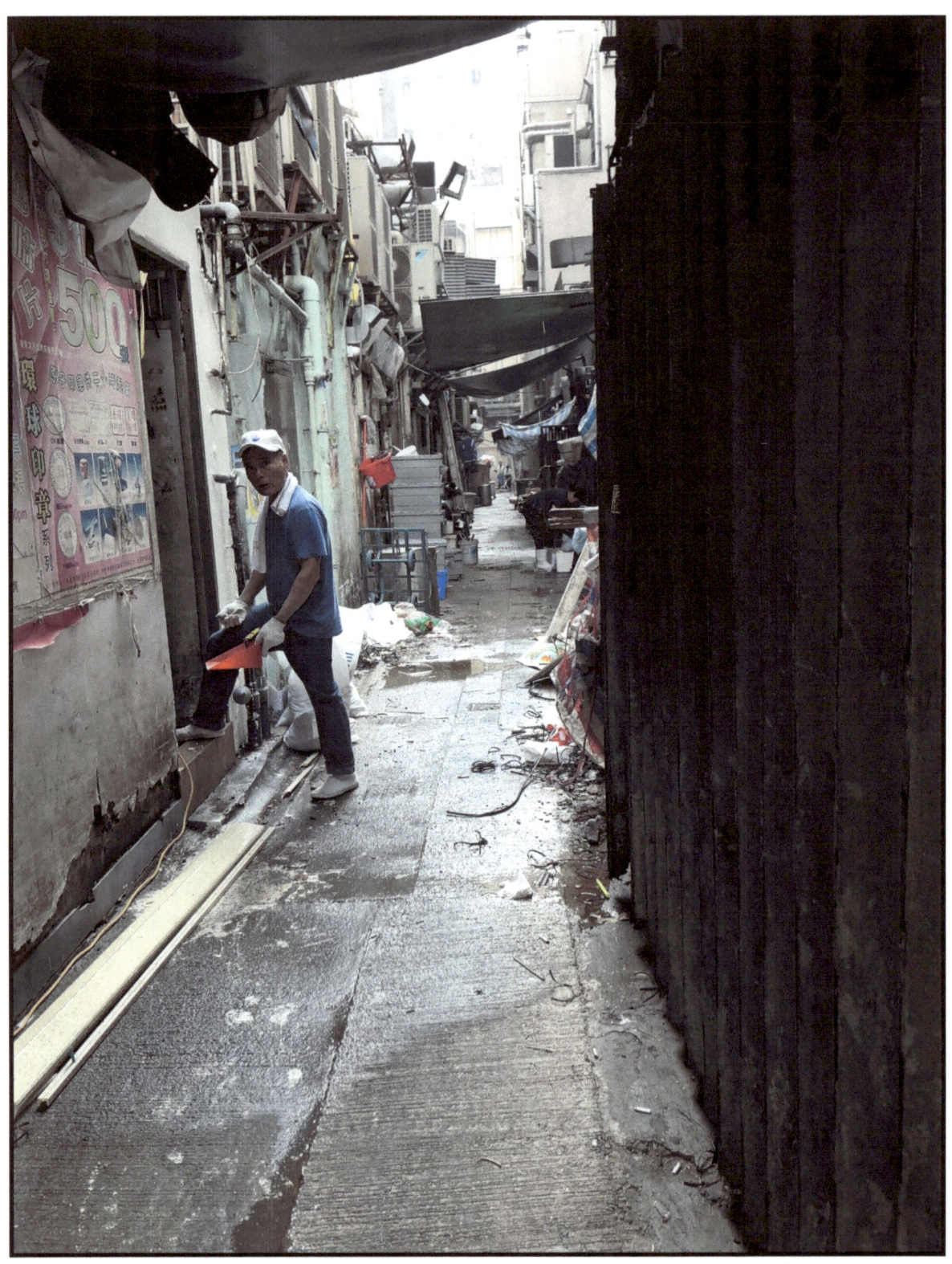

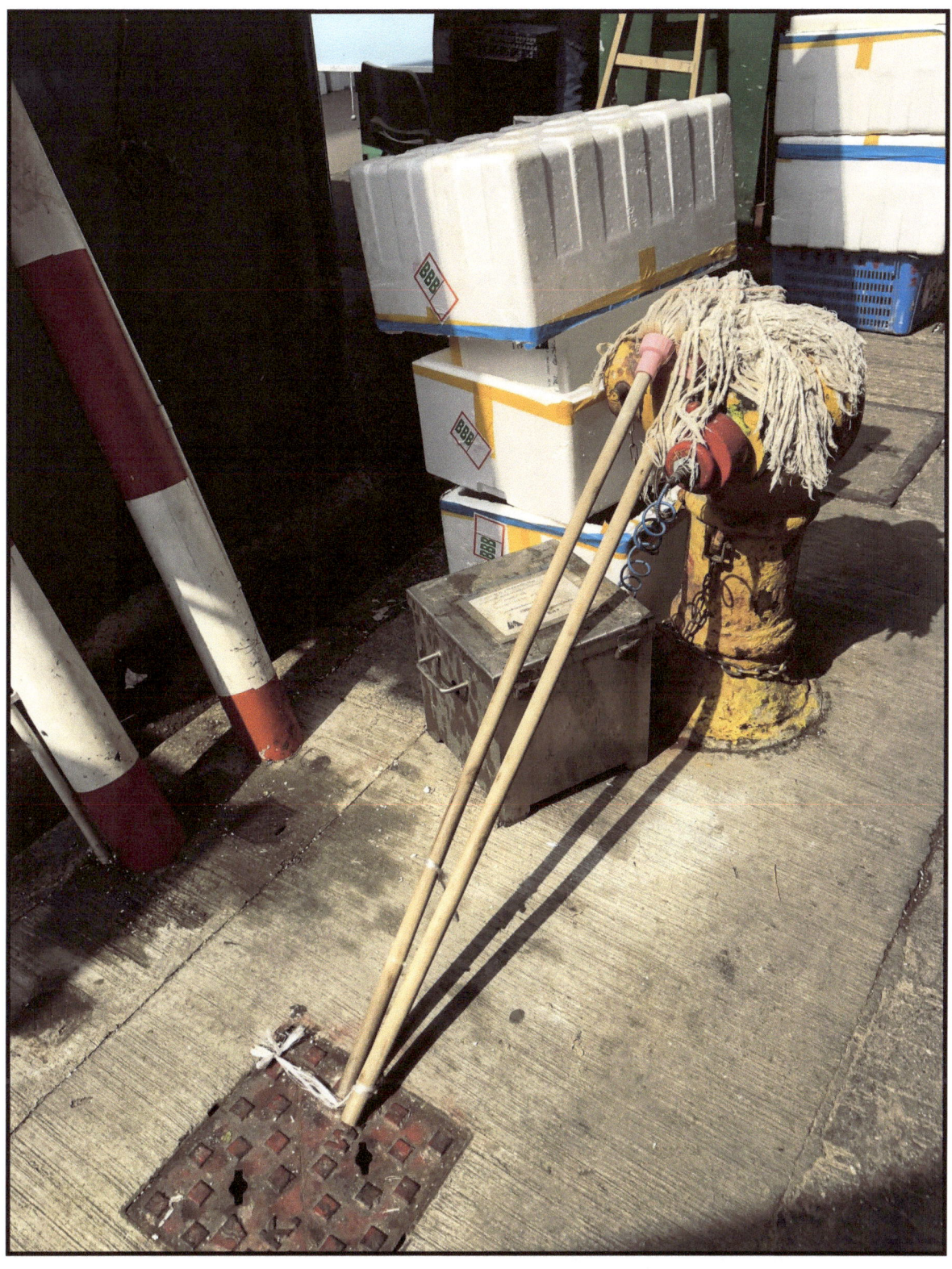

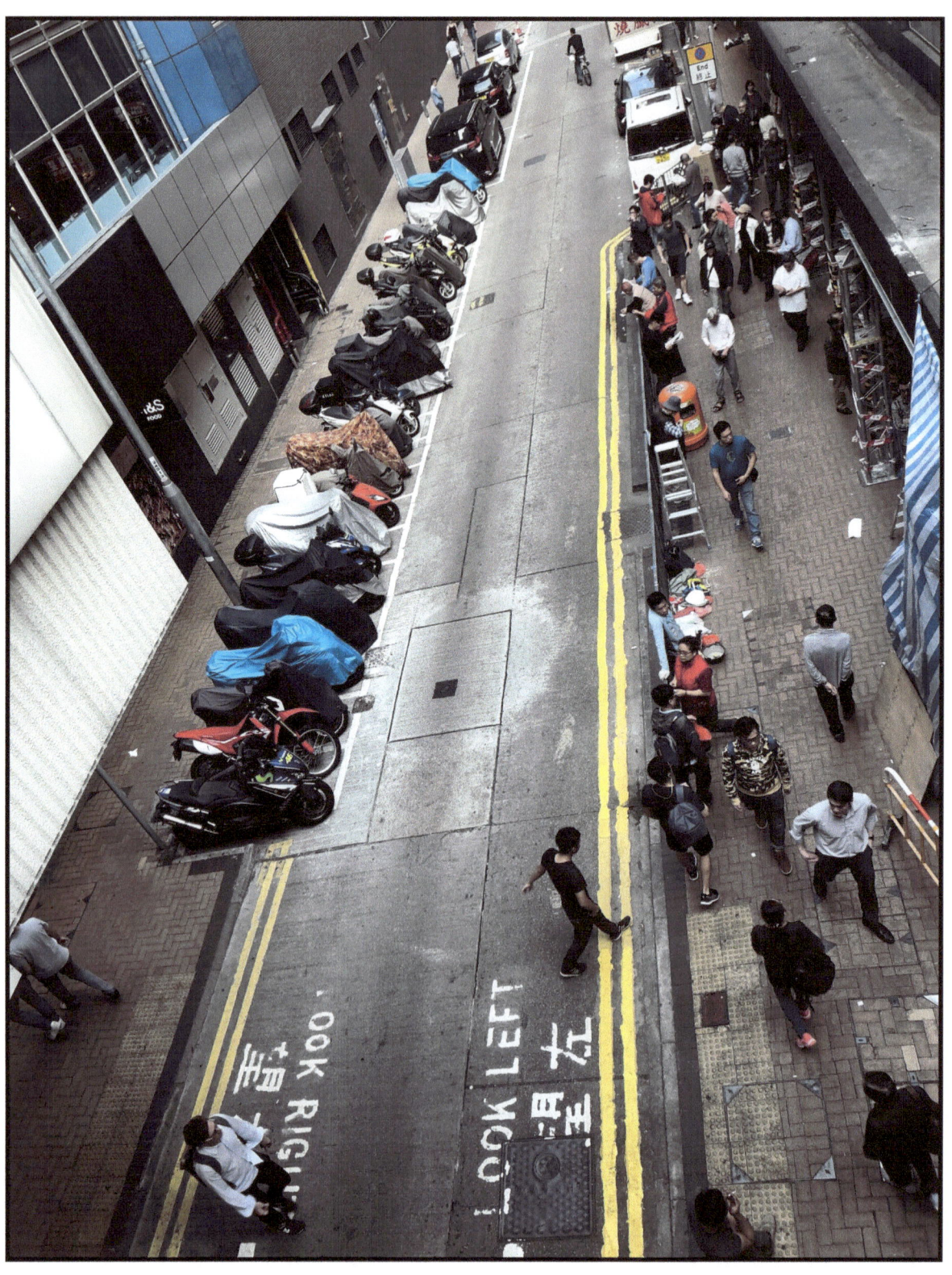

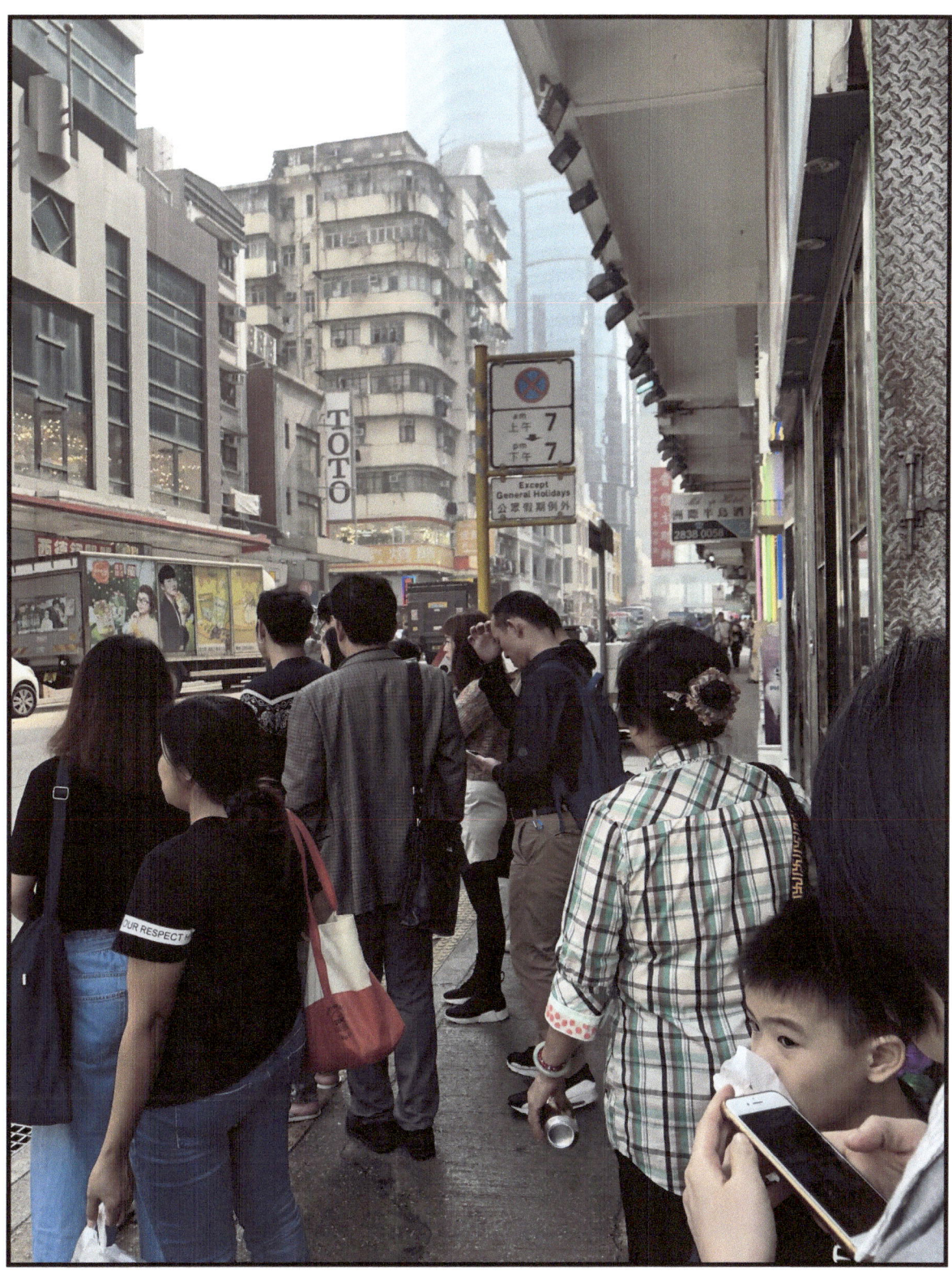

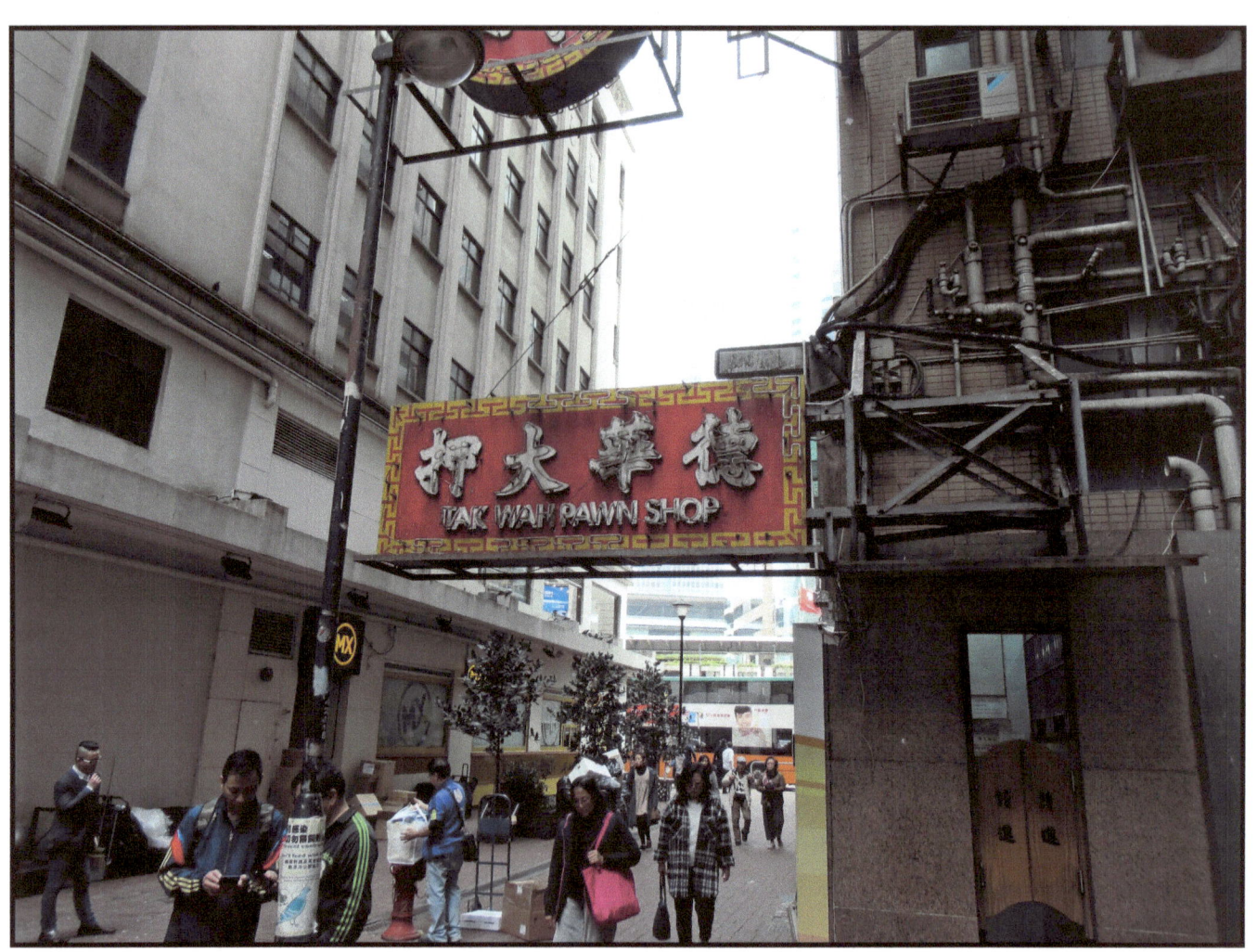

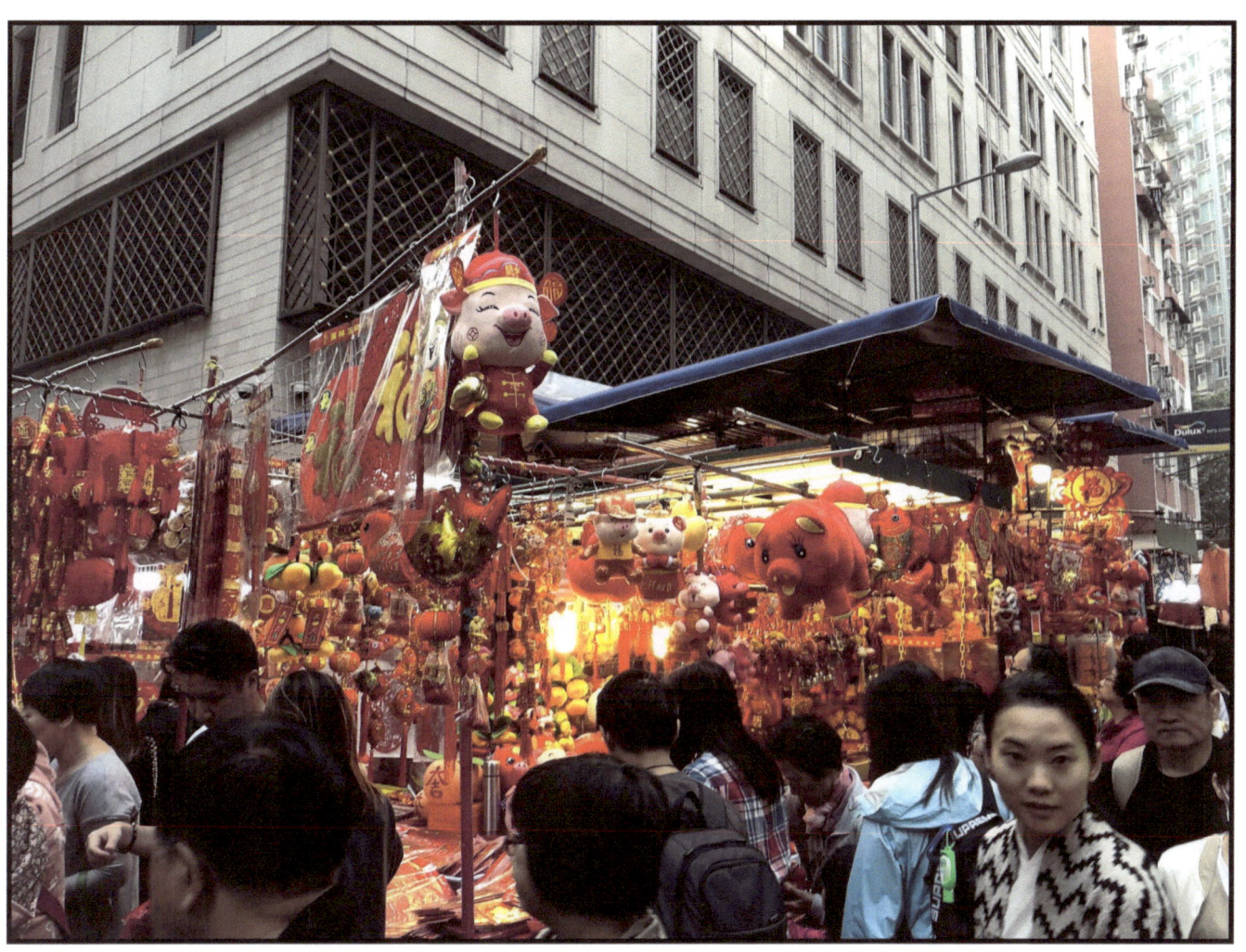

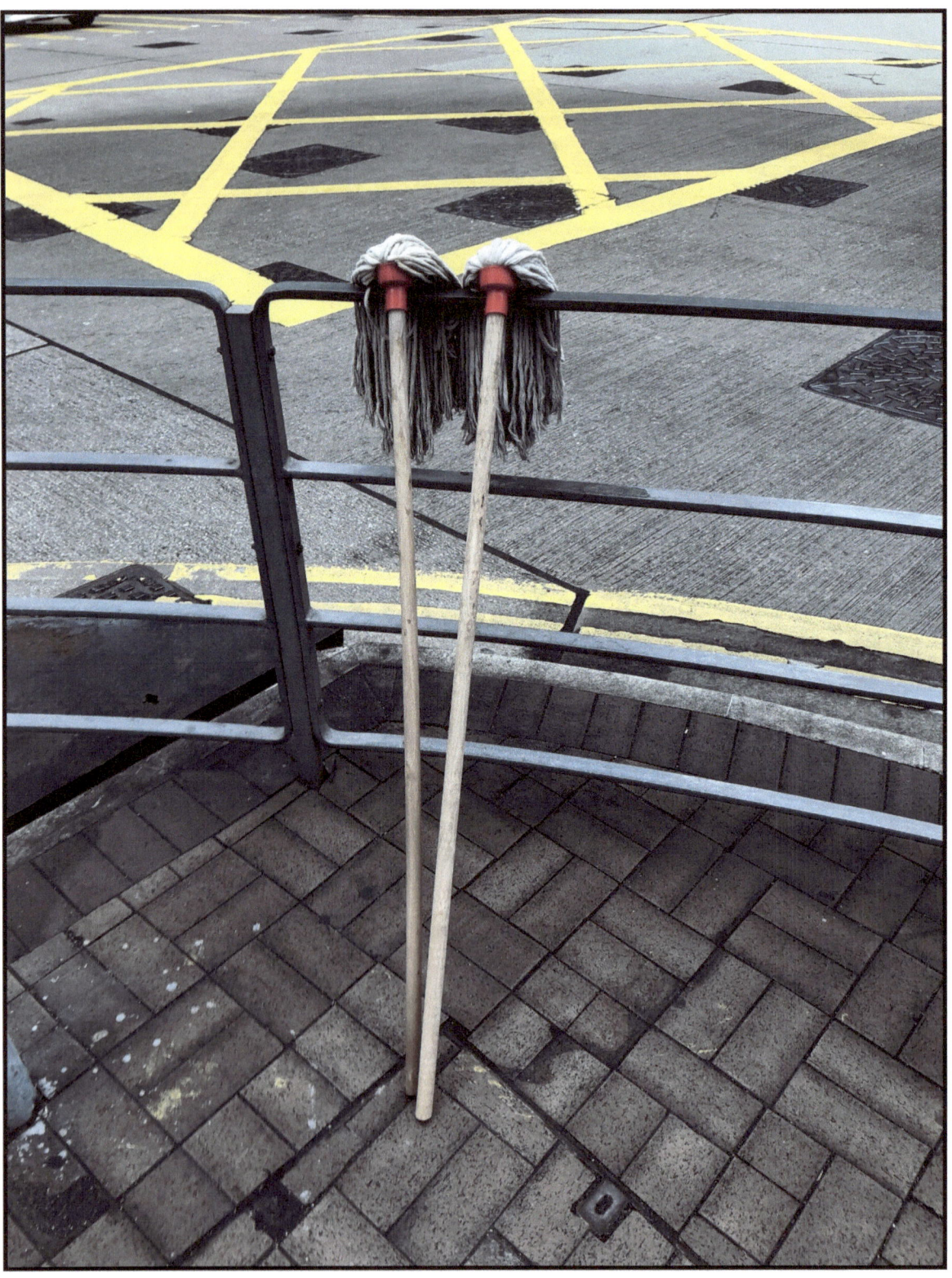

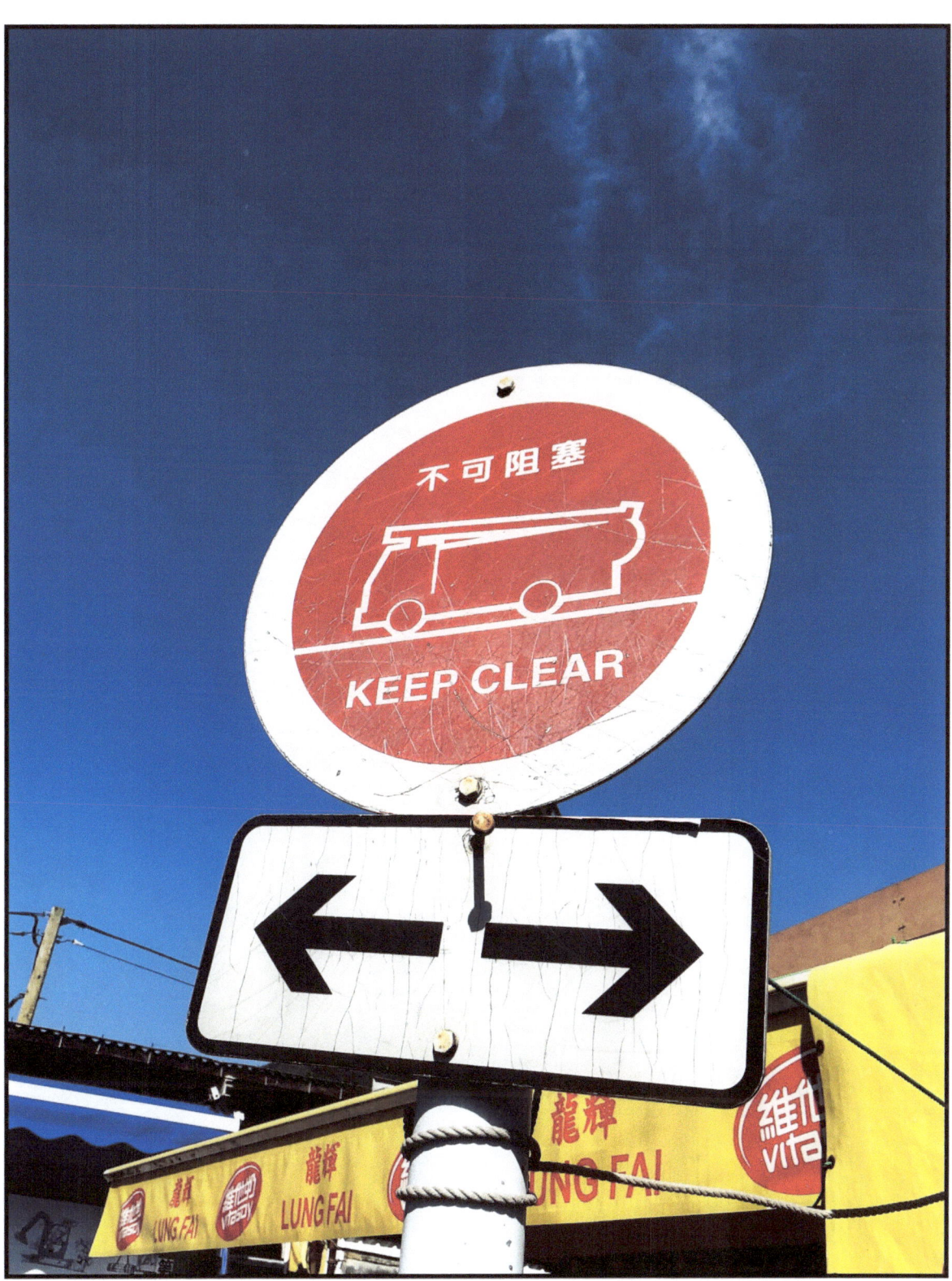

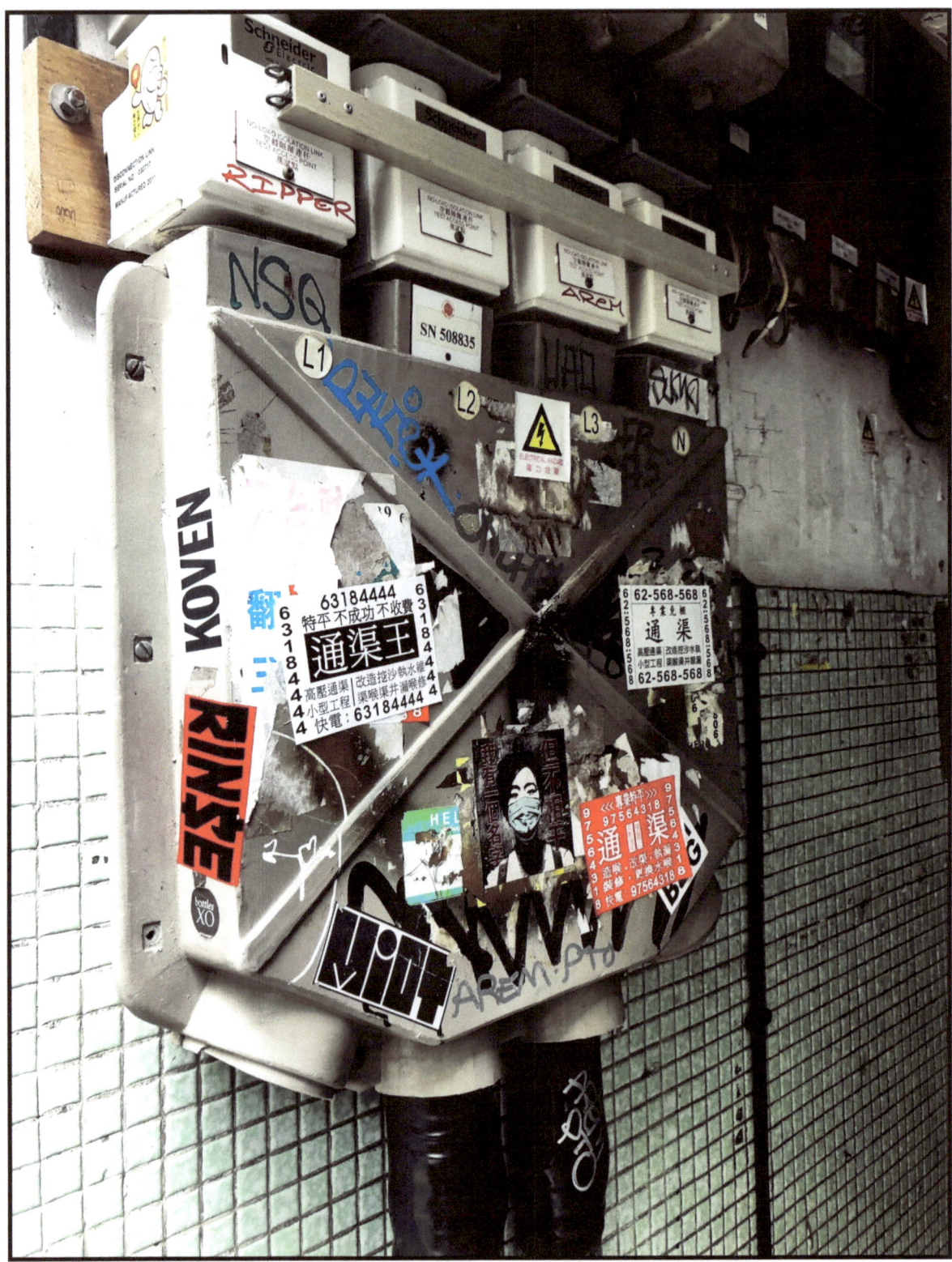

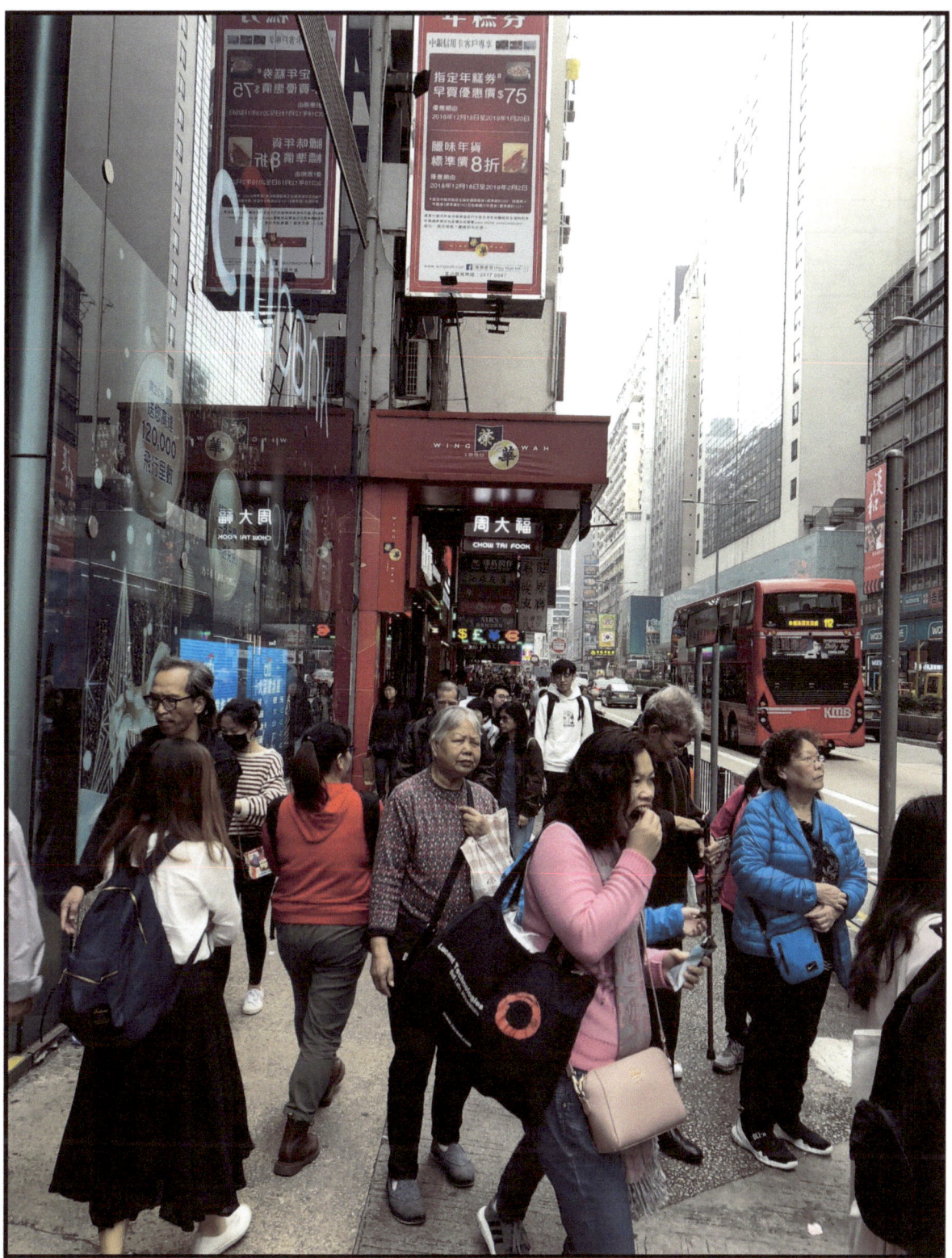

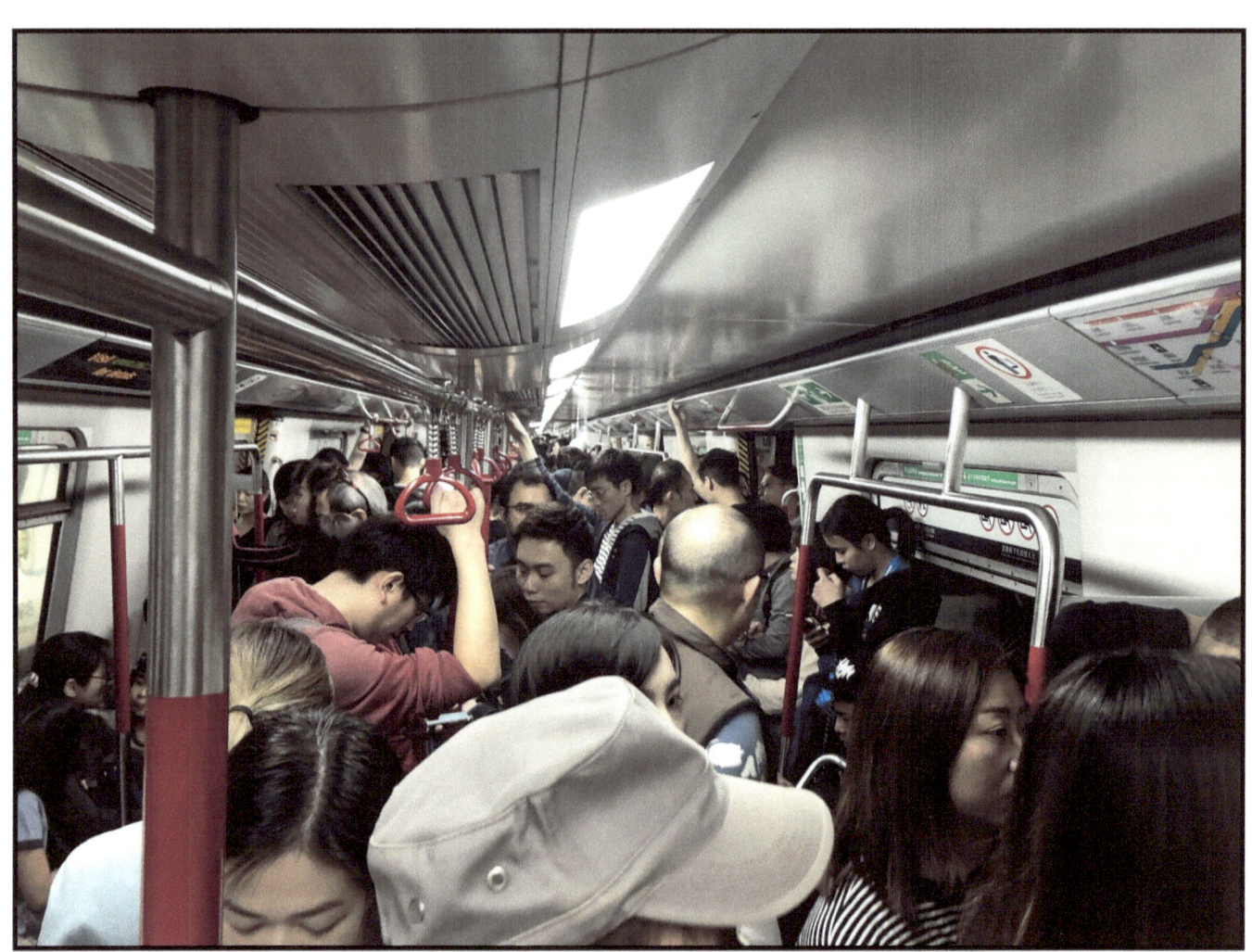

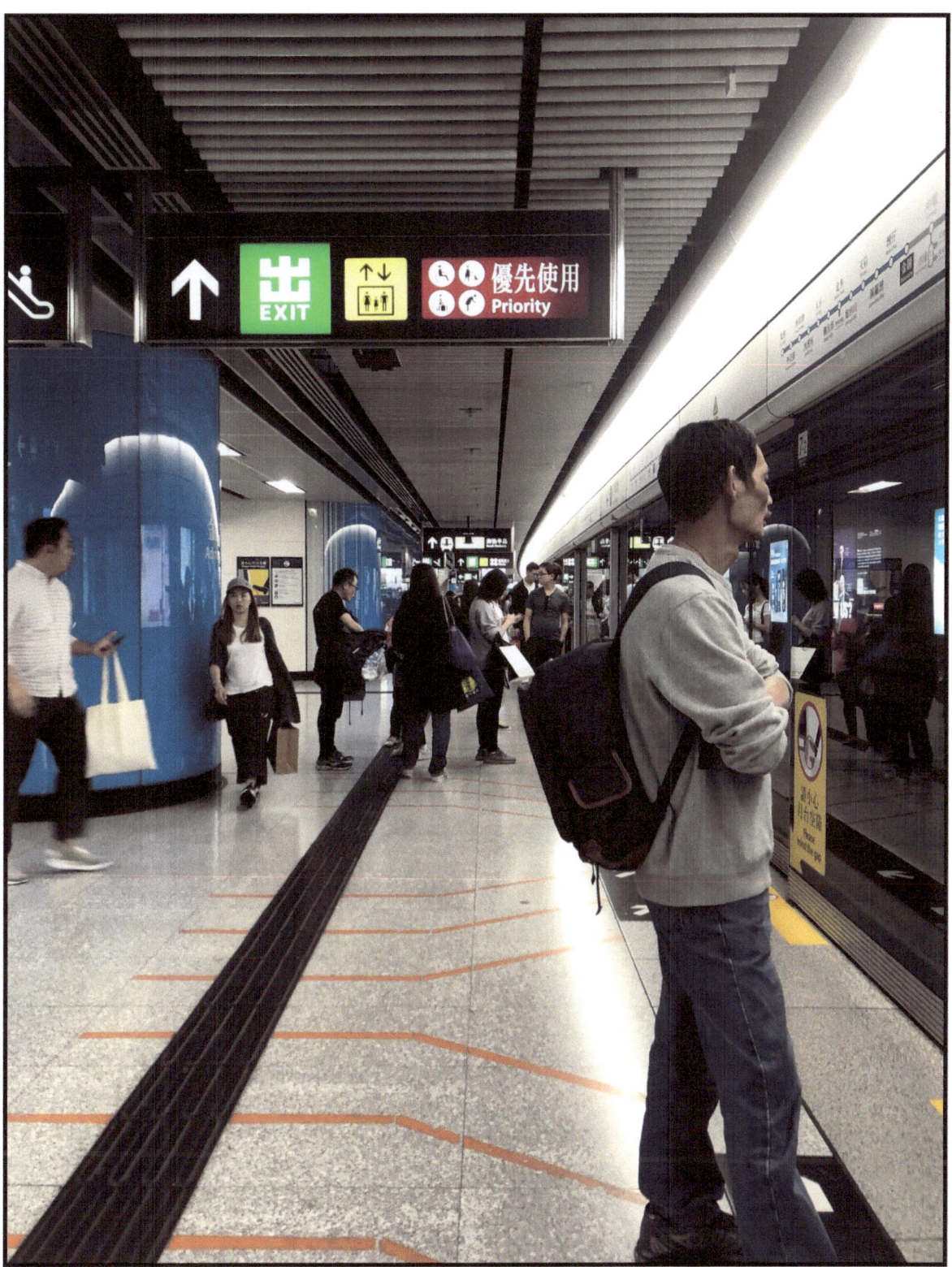

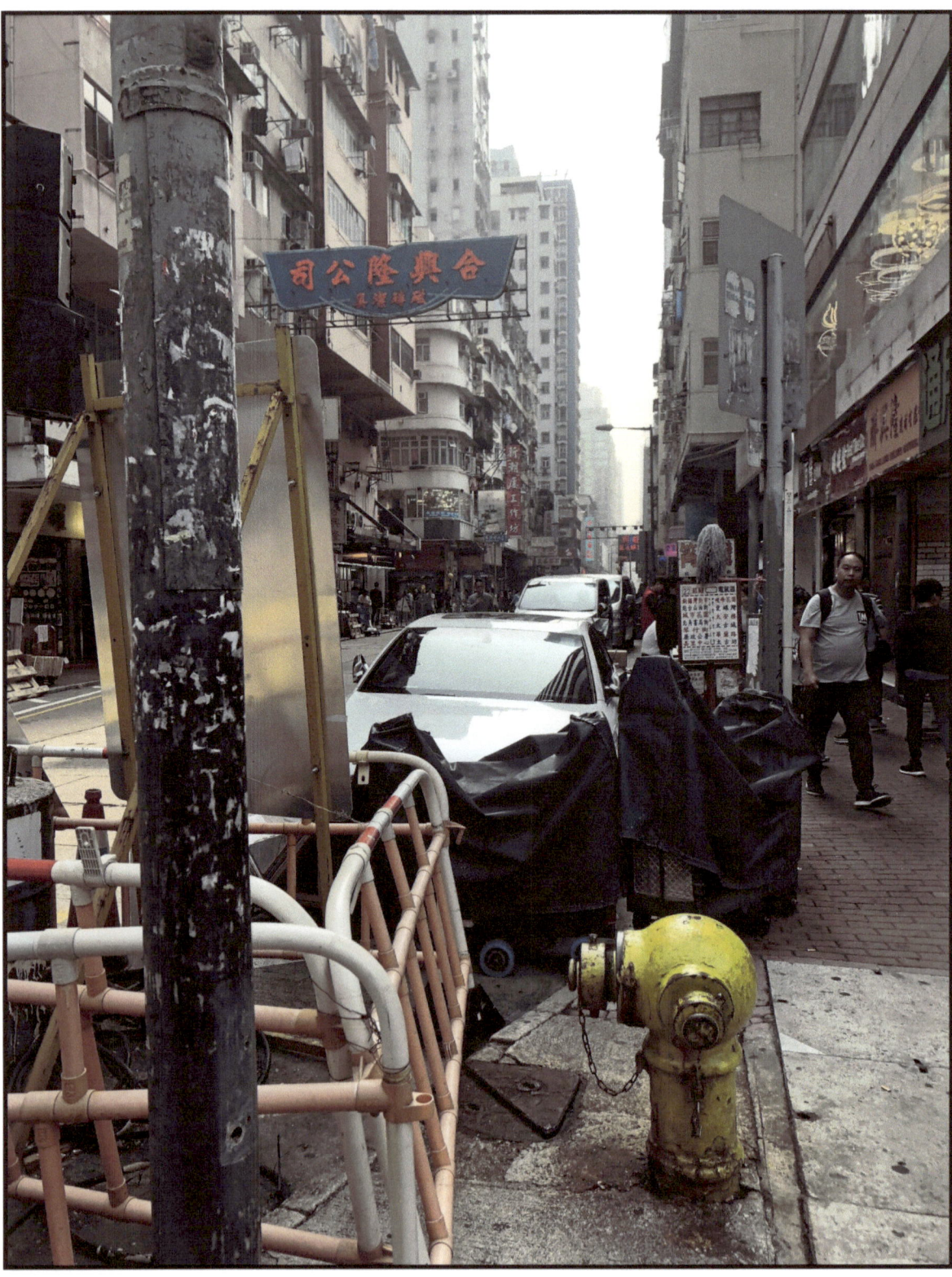

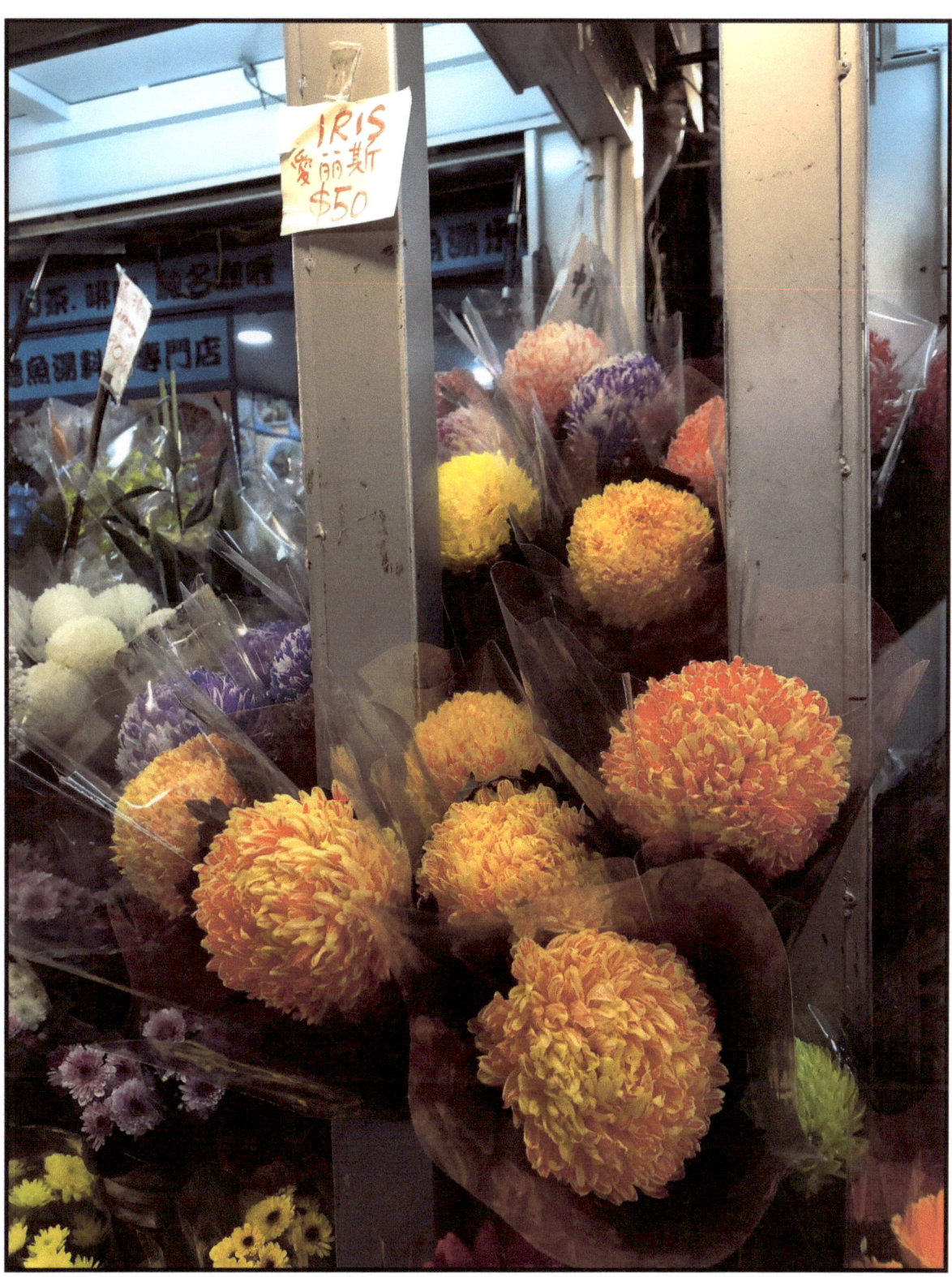

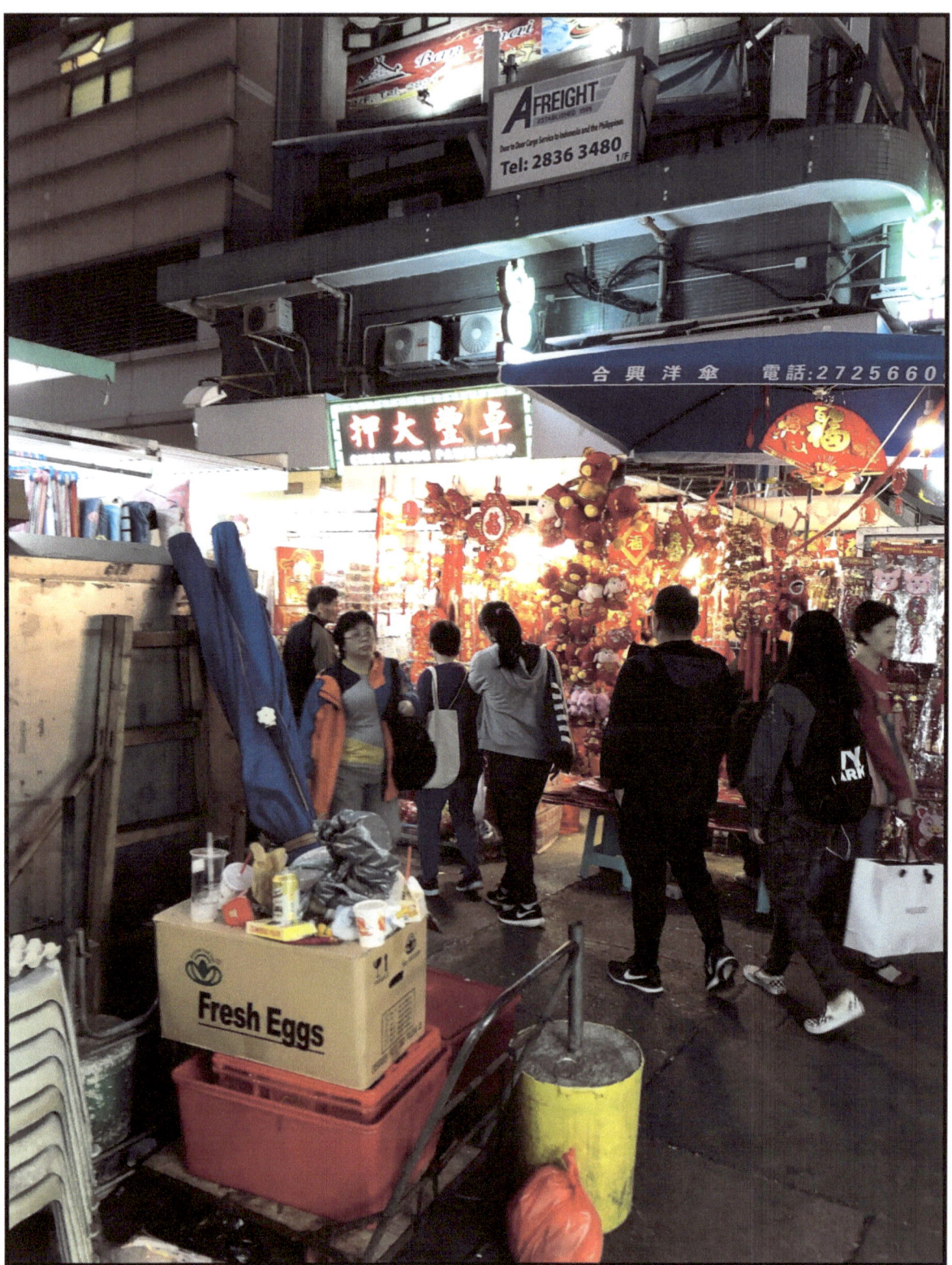

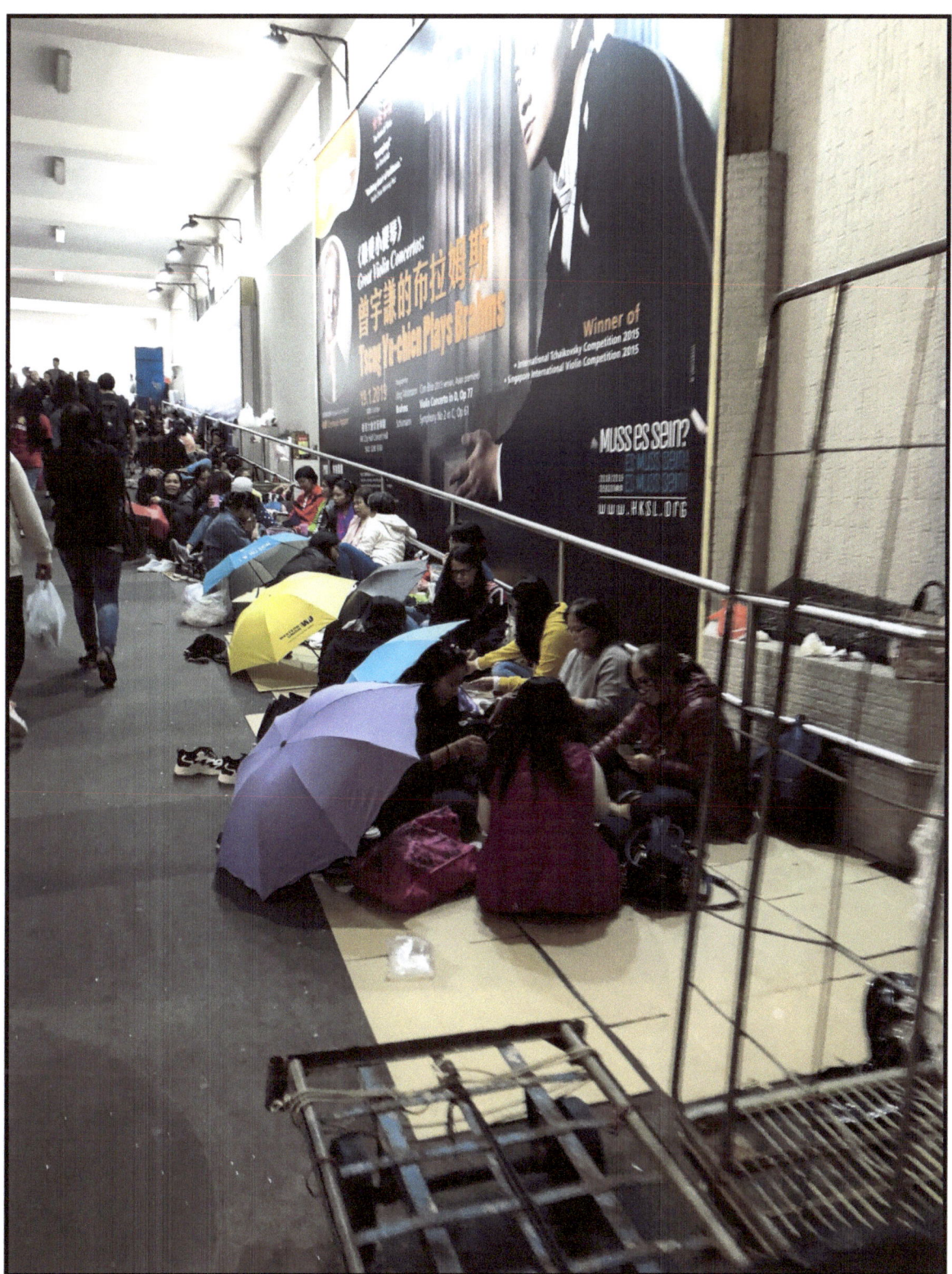

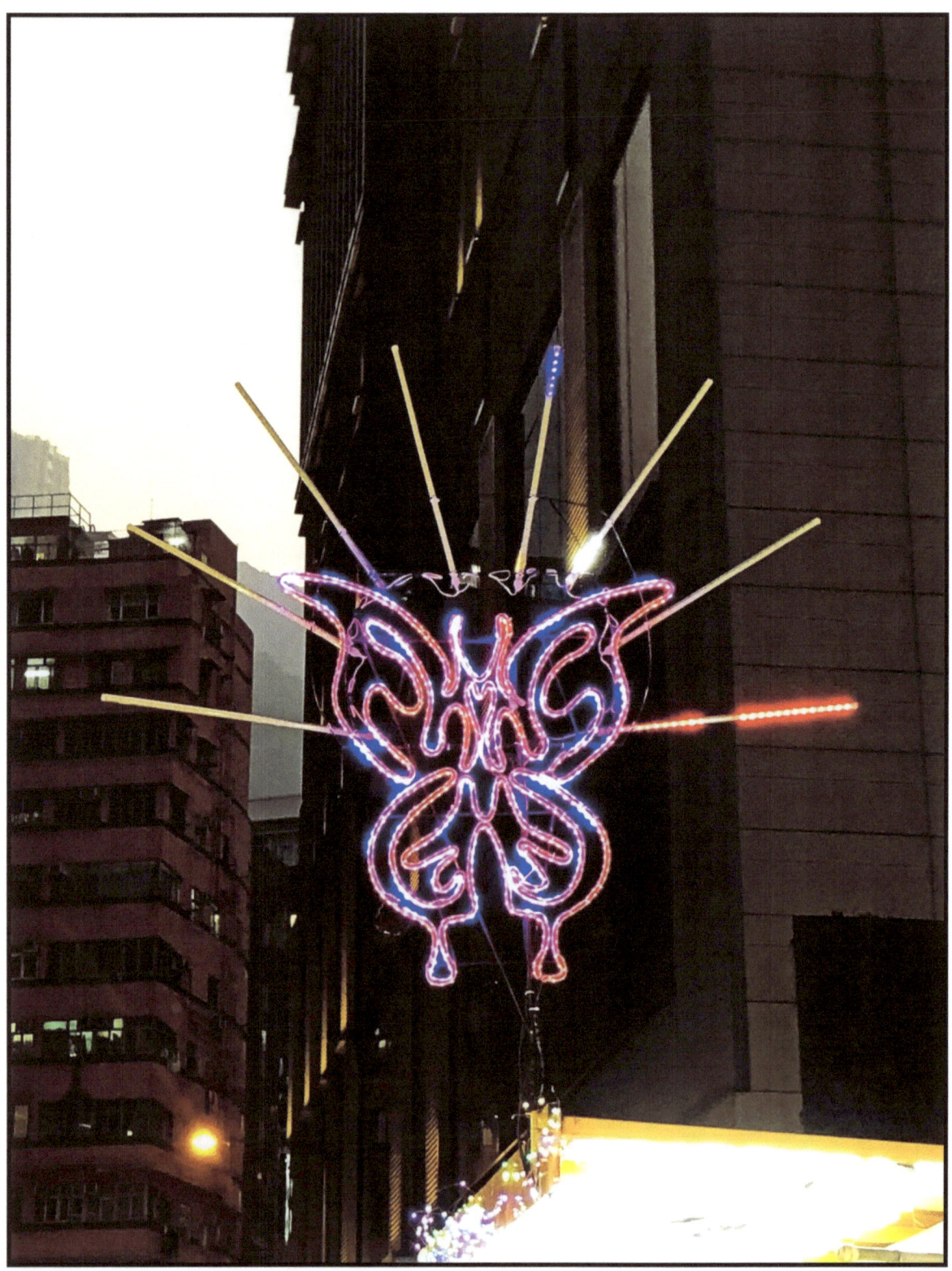

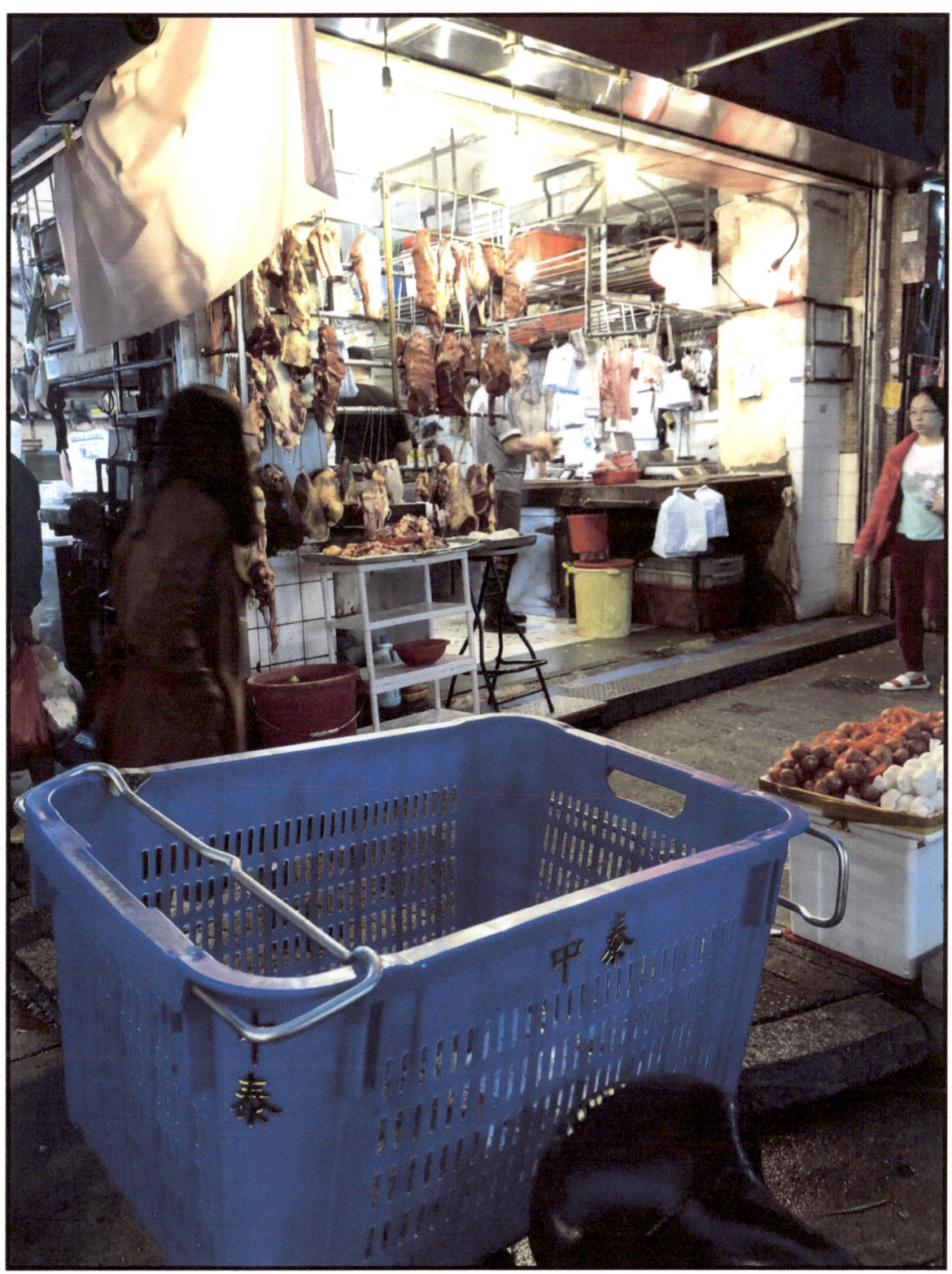

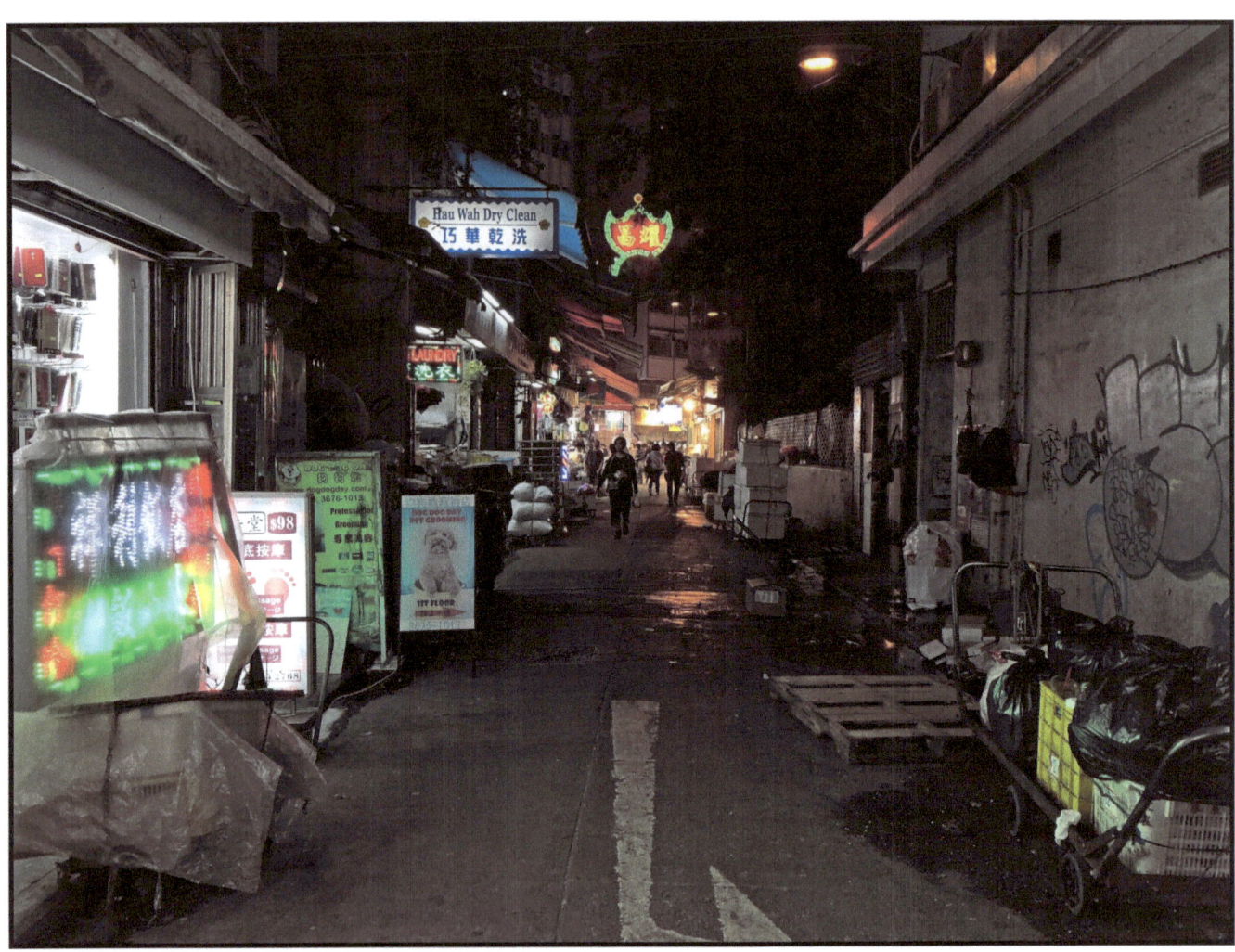

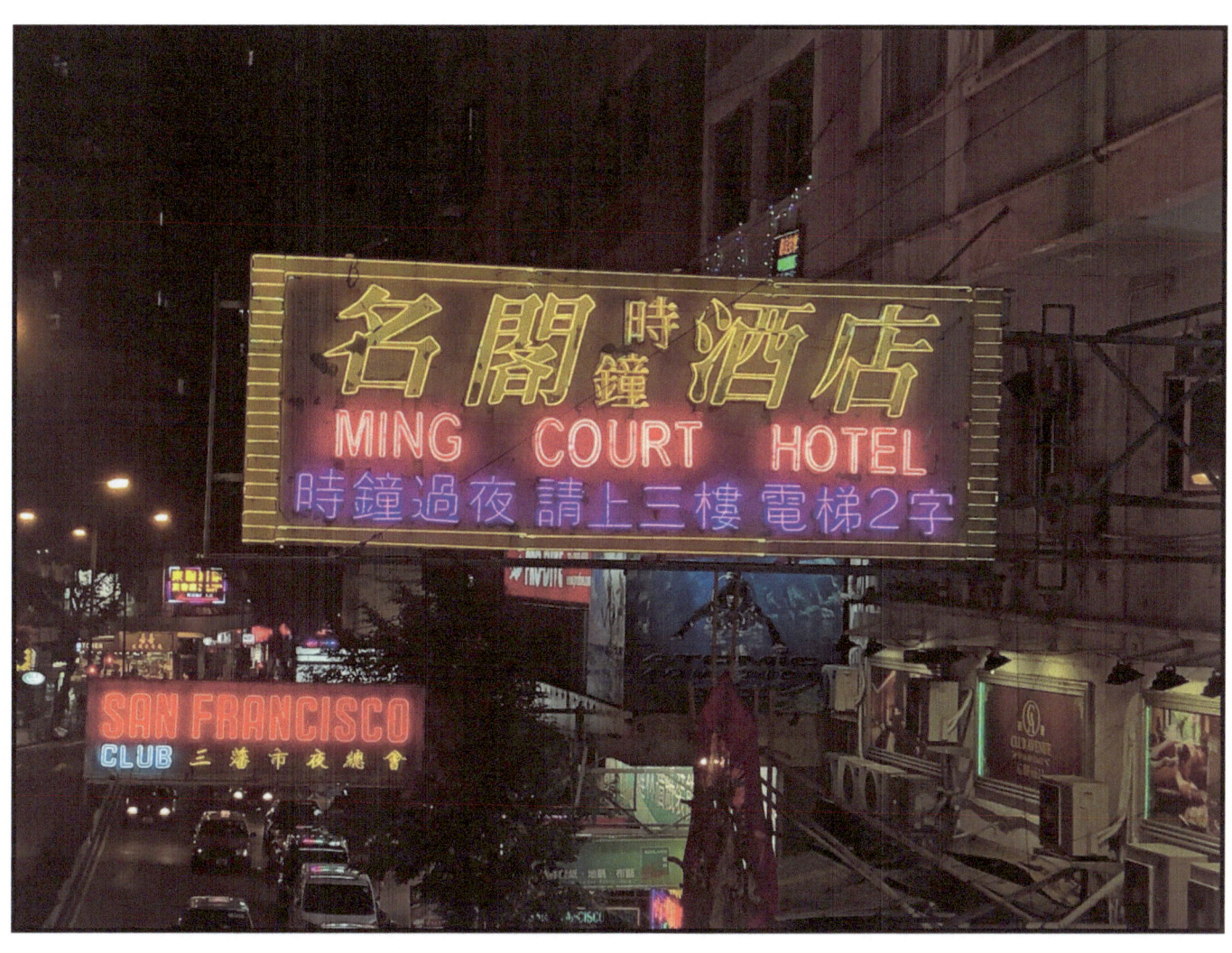

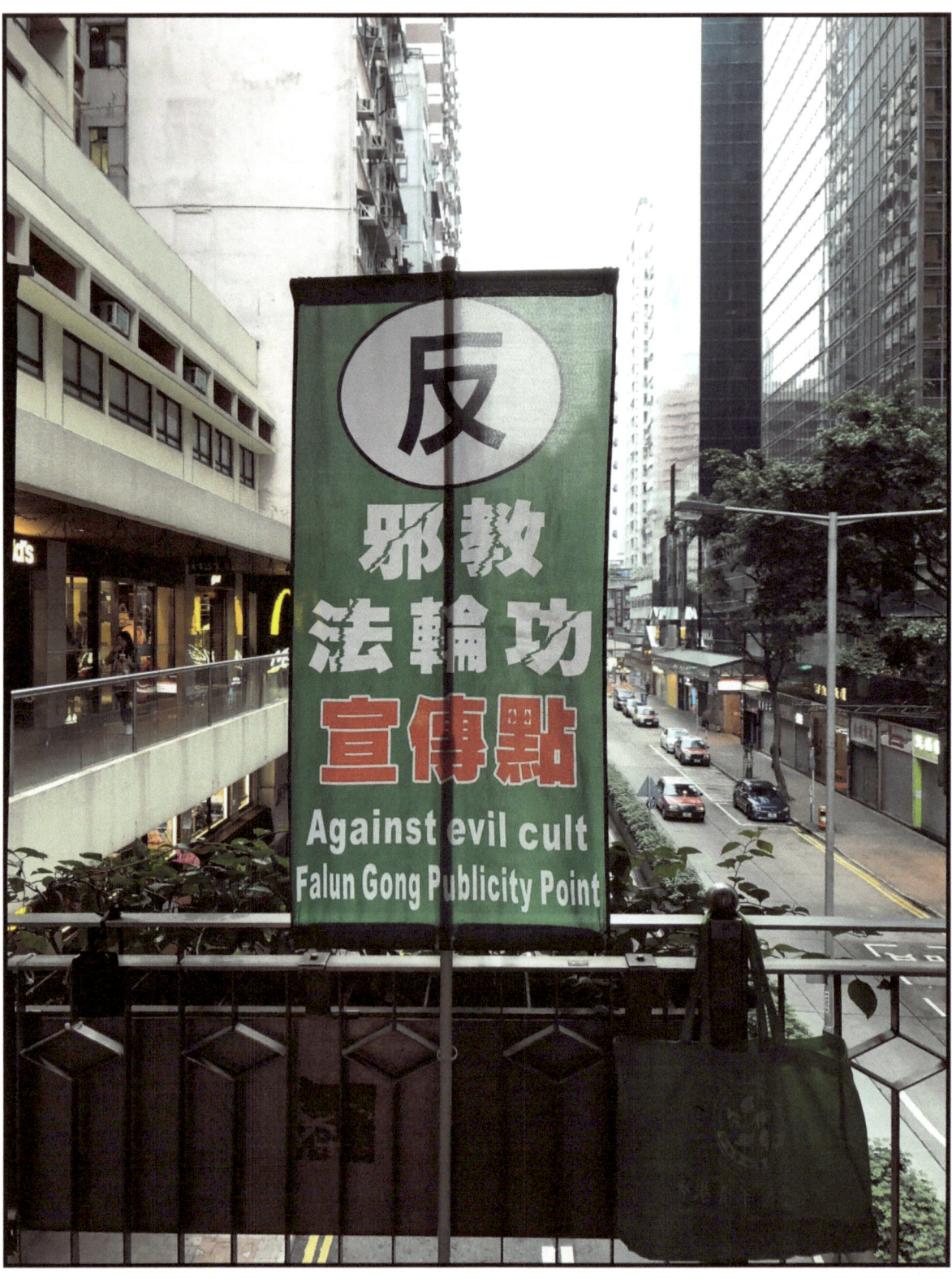

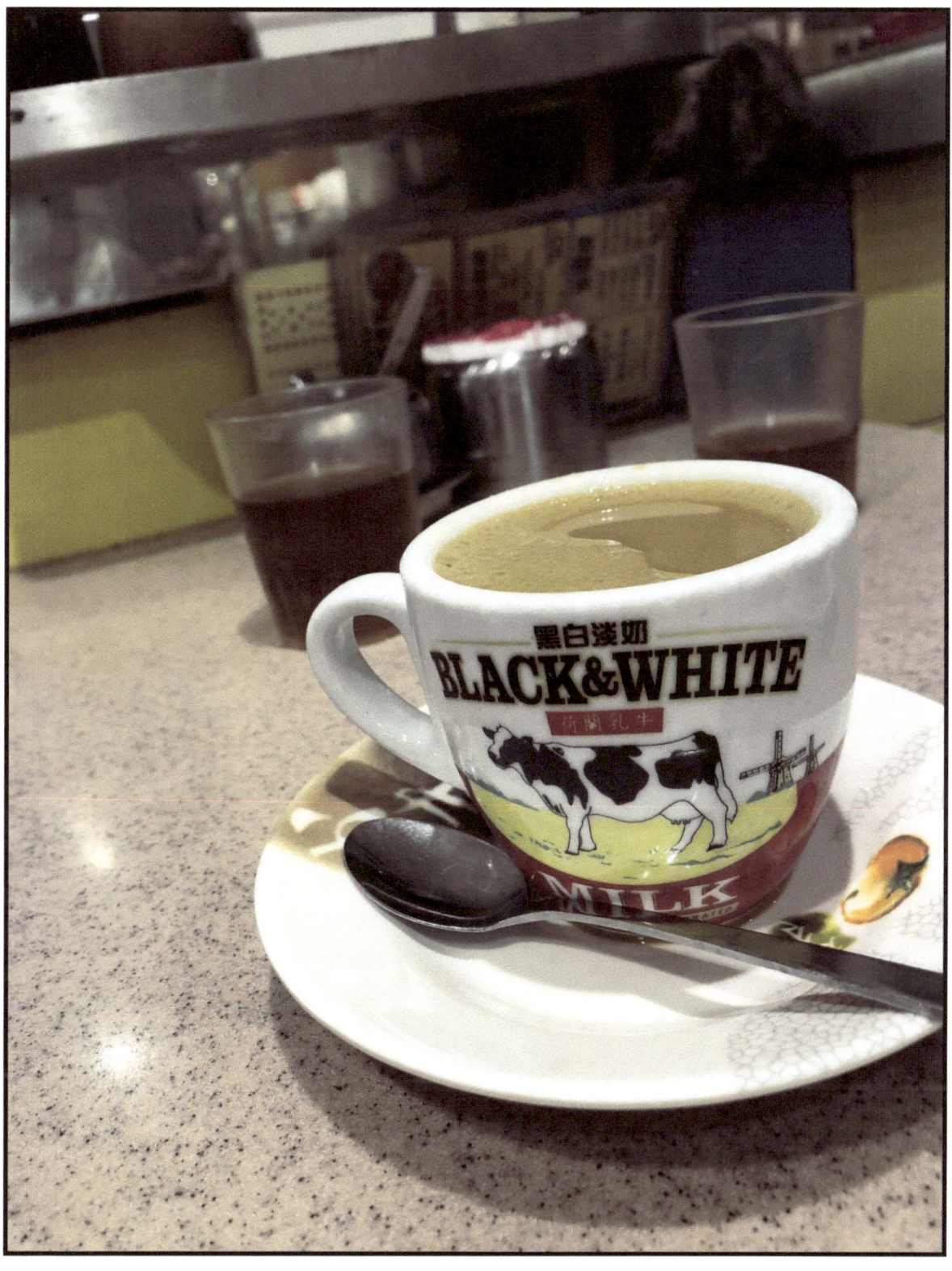

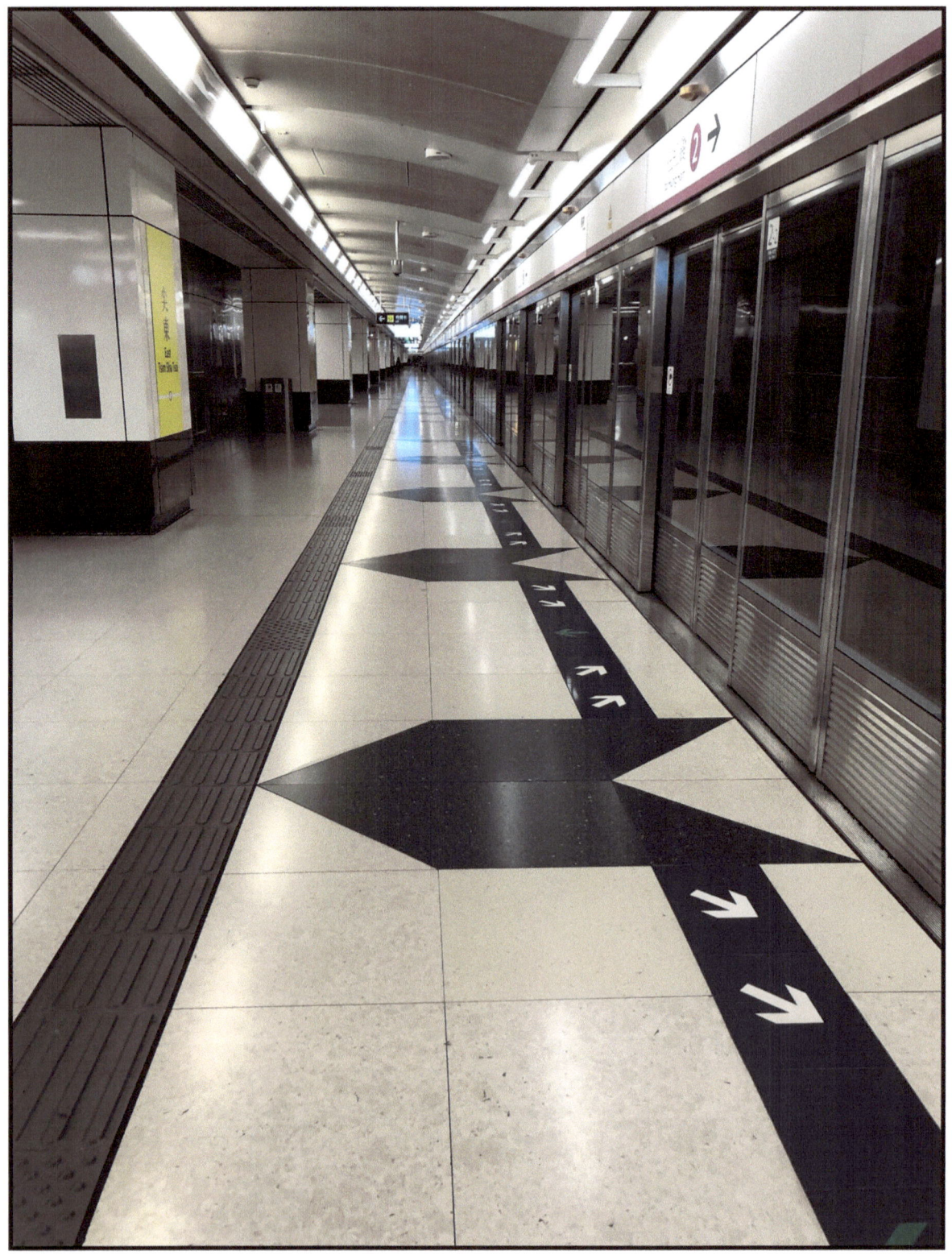

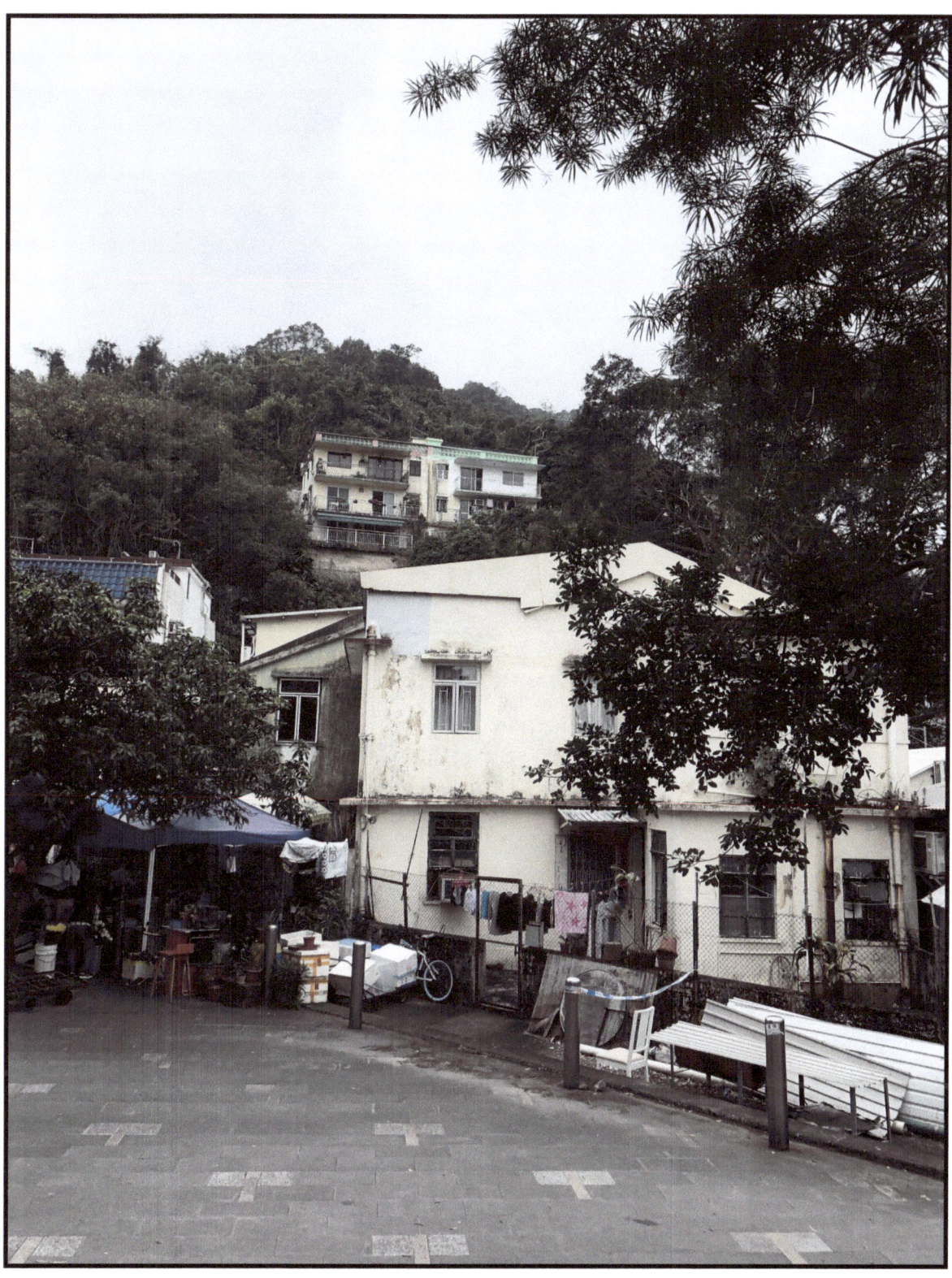

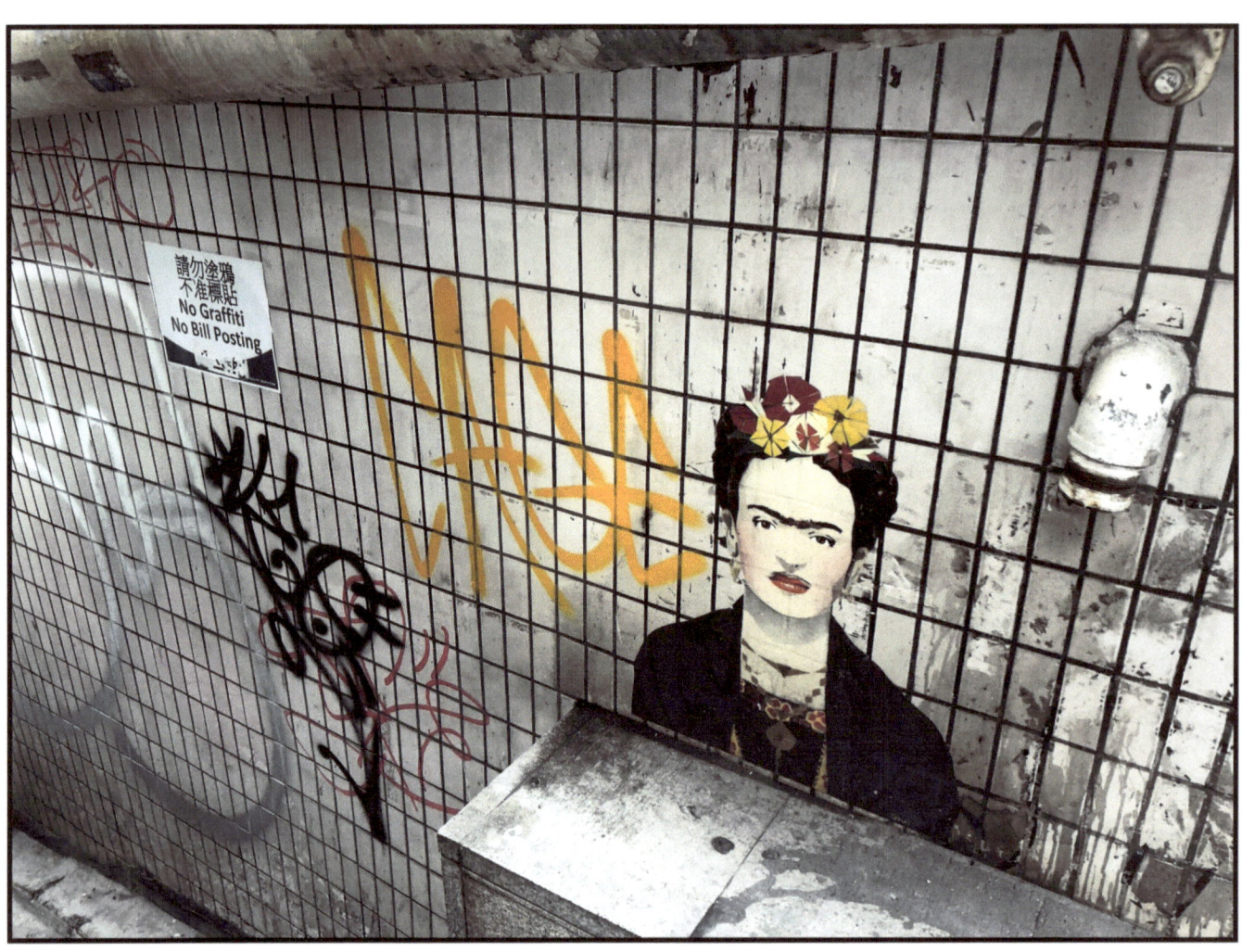

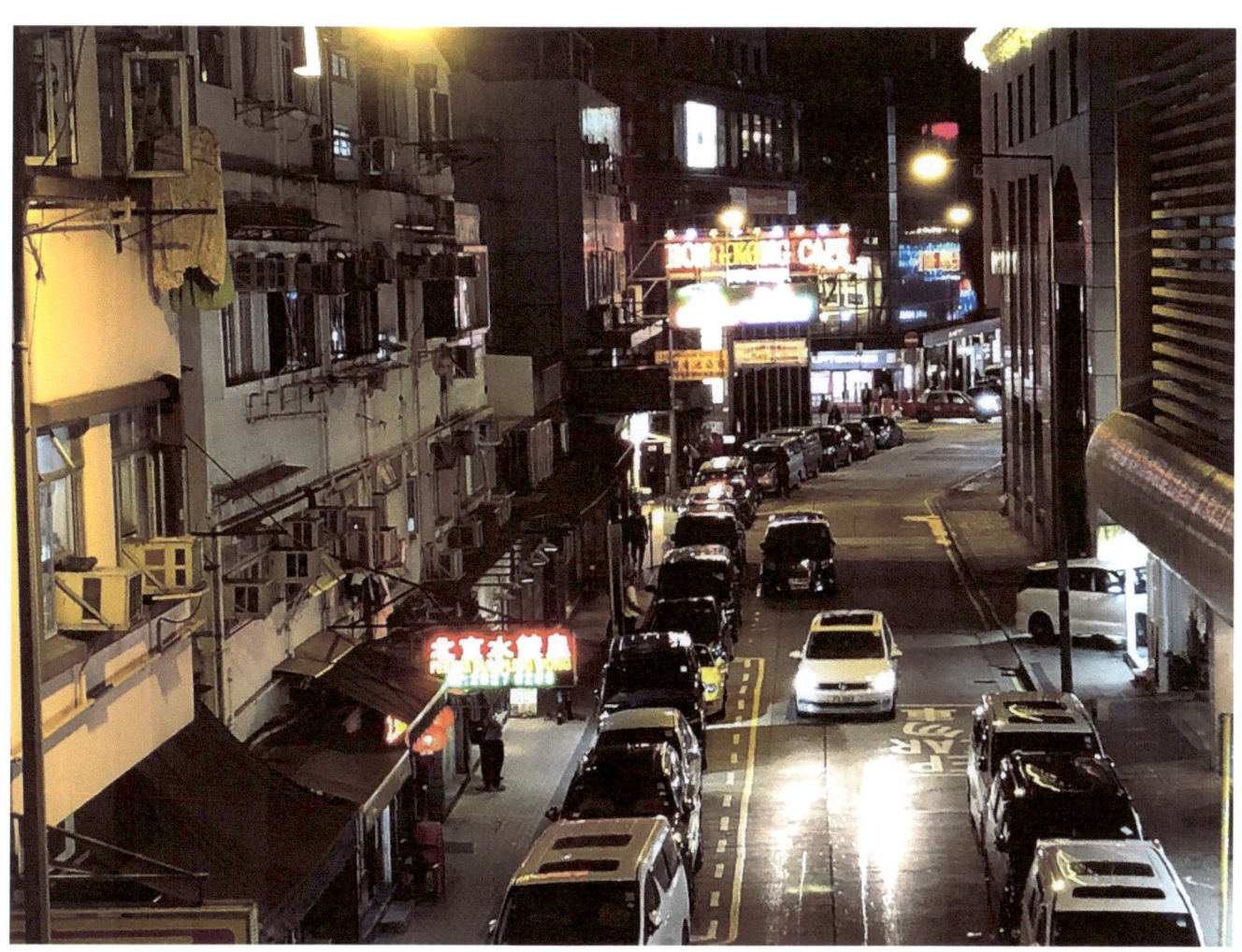

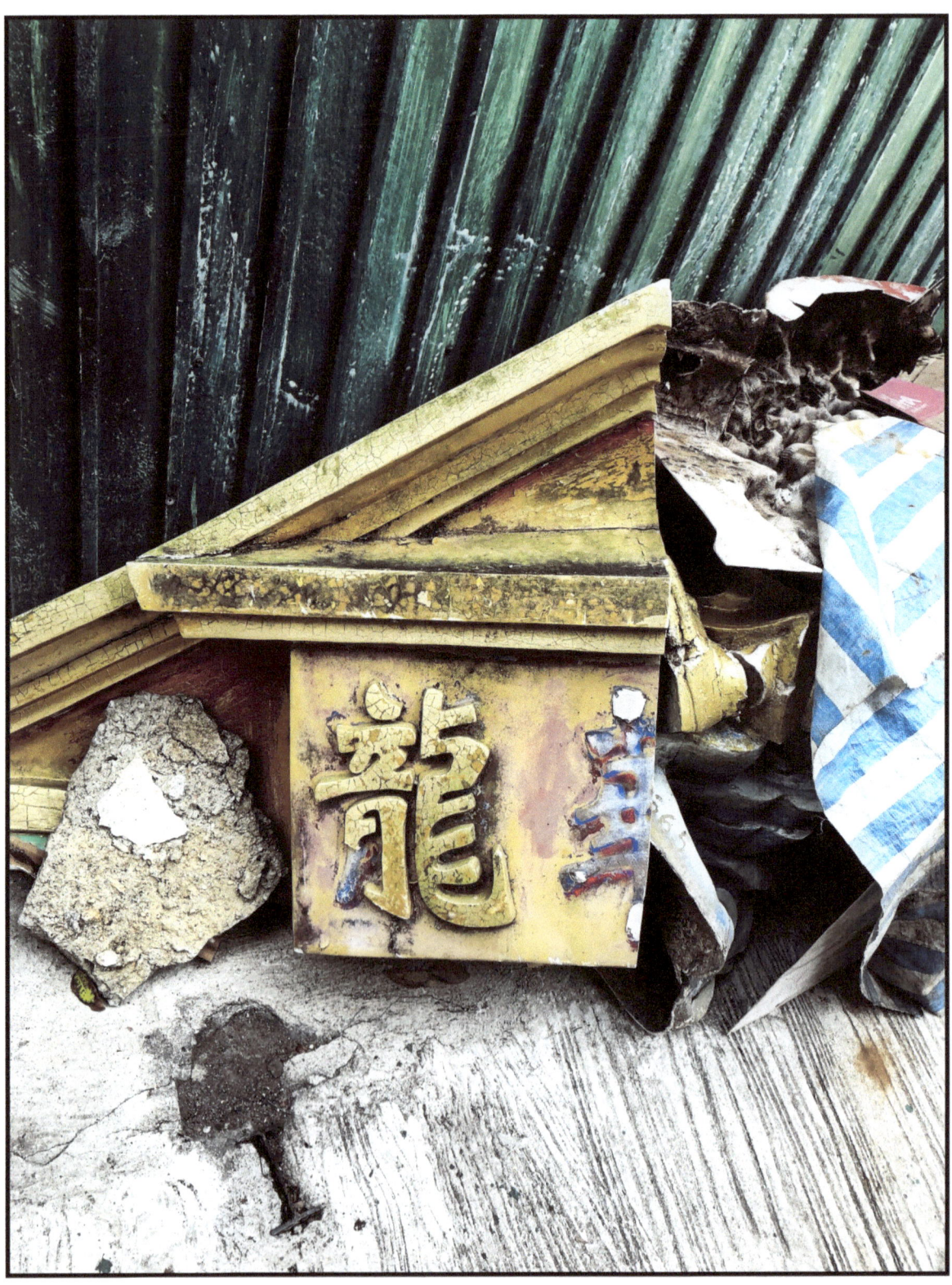

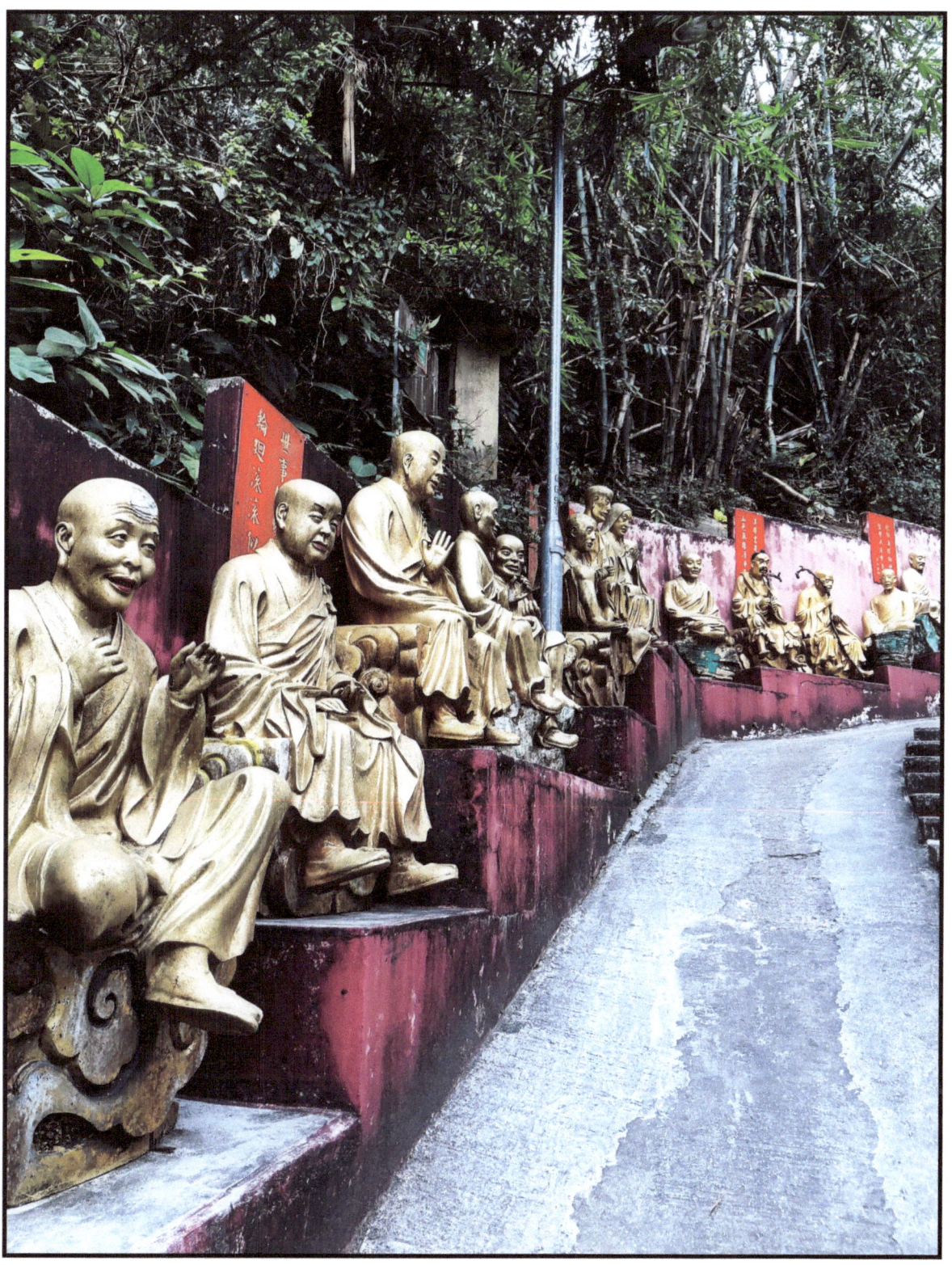

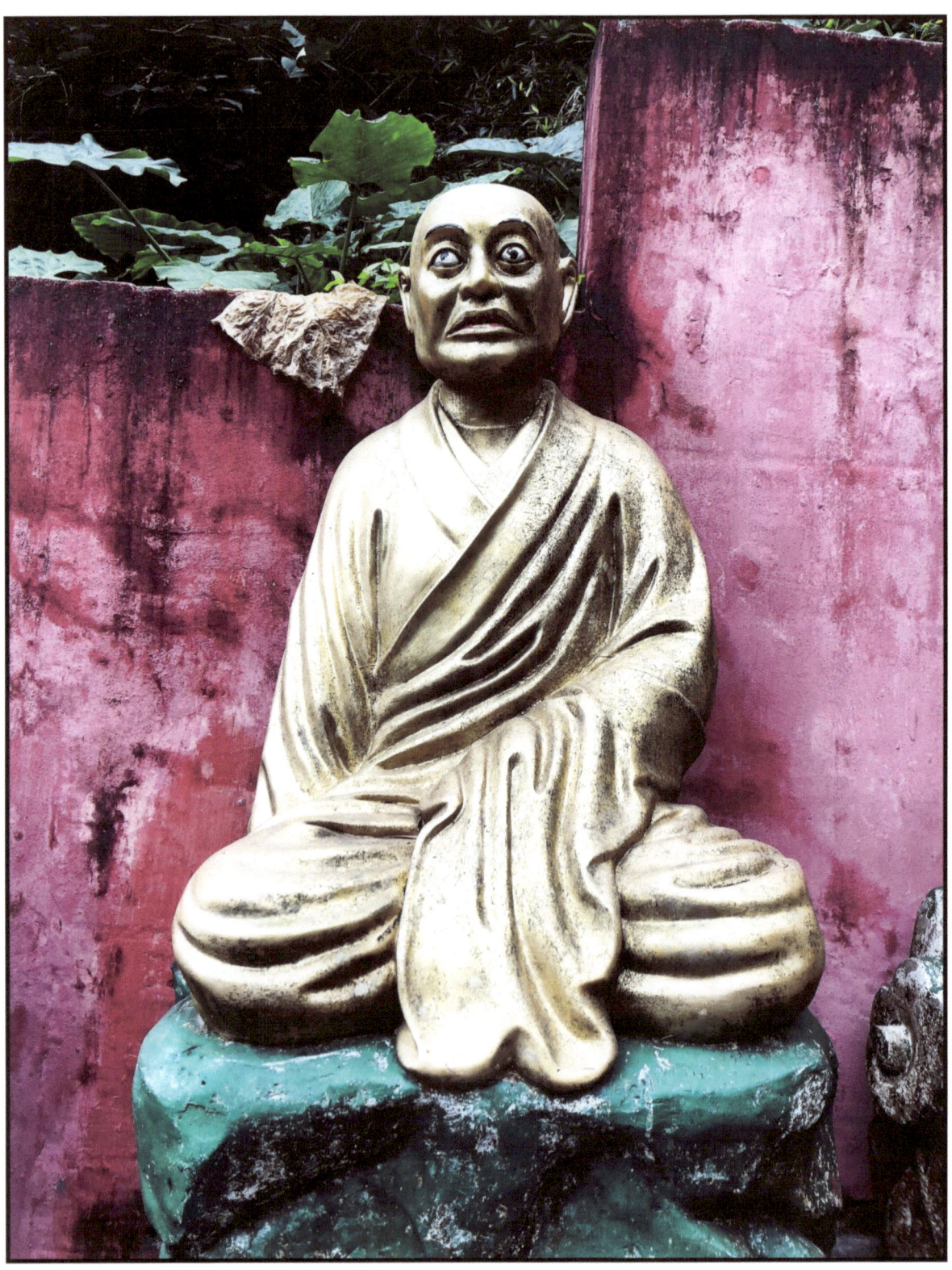

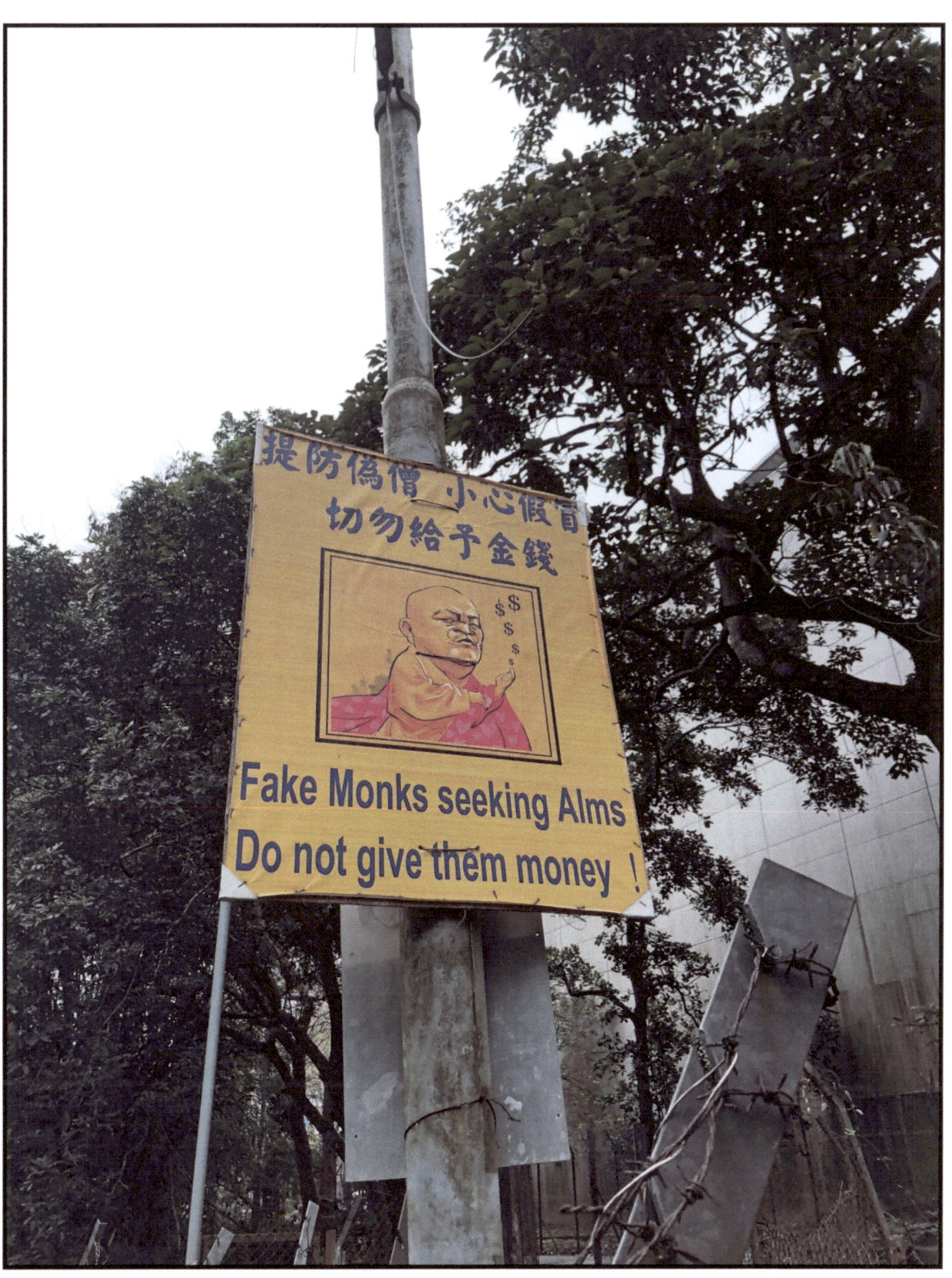

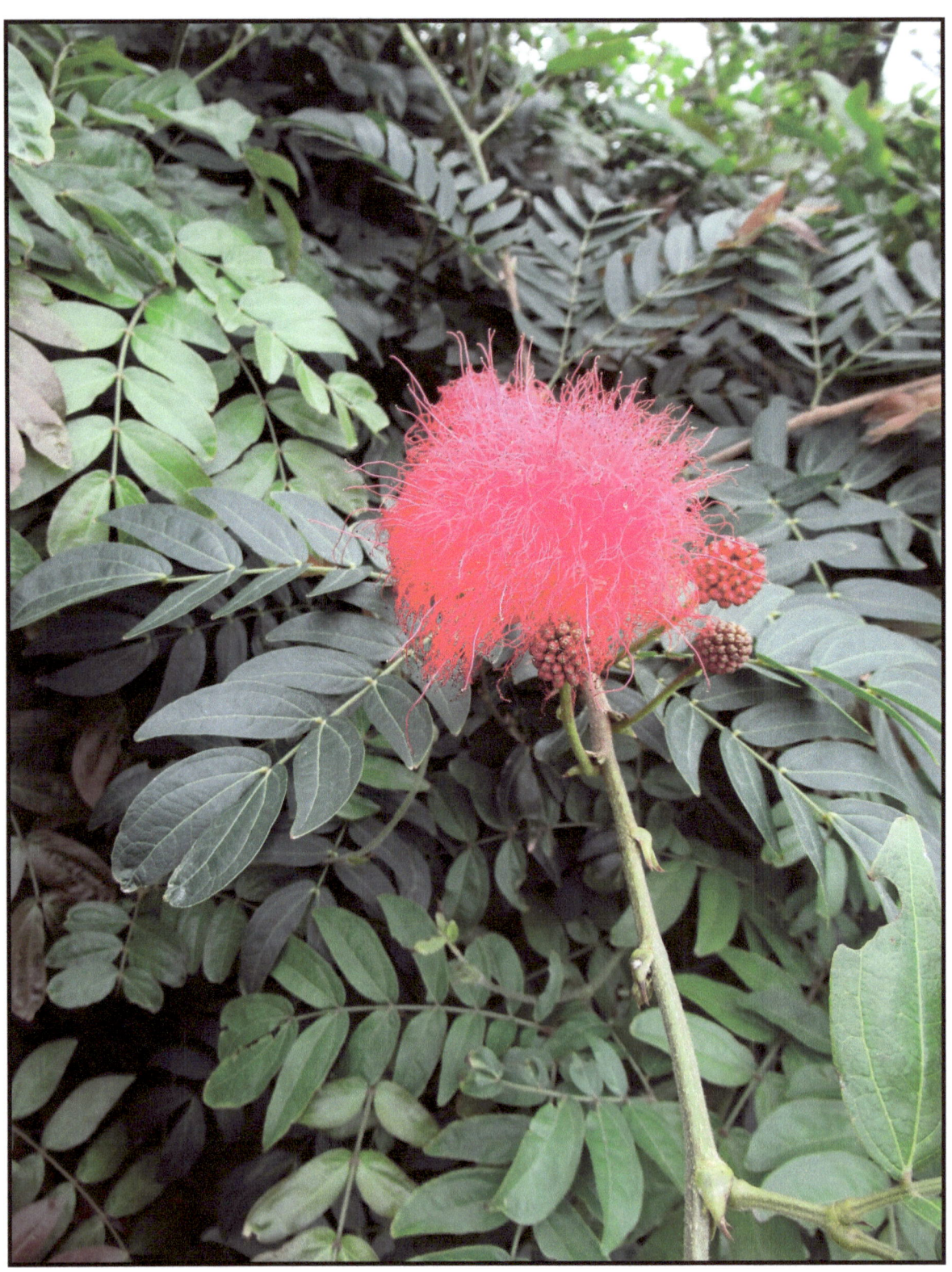

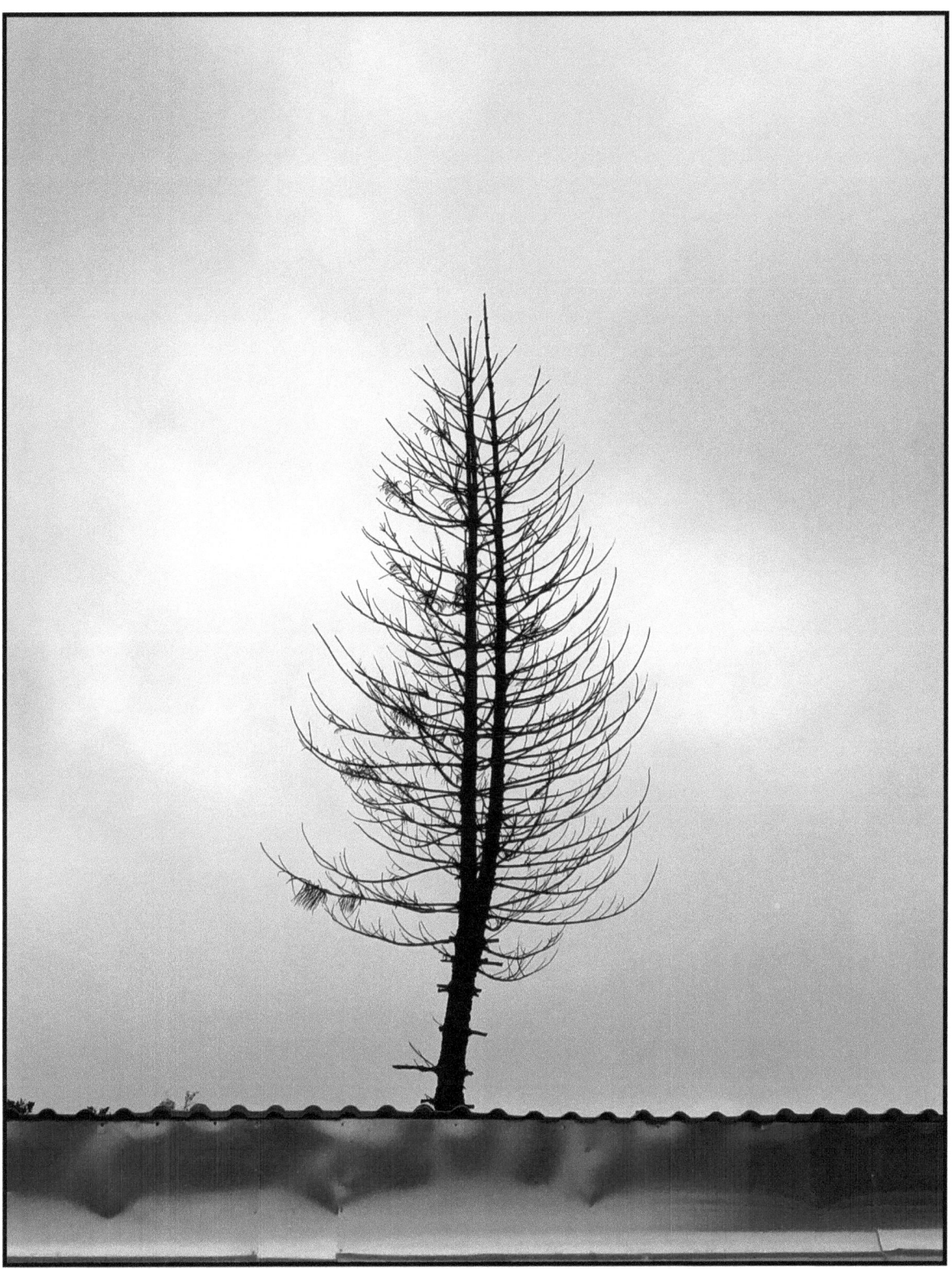

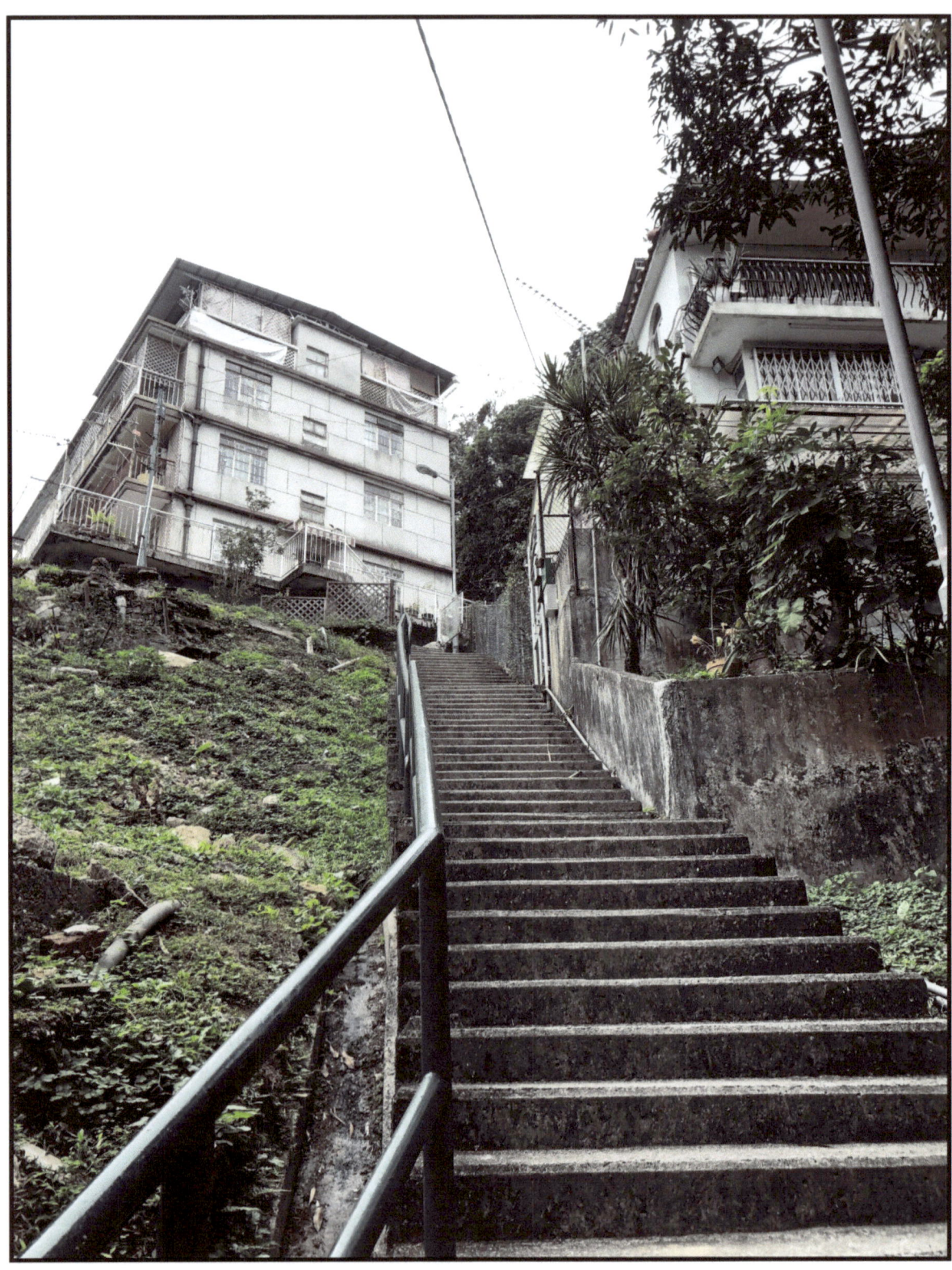

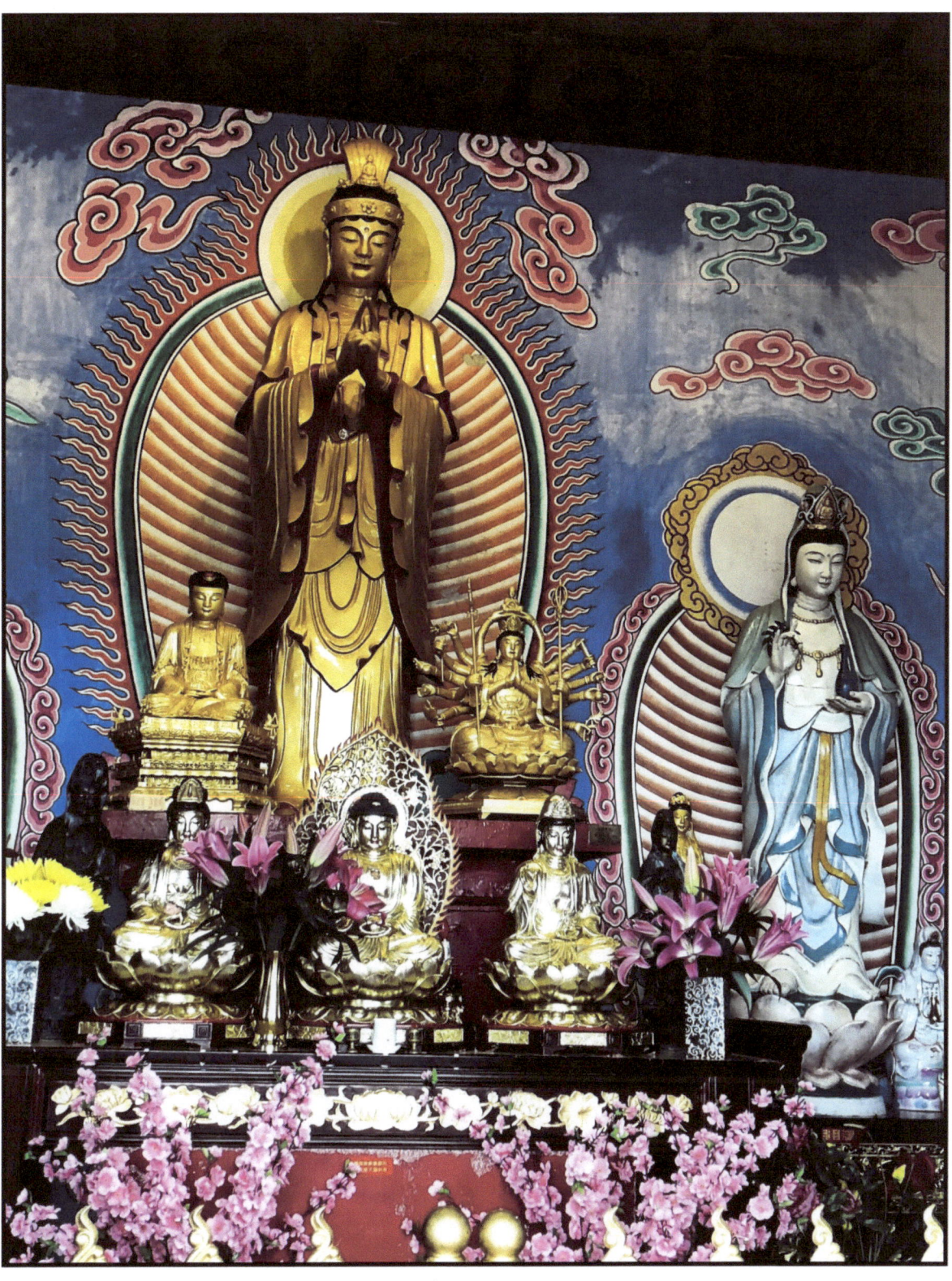

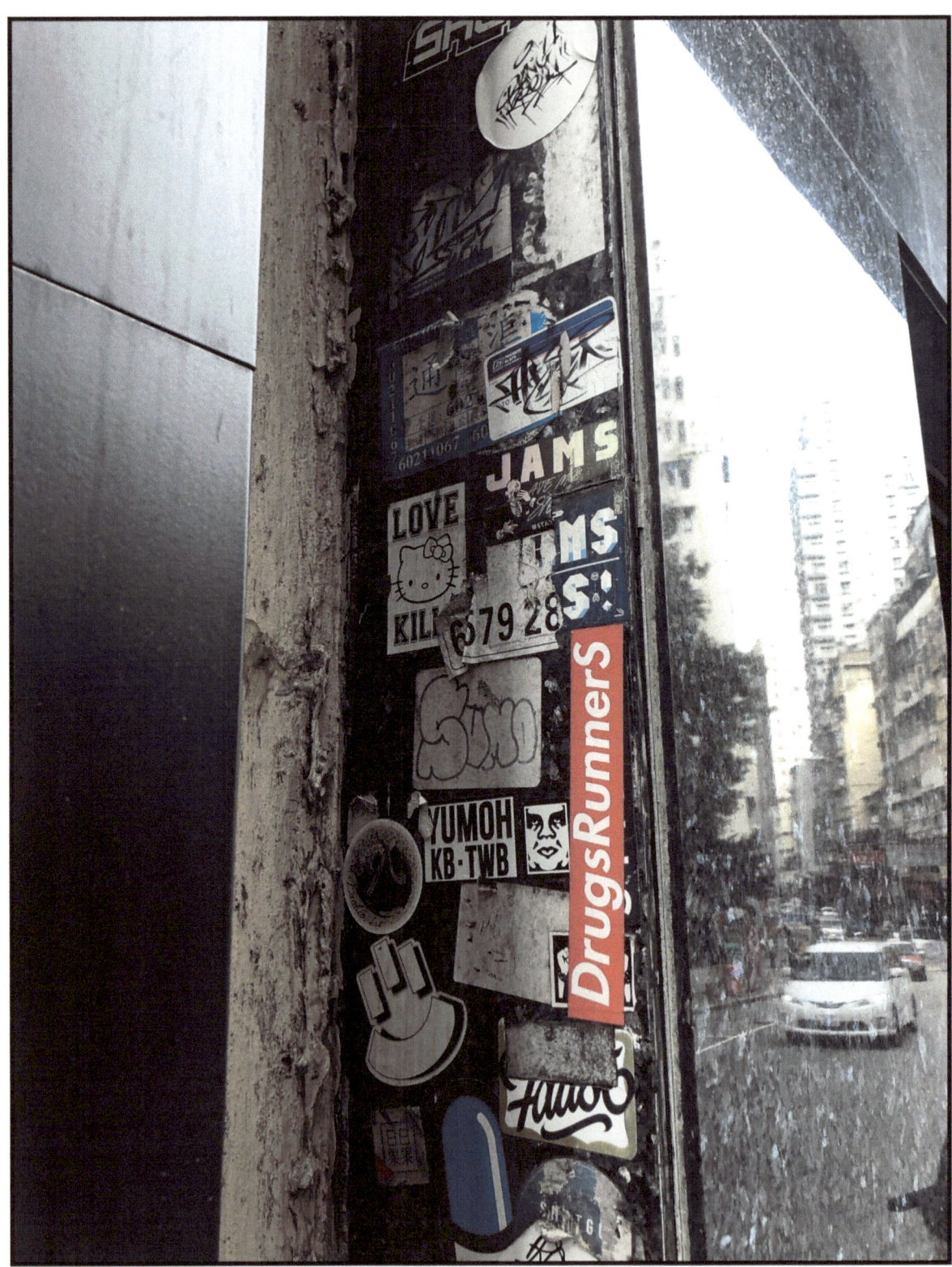

如身體不適請在下一站
要求車站職員協助

If you feel unwell
please contact staff
at the next station

非法使用罰款 5,000 元
Penalty for improper use $5,000

危急時按破封條使用
Break seal and use
when in danger

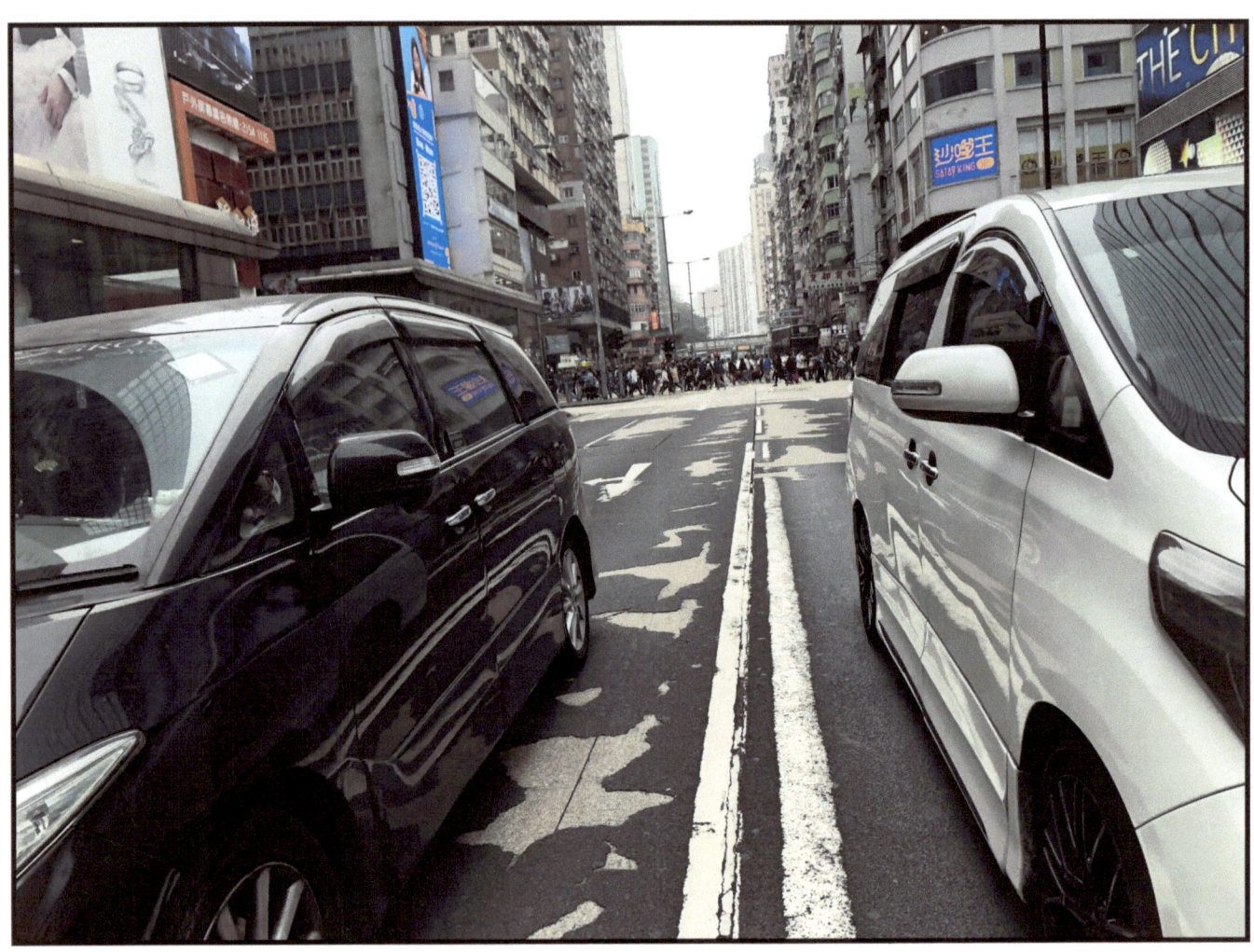

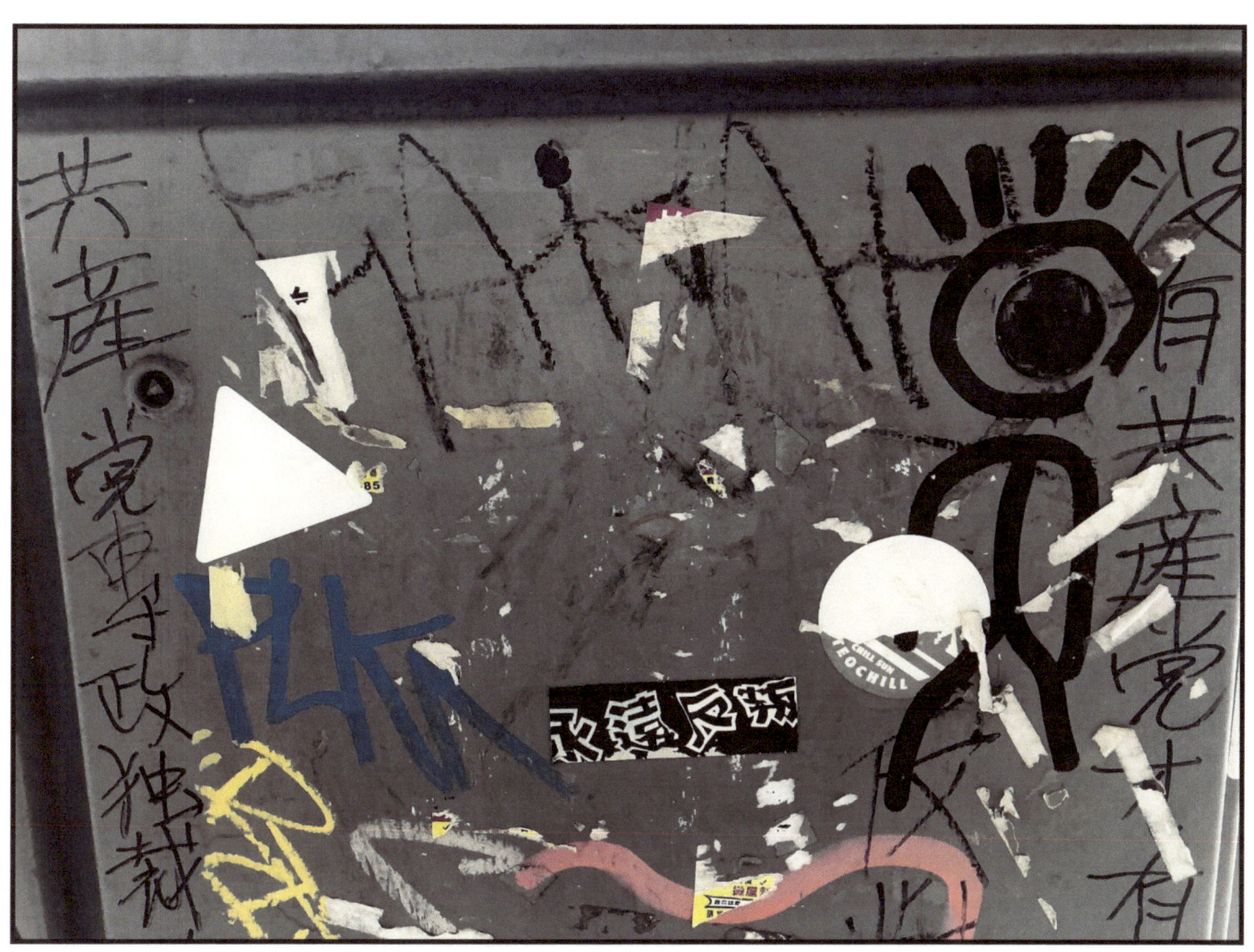

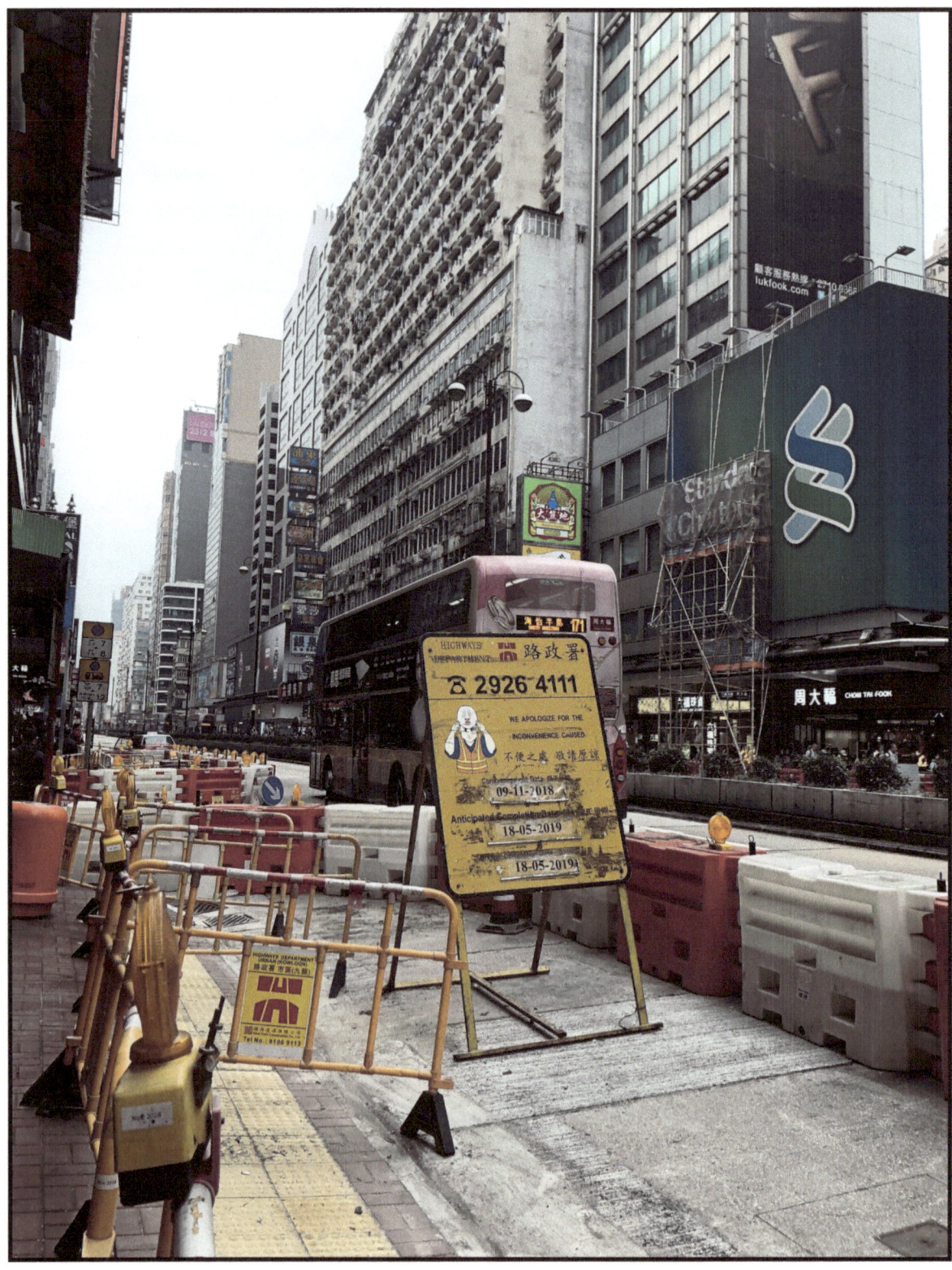

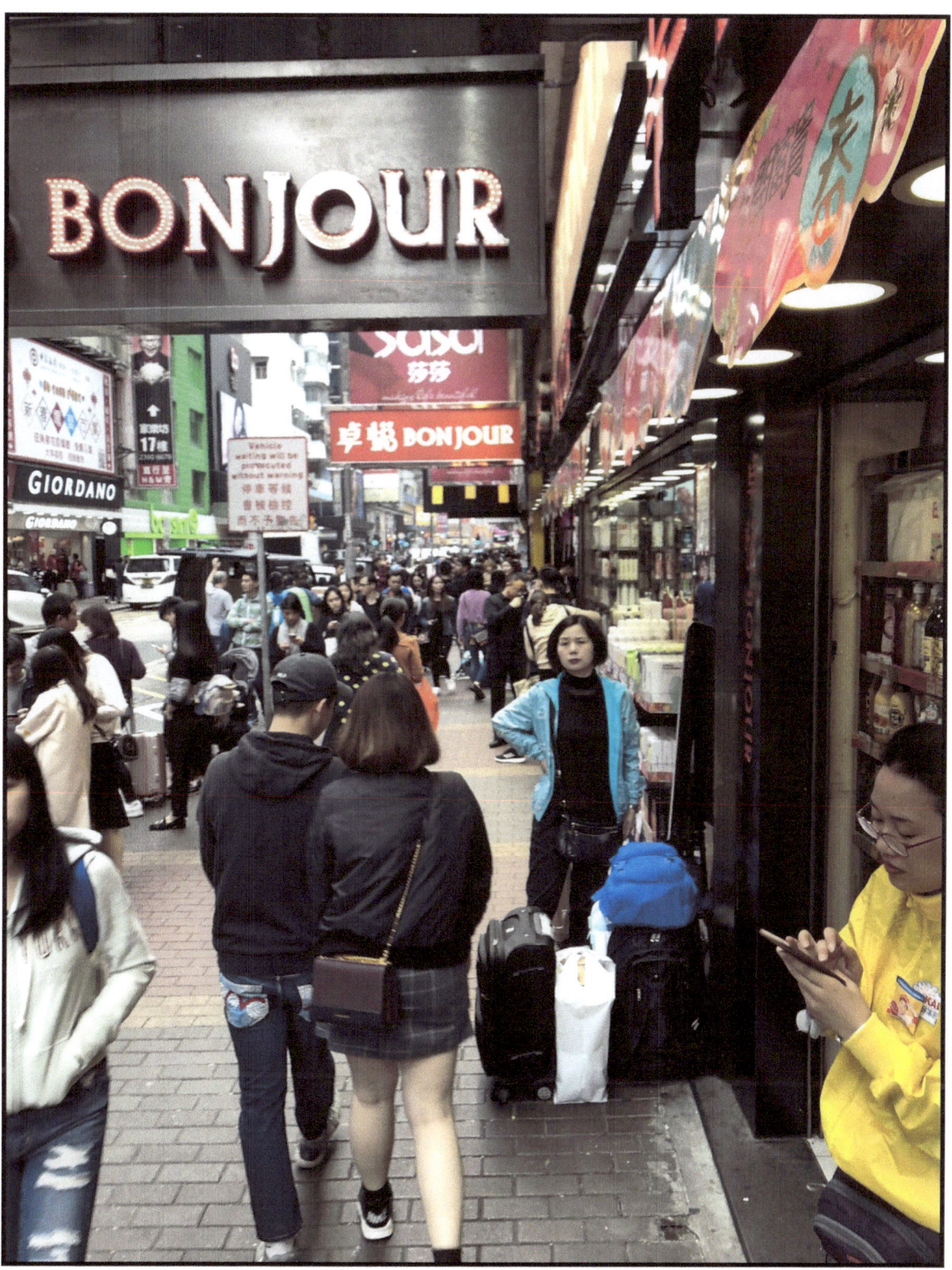

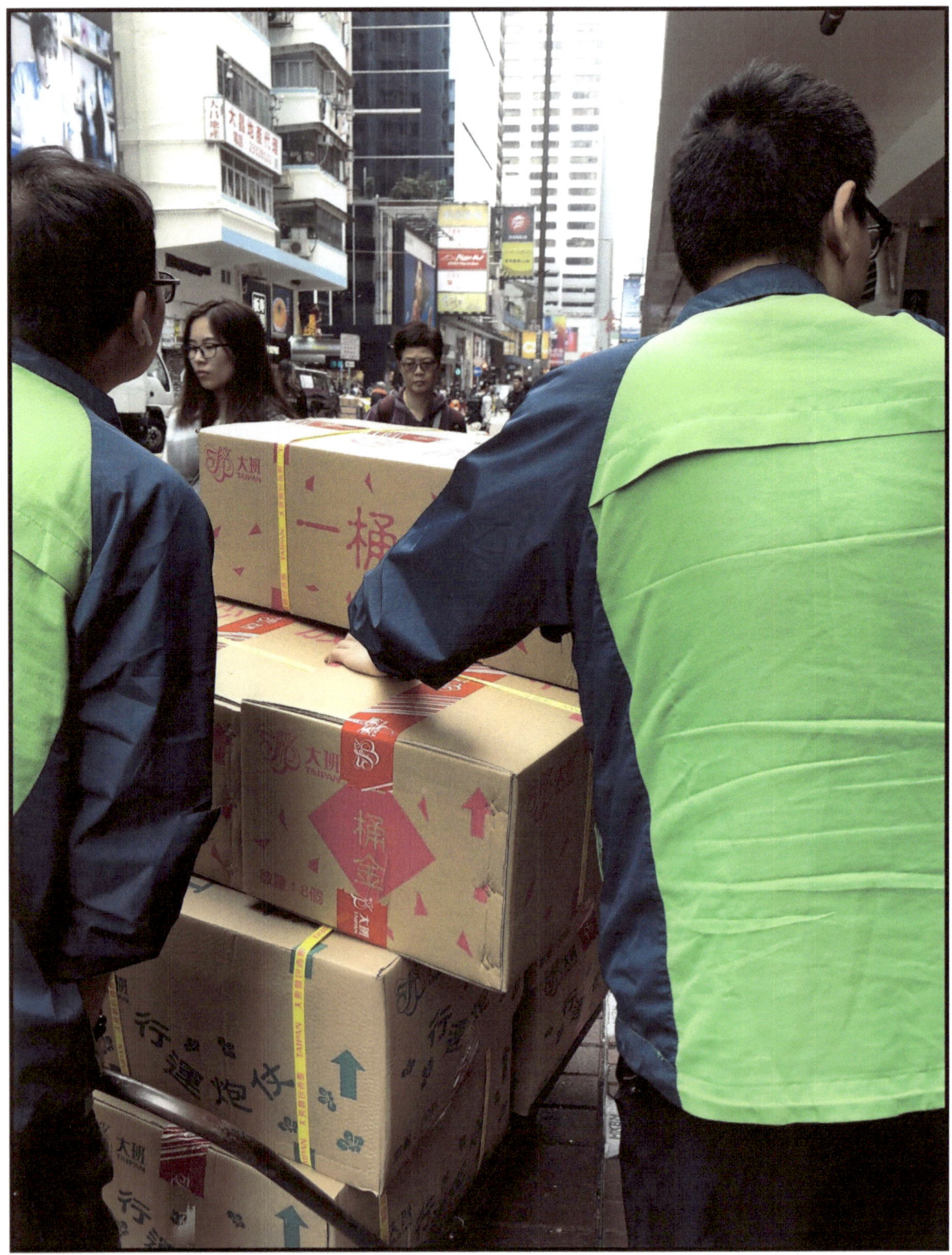

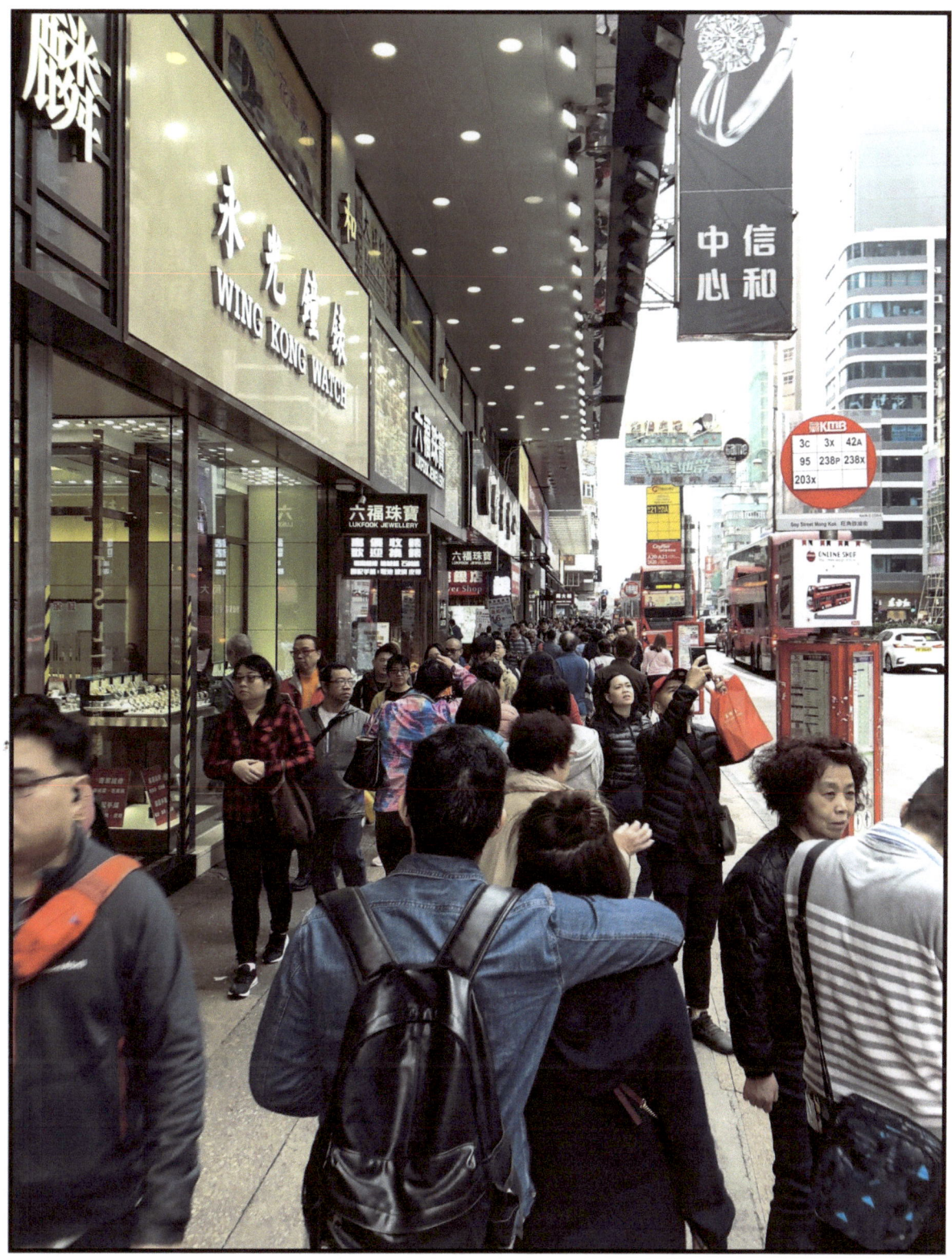

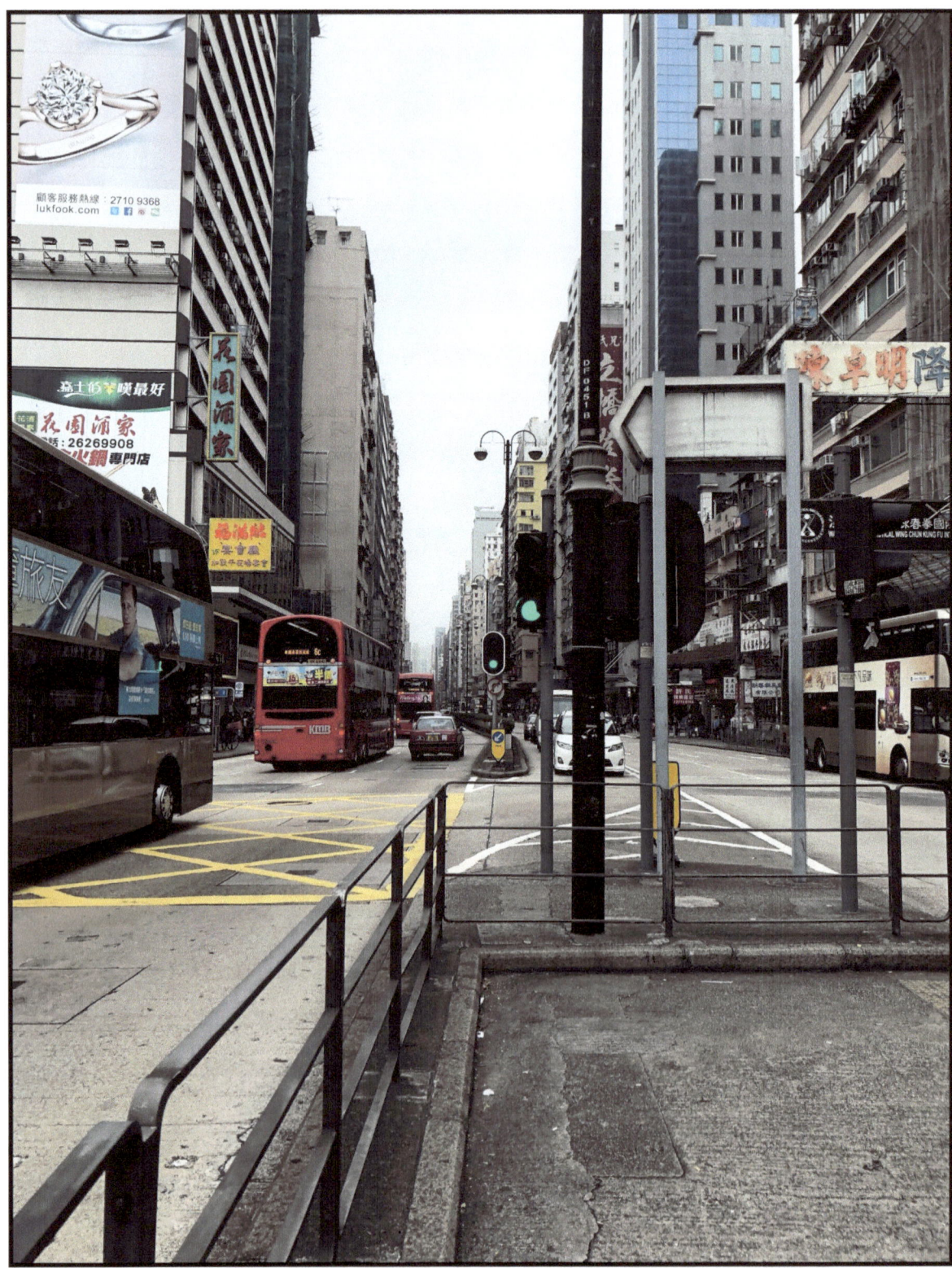

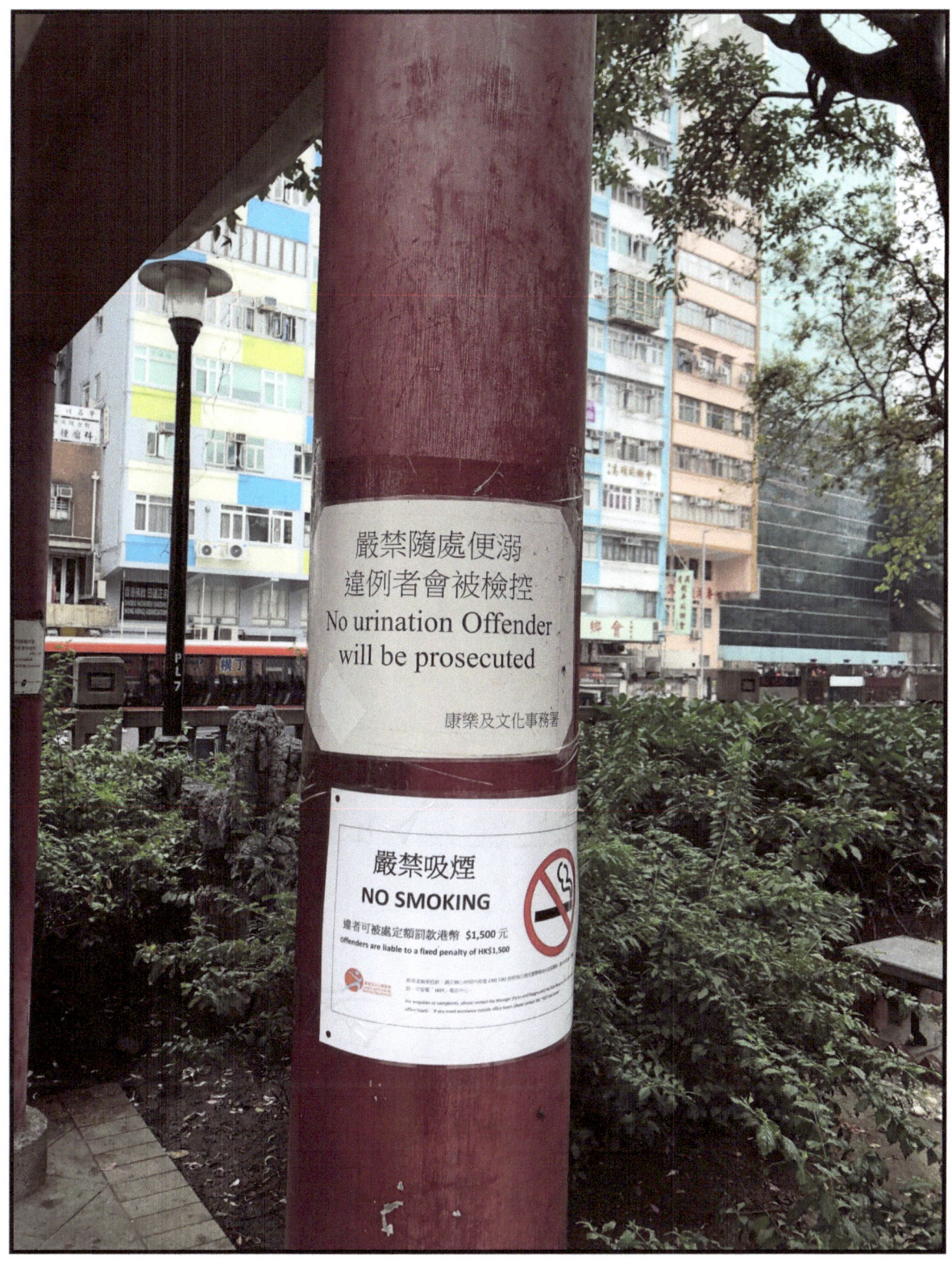

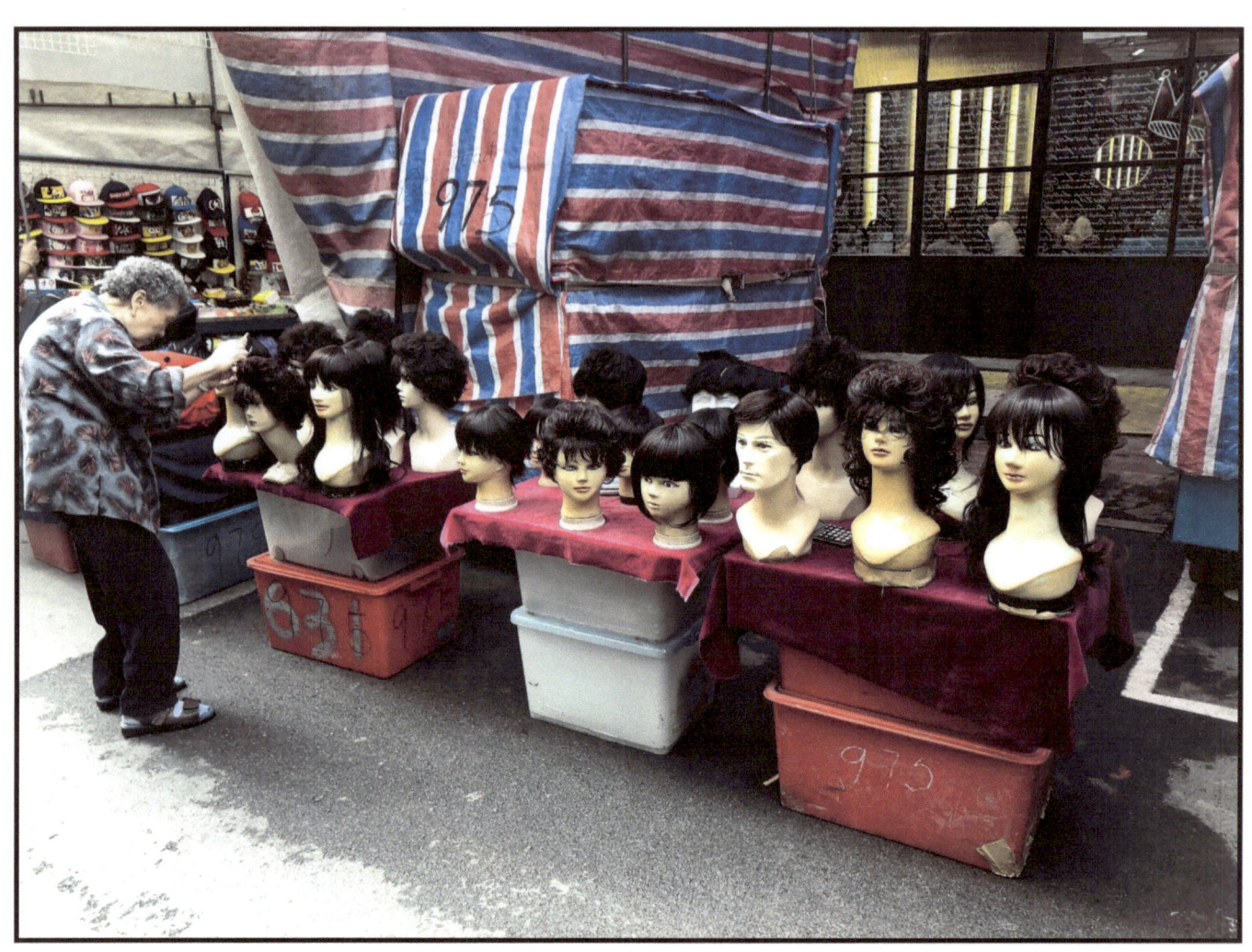

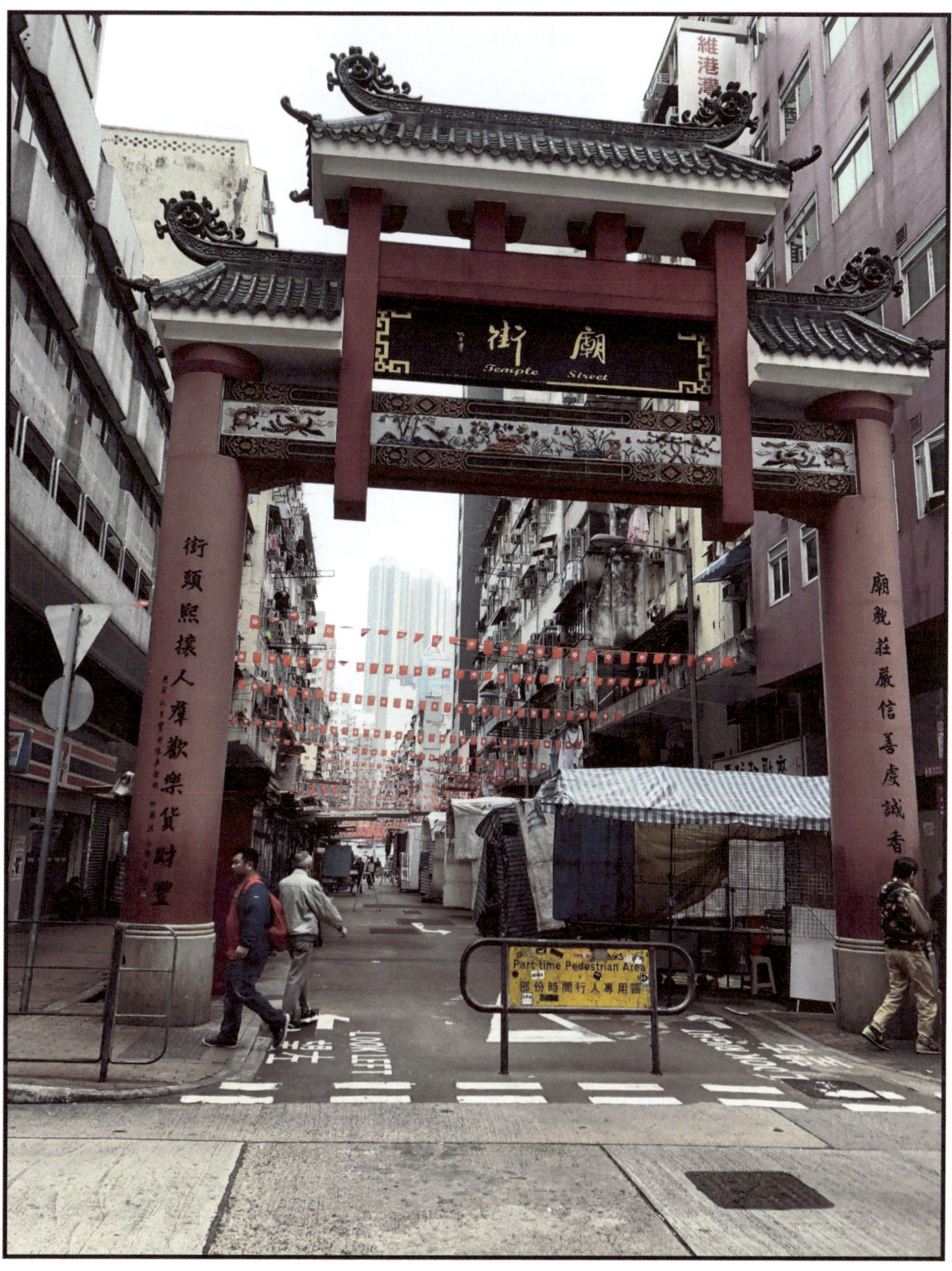

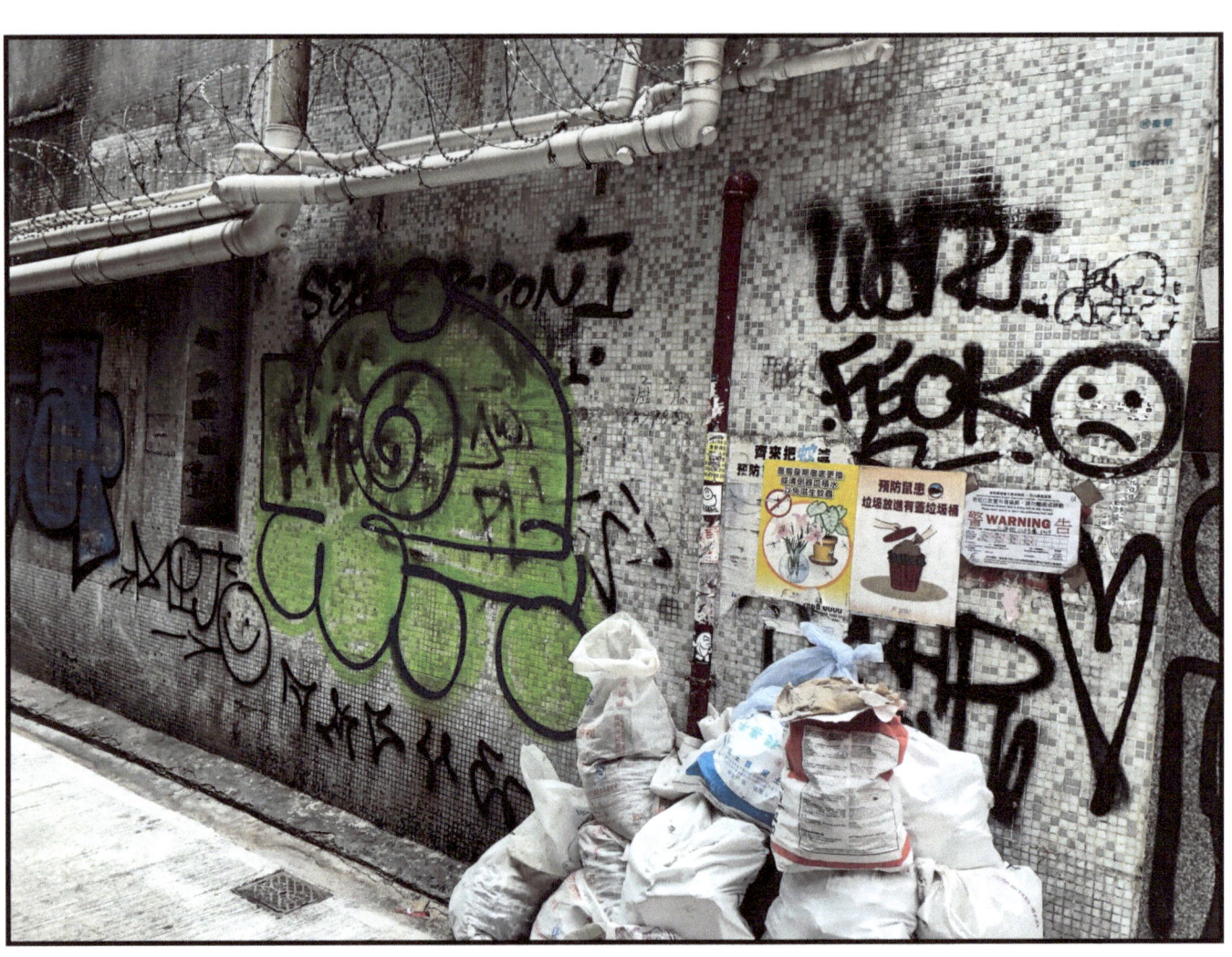

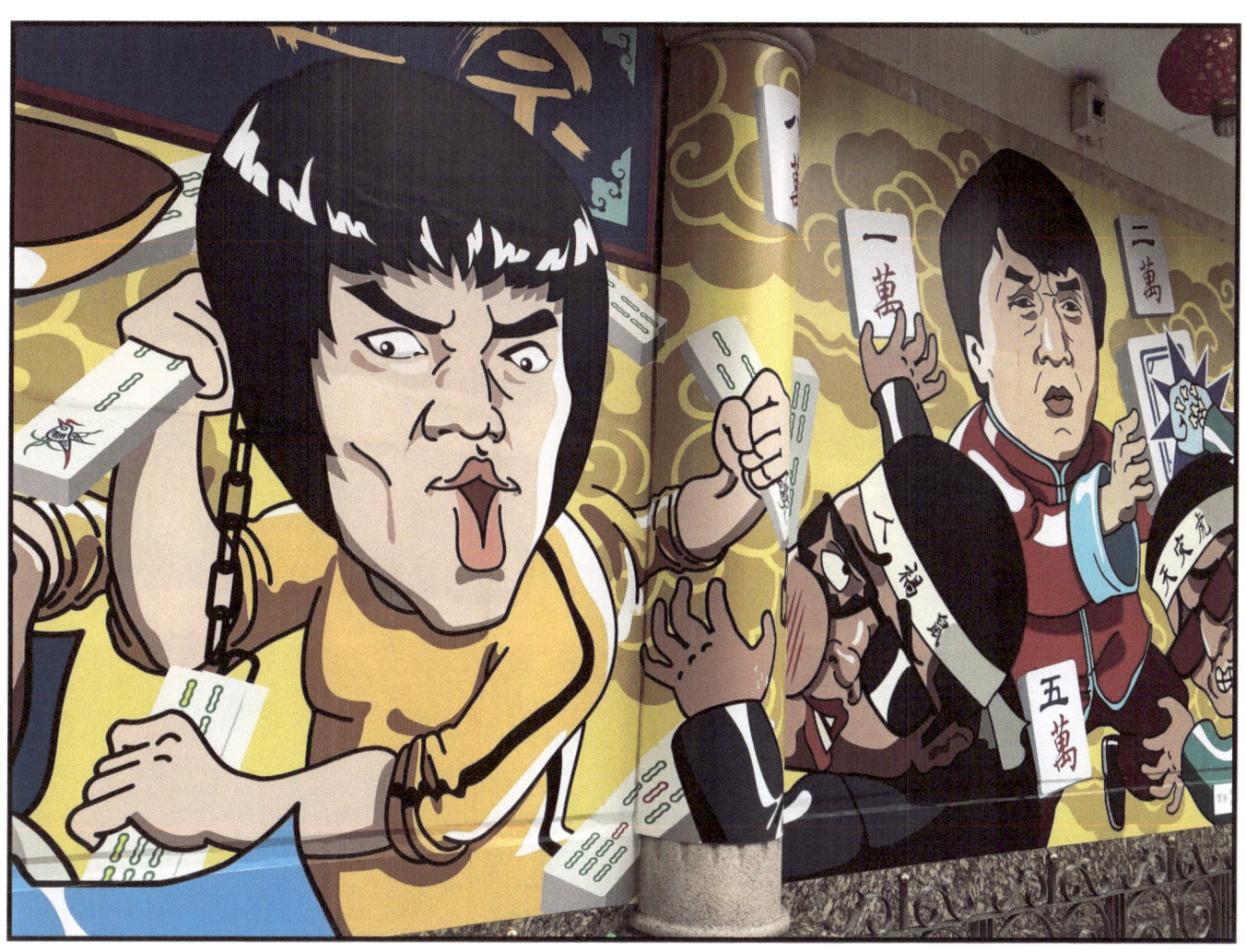

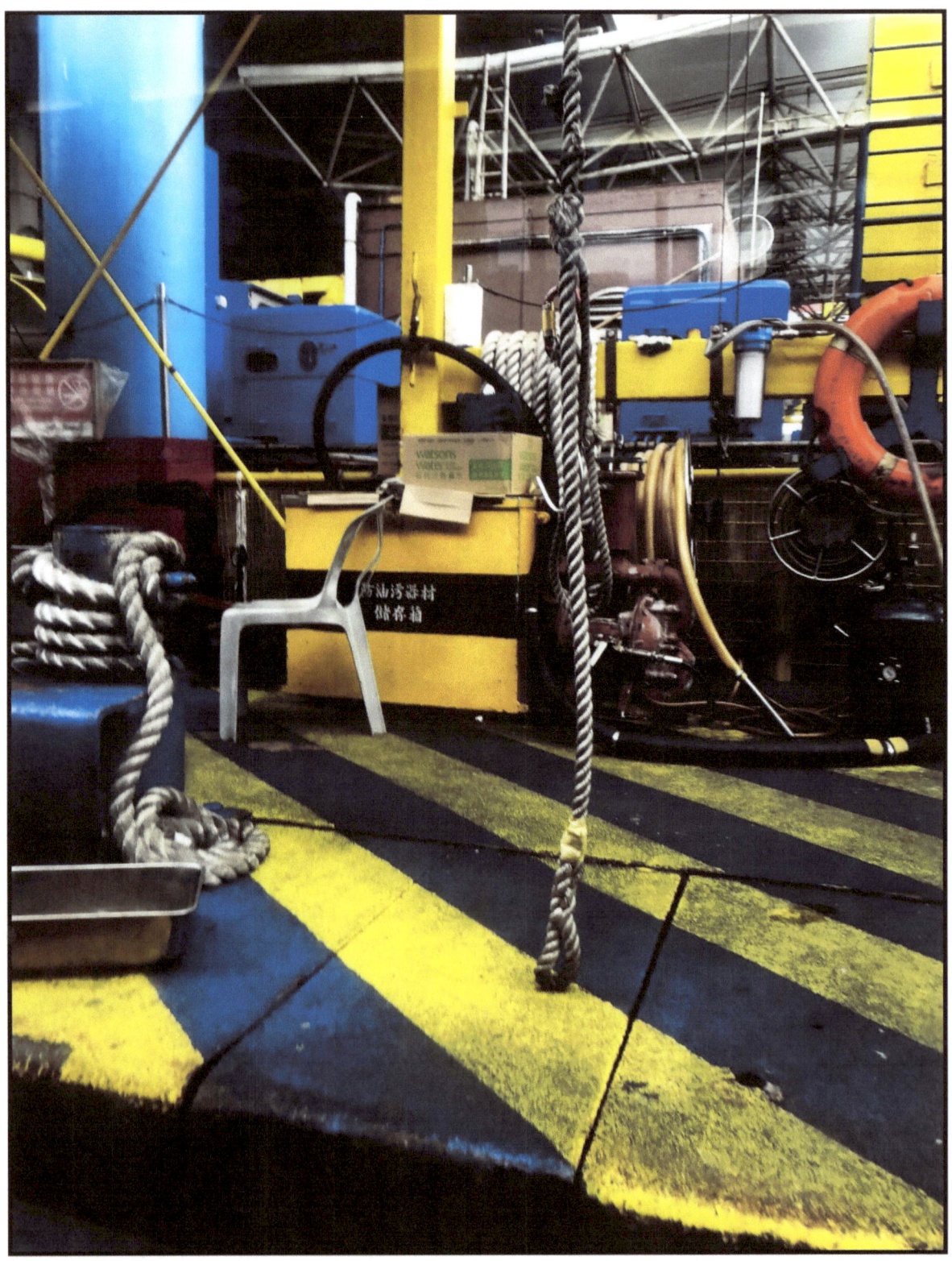

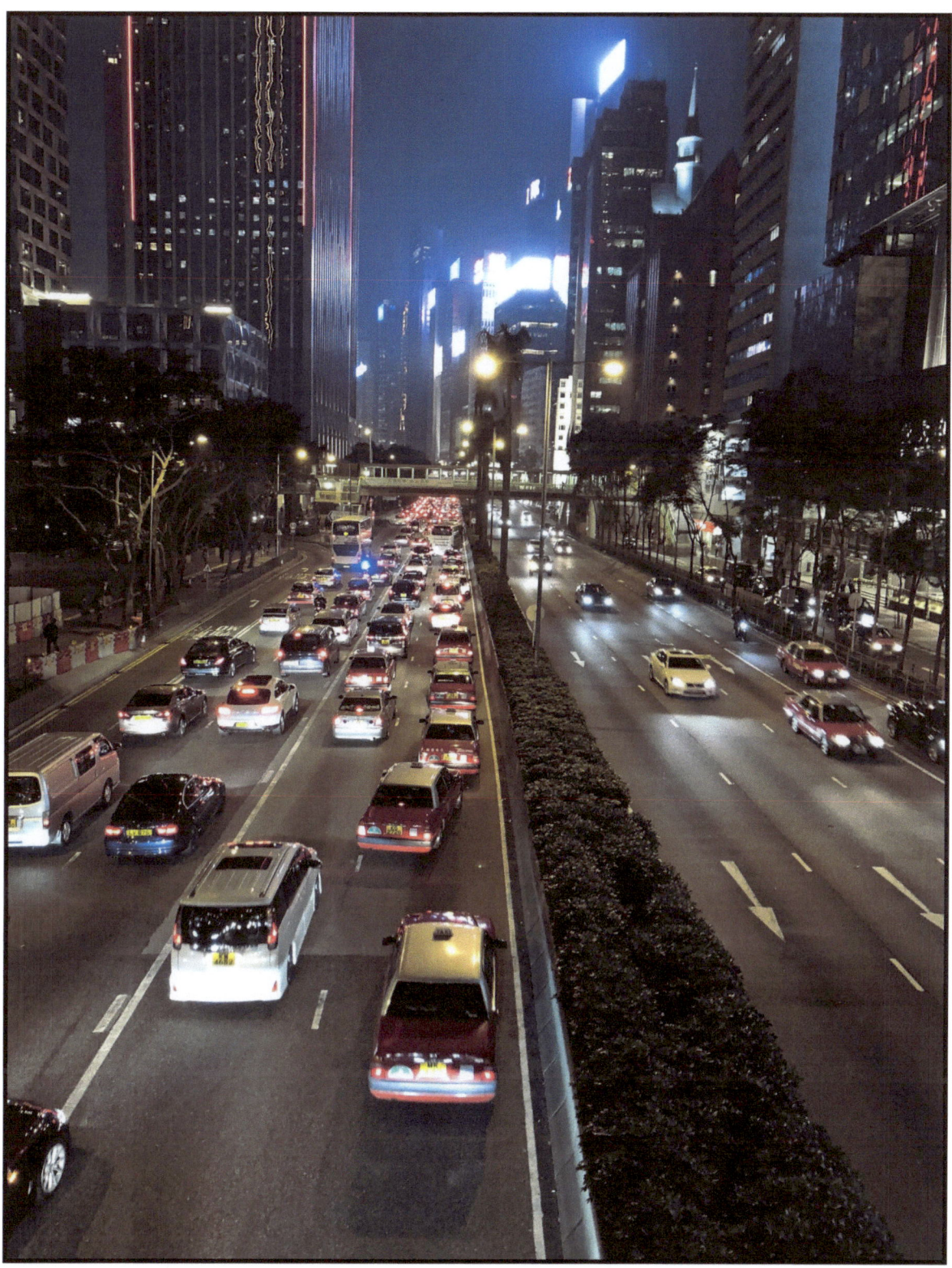

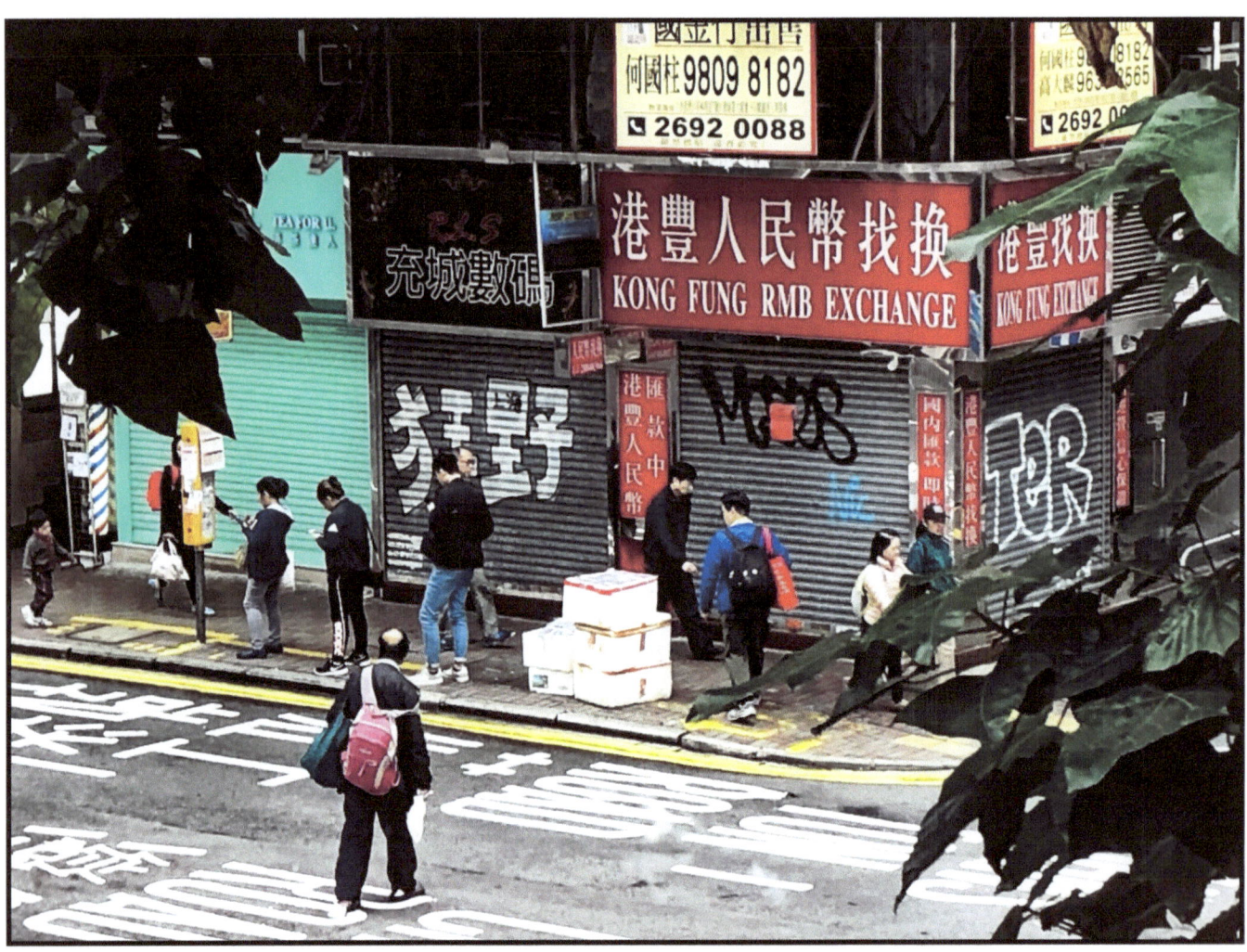

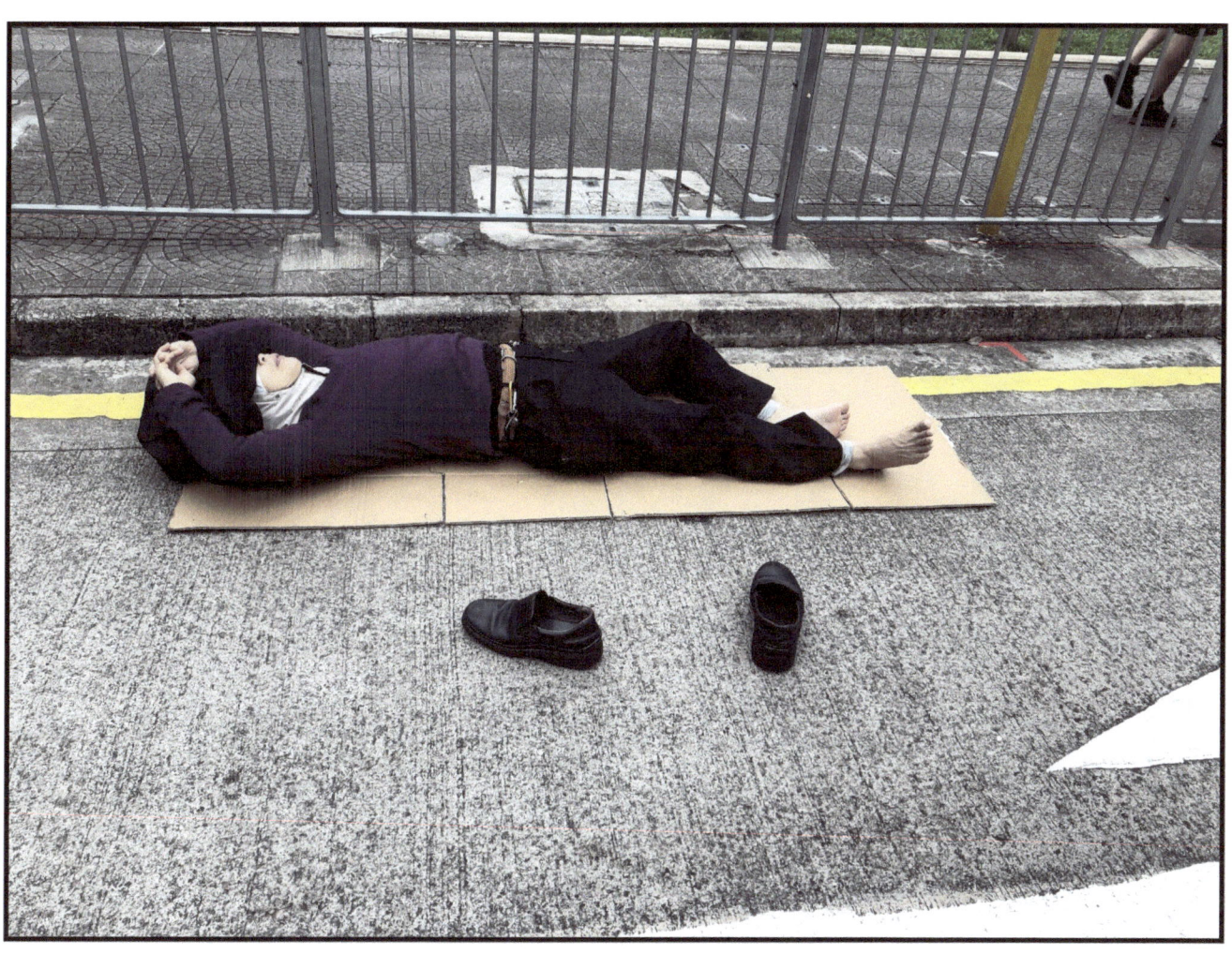

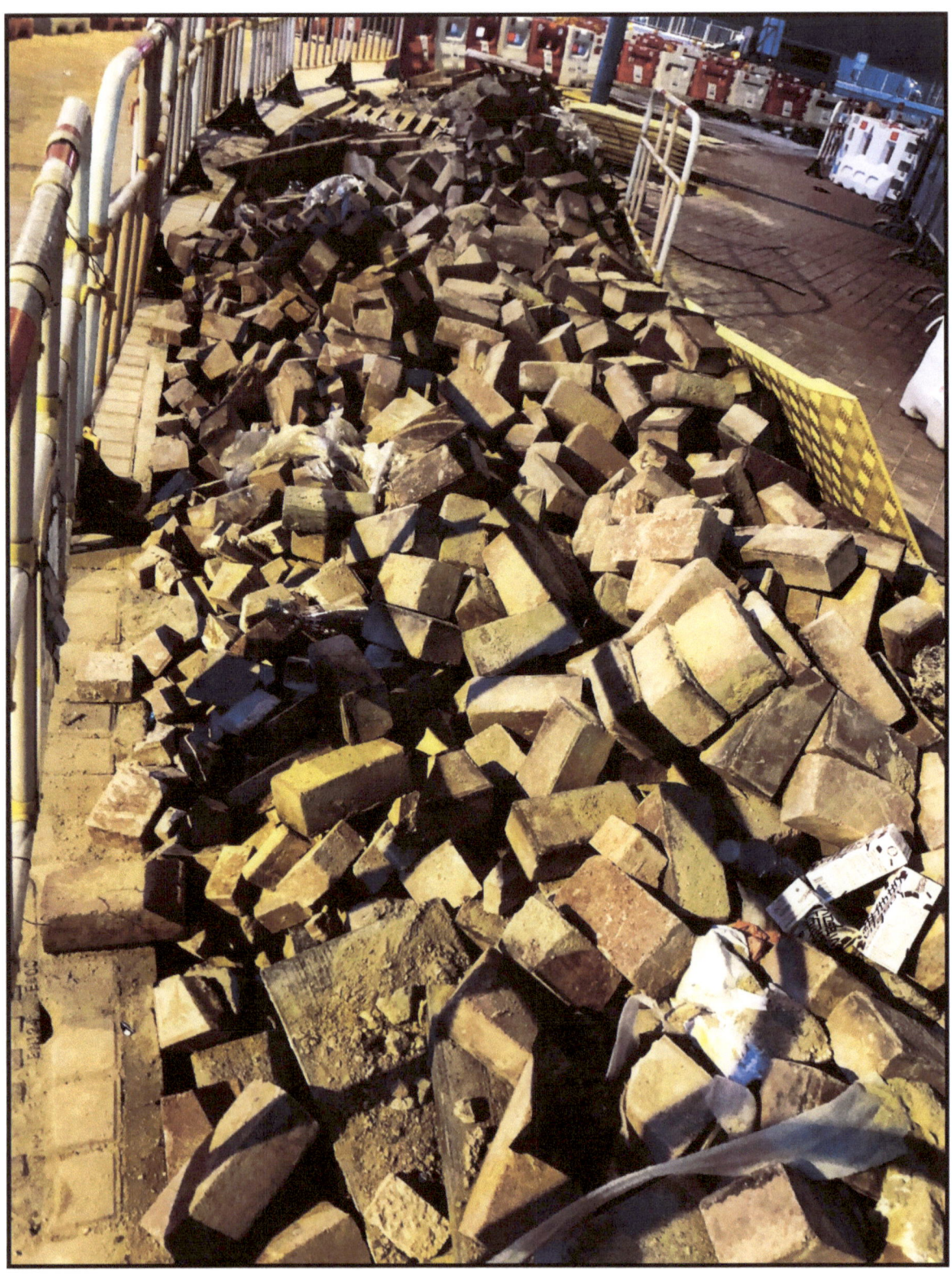

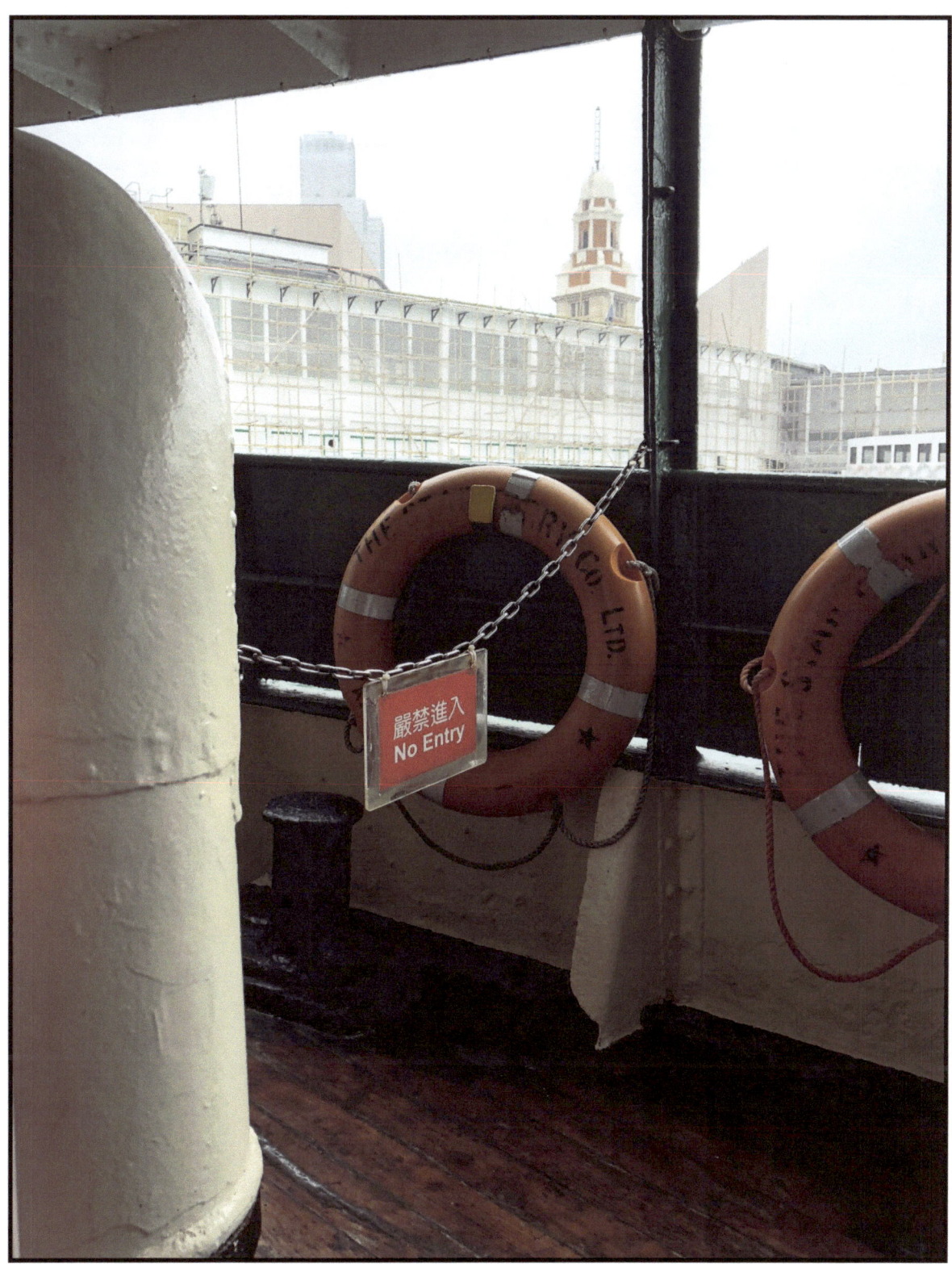

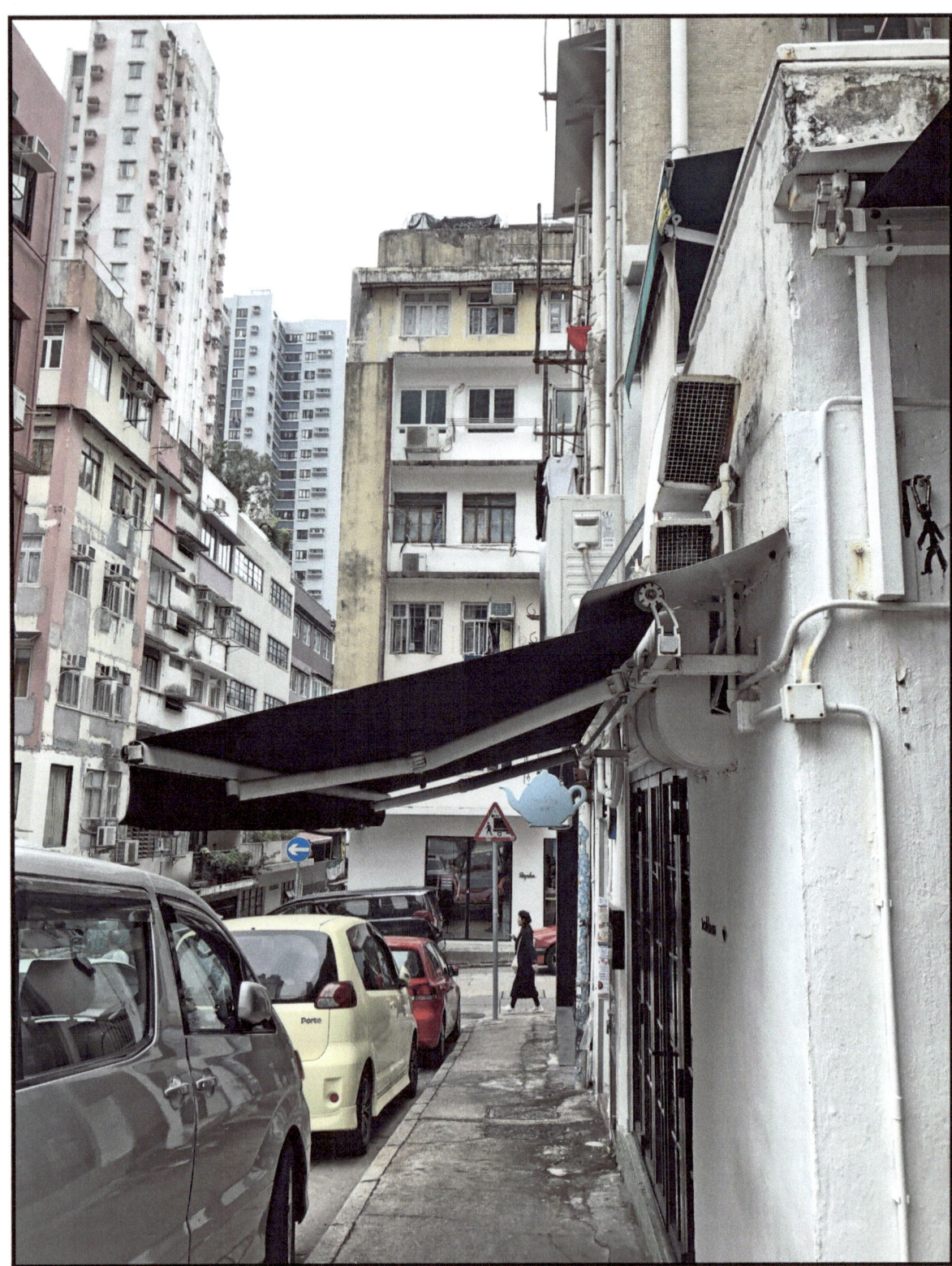

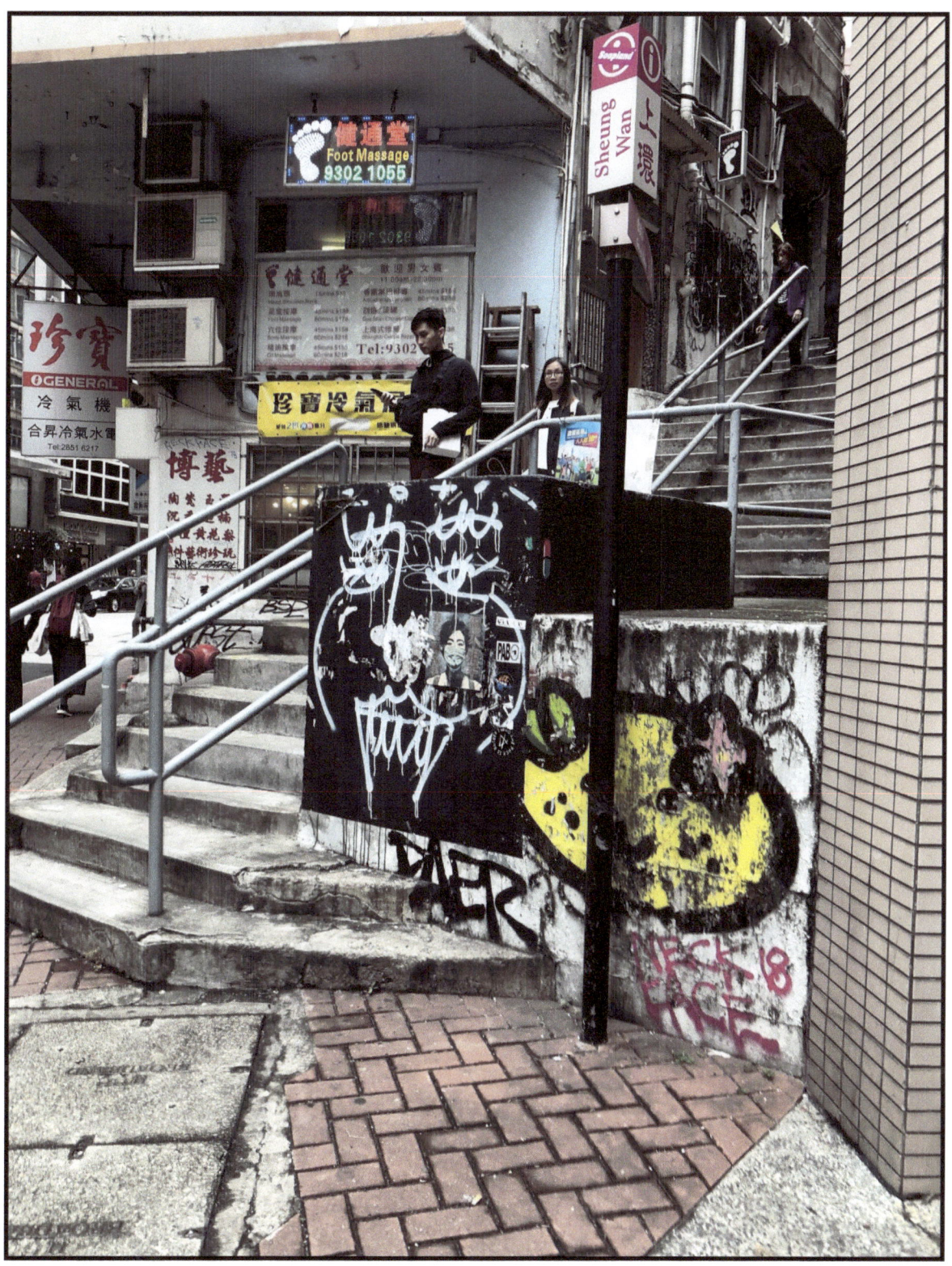

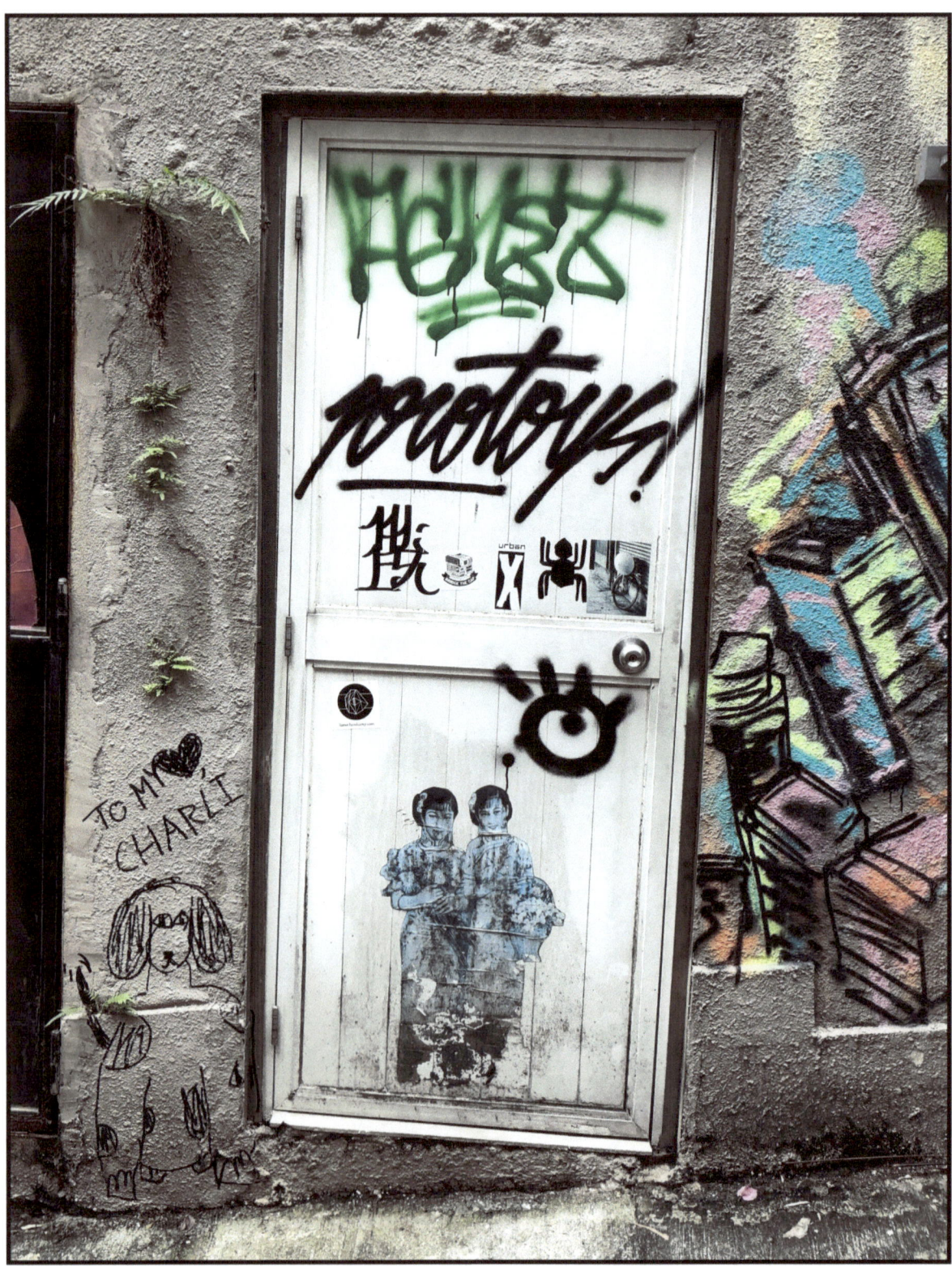

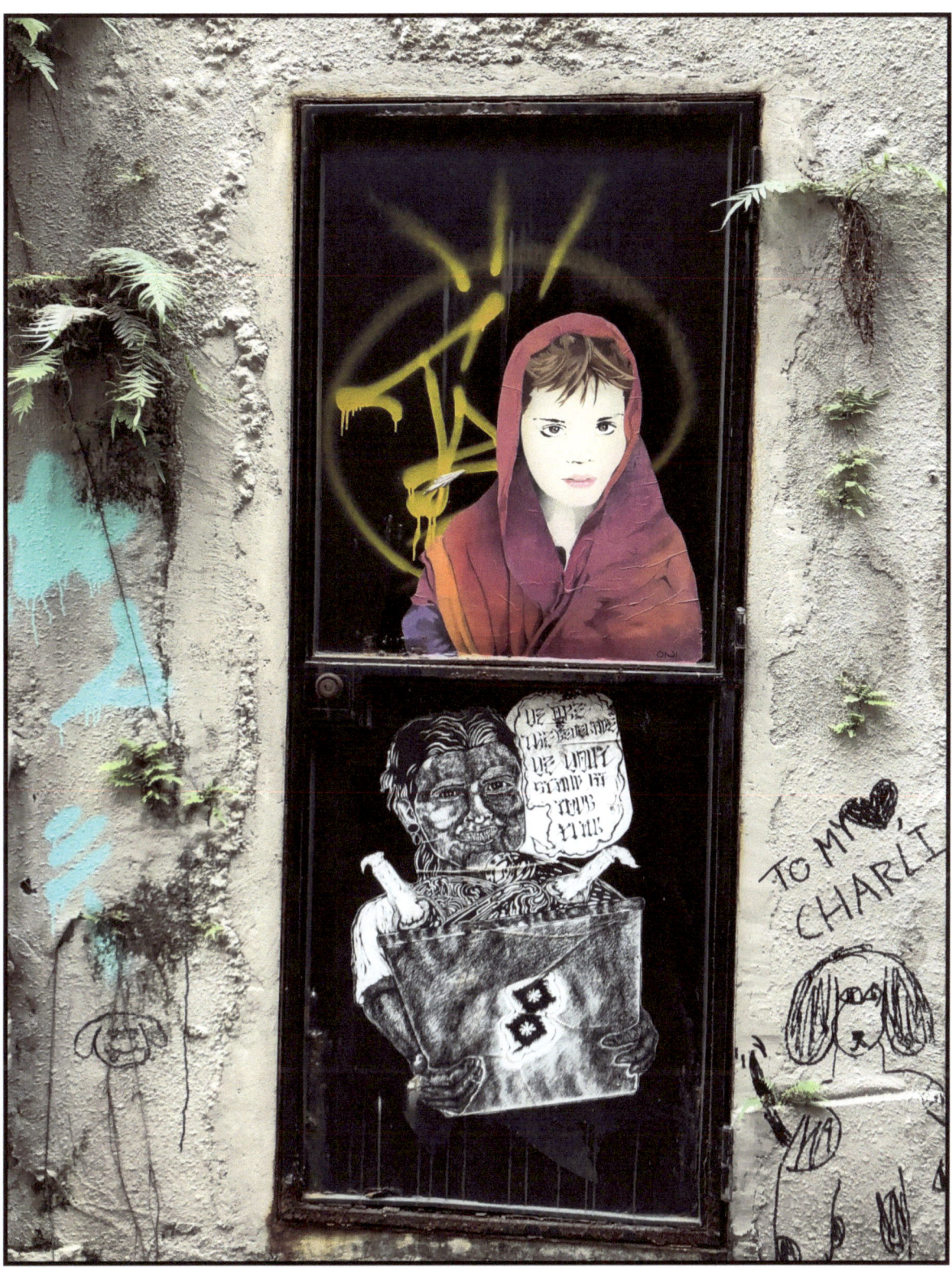

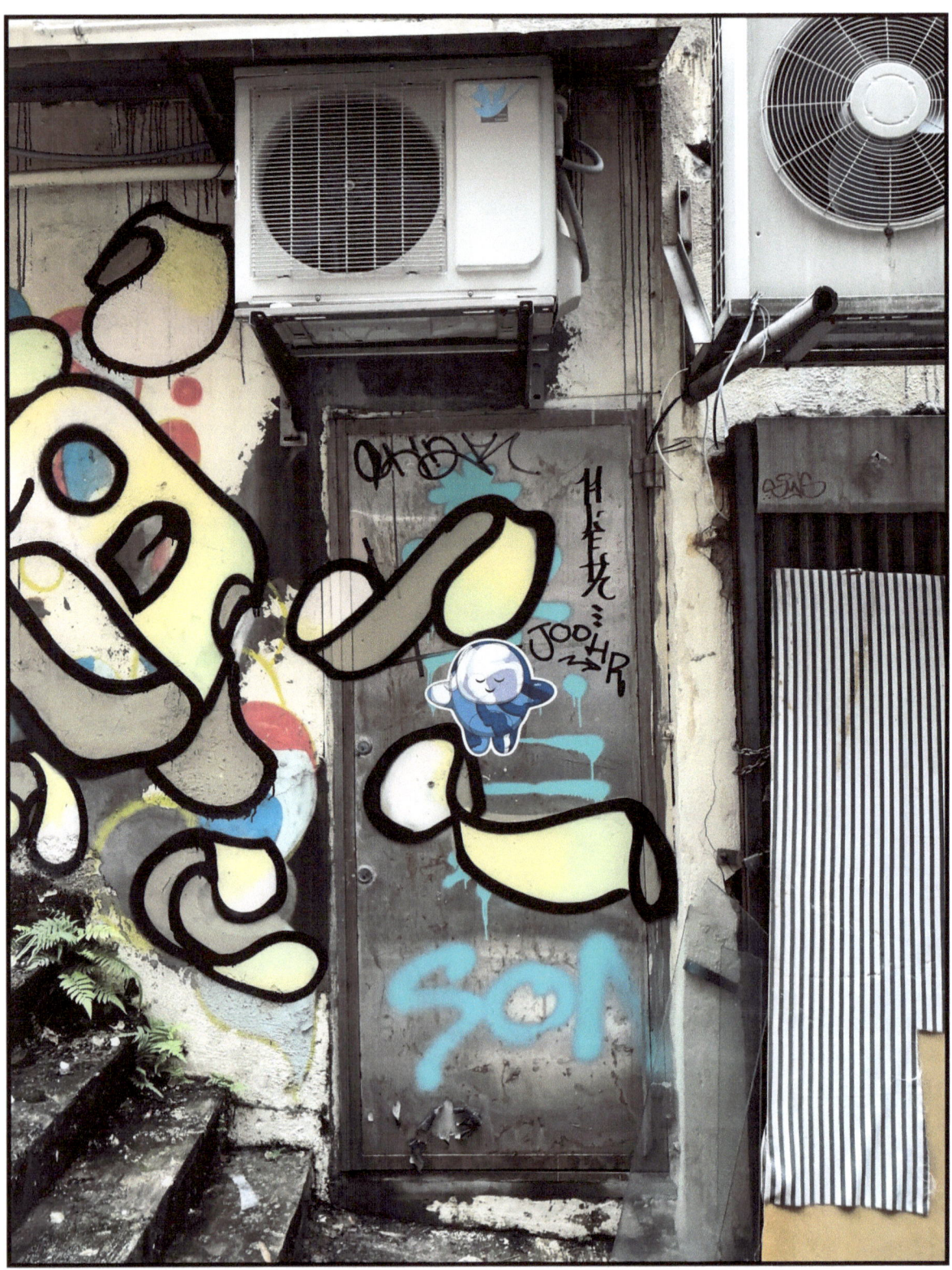

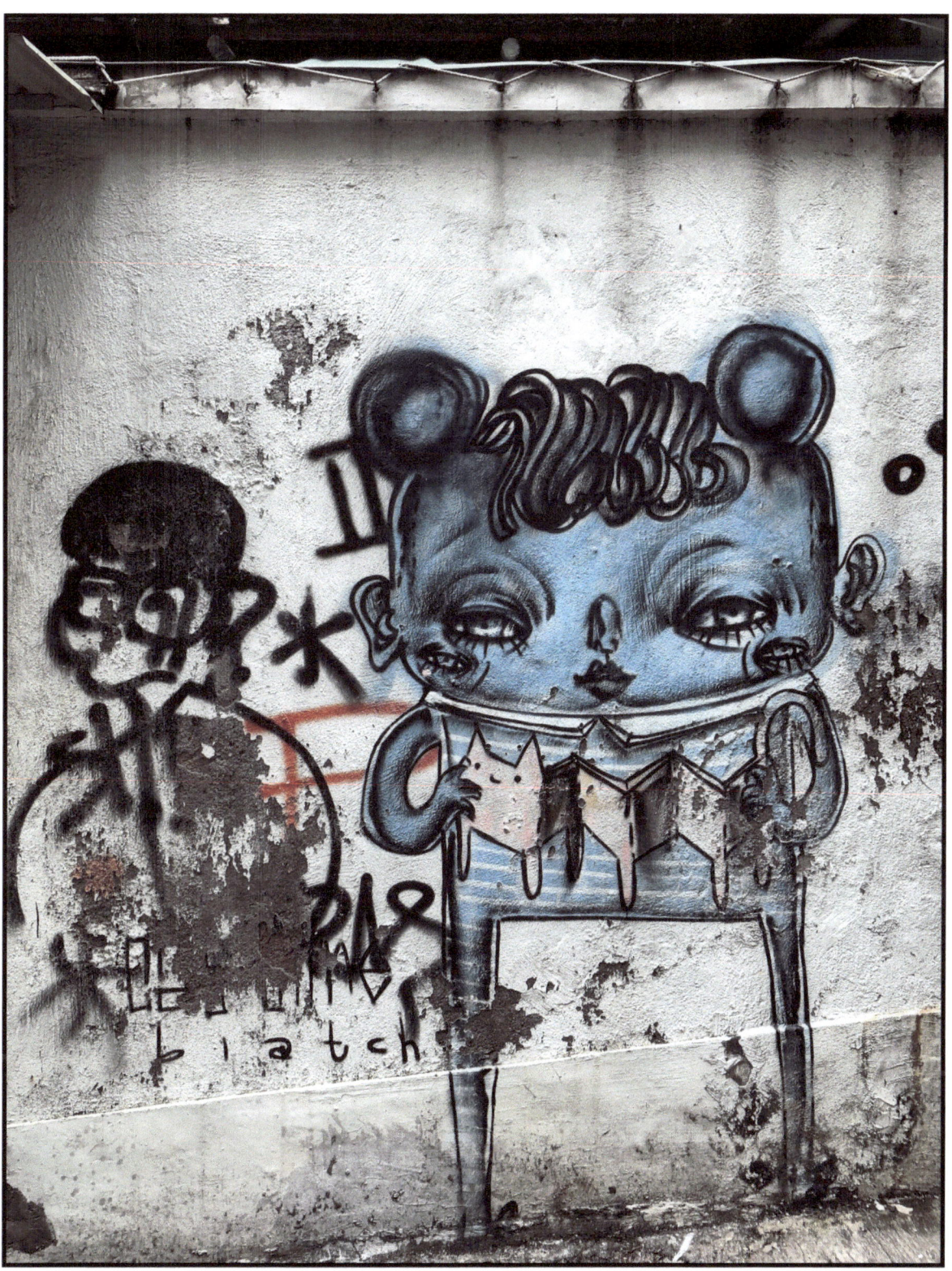

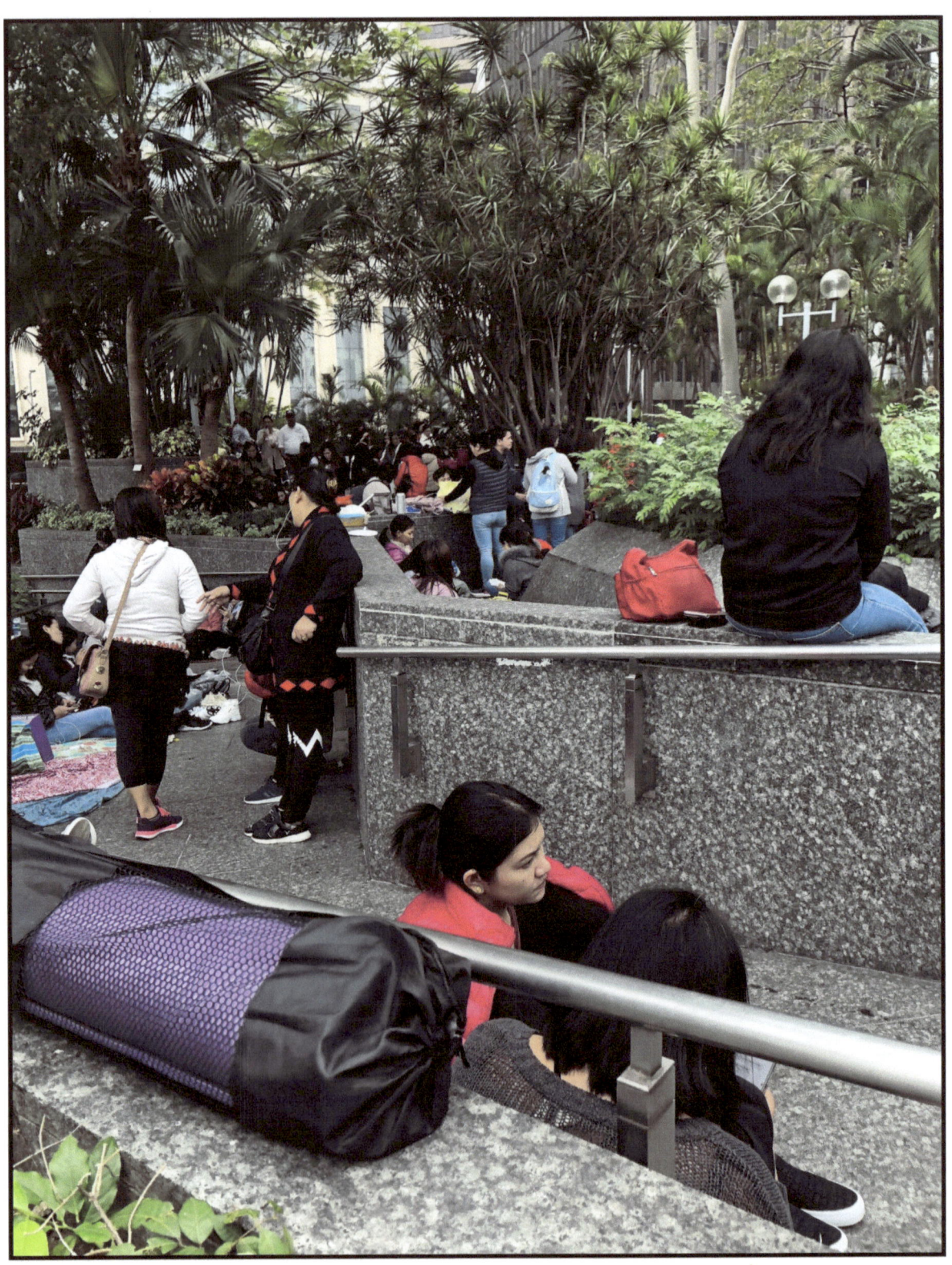

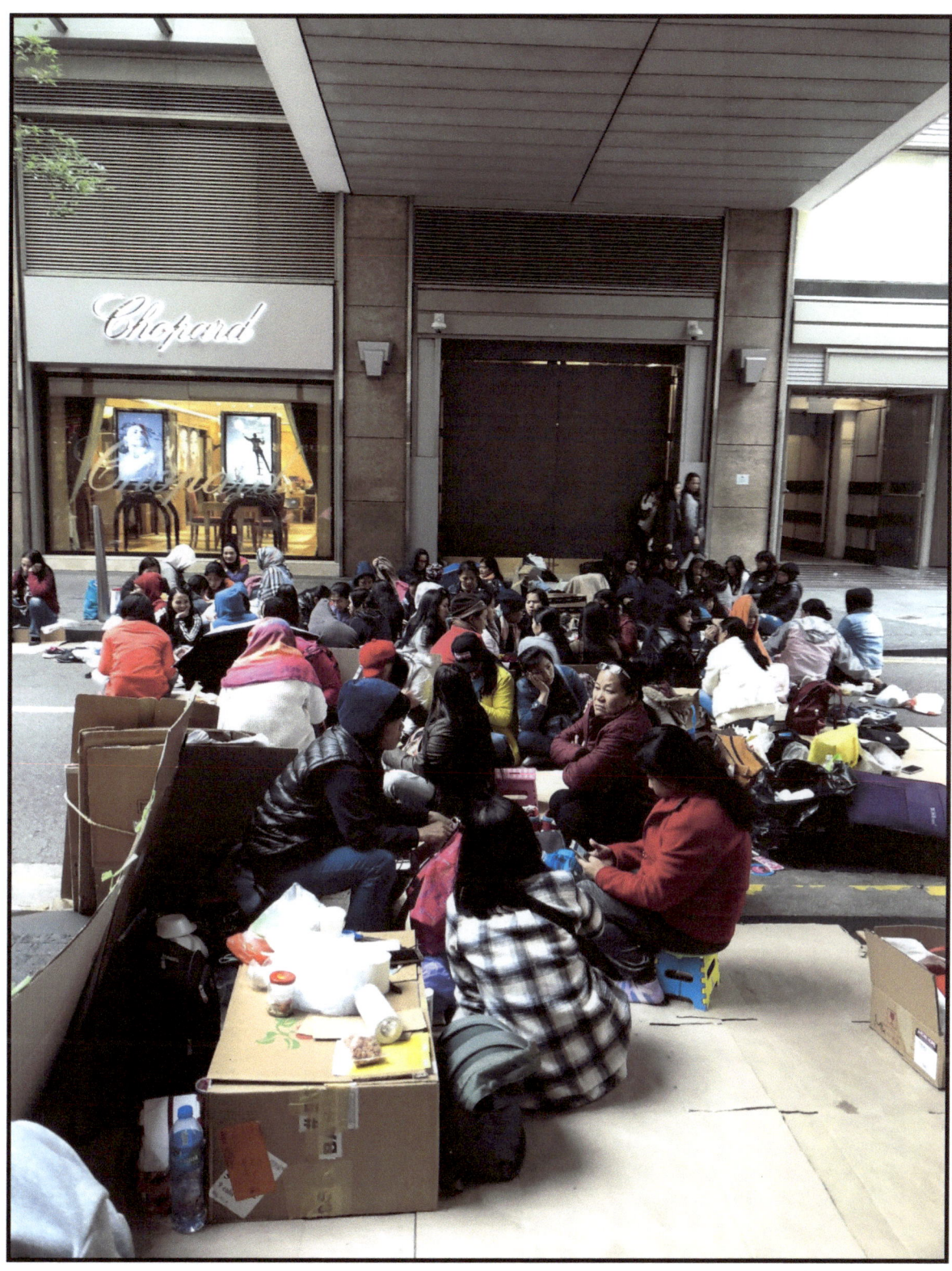

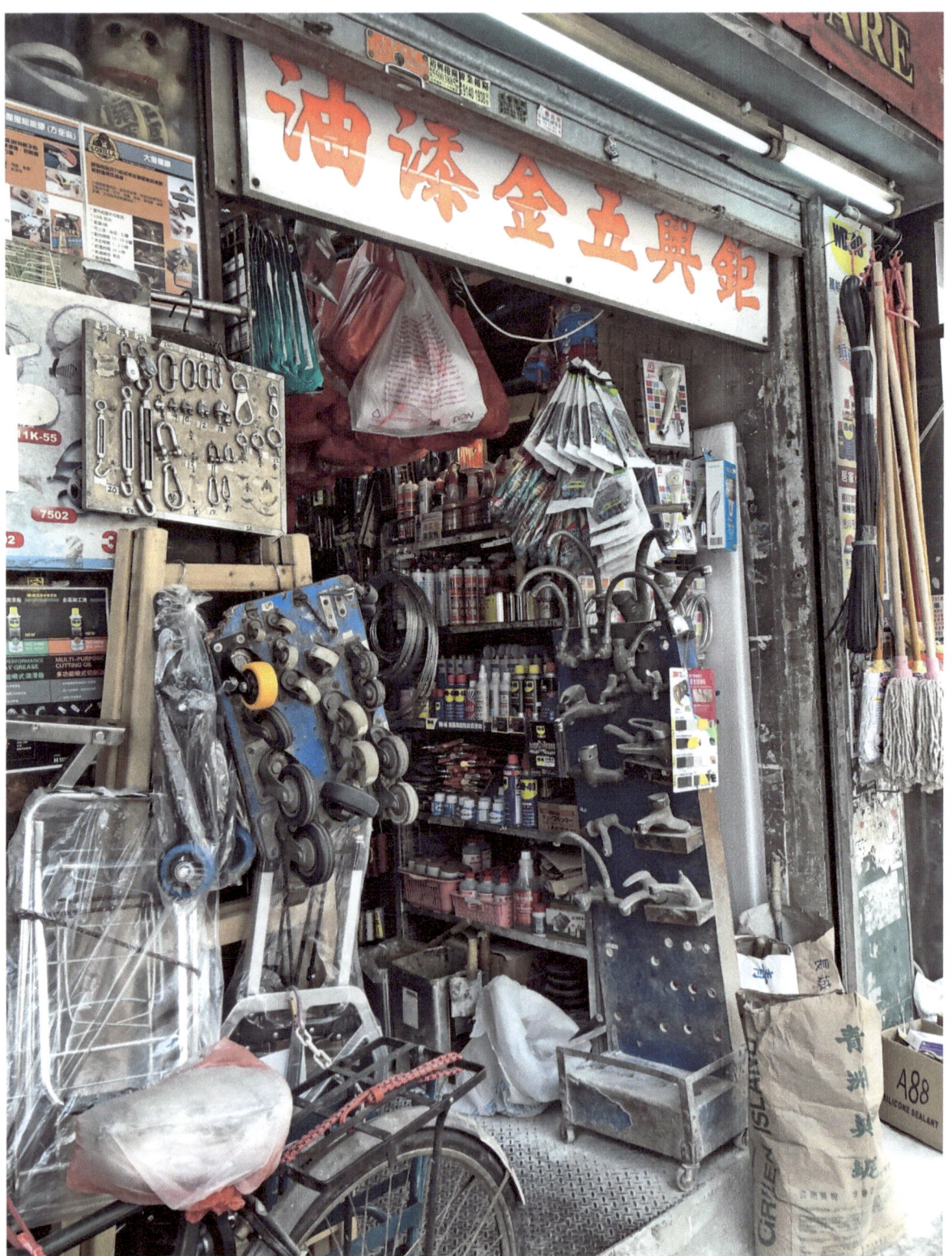

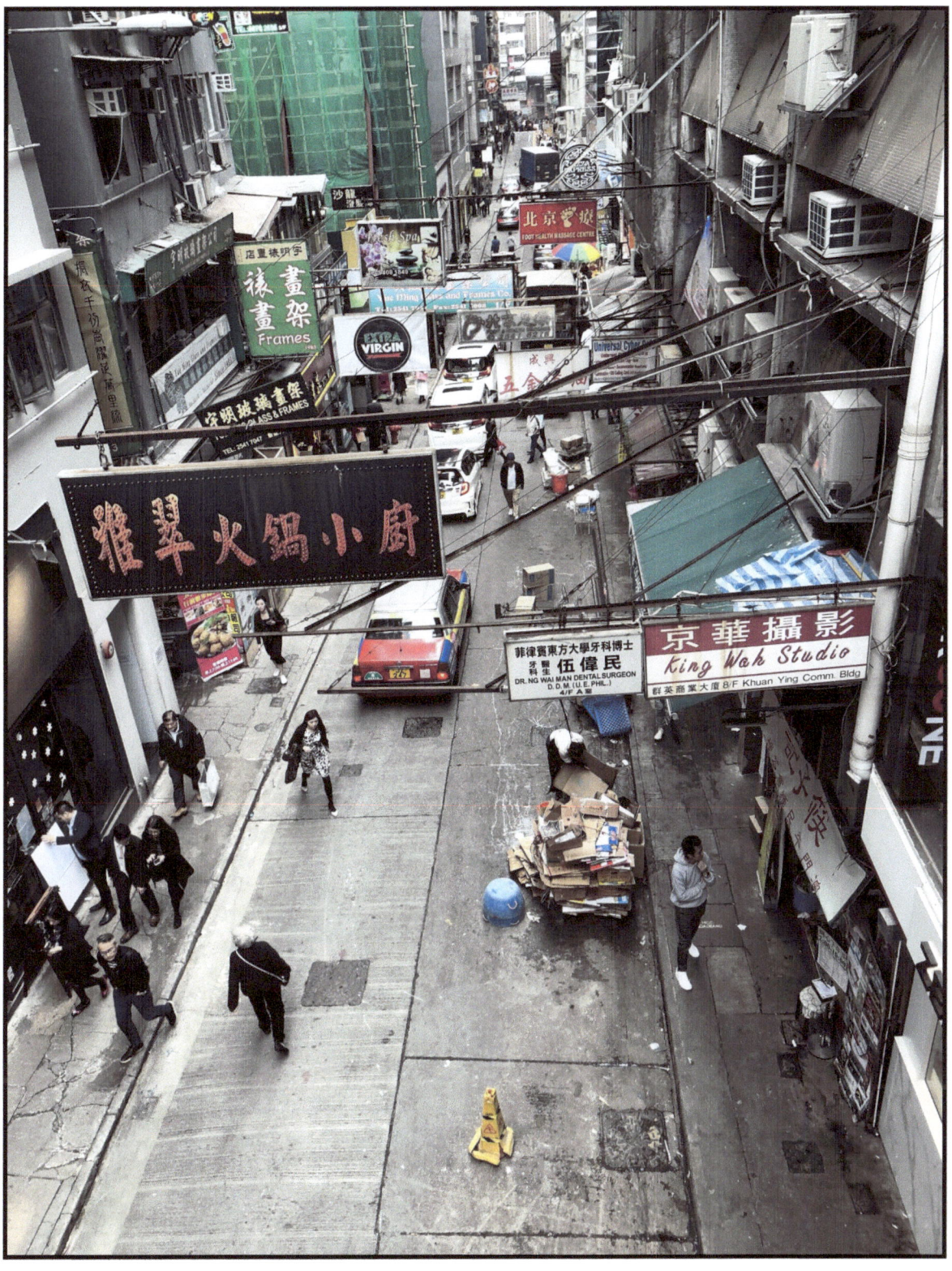

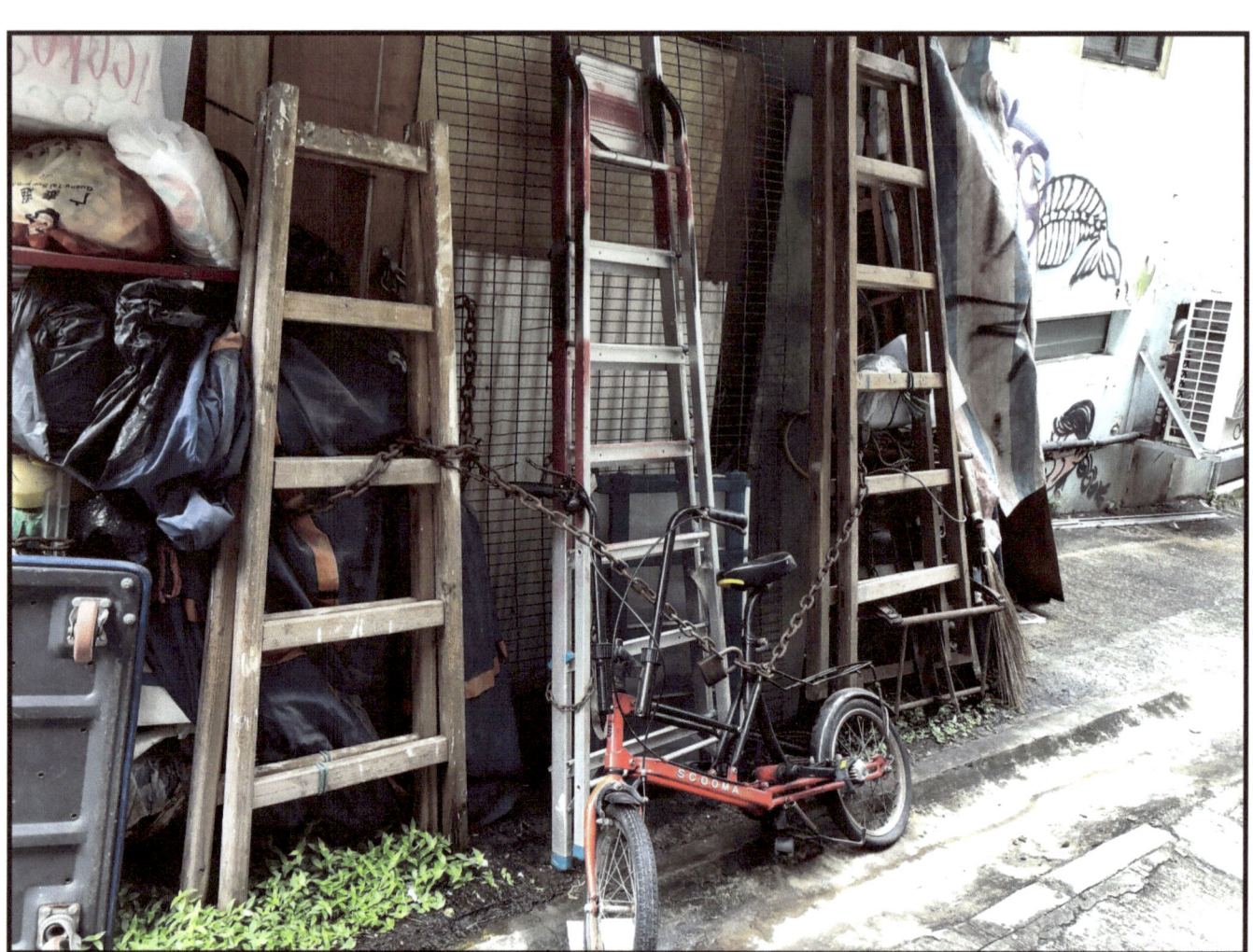

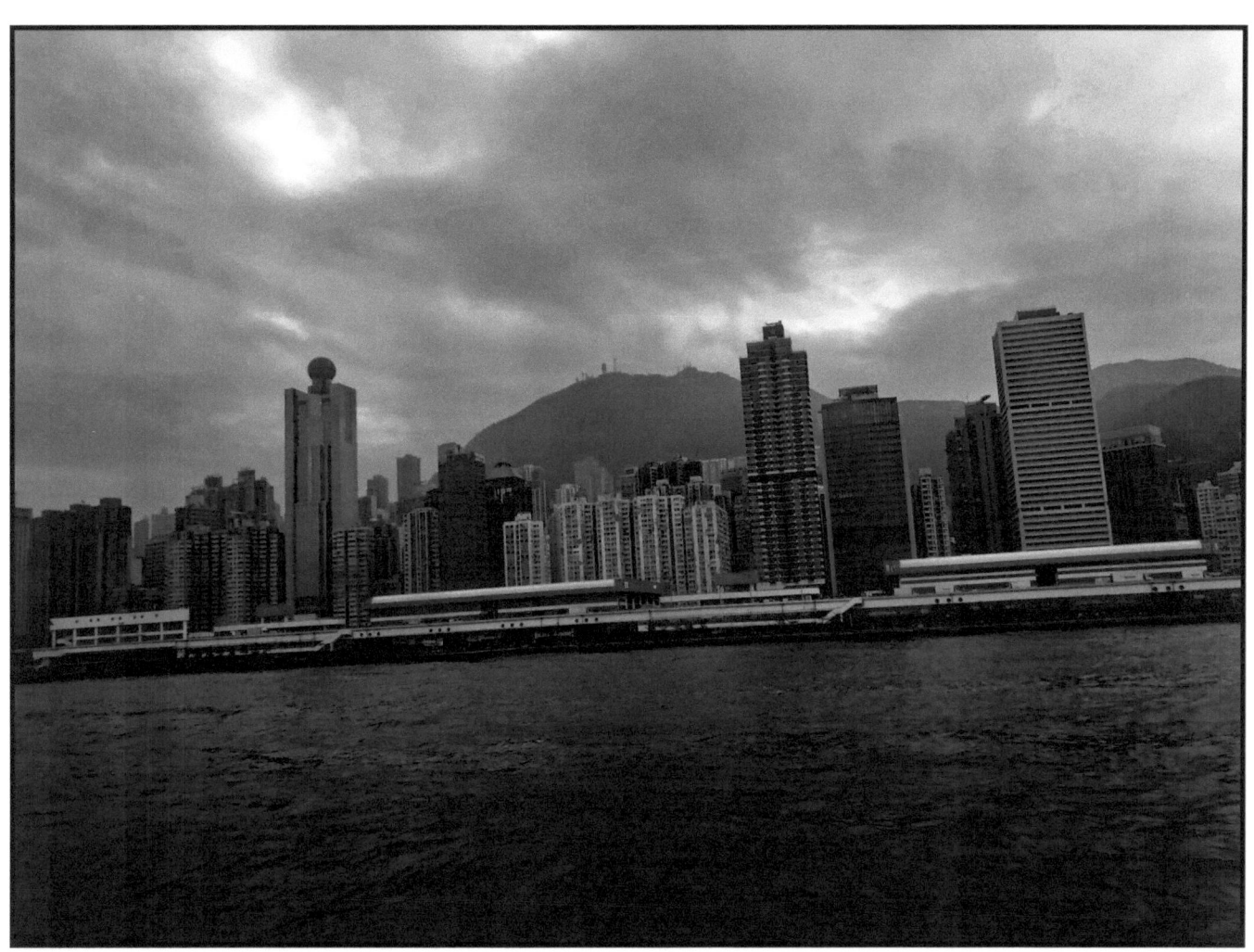

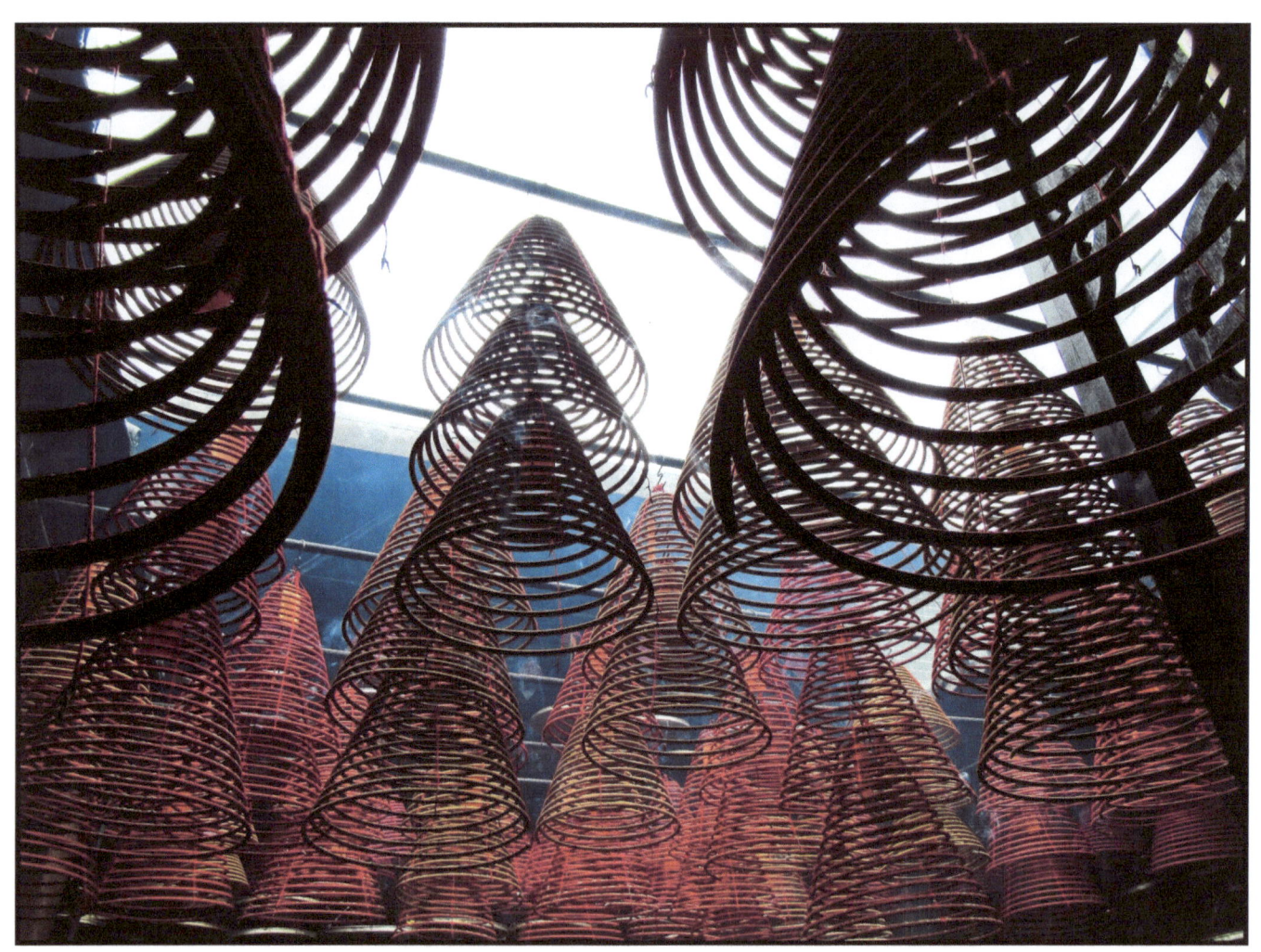

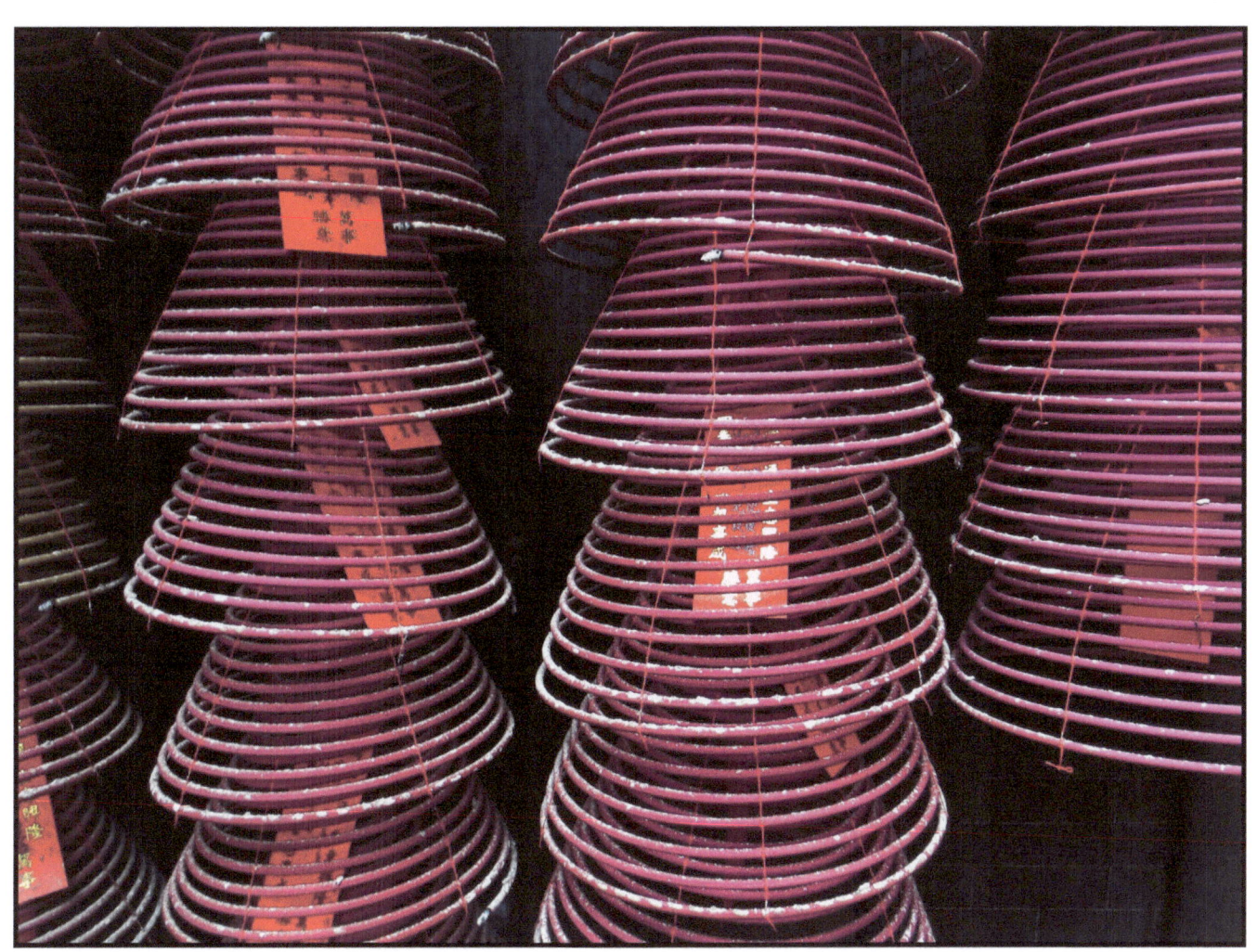

www.ingramcontent.com/pod-product-compliance
Lightning Source LLC
Chambersburg PA
CBHW051145220526
45473CB00003B/662